BURMESE

An Introduction
to the Spoken Language

BOOK ONE

Parallel with this course

Burmese—An Introduction to the Spoken Language, Book 2

Burmese—An Introduction to the Script

Burmese—An Introduction to the Literary Style

(Myanmar)

An Introduction to the Spoken Language

BOOK 1

John Okell

With assistance from U Saw Tun
and Daw Khin Mya Swe

Northern
Illinois
University
Press
DeKalb

Published by the Northern Illinois University Press in conjunction with the

Center for Southeast Asian Studies, DeKalb, Illinois   60115

Manufactured in the United States using postconsumer-recycled, acid-free paper.

Cover Design: Shaun Allshouse

ISBN:978-0-87580-642-6

Series: Southeast Asian language text series

LC Control No.: 2010939679

Front Cover Photo—Kalaga or Burmese tapestry representing a court scene.

BC90.02.01 from the Burma Art Collection at NIU.

CONTENTS

PART 1: GROUNDWORK

Introduction

The lessons

Common Phrases Supplement   182

PART 2: DIALOGUES
Introduction

The Topics: Level 1

Levels 2 to 5 of Part 2 are bound separately in Book 2

Appendices

ACKNOWLEDGMENTS

Funds from the Center for Southeast Asian Studies at Northern Illinois University, part of a grant made to them by the Henry Luce Foundation, allowed me to take time away from my normal duties in order to make a start on writing new courses for beginners in Burmese. During this time the School of Oriental and African Studies in the University of London kindly allowed me to continue to use its equipment and facilities (room, computers, printers, xeroxing, recording, photography, telephone, mail, fax, stationery and so on). A visit to Burma was funded by money from both the Center and SOAS, and supplemented by a grant from the British Academy. I am particularly grateful to Dr. Michael Aung-Thwin, director of the Center, who successfully applied for the grant, and chose me to write the book; and to Dr. Haig D. Roop, coauthor of *Beginning Burmese*, the standard textbook for 25 years, for his encouragement.

Many of the ideas, and some actual material, contained in this course were used in my *First steps in Burmese*, a short text and tape course published by the School of Oriental and African Studies in 1989. I am grateful to the School for allowing me to use some of that material again in the present course.

I would also like to acknowledge the part played by my colleague at SOAS, Mrs. Anna Allott, who heroically shouldered a heavy load of teaching and other duties for part of the time I had arranged to be away; and the contribution of my wife Sue, who generously and without complaint took on more than her share of the care of the house and family so that I could make progress with writing.

Many friends and colleagues have contributed to the course, directly or indirectly. U Saw Tun, a long-standing friend and a teacher of Burmese to foreigners, most recently at NIU, helped construct dialogues and check that they were natural and authentic. Daw Khin Mya Swe, an old friend, has also checked portions of the draft. Others who have given much helpful advice include Daw San San Me, a librarian at SOAS; Dr. Khin Maung Win, during his year of study in London; Than Than Win, who was then a student at NIU; U Oung Myint Tun, and Daw Kyi Kyi Me, of the BBC in London. All of these have patiently and generously, and on many occasions, answered my questions on matters of usage and pronunciation.

The recordings were made at SOAS under the supervision of the Technician Jahan Latif, and the speakers were —

U Aung Khin	Dr. Daw Khin Hla Thi	Ma Thuza
U Aung Naing	Daw Khin Mya Swe	Ma Tin May Aye
Dr. Ba Maw	Ma Khin Nan Oo	U Tun Min
Ma Kay Thwe	Dr. Nay Tun	Wa Wa Tin
U Khin	Daw San San Me	Daw Yi Yi Mya
	Saw Yu Win	

I am grateful to them all for their willing cooperation and perseverance: the second and third hours in a stuffy recording studio with pernickety microphones demand a high degree of concentration and discipline.

Prototype versions of the course were used by the beginners' classes at SOAS in the four years from 1990-91 to 1993-94, and at the SEASSIs held at Cornell University in 1990 and at the University of Washington in 1992. Members of all these classes made many helpful comments, as well as finding numerous typing errors, and I would like to thank them for being so tolerant and constructive.

The photograph used for the cover is ofpersnicketywooden doorway in the Shwe Inbin Monastery in Mandalay. It was taken by Dr. Elizabeth Moore of SOAS, and the design of the cover was implemented by Alfred Birnbaum, who was attending my class at the time. The photographs used in the text were taken on my visit to Burma in 1991. The remaining illlustrations are from books, magazines and other material published in Burma.

My greatest debt is to many friends in Burma, who not only answered my questions about their language and customs with immense patience and goodwill, but also made me welcome in their homes and daily lives, and went to staggering lengths to ensure that my needs were met in generous measure. To them all I extend my heartfelt thanks.

---

illustrations

I am responsible for typesetting the text, which includes three home-made fonts, and for editing the tapes. Professionals would have been more skilled but also more costly, so readers are asked to be indulgent when my lack of expertise shows through.

A NOTE FROM THE AUTHOR

Change of publisher

Publication of all four volumes of *Burmese: An Introduction,* first published in 1994, has been transferred to the Northern Illinois University Press and the books are now re-issued with minor revisions.

Change of audio format

At the time of initial publication, the audio component of Burmese: An Introduction was issued on cassette tapes. Now that digital recordings are more widely used than tapes, the audio material has been converted to digital. Two advantages of this change are, first, that digital files are less bulky to store and transport than cassette tapes and, second, that it is far easier to find a particular section in the audio.

Neither the printed text nor the audio files have been changed to reflect the transfer from tape to digital. So when you read or hear a reference to a particular tape, please understand it as referring to the corresponding track in the audio files.

Changes in Burma since the publication of this course

Sixteen years have passed since the first publication of this course. During that time several aspects of life in Burma have changed.

First and most obvious are price levels:
- A cup of tea that cost K4 in 1993 now costs K150, and costs may well rise further. So, when practicing prices in the exercises, bear in mind that most prices need to be multiplied by 30 or 40 to correspond with the cost of living today.

Second, some institutions that appear in the course have been renamed, relocated, or discontinued. For example:
- Tourist Burma has been renamed Myanmar Travel and Tours.
- The National Museum has moved from Pansodan to Pyay Road.
- The Diplomatic Store is no longer operating.

If you search in Burma for places mentioned in the course, remember that they may no longer be there.

Third, digital cameras have largely replaced film cameras, and most telephones now have keys to press rather than dials to turn. References in the Lessons to film and dialing should be understood as reflecting technology at the time of writing.

Apart from such obvious physical changes in the life of the country, the language of the course is still the language that you will hear and read in Burma today.

Errata lists

While using the course over the years, teachers, colleagues, and students have helpfully pointed out some errors and inconsistencies in the text. These have been listed and are to be found, with their corrections, on a page at the end of each volume.

GENERAL INTRODUCTION

Scope of the four volumes

This volume is one of a set of four:
1. *Burmese: An Introduction to the Spoken Language, Book 1*
2. *Burmese: An Introduction to the Spoken Language, Book 2*
3. *Burmese: An Introduction to the Script*
4. *Burmese: An Introduction to the Literary Style*

The spoken language

Among those I have met, the great majority of people interested in learning Burmese are people who are planning to go to Burma, or are already there, and want to be able to speak to Burmans in their own language. That is why this course takes the spoken language as its starting point, and why the spoken language volumes focus on early encounters with Burmese speakers in Burma or abroad.

It does not follow that the course is irrelevant to the needs of learners with other plans. They will gain from it a solid grounding in the grammar and sound system of Burmese, which will be useful to them whatever they intend to talk or read about. After all, choosing a Shan bag in a shop in Rangoon needs just as much grammar as studying approaches to Buddhist meditation, and much of the vocabulary of everyday life crops up in conversations about even quite specialized topics.

The literary style

The Burmese language has two different "styles": a "colloquial" style for speaking (and for writing personal letters) and a "literary" style for writing books, newspaper reports, official correspondence and so on. In novels, Burmese authors use the literary style for their narrative and descriptive passages, and the colloquial style for the dialogue. The spoken language volumes therefore teach you the colloquial style.

Learners who would like to be able to read the literary style are advised to acquire a grounding in the colloquial style first. It is hard to learn to read a language if you don't know what it sounds like. When you have a grasp of the material presented in *An Introduction to the Spoken Language, Book 1*, you will be equipped to move on to *Burmese: An Introduction to the Literary Style.*.

Learning Burmese script

It is possible to write Burmese words in the roman script, but there is no standard system for doing so, and all systems that have been tried suffer from serious defects. The best plan for beginning students of Burmese is to learn to read the script as quickly as they can. The volume called *Burmese: An Introduction to the Script* is intended to meet this need.

There is inevitably an initial phase during which the learner needs to practise speaking Burmese but doesn't yet know enough script to be able to read or make notes. All the written material in the first half of *An Introduction to the Spoken Language* is presented in both script and a romanization, so that you can read the examples and notes before you know the script, but you can start using the script as soon as you are ready. We hope that you will have learned to read the script by the time you reach the end of *Book 1*, if not before, so at that point we stop using the romanization for the notes and vocabulary, but, as a concession to stragglers, we do provide romanized versions of the new words and sample dialogues.

Time required

The following figures are estimates, and your experience may be quite different. I anticipate that most students will need to spend the equivalent of five to six weeks full time on the script and *Spoken Language Book 1* together, followed by a further five to six weeks on the literary style and *Spoken Language Book 2* together — and you'll probably find the literary style runs on beyond that estimate. This is based on a 40-hour working week, including both class and homework time. If you only have 20 hours a week to spend on Burmese, then you can expect to take twice as long to get through all four components of the course.

Words of advice

Confidence

When you are in Burma and using phrases from this course you may from time to time come across a Burman who says "Oh. Don't say it that way. Burmese people never use that phrase." Be grateful, and use the alternative he offers, but don't lose confidence in what you know. The chances are that you will soon meet another Burman who regularly uses your original phrase himself, and even thinks your new alternative sounds unnatural. Such experiences only go to show that there are Burmese — as there are speakers of all languages — who are eager to be helpful but are not very observant about the way other people speak.

Going further

If you have enjoyed learning some Burmese and would like to learn some more, you could follow up some of the text books and courses listed in Appendix 2 at the end of this book. Some of the learning aids in the list are only in the planning stage at the time of writing this introduction, but by the time you read this, some of them may have seen the light of day.

Bon voyage

You must be keen to learn some Burmese, otherwise you wouldn't have read this far. You need have no fear that the effort will be wasted. You will be able to communicate with people in Burma instead of being thrown back on helpless smirks and gestures. And you will immediately endear yourself to the Burmese: most Burmese are delighted to meet a foreigner who has taken the trouble to learn a bit of their language. We wish you a happy stay in Burma: a land of much natural beauty and of many lively and generous people.

PART 1: GROUNDWORK

INTRODUCTION

1 "Groundwork" and "Dialogues"

Some language learners hope to pick up enough of a language from the first few lessons of a course to be able to get around in the country without too much difficulty. Speakers of English can manage this with languages related to English, like French, German and Italian; but when you are faced with an unrelated language like Burmese, where none of the words reminds you of English words, where the sound system includes distinctions unknown in the European languages (such as aspirate versus plain consonants, and high versus low syllable tone), and where the shape of the sentence differs radically from anything you regard as normal and natural, the phrase-book approach is very hard work. Despite heroic application to memorizing, you still find your hard-won phrases keep slipping out of your grasp.

It is for this reason that *Burmese: An Introduction to the Spoken Language* (hereafter abbreviated to *BISL*) is divided into Part 1 "Groundwork" and Part 2 "Dialogues." The Groundwork section familiarizes you with the unfamiliar sounds and structures of the language, and provides you with some relevant basic vocabulary. It covers questions and answers with *what, where, which, who, how much,* and so on; verb sentences with the Burmese equivalents of *does, did, will, not, want to, have to, please, don't,* and so on; numbers and prices; names of places and people in Burma; addresses, phone numbers, time-telling, and so on. With this foundation behind you, learning the language you need for survival (shops, taxis, cafés) and first conversations (Where are you from? How long have you been here?), which is the content of Part 2, is a much less frustrating task.

2 Lesson structure

New material in the Groundwork section is presented in small doses. A typical Lesson introduces no more than half a dozen new points to learn, and takes up between five and ten minutes on the tape. The idea is to enable you to proceed at your own pace: each learner (or class) can take as many of the short lessons at one time as they have stamina for.

The typical Lesson consists of —
(a) in the text:
- some information (such as a map, or a list of names* and phone numbers)
- a list of new words and structures
- some example sentences

- under the heading "Models for the exercises," the first exchange in each exercise (typically Question/Answer/Confirmation of answer), so that you know where to listen and where to speak
- and (where appropriate) notes on grammar or related vocabulary that are too detailed to present on the tape

(b) on the tape:

- an introduction to the new material, followed by
- a set of exercises, usually three or four for each Lesson.

* Sets of personal names for the Exercises and Dialogues are taken from the telephone directory, or in some cases they belong to people known to the author. The intention in choosing them in this way is to expose the learner a wide spread of authentic names. It should be clearly understood that all characters in the Exercises and Dialogues are entirely fictional. A list in *BISL* stating that U Hla Myint doesn't eat pork, or that Daw Thein Shin lives in/on Bogyoke Road, or that Kyi Kyi Myint has eight children, and so on, has no validity for any real person bearing such a name. It is there solely to provide material for practice in using the language.

Each Exercise typically takes this form:

1. Speaker 1 says (in Burmese):   *What's the phone number of the Strand Hotel?*
2. The learner (after consulting the list printed in the text) says: *81533.*
3. Speaker 2 then repeats the answer to confirm it: *81533.*

In Part 2 most of the practice is in the form of dialogues, where you ask for information or help, and discuss prices and so on. You will find more detail in the Introduction to Part 2.

3 Material supplementary to the Lessons

Pronunciation practice

Burmese makes important distinctions between several pairs of sounds which English treats as variations of the same sound. For example, in Burmese you can say —

thoun-nyá   "zero" and
thoùn-nyá   "three nights"

The only difference between the two phrases is in the pitch of the first syllable, and to many English speakers, at first hearing anyway, thoun sounds much the same as thoùn. To the Burmese ear they are entirely different sounds — they make the two words as far apart as a *shortfall* and a *short fall* in English. So it is vital, as you go through this course, to reproduce the sounds of the Burmese words and phrases as faithfully as you can — including the stress and pitch patterns. The more often you hear the unfamiliar distinctions the more obvious they will appear.

To help with this process, each of the first ten Lessons in Part 1 has a supplementary Pronunciation Section. This allows you to take a closer look at some of the unfamiliar sounds of Burmese that you have met in the Lesson and make sure you are hearing and saying them accurately. The recordings for the Pronunciation Sections are on a separate tape, so that you can use them independently of the main Lessons if you wish; and there is an overview of the sounds of Burmese, and the letters that are used to represent them in *BISL*, in an appendix to this book.

Review Lessons

At selected points along the way there is a Review Lesson, distinguished by an R after the Lesson number. Review Lessons serve two purposes. The first is the usual one: when you are working through the course for the first time, a Review Lesson serves to remind you of the material you have covered up to that point, and to revive skills that may be fading. The second use for Review Lessons arises when you want to brush up your command of Burmese after a break. In this situation you won't want to wade through all the explanations on the Lesson tapes: you just want to practise some questions and answers and dialogues. To enable you to do this, the Review Lessons are recorded on separate tapes. For brushing up purposes, these tapes are all you need.

Common Phrases Supplement

The question and answer format of Part 1 doesn't provide a natural place for phrases like "Hallo," "Goodbye," "Thank you," "Wait a minute." You certainly need such phrases for the dialogues in Part 2, and if you have a teacher you may wish to use some of them in class before you get to Part 2. A set of phrases is therefore presented and practised in the "Common Phrases Supplement."

The Common Phrases Supplement is self-contained: it doesn't assume any prior knowledge of the *BISL* material. The text is printed as a supplement in this book, and its oral exercises are on a separate tape, so you can start working on it as soon or as late as you like, and study it at your own pace — but make sure you know the phrases before you start work on the Dialogues. We recommend that you start work on the phrases when you have reached Lesson 11 in Part 1 (where the Pronunciation Sections end), and thereafter take them at a rate of about one to every two Part 1 Lessons. You will find a note in the Lessons reminding you how far on you should be in the Common Phrases Supplement if you are to finish it at the same time as the Lessons.

Classroom language

Classroom talk ("Is everyone here?", "Repeat after me," "That's right," and so on) is omitted from *BISL* on the grounds that it is not needed by the learner on his own (who would have no opportunity to practise it anyway), or by the recently arrived foreigner in Burma. Also classes vary greatly from one another in size, physical environment, age of students, style of teacher, and so on, so many phrases appropriate for one would be inappropriate for another.

The "Common phrases" supplement contains some material that can be useful in this context, but *BISL* leaves it to the teacher to introduce the classroom language appropriate to his or her situation.

4 How to use *BISL Part 1*

Equipment

A cassette tape player of some kind is essential. A pause button on the player is almost indispensable, for the occasions when you need a few seconds to decide what you are going to say. A "review" button also makes life easier when you want a quick repetition of some short phrase. (Otherwise you have to press "stop," press "rewind," press "stop" again, and then press "play." With a "review" button you can do all this with one touch.) Lastly, it is an advantage to have a machine that can record on one track and play on the other: you can then record your answers without risk of erasing the questions, and compare your recorded version with the versions of the Burmese speakers on the tape. However, a machine without these refinements also serves the purpose.

Strategies

This is not a course you can lie back and listen to with your eyes closed. It requires you not just to repeat what you hear, but to formulate your own answers; and to be able to do that you must be able to see the text while you listen to the tapes. Conversely, *BISL* won't help you much if you just peruse the text without listening to the tapes. You may increase your store of general knowledge by finding out a few disparate facts about the structure of Burmese, but without the spoken practice you won't be learning to use the language. Language teachers make much of the distinction between learning a language and learning *about* a language. *BISL* is constructed to help you do the first, not the second.

Don't hesitate to use the pause button (or clumsier alternatives) freely while you are working through the Exercises and Practice Dialogues. Quite often you will need to scan a list for an address before you can respond, or search out a place on a map, or do a bit of mental arithmetic. It is intended that you should stop the tape while you do so and only start it again when you have the information you need. Don't feel that you ought to be able to answer without a break: looking up the facts has to take time. The best place to stop the tape is marked X on this diagram:

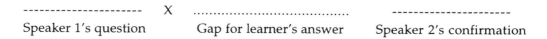

| ---------------------- | X | .... | ---------------------- |
| Speaker 1's question | | Gap for learner's answer | Speaker 2's confirmation |

Stopping the tape at this point (rather than later) means that when you start it going again you have the full length of the gap in which to speak your answer.

The quantity of drilling and repetition required in a language course inevitably varies from one learner to another. What this course includes is probably a minimum for most people. At some points you may feel that your memory of the material is weak. Don't let yourself get to the point of having to turn back the pages to look words up: wind back the tape instead, and do the exercises again until you are familiar with the ground covered.

5 Using Part 1 with a teacher

BISL is designed to be self-operating: learners can work through text and tapes on their own. When they do have an opportunity of working with a teacher, it is important that they should work through a section of the course on their own before coming to the classroom. Virtually all the learning goes on while you are working with the tapes.

So how can a teacher help? Firstly by providing encouragement and reassurance by practising in class the material the students have learned on their own, so that the students can check that they are getting the words, structures and pronunciation right.

Secondly the teacher can answer questions about the language that are not answered in the course, and provide further words and structures to suit the students' specific situation.

Thirdly, and most importantly, the teacher can make the course more fun by practising with real objects and real people in place of the fictions in the text: with real maps, town plans, and room plans; with real telephone directories, visiting cards, menus, money; and with the learners' own phone numbers, experiences, ages, families and so on.

Each Lesson in Part 1 includes a note suggesting activities for class.

One technique that works well in a small class (around 3 to 10 learners) is to have each learner ask the next one his address, phone number and so on. If all the learners make a note of the answers, you can get a further exercise — and a check on the accuracy of understanding of the first — by having the learners verify the answers with each other ("Is John's phone number 76113?" and so on).

Another useful activity is to provide one learner with a source of information (such as a phone directory), and the others with forms containing blanks, like this:

	name	address	phone	

Mandalay University —
     Rector:
     Registrar:
     Prof of Zoology:
     and so on.				

The class then has to ask for the details they need to fill in the blanks. And when that's done, they can verify with each other what they have written down.

6 Lesson contents: Finder list for Part 1

What is …?

Lesson 1. "What?" questions.

Practice:	What's that? — That's a hotel. ဒါ ဘာလဲ။ – ဒါ ဟိုတယ်ပါ။
Vocabulary:	ဒါ။ ဘာ။ –လဲ။ –ပါ။ Places: ဘုရား၊ ဈေး၊ ပြတိုက်၊ ဟိုတယ်၊ ပန်းခြံ။
Reference:	Rangoon map. Grammar notes.
Pronunciation:	a and à; p- and p'-; -o and -aw

Numbers

Lesson 2. Numbers 1-5.

Practice:	What is n° 1? — That's a museum. နံပါတ်(၁) ဘာလဲ။ – ဒါ ပြတိုက်ပါ။
Vocabulary:	နံပါတ်။ တစ်–နှစ်–သုံး–လေး–ငါး။
Reference:	Figures: ၁–၂–၃–၄–၅
Pronunciation:	-q; t- and t'-; n- and hn-

Lesson 3. "Yes/No" questions.

Practice:	Is that a pagoda? — Yes: it is/ No: it's a museum.
	ဒါ ဘုရားလား။ – ဟုတ်ကဲ့။ ဘုရားပါ။ /မဟုတ်ပါဘူး။ ပြတိုက်ပါ။
Vocabulary:	[sentence]–လား။ ဟုတ်ကဲ့ မဟုတ်ပါဘူး။
Reference:	Grammar notes.
Pronunciation:	e and -eh; -q and the next consonant; -q and tone

Lesson 4. Numbers 6-10. Contrasted subject.

	Weakening in တစ်ဆယ် (tăs'eh) and other numbers. တစ်ဆယ် ⇒ /တဆယ်/။
Practice:	Is n° 1 a hotel? နံပါတ်(၁)က ဟိုတယ်လား။
Vocabulary:	[subject]–က။ ခြောက်–ခုနှစ်–ရှစ်–ကိုး–တစ်ဆယ်။
Reference:	Figures: ၆–၇–၈–၉–၁၀
Pronunciation:	k- and k'-; c- and c'-; à and á

Lesson 5. What [noun]?

Practice:	What market is it? — It's Bogyoke Market. ဘာဈေးလဲ။ – ဗိုလ်ချုပ်ဈေးပါ။
Vocabulary:	ဘာ–[noun]. Places in Rangoon: ဗိုလ်ချုပ်ပြတိုက် ၊ ရွှေတိဂုံဘုရား ၊ ဗိုလ်ချုပ်ပန်းခြံ၊ သမတဟိုတယ် ၊ ဗိုလ်ချုပ်ဈေး ၊ သိမ်ကြီးဈေး ၊ ဆူးလေဘုရား၊ မဟာဗန္ဓုလပန်းခြံ ၊ အမျိုးသားပြတိုက်၊ စထရင်းဟိုတယ်။
Reference:	Grammar notes
Pronunciation:	-n; s- and s'-; à and á; th-

Lesson 6. Numbers 0 and short 7. Review of numbers 1-9-0. Checking questions.

Practice:	What's their phone number? — It's 71665.
	72665? — No: 71665.
	တယ်လီဖုန်းနံပါတ် ဘယ်လောက်လဲ။ – ၇၁၆၆၅–ပါ။
	၇၂၆၆၅–လား။ – မဟုတ်ပါဘူး။ ၇၁၆၆၅–ပါ။
Vocabulary:	တယ်လီဖုန်း။ ဘယ်လောက်။ သုည။ ခုန်
Reference:	List of phone nos. Grammar notes.
Pronunciation:	un; ny-; -n and the next consonant

Lesson 7. This [noun].

Practice: What road is this road? — It's Strand Road.
                ဒီလမ်း ဘာလမ်းလဲ။ – ကမ်းနားလမ်းပါ။

Vocabulary: ဒီ–[noun]. Rangoon roads: ဗိုလ်ချုပ်လမ်း၊ အနော်ရထာလမ်း၊ မဟာဗန္ဓုလလမ်း၊
                ကုန်သည်လမ်း၊ ကမ်းနားလမ်း။

Reference: Rangoon road names.

Pronunciation: th- and dh-; my- and py-; a and à

Lesson 8. Numbers in round hundreds. Weakening for 1, 2, 7.
                တစ် ⇒ /တ/။ နှစ် ⇒ /နှ/။ ခုနှစ် ⇒ /ခွန်နှ/။

Practice: တစ်ရာ၊ နှစ်ရာ၊ သုံးရာ စသည်။

Vocabulary: –ရာ။ တစ်ထောင်။

Reference: List of numbers.

Pronunciation: -e and -eh; -o and -aw; round-up of plain and aspirate

Lesson 9. Sentences without –ပါ -ba/-pa *"polite."*

Practice: What road is N° 500? — Strand Road.
                နံပါတ် ၅၀၀ ဘာလမ်းလဲ။ – ကမ်းနားလမ်း။

Vocabulary: Rangoon roads: ဗိုလ်အောင်ကျော်လမ်း၊ ပန်းဆိုးတန်း၊ ဆူးလေဘုရားလမ်း၊ ရွှေဘုံသာလမ်း၊
                [ရွှေတိဂုန်]ဘုရားလမ်း။

Reference: More Rangoon road names.

Pronunciation: hm-; a and à and á

Lesson 10. Numbers in round thousands. Voicing for ထောင် -t'aun thousand and other words.
                သုံးထောင်၊ လေးထောင် ⇒ /သုံးဒေါင်၊ လေးဒေါင်/

Practice: တစ်ထောင်၊ နှစ်ထောင်၊ သုံးထောင် စသည်။

Vocabulary: –ထောင်

Reference: List of numbers. Numbers over 10,000.

Pronunciation: hl-; round-up of breathed nasals; round-up of tones

Where is …?

Lesson 11. Which [noun]? In [place]. In which [place]?

Practice: Which road is the Strand Hotel in? — In/On Strand Road.
                စထရင်းဟိုတယ်က ဘယ်လမ်းမှာလဲ။ – ကမ်းနားလမ်းမှာ။

Vocabulary: ဘယ်–[noun]။ [noun]–မှာ။ ဘယ်–[noun]–မှာလဲ။

Reference: List of places and roads. Grammar notes.
                What [noun] versus Which [noun]: ဘယ်–[noun] versus ဘာ–[noun]

Lesson 12. Numbers in round tens. Voicing for ဆယ် (-s'eh) ten. သုံးဆယ်၊ လေးဆယ် ⇒ /သုံးဇယ်၊
                လေးဇယ်/

Practice: ၁၀၊ ၂၀၊ ၃၀ စသည်

Vocabulary: –ဆယ်

Reference: List of numbers.

Lesson 13. Names of some countries near Burma. Asking for a repeat.

Practice: What country is n° 20? — Bangladesh.

Could you please say that again? — Bangladesh.

နံပါတ်(၂၀)က ဘာနိုင်ငံလဲ။ – ဘင်္ဂလားဒေ့ရှ်နိုင်ငံပါ။

ထပ်ပြောပါအုံး။ – ဘင်္ဂလားဒေ့ရှ်နိုင်ငံ။

Vocabulary: Country names: အိန္ဒိယနိုင်ငံ၊ ဘင်္ဂလားဒေ့ရှ်နိုင်ငံ၊ မြန်မာနိုင်ငံ၊ ထိုင်းနိုင်ငံ၊ မလေးရှားနိုင်ငံ၊ ဗီယက်နမ်နိုင်ငံ၊ ဖိလစ်ပိုင်နိုင်ငံ၊ တရုပ်နိုင်ငံ၊ ဂျပန်နိုင်ငံ။

Reference: Asia map. Names of other countries. Burma, Myanmar, Bamar.

Lesson 14. Numbers in hundreds and tens. Joining numbers with "and" or creaky tone.

Practice: ၁၁၀၊ ၃၂၀၊ ၅၃၀ စသည်။

Vocabulary: ရှစ်ဆယ်နဲ့ ရှစ် or ရှစ်ဆယ့် ရှစ်

Reference: List of numbers.

Lesson 15. Names of some towns in countries near Burma.

Practice: What town is n° 140? — New Delhi.

နံပါတ်(၁၄၀)က ဘာမြို့လဲ။ – နယူးဒေလီပါ။

Vocabulary: မြို့။ Town names: နယူးဒေလီ၊ ဒက္ကား၊ ရန်ကုန်၊ ဘန်ကောက်၊ ကွာလာလမ်ပူ၊ ဟနွိုင်း၊ မနီလာ၊ ပီကင်း၊ တိုကျို။

Reference: Rangoon/Yangon.

Lesson 16. Numbers in tens and units. No တစ် (tă) in 11-19. တစ်ဆယ့် တစ် ⇒ ဆယ့် တစ် and so on.

Practice: ၁၉၊ ၂၆၊ ၃၇၊ စသည်။

Vocabulary: -

Reference: List of numbers.

Lesson 17. Informal names for countries.

Practice: Which country is Manila in? — In the Philippines.

မနီလာက ဘယ်နိုင်ငံမှာလဲ။ – ဖိလစ်ပိုင်မှာပါ။

Vocabulary: ဗမာပြည်။ ယိုးဒယား။ စသည်

Reference: -

Lesson 18. Numbers 1-9,999. Omitting တစ် (tă) in 1000-1999. တစ်ထောင့်တစ်ရာ ⇒ ထောင့်တစ်ရာ and so on.

Practice: ၁–၉၉၉၉

Vocabulary: ရှစ်ထောင့် ခြောက်ရာ့ သုံးဆယ့် ငါး စသည်

Reference: List of numbers.

Lesson 19. Names of some towns in Burma.

Practice: What town is n° 16? — Myitkyina.

နံပါတ်(၁၆)က ဘာမြို့လဲ။ – မြစ်ကြီးနားပါ။

Vocabulary: Burma towns: မြစ်ကြီးနား၊ မေမြို့၊ မန္တလေး၊ စစ်ကိုင်း၊ ပုဂံ၊ သာစည်၊ တောင်ကြီး၊ ပြည်၊ ရေနံချောင်း၊ သံတွဲ၊ ပဲခူး၊ ရန်ကုန်၊ မော်လမြိုင်။

Reference: Burma map. Names of states, divisions, and similar. Traditional and revised roman spellings.

Lesson 20. Where and here.
    Practice: Where is Maymyo? — It's here. မေမြို့ဘယ်မှာလဲ။ — ဒီမှာပါ။
    Vocabulary: ဘယ်မှာ။ ဒီမှာ။
    Reference: Grammar notes.

Lesson 20R. Review of material in Lessons 1-20.
    Overview of grammar, numbers and vocabulary for Lessons 1-20

Who is … ?
Lesson 21. Burmese personal names.
    Practice: Who's that? — It's Tin Aye. ဒါ ဘယ်သူလဲ။ — တင်အေးပါ။
    Vocabulary: ဘယ်သူ။
    Reference: Grammar notes. Burmese naming practice.

Lesson 22. Names with the prefixes U and Daw.
    Practice: Who's that? — It's U Tin Aye. နံပါတ်(၄) ဘယ်သူလဲ။ — ဒါက ဦးတင်အေးပါ။
    Vocabulary: ဦး–NAME။ ဒေါ်–NAME။
    Reference: Other prefixes to Burmese names

Counting: prices
Lesson 23. Prices in dollars and pounds (unround numbers). Weakening and voicing in prices.
                  နှစ်ပေါင်၊ သုံးပေါင် ⇒ /နှစ်ပေါင်၊ သုံးဘောင်/ စသည်။
    Practice: သုံးဒေါ်လာ။ နှစ်ရာ ကိုးဆယ့် ရှစ်ပေါင်။ စသည်။
    Vocabulary: ဒေါ်လာ။ ပေါင်။
    Reference: Price lists.

Lesson 24. Names with the prefixes Ko and Ma.
    Practice: Who is n° 1? — N° 1 is Ko Khin Maung Aye.
                  နံပါတ်(၁) ဘယ်သူလဲ။ — နံပါတ်(၁)က ကိုခင်မောင်အေးပါ။
    Vocabulary: ကို–NAME။ မ–NAME။
    Reference: -

Lesson 25. Review of names and prefixes.
    Practice: Who is n° 1? — That's Bo Ni. — Ah. U Bo Ni.
                  နံပါတ်(၁) ဘယ်သူလဲ။ — ဒါက ဗိုလ်နီပါ။ — အာ။ ဦးဗိုလ်နီ။
    Vocabulary: -
    Reference: -

Lesson 26. Prices in pounds and pya.
    Practice: Round and unround numbers, and ten. ပေါင် နှစ်ဆယ်။ ပြား နှစ်ဆယ်။ ဆယ်ပေါင်။
                  ဆယ်ပြား။
    Vocabulary: ပြား၊ ပဲနီ၊ ဆင့်။
    Reference: Price lists

Verb sentences

Lesson 27. Verbs in Which? questions.

Practice:	Which road does he live in/on? — He lives in/on Bogyoke St. ဘယ်လမ်းမှာ နေသလဲ။ – ဗိုလ်ချုပ်လမ်းမှာ နေပါတယ်။
Vocabulary:	[place]–မှာ နေတယ်။
Reference:	Pronouns: "he" and "she" are dispensable.

Lesson 28. Prices in pounds combined with pence. Round and unround numbers.

Practice:	How much is nº 1? — It's six pounds 45 pence. နံပါတ်(၁) ဘယ်လောက်လဲ။ – ခြောက်ပေါင် လေးဆယ့်ငါးပြား။
Vocabulary:	-
Reference:	Price lists

Lesson 29. Verbs in Yes/No questions.

Practice:	Does he live in Bogyoke St? — Yes, he does/ No, he doesn't. ဗိုလ်ချုပ်လမ်းမှာ နေသလား။ – ဟုတ်ကဲ့။ နေပါတယ်။/ မနေပါဘူး။
Vocabulary:	[verb]–သလား။ – [verb]–ပါတယ်။/ မ–[verb]–ပါဘူး။
Reference:	Names and addresses. Grammar notes.

Counting: streets

Lesson 30. Counting: practice with numbered streets. Round and unround numbers.

Practice:	Where does U Sein Myint live? — He lives at 180, 84th St. ဦးစိန်မြင့် ဘယ်မှာ နေသလဲ။ – အမှတ်–၁၈၀၊ ၈၄–လမ်းမှာ နေပါတယ်။
Vocabulary:	အမှတ်–၃၄၊ ၇၅–လမ်း
Reference:	Names and addresses

Lesson 31. Who comes from where.

Practice:	What country does he come from? — He comes from India. ဘယ်နိုင်ငံက လာသလဲ။ – အိန္ဒိယနိုင်ငံက လာပါတယ်။
Vocabulary:	[country]–က လာ–။
Reference:	Names and countries. Grammar notes.

Lesson 32. Prices in Burmese currency. Round, unround, and ten.

Practice:	How much is nº 1? — It's three kyats. နံပါတ်(၁) ဘယ်လောက်လဲ။ – သုံးကျပ်ပါ။
Vocabulary:	ကျပ်။ ပြား။ ဗမာငွေ။
Reference:	Price list. Burmese currency notes.

Counting: telling the time

Lesson 33. Clock times (hours). Who came when.

Practice:	What time did she come? — She came at 3.00. ဘယ်အချိန် လာသလဲ။ – ၆–နာရီမှာ လာပါတယ်။
Vocabulary:	TIME–မှာ လာ–။ အချိန်။ နာရီ။
Reference:	Names and times

Lesson 34. Going to [place]. Who went where.
Practice: Which town did she go to? — She went to Maymyo.
                 ဘယ်မြို့ သွားသလဲ။ – မေမြို့ သွားပါတယ်။
Vocabulary: [place] သွား–။ More names of countries.
Reference: Grammar notes. Names and destinations.

Lesson 35. More practice with going to.
Practice: Where did she go? — She went to the library.
                 ဘယ် သွားသလဲ။ – စာကြည့်တိုက် သွားပါတယ်။
Vocabulary: ဘယ် သွား–။ Places: အိမ်သာ၊ စာကြည့်တိုက်၊ စားသောက်ခန်း၊ အပြင်၊
                 သံတမန်ကုန်တိုက်၊ ကုန်တိုက်။
Reference: Names and destinations

Lesson 36. Asking people's names.
Practice: What's your name? — It's Aung San.
                 နာမည် ဘယ်လို ခေါ်သလဲ။ – အောင်ဆန်းလို့ ခေါ်ပါတယ်။
Vocabulary: နာမည်။ ဘယ်လို။ ခေါ်–။ –လို့။
Reference: List of names. Grammar notes.

Lesson 37. Clock times: hours and minutes. Where did he go and when?
Practice: What time did Ma San San Hlaing go? — She went at 7.45.
                 မစံစံလှိုင် ဘယ်အချိန် သွားသလဲ။ – ၇-နာရီ ၄၅-မိနစ်မှာ သွားပါတယ်။
Vocabulary: မိနစ်။ –ခွဲ။
Reference: Name, place, time

Lesson 38. Burmese currency: parts of a kyat.
Practice: How much is this? — K1/50.
                 ဒါ ဘယ်လောက်လဲ။ – သုံးကျပ်ခွဲ။
Vocabulary: –ခွဲ။
Reference: Price list. Burmese coins.

Lesson 39. Paying a price. Who paid what.
Practice: How much did you pay for that? — I paid K45.
                 အဲဒါ ဘယ်လောက် ပေးရသလဲ။ – ၄၅-ကျပ် ပေးရပါတယ်။
Vocabulary: PRICE ပေးရ–။ အဲဒါ။
Reference: People and prices. Pronouns: "you" and "I" are dispensable.

Lesson 40. Asking for words.
Practice: What's that called in Burmese? — It's called စာအိတ် (sa-eiq)
                 အဲဒါ ဗမာလို ဘယ်လို ခေါ်သလဲ။ – စာအိတ်လို့ ခေါ်ပါတယ်။
Vocabulary: ဗမာလို ခေါ်–။ Things: ဘောပင်၊ ပုံစကန်ဒ်၊ ဖလင်၊ ဆယ်လိုတိပ်၊ တိပ်ခွေ၊ ဘီစကွတ်၊
                 ကော်ဖီမှုန့်၊ မြေပုံ၊ နို့မှုန့်၊ စာအိတ်၊ စာရွက်။
Reference: Things and prices. Grammar notes.

Lesson 41. Buying things. Who bought what.
Practice:	What did he buy? — He bought a map and some sellotape/Scotchtape.
	ဘာ ဝယ်သလဲ။ – မြေပုံနဲ့ ဆယ်လိုတိပ် ဝယ်ပါတယ်။
Vocabulary:	[thing] ဝယ်–။ [thing-1]–နဲ့ [thing-2]
Reference:	Names and things

Lesson 41R. Review of material in Lessons 1-41

Lesson 42. Want to [verb].
Practice:	Where did he want to go? — He wanted to go to Peking.
	ဘယ် သွားချင်သလဲ။ – ပီကင်း သွားချင်ပါတယ်၊
Vocabulary:	[verb]–ချင်–။
Reference:	People, places, times, things. Grammar notes.

Lesson 43. Practice with want to [verb]. More verbs: sit, open, close.
Practice:	Where do you want to sit? Do you want the fan on?
	ဘယ်မှာ ထိုင်ချင်သလဲ။ ပန်ကာ ဖွင့်ချင်သလား။
Vocabulary:	ထိုင်–။ ဖွင့်–။ ပိတ်–။ စားပွဲ။ ပြတင်းပေါက်၊ တံခါး၊ ပန်ကာ၊ မီး။
Reference:	Names and preferences

Lesson 44. Going to [verb].
Practice:	Where is he going to sit? — He's going to sit here.
	ဘယ်မှာ ထိုင်မလဲ။ – ဒီမှာ ထိုင်မယ်။
Vocabulary:	[verb]–မယ်။
Reference:	Grammar notes. Names and plans.

Lesson 45. Will have to [verb].
Practice:	Where is he going to have to live? — He'll have to live in Taunggyi.
	ဘယ်မှာ နေရမလဲ။ – တောင်ကြီးမှာ နေရမယ်။
Vocabulary:	[verb]–ရမယ်။
Reference:	Grammar notes. Names and obligations.

Lesson 46. Requests: Please [verb]/ Please don't [verb].
Practice:	Should I sit here? — Yes, please do/ No, please don't.
	ဒီမှာ ထိုင်ရမလား။ – ဟုတ်ကဲ့။ ထိုင်ပါ။/ မထိုင်ပါနဲ့။
Vocabulary:	[verb]–ပါ။/ မ–[verb]–ပါနဲ့။
Reference:	Grammar notes. Names and preferences.

Lesson 46R. Review of material in Lessons 1-46.

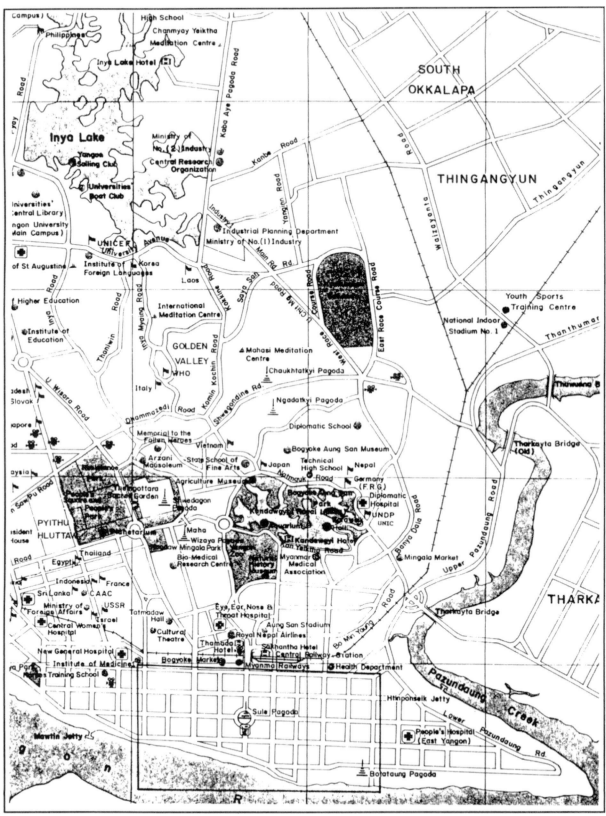

From a tourist map of Rangoon (Yangon).
The downtown section is shown separately.

THE LESSONS

To start using *BISL*, put the book where you can see the street plan of Rangoon, and start listening to Lesson 1 on the tape.

The tapes

The main function of the tapes is to introduce new words and structures to you and to give you opportunities to practise them. Many of the exercises ask questions for you to answer (like "What's the phone number of the Strand Hotel?"), and one of the functions of the book is to give you the facts you need for your answers (like "81533"). So it is important to look at the book while you do the exercises on the tape. The book also gives you notes and explanations of points that are too detailed or lengthy to be delivered by word of mouth.

The tapes in this set are called "Lesson Tapes," because they provide explanations and comments as well as exercises. This is all very well when you're meeting the material for the first time. But when you've got some way through *BISL* and you want to review some of the material you've learned, you won't need the explanations — at that stage they are unnecessary and even irritating. So what you can do is to use a different set of tapes — called "Review Tapes" — where you will find exercises for review unimpeded by explanation.

Having much leisure during this six weeks' voyage I now set myself with great industry to acquire the language. ... By the time I reached Amerapoorah I had the gratification to find that I could express myself on common topics with some degree of fluency and correctness.

From: Henry Gouger: *A Personal Narrative of Two Years Imprisonment in Burmah.* London 1864. p. 22

Rangoon sites and streets: plan

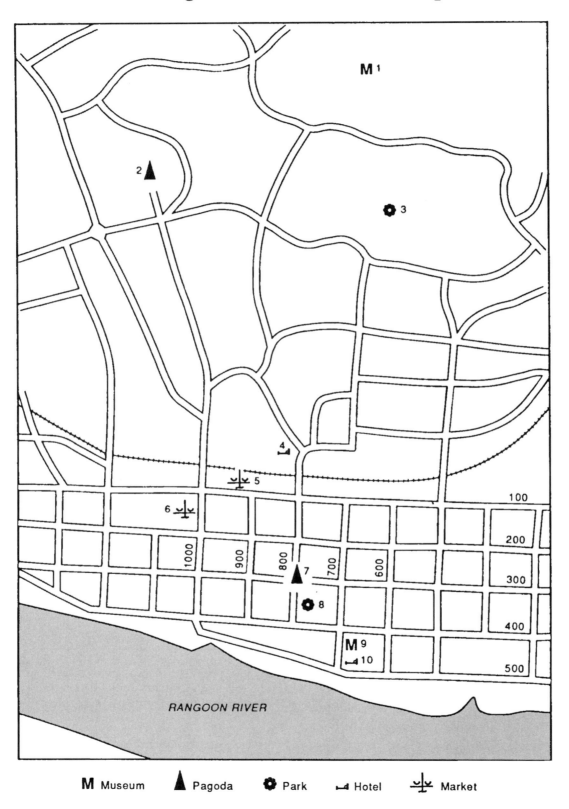

M Museum   ▲ Pagoda   ✿ Park   ⊶ Hotel   ⥽ Market

Diphthongs in the roman transcription:
pronounce ei as in *vein*, ai as in *Thailand*, ou as in *though*, au as in *Sauerkraut*.

Rangoon sites and streets: key

Sites

n°	symbol	script	meaning	pronunciation — (1) script	roman
1.	**M**	ပြတိုက်	museum	/ပျာ့ဒိုက်/	pyá-daiq
2.	▲	ဘုရား	pagoda	/ဖယား/	p'ăyà
3.	✿	ပန်းခြံ	park	/ပန်းဂျန်/	pàn-jan
4.	⊔	ဟိုတယ်	hotel	as written	ho-teh
5.	⸽	ဈေး	market	as written	zè

Numbered sites

n°	script	English equivalent	pronunciation in roman [1]
1.	ဗိုလ်ချုပ်ပြတိုက်	Bogyoke Museum	Bo-jouq Pyá-daiq
2.	ရွှေတိဂုံ ဘုရား	Shwedagon Pagoda	Shwe-dăgoun P'ăyà
3.	ဗိုလ်ချုပ်ပန်းခြံ	Bogyoke Park	Bo-jouq Pàn-jan
4.	သမ္မတဟိုတယ်	President Hotel	Thămădá Ho-teh
5.	ဗိုလ်ချုပ်ဈေး	Bogyoke Market	Bo-jouq Zè
6.	သိမ်ကြီးဈေး	Thein-gyi Market	Thein-jì-zè
7.	ဆူးလေဘုရား	Sule Pagoda	S'ù-le P'ăya
8.	မဟာဗန္ဓုလပန်းခြံ	Maha Bandoola Park	Măha Ban-dú-lá Pàn-jan
9.	အမျိုးသားပြတိုက်	National Museum	Ămyò-thà Pyá-daiq
10.	စထရင်းဟိုတယ်	Strand Hotel	Săt'ărìn Ho-teh

Numbered streets

n°	script	English equivalent	pronunciation in roman [1]
100	ဗိုလ်ချုပ်လမ်း	Bogyoke Street	Bo-jouq Làn
200	အနော်ရထာလမ်း	Anawrahta Street	Ănaw-yăt'a Làn [2]
300	မဟာဗန္ဓုလလမ်း	Maha Bandoola Street	Măha Ban-dú-lá Làn
400	ကုန်သည်လမ်း	Merchant Street	Koun-dheh Làn
500	ကမ်းနားလမ်း	Strand Road	Kàn-nà Làn
600	ဗိုလ်အောင်ကျော်လမ်း	Bo Aung Kyaw Street	Bo Aun Jaw Làn
700	ပန်းဆိုးတန်း	Pansodan Street	Pàn-s'ò-dàn or Pàn-zò-dàn
800	ဆူးလေဘုရားလမ်း	Sule Pagoda Road	S'ù-le P'ăyà Làn
900	ရွှေဘုံသာလမ်း	Shwebontha Street	Shwe-boun-dha Làn
1000	[ရွှေတိဂုံ]ဘုရားလမ်း	Shwedagon Pagoda Rd	[Shwe-dăgoun] P'ăyà Làn

1. On "pronunciation in roman" and "pronunciation in script" see Appendix 3.
2. Also pronounced Ănaw-răt'a Làn

Diphthongs in the roman transcription:
pronounce ei as in *vein*, ai as in *Thailand*, ou as in *though*, au as in *Sauerkraut*.

Rangoon names with pronunciation represented in Burmese script

Sites

n°	script	English equivalent	pronunciation in script [1]
1.	ဗိုလ်ချုပ်ပြတိုက်	Bogyoke Museum	/ဗိုဂျုတ်ပျှဒိုက်/
2.	ရွှေတိဂုံ ဘုရား	Shwedagon Pagoda	/ရွှေဒဂုန်ဖယား/
3.	ဗိုလ်ချုပ်ပန်းခြံ	Bogyoke Park	/ဗိုဂျုပ်ပန်းဂျန်/
4.	သမ္မတဟိုတယ်	President Hotel	/သမဒါ့ဟိုတယ်/
5.	ဗိုလ်ချုပ်ဈေး	Bogyoke Market	/ဗိုဂျုတ်ဇေး/
6.	သိမ်ကြီးဈေး	Thein-gyi Market	/သိန်ကြီးဇေး/
7.	ဆူးလေဘုရား	Sule Pagoda	/ဆူးလေဖယား/
8.	မဟာဗန္ဓုလပန်းခြံ	Maha Bandoola Park	/မဟာဗန်ဒုလ့ပန်းဂျန်/
9.	အမျိုးသားပြတိုက်	National Museum	/အမျိုးသားပျဒိုက်/
10.	စထရင်းဟိုတယ်	Strand Hotel	as written

Streets

n°	script	English equivalent	pronunciation in script [1]
100	ဗိုလ်ချုပ်လမ်း	Bogyoke Street	/ဗိုဂျုတ်လန်း/
200	အနော်ရထာလမ်း	Anawrahta Street	/အနော်ယထာလန်း/ [2]
300	မဟာဗန္ဓုလလမ်း	Maha Bandoola Street	/မဟာဗန်ဒုလ့လန်း/
400	ကုန်သည်လမ်း	Merchant Street	/ကုန်သုယ်လန်း/
500	ကမ်းနားလမ်း	Strand Road	as written
600	ဗိုလ်အောင်ကျော်လမ်း	Bo Aung Kyaw Street	/ဗိုအောင်ကျော်လန်း/
700	ပန်းဆိုးတန်း	Pansodan Street	/ပန်းဆိုးဒန်း/ or /ပန်းဇိဒန်း/
800	ဆူးလေဘုရားလမ်း	Sule Pagoda Road	/ဆူးလေဖယားလန်း/
900	ရွှေဘုံသာလမ်း	Shwebontha Street	/ရွှေဘုံသာလန်း/
1000	[ရွှေတိဂုံ]ဘုရားလမ်း	Shwedagon Pagoda Rd	/[ရွှေဒဂုန်]ဘုရားလန်း/

1. On "pronunciation in roman" and "pronunciation in script" see Appendix 3. The paucity of "as written" entries shows how many mismatches there are between sound and script.
2. Also pronounced /အနော်ရထာလန်း/။

In the precincts of a pagoda
From the children's comic ရွှေသွေး

Diphthongs in the roman transcription:
pronounce ei as in *vein*, ai as in *Thailand*, ou as in *though*, au as in *Sauerkraut*.

LESSON 1

"What?" questions.
What's that? — That's a hotel.

New words

script	English	pronunciation [1]
ပြတိုက် /ပြွဲဒိုက်/ [2]	museum	pyá-daiq [3]
ပြ– /ပြွဲ/	to show, exhibit	pyá-
တိုက်	building	taiq [3]
ဘုရား /ဖယား/	lord, pagoda, Buddha image	p'ăyà
ပန်းခြံ /ပန်းဂျန်/	park, garden	pàn-jan
ပန်း	flower	pàn
ခြံ /ချန်/	enclosure, garden	c'an
ဟိုတယ်	hotel [from English]	ho-teh
ဈေး /ဇေး/	market	zè
ဒါ	that thing, this thing	ɟa
ဘာ	what?	ba
–လဲ	suffix: "question [4]	-lèh
–ပါ /–ဘာ or –ပါ/ [5]	suffix: "polite" [6]	-ba or -pa[5]

1. For notes on the roman transcription and its limitations see Appendix 3.

2. Words between /.../ show the pronunciation written in Burmese script. It is shown only when the pronunciation of the word doesn't match its spelling. Words without a /.../ entry are pronounced as written.

3. Diphthongs in the roman transcription: pronounce ai as in *Thailand*. See also the Note on diphthongs below, and the reminder at the foot of the page.

4. The suffix –လဲ (-lèh) in ဘာလဲ (ba-lèh) "What?" shows that the speaker is asking a question. It is as if the "?" were spoken aloud.

5. This suffix is pronounced /–ပါ/ (-pa) after a glottal stop, for example in —
ဒါ ပြတိုက်ပါ   /ဒါ ပြွဲဒိုက်ပါ/   Da pyá-daiq-pa   That's a museum.
but /–ဘာ/ (-ba) elsewhere; for example in —
ဒါ ဘုရားပါ   /ဒါ ဖယားဘာ/   Da p'ăyà-ba   That's a pagoda.
At this stage the difference is not crucial. It is an example of a rule that is given full coverage in Lesson 10. When people are speaking fast, the voiced form /–ဘာ/ (-ba) often sounds like -va. Don't be misled into thinking this is a new word. Burmese doesn't have a V sound anyway: -va is just a variant of /–ဘာ/ (-ba).

| Diphthongs in the roman transcription: pronounce ei as in *vein*, ai as in *Thailand*, ou as in *though*, au as in *Sauerkraut*. | 5 |

6. The suffix –ပါ (-ba) in [sentence]–ပါ ([sentence]-ba) shows you are being polite to the person you are talking to. You'll hear more about it in Lesson 9.

Example sentences

Speaker 1: ဒါ ဘာလဲ။   What's that?   Da ba-lèh?

Speaker 2: ဒါ ဟိုတယ်ပါ။   That's a hotel.   Da ho-teh-ba.

In later lessons "Speaker 1" and "Speaker 2" will be shortened to "S1" and "S2"

Models for the exercises

In the models showing the format for each Exercise
    S1 means Speaker 1
    S2 means Speaker 2
    L means you the Learner
Where you see L in the model there is a gap on the tape to give you time to say your response aloud — and record it on a student track, if you are using a machine that can do that.

In almost all exercises, your response is followed by the same response spoken by one of the speakers on the tape. This is a "confirmation response": it is to confirm your response, or to show you how to correct it if you need to. In the models, when your answer is followed by a confirmation response you will find it marked L/S2 (or L/S1, if S1 is making the confirmation).

In a few exercises you are asked to say the phrase again after a response and confirmation. In that case the three responses will be marked L/S2/L (or L/S1/L).

For the Exercises in Lesson 1 you need to be looking at the map of Rangoon in the text.

Ex. 1: Prompt: S1 points to Number 1 and asks
    S1/L [representing: S1 asks and you repeat]:   ဒါ ဘာလဲ။   Da ba-lèh?
    S2/L [representing: S2 answers and you repeat]:   ဒါ ပြတိုက်ပါ။   Da pyá-daiq-pa.

Ex. 2: Prompt: Point to Number 5 and ask what it is (ဒါ ဘာလဲ)
    L/S1 [short for: you ask and S1 repeats]:   ဒါ ဘာလဲ။   Da ba-lèh?
    S2:   ဒါ ဈေးပါ။   Da zè-ba.
    L/S2/L: ဈေး။   Zè.
[short for: (1) you repeat the word, (2) S1 confirms, (3) you say the word again]

Diphthongs in the roman transcription:
pronounce ei as in *vein*, ai as in *Thailand*, ou as in *though*, au as in *Sauerkraut*.

Ex. 3: Prompt: S1 points to Number 1 and says:

S1: ဒါ ဘာလဲ။ Da ba-lèh?

L/S2 [= you answer and S2 confirms]: ဒါ ပြတိုက်ပါ။ Da pyá-daiq-pa.

In class:

Ask each other questions pointing to the map (Learner and Teacher, Learner and Learner). For a large class copy the map to a transparency and use an overhead projector.

Notes

Grammar. In questions and answers of the type you meet in this Lesson ("*is* sentences") there is no Burmese word corresponding to the English word *is*. Word by word the Burmese says:

ဒါ – ဘာ–လဲ။ That — what-*question?* da — ba-lèh

ဒါ – ဈေး–ပါ။ That — market-*polite.* da — zè-ba

There is a word for "is" in Burmese, but most of the time people prefer to leave it out. The same goes for "are" and for "was" and "were."

Notice also the neat parallel between the question and the answer. Both begin with ဒါ da "this/that" and then go on to ask or state something about "this/that." As a way of showing that the *"is"* is needed in English but is not expressed in Burmese, we put it in <...>.

The question says — "This/that <is> what *-question*"

and the answer says — "This/that <is> market *-polite*"

Looked at as a formula, the structure is

NOUN1	<is>	NOUN2		SUFFIX

In this formula NOUN and SUFFIX are like slots or containers: you can drop (almost) any actual noun or suffix into the appropriate container and end up with a grammatical sentence. Here are some examples:

NOUN1	<is>	NOUN2		SUFFIX
This/that		his office		*polite*
That building		a school		*right?*
N° 4		the university		*of course*
The nearer one		a pagoda		*you see*

You can swap the NOUN1 from one of these sentences with the NOUN1 from any other and the sentence still makes sense. And you can do the same with the NOUN2s; and the same again with the suffixes. Burmese has a suffix for each of the meanings listed here. There is only one restriction: if the NOUN2 container is filled with a question-word, like "what" or "where" or "which one" and so on, then the suffix has to be –လဲ -lèh *question.*

NOUN1	<is>	NOUN2		SUFFIX
This/that		what		*question*
That building		where		
N° 4				
The nearer one				

Diphthongs in the roman transcription:
pronounce ei as in *vein,* ai as in *Thailand,* ou as in *though,* au as in *Sauerkraut.*

Two ba-s? Take care not to confuse သာ ba "what?" (which goes in the NOUN2 container), with –ပါ -ba *"polite"* (which goes in the SUFFIX container):

NOUN1 <is>	NOUN2	SUFFIX
ဒါ	သာ	–လဲ
D a	ba	-lèh
This/that <is>	what	*question*
ဒါ	ဟိုတယ်	–ပါ
D a	ho-teh	-ba
This/that <is>	hotel	*polite*

Pagodas. Pagodas in Burma take various forms, but the usual shape is like a bell built of stone or brick and topped by an ornate finial. They are often sited on high ground where they can be seen from far and wide. Many pagodas are whitewashed, but very popular ones, like the Shwedagon and Sule Pagoda, are covered with gold leaf. They form a focus for Buddhist devotion.

Hotel. Foreign words in Burmese (like "hotel") are pronounced by some speakers with a good English accent, mainly following the British model, and by others with a strong Burmese accent. Most speakers produce something between the two extremes. For *BISL* we have tried to give you a fairly strong Burmese accent (like ho-teh) with the idea of giving you some practice in recognizing familiar words with an unfamiliar pronunciation.

Diphthongs in the roman transcription. The choice of ei, ai, au and ou to represent the four diphthongs of Burmese is influenced both by standard phonetic transcriptions of such sounds and by the conventions of traditional romanization in Burma. They are all ambiguous in English: compare *vein* and *receive*, *Thai* and *tail*, *Gauss* and *Gaul*, *though* and *thought* and *through*. It is not easy for beginners to remember which pronunciation to attach to each written diphthong, so for the first few Lessons a reminder is printed at the foot of each page.

Pronunciation section for Lesson 1

Introduction

There is a section for pronunciation practice in each of the first ten Lessons of *BISL*. The Pronunciation Section comments on and provides practice in pronunciation points that arise in the words introduced in the Lesson. Happily, not all the sounds of Burmese are alien to speakers of English. Burmese and English both have a "m" sound and a "l" sound, for example, and it would be pointless to make English-speaking learners of Burmese work through exercises on sounds like those. The Pronunciation Sections therefore pick out the sounds in Burmese which speakers of English find unfamiliar, or pairs of sounds they find hard to distinguish, and provide exercises in listening to, discriminating between, and pronouncing those.

Diphthongs in the roman transcription:
pronounce ei as in *vein*, ai as in *Thailand*, ou as in *though*, au as in *Sauerkraut*.

The comments and exercises are all on tape: the text below only provides written representations of the words and sounds you will be practising. All the Pronunciation Sections are recorded together on their own separate tape, so at this point you will need to take out the main Groundwork tape, load the Pronunciation tape, and wind it to the Pronunciation Section for Lesson 1.

For a list of all the sounds in the Burmese sound system, with some examples, see Appendix 1 at the end of this book.

Text for use with the tape

For the pronunciation of ai, ei, ou, au in the roman transcription,
see the reminder at the foot of the page.

Point 1: high and low pitch: **a and à**

1.	pàn-jan (hi-lo), ho-teh (lo-lo)	park, hotel	ပန်းခြံ၊ ဟိုတယ်။
2.	A. Da maùn-ba (lo hi-lo)	That's a gong.	ဒါ မောင်းပါ။
	B. Da maun-ba (lo lo-lo)	That's her brother.	ဒါ မောင်ပါ။
3.	Da pàn-jan-ba. (lo hi-lo-lo)	That's a park.	ဒါ ပန်းခြံပါ။
4.	Da ho-teh-ba. (lo lo-lo-lo)	That's a hotel.	ဒါ ဟိုတယ်ပါ။
5.	Da zè-ba. (lo hi-lo)	That's a market.	ဒါ ဈေးပါ။

Point 2: plain and aspirate: **p- and p'-**

1. ăpaw, ăp'aw (English paw)   above, companion   အပေါ်၊ အဖော်
2. *A pair of pink pants*
3. The mechanics of aspirate, plain and voiced

	closure	release	voice	
p'-	—————— ! hhhh	....	(aspirate)
p-	—————— !	....	(plain)
b-	—————— !	....	(voiced)

4. English: *Pore, Bore*
5. ăp'aw, ăpaw, ăbaw   အပေါ်၊ အဖော်၊ အဘော်
6. pèh, p'èh   beans, silk   ပဲ၊ ဖဲ
   pù-deh, p'ù-deh *   to attach, to worship   ပူးတယ်၊ ဖူးတယ်
   pó-deh, p'ó-deh *   to send, to block up   ပို့တယ်၊ ဖို့တယ်
   peiq-teh, p'eiq-teh*   to close, to invite   ပိတ်တယ်၊ ဖိတ်တယ်

   *-deh (sometimes pronounced -teh) is a suffix attached to verbs.
   You will find a full explanation in Lesson 27.

7. p'ăyà   pagoda   ဘုရား (/ဖယား/)
8. pàn-jan, pyá-daiq   park, museum   ပန်းခြံ၊ ပြတိုက်

Point 3: vowels: **-o and -aw**

1. ho-teh   hotel   ဟိုတယ်
2. ki-mo-no   kimono   ကီမိုနို

Diphthongs in the roman transcription:	9
pronounce ei as in *vein*, ai as in *Thailand*, ou as in *though*, au as in *Sauerkraut*.	

3. A-ji-no-mo-to [name of a brand of MSG] အာဂျိနိုမိုတို

4. Bămaw, Maw-lămyain Bamaw, Moulmein [Burma towns] ဗန်းမော်၊ မော်လမြိုင်

English: *jackdaw*

5. A. Sàw-deh. B. Sò-deh. A. He's early. B. He worries. စောတယ်၊ စိုးတယ်

LESSON 2

Numbers 1 to 5.
What is nº 1? — It's a museum.

၁	၂	၃	၄	၅
1	2	3	4	5

New words

figures	script	English	pronunciation
	နံပါတ် /နန့်ဗတ်/	number	nan-baq
၁	တစ်	one	tiq
၂	နှစ်	two	hniq
၃	သုံး	three	thoùn [1]
၄	လေး	four	lè
၅	ငါး	five	ngà

1. For the pronunciation of diphthongs see the reminder at the foot of the page.

Writing the figures

In these diagrams the blob shows where to place the pen to start drawing the figure, and the arrowhead shows where you end the stroke. Note that the figures ၂ ၃ ၄ ၅ all have a tail that drops below the line: ၂ ၃ ၄ ၅

Diphthongs in the roman transcription:
pronounce ei as in *vein,* ai as in *Thailand,* ou as in *though,* au as in *Sauerkraut.*

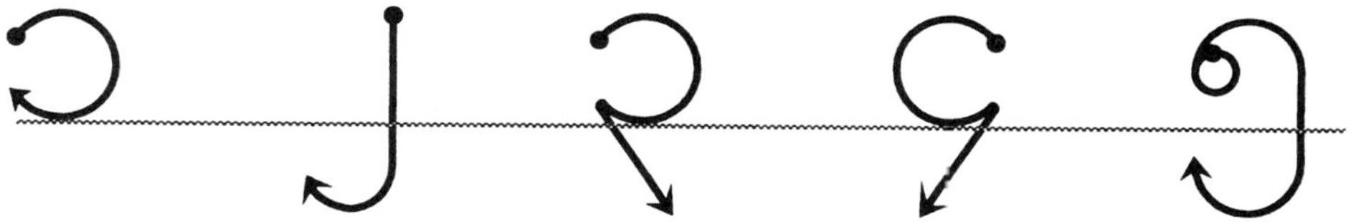

Models for the exercises

Ex. 1: Repeat and add one

S1:	တစ်။	Tiq.
L/S2/L:	တစ်၊ နှစ်။	Tiq, hniq.

(short for: L responds and S2 confirms the response, and L repeats)

Ex. 2: Add one

S1:	တစ်။	Tiq.
L/S2/L:	နှစ်။	Hniq.

Ex. 3: Looking at the map.

S1:	နံပါတ်(၁) ဘာလဲ။	Nan-baq-tiq ba-lèh?
L/S2:	ဒါ ပြတိုက်ပါ။	Da pyá-daiq-pa.

Ex. 4 (for reading the figures)

Prompt: What's the figure under A? (see the chart below)

L/S:	တစ်	Tiq.

Chart for Ex. 4

	A	B	C	D	E
Line 1:	၁	၅	၃	၄	၂
Line 2:	၃	၂	၅	၁	၄

Ex. 5 (for writing the figures)

S1/L:	တစ်	Tiq.

L: stops tape and writes: ၁

There is a key to this exercise at the end of the Lesson.

In class: Exercises as above. Teacher or Learner writes figures on the board, and other Learners read them aloud. Teacher or Learner says numbers aloud, and other Learners write down the corresponding figures.

Keys to the Exercises: Ex. 5

၁ ၂ ၄ ၃ ၁
၅ ၃ ၂ ၅ ၄
၂ ၃ ၁ ၄ ၅

Diphthongs in the roman transcription:
pronounce ei as in *vein,* ai as in *Thailand,* ou as in *though,* au as in *Sauerkraut.*

Pronunciation section for Lesson 2

For the pronunciation of ai, ei, ou, au in the roman transcription,
see the reminder at the foot of the page.

Point 1: finals: -q

1. nan-baq   number   နံပါတ်
2. A. The caq saq on the maq.
    B. Iq wenq righq inqa qa waqer.
3. nan-baq, bo-jouq,   number, general,   နံပါတ်၊ ဗိုလ်ချုပ်
    pyá-daiq, Mò-gouq   museum, Mogok (town)   ပြတိုက်၊ မိုးဂုတ်

Point 2: plain and aspirate: t- and t'-

1. Taùn-ba. T'aùn-ba.   Please ask. Please thump.   တောင်းပါ၊ ထောင်းပါ
    Time for tea
2. A. Ko Tin. B. Ko T'in.   [names of people]   ကိုတင်၊ ကိုထင်
3. tiq   one   တစ်

Point 3: breathed nasal: n- and hn-

1. N word: niq.   HN word: hniq.   နှစ်၊ နှစ်
2. Phases of niq   1. n-   2. -iq
    Phases of hniq   1. hn-   2. -n-   3. -iq
3. na, hna   နာ၊ နှာ
4. nàn, hnàn   palace, sesame   နန်း၊ နှမ်း

Point 4: velar nasal: ng-

1. ngà   five   ငါး၊ နား
2. singer, si-nger, si--nger; si, nger
3. A. nà—ngà   B. nà—nà   C. ngà—nà   D. ngà—ngà
    A. နား–ငါး   B. နား–နား   C. ငါး–နား   D. ငါး–ငါး

LESSON 3

Yes/No questions.
Is that a pagoda? — Yes: it is/ No: it's a museum.

New words

–လား	*suffix: "question"* [1]	-là
ဟုတ်ကဲ့	It is so.	houq-kéh [2]
မဟုတ်ပါဘူး	It is not so.	măhouq-pa-bù
ဟုတ်–	to be so	houq-

1. For the difference between –လား (-là) and –လဲ (-lèh) see the note below.
2. For the pronunciation of diphthongs see the reminder at the foot of the page.

Diphthongs in the roman transcription:
pronounce ei as in *vein,* ai as in *Thailand,* ou as in *though,* au as in *Sauerkraut.*

The Sule Pagoda, Rangoon
The temporary scaffolding at the top of the spire is there to protect regilding work

Example sentences

S1: ဒါ ပြတိုက်လား။   Is that a museum?   Da pyá-daiq-là?

S2: ဟုတ်ကဲ့။ ဒါ ပြတိုက်ပါ။   Yes. That's a museum.   Houq-kéh. Da pyá-daiq-pa.

S1: ဒါ ဘုရားလား။   Is that a pagoda?   Da p'ăyà-là?

S2: မဟုတ်ပါဘူး။ ဒါ ဈေးပါ။   No. That's a market.   Măhouq-pa-bù. Da zè-ba.

Models for the Exercises

Using the map of Rangoon

Ex. 1: Looking at the Rangoon map
    S1:   ဒါ ဘုရားလား။   Da p'ăyà-là?
    L/S2/L: ဟုတ်ကဲ့။ ဒါ ဘုရားပါ။   Houq-kéh. Da p'ăyà-ba.

Ex. 2: Prompt: S1 points to N° 2 and asks you
    S1:   ဒါ ပြတိုက်လား။   Da pyá-daiq-là?
    L/S2/L: ဟုတ်ကဲ့။ ဒါ ပြတိုက်ပါ။   Houq-kéh. Da pyá-daiq-pa.
    — or
    L/S2/L: မဟုတ်ပါဘူး။ ဒါ ပန်းခြံပါ။   Măhouq-pa-bù. Da pàn-jan-ba.

Diphthongs in the roman transcription:
pronounce ei as in *vein,* ai as in *Thailand,* ou as in *though,* au as in *Sauerkraut.*

In class: Exercises as above. Also use a map of your own town, your university campus and so on, and use English words where the Burmese is not yet known:

L1: ဒါ swimming pool–လား။ Da swimming pool-là?

and so on.

Notes

Grammar. The difference between –လား -là "question" and –လဲ -lèh "question" is that –လဲ -lèh is used to mark questions that require an informative answer (questions containing words like What? Which? Where?), while –လား -là is used to mark questions that can be answered by Yes or No. Compare questions 1 and 2 below:

NOUN1 <is>	NOUN2	SUFFIX
ဒါ	ဘာ	–လဲ။
Da	ba	-lèh?
This/that <is>	what	*question*

"What is that?" [Answer: It's a ...]

ဒါ	ဘုရား	–လား။
Da	p'ăyà	-là?
This/that <is>	pagoda	*question*

"Is that a pagoda?" [Answer: Yes or No]

Note that Yes or No questions (the ones that end in –လား -là) fit neatly into the formula set out in the note to Lesson 1. They are not restricted like information questions (ending in –လဲ -lèh).

NOUN1 <is>	NOUN2	SUFFIX
This/that <is>	his office	*polite*
That building <is>	a school	*question* (–လား -là)
N° 4 <is>	the university	*of course*
The nearer one <is>	a pagoda	*you see*

You could use *question* (–လား -là) after any of the NOUN1 <is> NOUN2 combinations.

Yes and No. ဟုတ်ကဲ့ houq-kéh and မဟုတ်ပါဘူး măhouq-pa-bù: phrases meaning "It is so, That's right" and "It's not so, That's not right" respectively. As answers to questions like the ones above ("Is this a pagoda?" and so on) these two phrases correspond to Yes and No in English; but Burmese has other ways of saying Yes and No: we'll come to those later.

Pronunciation Section for Lesson 3

For the pronunciation of diphthongs see the reminder at the foot of the page.

Point 1: vowels: -e and -eh

1.	ho-teh, Da ba-lèh, houq-kéh	hotel, What is that?, Yes	ဟိုတယ်၊ ဒါ ဘာလဲ၊ ဟုတ်ကဲ့
2.	zè, lè	market, four	ဈေး၊ လေး

Diphthongs in the roman transcription:
pronounce ei as in *vein*, ai as in *Thailand*, ou as in *though*, au as in *Sauerkraut*.

3.	Theh-pè-ba. *	Please carry it for me.	သယ်ပေးပါ။
	The-pè-ba. *	Please die for me.	သေပေးပါ။
4.	le, leh	air, paddy field	လေ၊ လယ်
5.	A. le—leh B. leh—le C. le—le D. leh—leh		
	A. လေ—လယ် B. လယ်—လေ C. လေ—လေ D. လယ်—လယ်		

* -ba (sometimes pronounced -pa) is a suffix you attach to verbs when you are making a request.

Point 2: finals: -q and the next consonant

1.	Houq-kéh. Măhouq-pa-bù.	Yes. No.	ဟုတ်ကဲ့၊ မဟုတ်ပါဘူး၊
	Houq-teh.	It is so.	ဟုတ်တယ်
2.	Houk-kéh. Măhoup-pa-bù. Hout-teh.		

Point 3: tone: -q

1.	pàn-jan (hi-lo)	park	ပန်းခြံ
2.	lin-bàn	tray	လင်ဗန်း
3.	nan-baq	number	နံပါတ်
4.	pàn-jan, nan-baq	park, number	ပန်းခြံ၊ နံပါတ်
5.	lin-bàn, nan-baq	tray, number	လင်ဗန်း၊ နံပါတ်
6.	Da tiq-pa.	That's a one.	ဒါ တစ်ပါ။
7.	Da thoùn-ba.	That's a three.	ဒါ သုံးပါ။
8.	Da hniq-pa.	That's a two.	ဒါ နှစ်ပါ။
9.	Da lè-ba.	That's a four.	ဒါ လေးပါ။
10.	Houq-kéh.	Yes.	ဟုတ်ကဲ့။
11.	Măhouq-pa-bù.	No.	မဟုတ်ပါဘူး။

[On the six week voyage up the Irrawaddy] My ear, too, was rarely greeted by any other sounds than those of the Burmese, an advantage in acquiring this language beyond most others, as it possesses a peculiarity of emphasis and intonation, and a nice precision of sounds, most difficult to attain by anyone living among Europeans and taking up the language as a mere study. I have heard even Dr Judson, whose grammatical knowledge of it was perfect, but whose ear was not good, lament that he had never been able to conquer this difficulty, and that he never expected to do so. For want of this peculiarity of emphasis, or intoning, his addresses to the natives lost much of their power.

From: Henry Gouger: *A Personal Narrative of Two Years Imprisonment in Burmah.* London 1864. p. 22

Diphthongs in the roman transcription:
pronounce ei as in *vein,* ai as in *Thailand,* ou as in *though,* au as in *Sauerkraut.*

LESSON 4

Numbers 6 to 10.
[subject]–က ([subject]-gá).

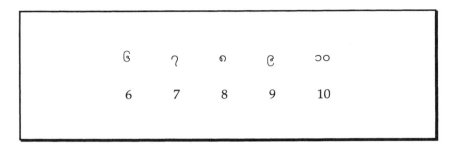

၆	၇	၈	၉	၁၀
6	7	8	9	10

Writing the figures

In these diagrams, as before, the blob shows where to place the pen to start drawing the figure, and the arrowhead shows where you end the stroke. Note that the figures ၇ and ၉ both have a tail that drops below the line: ၇၉

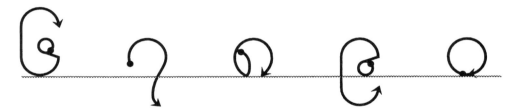

New words

figure	*script*	*English*	*pronunciation*
၆	ခြောက်	six	c'auq
၇	ခုနစ် /ခွန်နှစ်/	seven	k'un-hniq or k'un-niq [1]
၈	ရှစ်	eight	shiq
၉	ကိုး	nine	kò
၁၀	တစ်ဆယ် /တဆယ်/	ten	tăs'eh
–က		*suffix: "subject"*	-gá or -ká [2]

emphasizing the subject of the sentence

1. k'un-hniq is the purist pronunciation. In fast speech you will more often hear k'un-niq.

2. This suffix is pronounced /–က/ -ká after a glottal stop (for example after တစ်၊ နှစ်၊ ခြောက်၊ ခုနစ်၊ ရှစ် = tiq, hniq, c'auq, k'un-hniq, shiq) but /–ဂ/ -gá elsewhere (for example after သုံး၊ လေး၊ ငါး၊ ကိုး၊ တစ်ဆယ် = thoùn, lè, ngà, kò, tăs'eh). As noted for the suffix –ပါ

Diphthongs in the roman transcription:
pronounce ei as in *vein*, ai as in *Thailand*, ou as in *though*, au as in *Sauerkraut*.

-pa/-ba in Lesson 1, the difference is not crucial at this stage. This note is here only to assuage curiosity. You will find the details in Lesson 10.

Example sentences

S1: နံပါတ်(၁)က ပြတိုက်လား။   Nan-baq tiq-ká pyá-daiq-là?   N° 1, is that a museum?

S2: ဟုတ်ကဲ့။ ပြတိုက်ပါ။   Houq-kéh. Pyá-daiq-pa.   Yes, it's a museum.

Models for the exercises

Ex. 1: add one
    S1:   ခြောက်   C'auq.
    L/S2/L: ခုနစ်   K'un-hniq.

Ex. 2: say the next two up
    S1:   လေး   Lè.
    L/S2:   ငါး ခြောက်   Ngà, c'auq.

Ex. 3: looking at the Rangoon map
    S1:   နံပါတ်(၁)က ပြတိုက်လား။   Nan-paq-tiq-ká pyá-daiq-là?
    L/S2:   ဟုတ်ကဲ့။ ပြတိုက်ပါ။   Houq-kéh. Pyá-daiq-pa.

Ex. 4: for reading the figures
    Prompt: What's the figure under A?
    L/S: ခြောက်   C'auq.

Chart for Ex. 4:

	A	B	C	D
line 1	၆	၈	၃	၇
line 2	၃	၇	၆	၈
line 3	၁	၂	၅	၆
line 4	၈	၄	၃	၂

Ex. 5: for writing the figures
S1/L: ကိုး   Kò.
L: stops tape and writes: ၉
There is a key to this exercise at the end of the Lesson.

In class: Exercises as above.
Also with (easy!) additions:
L1: သုံးနဲ့ တစ် ပေါင်း ဘယ်လောက်လဲ။   Thoùn-néh tiq paùn beh-lauq-lèh?
L2: လေး။   Lè.
L3: သုံးနဲ့ တစ် ပေါင်း လေးလား။   Thoùn-néh tiq paùn lè-là?
L2: ဟုတ်ကဲ့။ လေးပါ။   Houq-kéh. Lè-ba.
or No, as the case may be.

Diphthongs in the roman transcription:
pronounce ei as in *vein*, ai as in *Thailand*, ou as in *though*, au as in *Sauerkraut*.

Vocabulary:

| [noun1]-နဲ့ [noun2] | [noun1] and [noun2] | [noun1]-néh [noun2] |
| [N°1]-နဲ့ [N°2] ပေါင်း | [N°1] and [N°2] added together | [N°1]-néh [N°2] paùn |

Notes

Suffix –က -gá. This suffix is tacked on to the subject of a sentence and highlights it. There is nothing in English that corresponds precisely to –က -gá, but you can think of it as like saying "as for [subject]," or like using a more lively intonation. For this reason it is often used when you are picking out one member of a group from the rest. There is more about –က -gá on the tape for this Lesson.

Spelling. There are some words in Burmese that are spelled one way by some people and another way by others, like *grey* and *gray* in English. Scholars in the past compiled spelling books to try and standardize the words in doubt, and in the 1970s the government adopted measures to enforce standard spelling in published material. Nonetheless, every now and again a revised standard spelling for some word is announced, and the word for "seven" is one of those. While many people write ခုနှစ် the current officially approved spelling is ခုနစ်။

Weakening. Notice that in writing the word for ten is made up of တစ် tiq "one" and ဆယ် s'eh "ten." In pronunciation the တစ် tiq "one" is shortened to /တ/ tă: so you hear, not /တစ်ဆယ်/ tiq-s'eh but /တဆယ်/ tăs'eh. The change of pronunciation from /တစ်/ tiq to /တ/ tă is an example of a full syllable being pronounced (usually in defined circumstances) as a short "weak" syllable with the vowel ă. When a syllable gets reduced in this way we say it is "weakened."

Spelling again. The weakening of /တစ်/ tiq "one" takes place not only in တစ်ဆယ် /တဆယ်/ tăs'eh "one ten" but also in all other counting phrases that contain "one"; for example:

တစ်ရာ	/တယာ/	tăya	one hundred
တစ်ထောင်	/တထောင်/	tăt'aun	one thousand
တစ်နာရီ	/တနာယီ/	tăna-yi	one hour
တစ်ခွက်	/တခွက်/	tăk'weq	one cupful

This change is so widespread and so commonly encountered that for many years people wrote these phrases as they are pronounced. Instead of writing the longer form တစ် —

| တစ်ဆယ် | တစ်ရာ | တစ်ထောင် | တစ်နာရီ | တစ်ခွက် |

people wrote the shorter form တ —

| တဆယ် | တစ်ရာ | တထောင် | တနာရီ | တခွက် |

However, in the mid-1980s the government ruled that the longer form should be the correct spelling, so most texts printed since that time write the longer form တစ်ဆယ် in place of the shorter form တဆယ်, and likewise for all the other phrases that contain တစ် meaning "one." In earlier printed texts, and in documents handwritten by people who resist the change, or don't remember to make it, you will still find "one ten" written တဆယ်, and "one" anything else will also be written with the shorter form.

Diphthongs in the roman transcription:
pronounce ei as in *vein*, ai as in *Thailand*, ou as in *though*, au as in *Sauerkraut.*

Keys to the Exercises

Key to Ex. 5 in Lesson 4

line 1	S1:	၉	၆	၃	၁	၈
line 2	S1:	၆	၄	၂	၃	၅
line 3	S1:	၈	၄	၉	၁	၉
line 4	S1:	၈	၂	၇	၁	၂
line 5	S1:	၅	၇	၆	၅	၇

Pronunciation Section for Lesson 4

Point 1: plain and aspirate: k- and k'-

1. k'un-hniq, kò — seven, nine — ခုနစ်၊ ကိုး
2. Kù-ba. K'ù-ba — Please copy it. Please dish it out. — ကူးပါ၊ ခူးပါ
3. A. kù-ba—k'ù-ba   B. k'ù-ba—k'ù-ba   C. k'ù-ba—kù-ba   D. kù-ba—kù-ba
   A. ကူးပါ–ခူးပါ   B. ခူးပါ–ခူးပါ   C. ခူးပါ–ကူးပါ   D. ကူးပါ–ကူးပါ
4. Ko-ka-ko-la — Coca-cola — ကိုကာကိုလာ

Point 2: plain and aspirate: c- and c'-

1. c'auq — six — ခြောက်
2. c'auq, cauq — six, stone — ခြောက်၊ ကျောက်
   Italian: *ciao, Cellini*
3. c'auq-teh, cauq-teh — be dry, be afraid — ခြောက်တယ်၊ ကြောက်တယ်
4. c'àn-deh, càn-deh — feel cold, be rough — ချမ်းတယ်၊ ကြမ်းတယ်
5. A. c'a—ca   B. c'a—c'a   C. ca—c'a   D. ca—ca
   A. ချာ–ကျာ   B. ချာ–ချာ   C. ကျာ–ချာ   D. ကျာ–ကျာ
6. Daw Aun S'àn Sú Ci — Daw Aung San Suu Kyi — ဒေါ်အောင်ဆန်းစုကြည်

Point 3: tone: à and á

1. Ko Thàn.   Ko Thán. — "Mr. Million," "Mr. Clean" — ကိုသန်း၊ ကိုသန့်
   [names of people: compare U Thant]
2. ăthì, ăthí — fruit, friend — အသီး၊ အသိ
3. A. ăthì—ăthì   B. ăthí—ăthí   C. ăthì—ăthí   D. ăthí—ăthì
   A. အသီး–အသီး   B. အသိ–အသိ   C. အသီး–အသိ   D. အသိ–အသီး
4. da-gá, houq-kéh, pyá-daiq — as for that, yes, museum — ဒါက၊ ဟုတ်ကဲ့၊ ပြတိုက်
5. Daw Aun S'àn Sú Ci — Daw Aung San Suu Kyi — ဒေါ်အောင်ဆန်းစုကြည်

Diphthongs in the roman transcription:
pronounce ei as in *vein*, ai as in *Thailand*, ou as in *though*, au as in *Sauerkraut*.

LESSON 5

What [noun]: သာ–[noun]: ba-[noun].
What market is it? — It's Bogyoke Market.

Place names

n°	script	English equivalent	pronunciation — script	roman
1.	ဗိုလ်ချုပ်ပြတိုက်	Bogyoke Museum	/ဗိုဂျုတ်ပျာ့ဒိုက်/	Bo-jouq Pyá-daiq
2.	ရွှေတိဂုံဘုရား	Shwedagon Pagoda	/ရွှေဒဂုန်ဖယား;/	Shwe-dăgoun P'ăyà
3.	ဗိုလ်ချုပ်ပန်းခြံ	Bogyoke Park	/ဗိုဂျုပ်ပန်း;ဂျန်/	Bo-jouq Pàn-jan
4.	သမ္မတဟိုတယ်	President Hotel	/သမဒါ့ဟိုတယ်/	Thămădá Ho-teh
5.	ဗိုလ်ချုပ်ဈေး	Bogyoke Market	/ဗိုဂျုတ်ဇေး;/	Bo-jouq Zè
6.	သိမ်ကြီးဈေး	Thein-gyi Market	/သိန်ဂျီး;ဇေး;/	Thein-jì-zè
7.	ဆူးလေဘုရား	Sule Pagoda	/ဆူး;လေဖယား;/	S'ù-le P'ăya
8.	မဟာဗန္ဓုလပန်းခြံ	Maha Bandoola Park	/မဟာဗန်ဒုလာ့ပန်း;ဂျန်/	Măha Ban-dú-lá Pàn-jan
9.	အမျိုးသားပြတိုက်	National Museum	/အမျိုး;သား;ပျဒိုက်/	Ămyò-thà Pyá-daiq
10.	စထရင်းဟိုတယ်	Strand Hotel	as written	Săt'ărìn Ho-teh

The front of
Bogyoke Aung San
Market, Rangoon

New words

အော်	Oh	Aw

[used when you have just been given some information, like "Oh, I see" or "Really?" or "Oh, is it?"]

သာ–[noun]	What [noun]?	ba-[noun]
ဘာဈေး;	What market?	ba-zè
ဘာဘုရား;	What pagoda?	ba-p'ăyà

Diraphthongs in the roman transcription:
pronounce ei as in *vein*, ai as in *Thailand*, ou as in *though*, au as in *Sauerkraut.*

Example sentences

S1: ဒါ ဘာလဲ။	What <is> that?	Da ba-lèh?
S2: ဒါ ပြတိုက်ပါ။	That's a museum.	Da pyá-daiq-pa.
S1: အော်။ ဘာပြတိုက်လဲ။	Oh. What museum [is it]?	Aw. Ba-pyá-daiq-lèh?
S2: ဗိုလ်ချုပ်ပြတိုက်ပါ။	[It's the] Bogyoke Museum.	Bo-jouq Pyá-daiq-pa.
S1: ဗိုလ်ချုပ်ပြတိုက်။	The Bogyoke Museum.	Bo-jouq Pyá-daiq.

Models for the exercises

Ex. 1: Looking at the Rangoon map

Prompt: Point to n° 1 and ask what it is

L/S2: ဒါ ဘာလဲ။	Da ba-lèh?
S1: ဒါ ပြတိုက်ပါ။	Da pyá-daiq-pa.
L/S2: အော်၊ ဘာပြတိုက်လဲ။	Aw. Ba pyá-daiq-lèh?
S1: ဗိုလ်ချုပ်ပြတိုက်ပါ။	Bo-jouq Pyá-daiq-pa.
L/S2: ဗိုလ်ချုပ်ပြတိုက်။	Bo-jouq Pyá-daiq.

Ex. 2: Prompt: Ask what N° 1 is.

L/S2: နံပါတ်(၁) ဘာလဲ။	Nan-baq-tiq ba-lèh?
S1: ဗိုလ်ချုပ်ပြတိုက်ပါ။	Bo-jouq Pyá-daiq-pa.
L/S2: အော်။ ဗိုလ်ချုပ်ပြတိုက်။	Aw. Bo-jouq Pyá-daiq.

Ex. 3

S1: နံပါတ်(၂) ဈေးလား။	Nan-baq-hniq zè-là?
L/S2: မဟုတ်ပါဘူး။ ဘုရားပါ။	Măhouq-pa-bù. P'ăyà-ba.
S1: အော်။ ဘာဘုရားလဲ။	Aw. Ba p'ăyà-lèh?
L/S2: ရွှေတိဂုံဘုရားပါ။	Shwe-dăgoun P'ăyà-ba.

Ex. 4: Prompt: Ask S1 if N° 2 is the Shwedagon Pagoda:

L/S2: နံပါတ်(၂)က ရွှေတိဂုံဘုရားလား။	Nan-baq-hniq-ká Shwe-dăgoun P'ăyà-là?
S1: ဟုတ်ကဲ့။ ရွှေတိဂုံဘုရားပါ။	Houq-kéh. Shwe-dăgoun P'ăyà-ba.

Ex. 5 For written answer: not on the tape.

The words in the following questions and answers have been split up and jumbled. Rearrange them to form meaningful sentences. There is a Key to this Exercise at the end of the Lesson.

You may find it helpful to copy the words for each sentence onto a separate sheet of paper, then cut the paper so that each word is on a separate slip. Then you can reorder the slips by sliding them around on a table until you hit on an acceptable order.

Diphthongs in the roman transcription:
pronounce ei as in *vein,* ai as in *Thailand,* ou as in *though,* au as in *Sauerkraut.*

Ex. 5 in Lesson 5 (script)

S1: — က — နံပါတ်(၂) — လား — ဈေး   S2: — ပါ — ဘုရား — မဟုတ်ပါဘူး;
S1: — လဲ — ဘာဘုရား — အော်   S2: — ရွှေတိဂုံ — ပါ — ဘုရား
S1: — နံပါတ်(၄) — လား — ဟိုတယ် — က   S2: — ဟိုတယ် — ဟုတ်ကဲ့ — ပါ
S1: — ဘာ — အော် — လဲ — ဟိုတယ်   S2: — ပါ — ဟိုတယ် — သမ္မတ

Ex. 5 in Lesson 5 (romanization)

S1: — ká — nan-baq(2) — là — zè   S2: — ba — p'ăyà — măhouq-pa-bù.
S1: — lèh — ba-p'ăyà — aw.   S2: — Shwe-dăgoun — ba — p'ăyà
S1: — nan-baq(4) — là — ho-teh — ká   S2: — ho-teh — houq-kéh. — ba
S1: — ba — aw. — lèh — ho-teh   S2: — ba — ho-teh — thămădá

In class: Question and answer with a big map. Also with your own town and similar.

Notes

Grammar. Note that the "[noun1] <is> [noun2]" formula is still all you need for the longer exchanges in the Examples and Exercises — though there are a couple of small modifications: in the last Lesson you met –က -gá "as for," which may be suffixed to [noun1] in the formula; so the formula needs to be be adapted to include that. And the appearance of –က -gá "as for" brings to light a distinction we didn't need earlier: while –က -gá "as for" only concerns the noun it is attached to, the suffix at the end of the sentence affects the whole sentence. To keep the distinction clear, we shall henceforth call the end-of-sentence suffix a "sentence suffix" (abbreviated to STC SFX). Here is the formula revised to take account of the new elements.

NOUN1+SUFFIX	<is>	NOUN2		STC SFX

S1:   နံပါတ်(၁)[+က]   ဘာ   –လဲ။
     Nan-baq-tiq[+ká]   ba   -lèh?
     N° 1[+*as for*] <is>   what   *question*
        "What is n° 1?"

S2:   ဒါ[+က]   ဟိုတယ်   –ပါ။
     Da[+gá]   ho-teh   -ba.
     This/that [+*as for*] <is>   hotel   *polite*
        "It's a hotel."

The suffix –က -gá "as for" is written in brackets to show that it may be put in or left out according to mood and context

This Lesson also introduces a variation to the standard formula for "*is* sentences." Here's a possible follow-up to the exchange above:

S1:   –   ဘာဟိုတယ်   –လဲ။
     –   Ba Ho-teh   -lèh?
     – <is>   What hotel   *question*
        "What hotel [is it]?"

Diphthongs in the roman transcription:
pronounce ei as in *vein*, ai as in *Thailand*, ou as in *though*, au as in *Sauerkraut*.

S2:   –   သမ္မတဟိုတယ်   –ပါ။
      –   Thămădá Ho-teh   -ba.
      – <is>   President Hotel   *polite*
                    "[It's] the President Hotel."

As you can see, NOUN1, which is the subject of discussion, can be omitted when both speakers know what it is. Spoken English often leaves out "it" in the same circumstances.

Romanization. Burmese place names are given here in both a "systematic" romanization and a "traditional" romanization. For the difference between the two see the section on script and transcription in Appendix 3. The first gives you a guide to the way the names are pronounced, and the second lets you see how people romanize them in practice.

The place names. ဗိုလ်ချုပ် /ဗိုဂျုတ်/ Bo-jouq "Bogyoke," "General": Without a name following, this word normally refers to "The General": ဗိုလ်ချုပ်အောင်ဆန်း Bo-jouq Aun S'àn General Aung San: a national hero of modern times. He led the Burmese in their campaign for independence from British rule in the 1940s, and was assassinated by a rival in 1947. His picture is to be seen in schools and government offices, and his name is used for roads and other places in the same way as "Washington" is used in the USA. The Bogyoke Museum is in the house where General Aung San used to live, and the Bogyoke Market is one of the great covered markets of Rangoon. Their full names are Bogyoke Aung San Museum and Bogyoke Aung San Market, but in ordinary conversation people refer to them without the "Aung San." In older books on Burma you'll find the Bogyoke Market referred to as Scott Market, after Sir J. G. Scott, a distinguished British administrator and writer.

မဟာဗန္ဓုလ Măha Ban-dú-lá Maha Bandula: was a skilled general. After many victorious battles he was killed in the Anglo-Burmese war of 1824 to 1826.

သိမ်ကြီးဈေး Thein-jì Zè Theingyi Market: another great covered market. A သိမ် thein is a hall for the ordination of Buddhist monks (from the Pali word sīma). သိမ်ကြီး Thein-jì means "the great thein": there must have been one on or near the site of the present market.

အမျိုးသားပြတိုက် Ămyò-thà Pyá-daiq National Museum: အမျိုး ămyò means "race" and သား thà means "son, scion, descendant, member," so အမျိုးသား ămyò-thà means "descendant of the race" and hence "national." Later we shall meet the same word with the meaning "man, male."

စထရင်းဟိုတယ် Săt'ărìn Ho-teh Strand Hotel: for the pronunciation of foreign words like "Strand" see the note on "hotel" in Lesson 1.

Diphthongs in the roman transcription: 23
pronounce ei as in *vein*, ai as in *Thailand*, ou as in *though*, au as in *Sauerkraut*.

Keys to the Exercises: Ex. 5

script

S1:— နံပါတ်(၂) — က — ဈေး — လား။ S2:— မဟုတ်ပါဘူး။ — ဘုရား — ပါ။

S1:— အော်။ — ဘာဘုရား — လဲ။ S2:— ရွှေတိဂုံ — ဘုရား — ပါ။

S1:— နံပါတ်(၄) — က — ဟိုတယ် — လား။ S2:— ဟုတ်ကဲ့။ — ဟိုတယ် — ပါ။

S1:— အော်။ — ဘာ — ဟိုတယ် — လဲ။ S2:— သမ္မတ — ဟိုတယ် — ပါ။

Romanization

S1: — nan-baq(2) — ká — zè — là S2: — măhouq-pa-bù. — p'ăyà — ba

S1: — aw. — ba-p'ăyà — lèh S2: — Shwe-dăgoun — p'ăyà — ba

S1: — nan-baq(4) — ká — ho-teh — là S2: — houq-kéh. — ho-teh — ba

S1: — aw. — ba — ho-teh — lèh S2: — thămădá — ho-teh — ba

Pronunciation Section for Lesson 5

Point 1: finals: -n

1. Shwe-dăgoun [name of pagoda] ရွှေတိဂုံ

2. French: *bon, vin, Lyons, printemps*

3. Shwe-dăgoun, thoùn, pàn-jan Shwedagon, three, park ရွှေတိဂုံ၊ သုံး၊ ပန်းခြံ

4. nan-(baq), Ban-(dú-lá), number, Bandoola, နံ(ပါတ်)၊ ဗန်(ဒုလ)
   Thein-(jì) Theingyi သိမ်(ကြီး)

Point 2: plain and aspirate: s- and s'-

1. seiq, s'eiq mind, goat စိတ်၊ ဆိတ်

2. seiq, s[cut]'eiq (leaves s/heiq)

3. saùn, s'aùn harp, winter စောင်း၊ ဆောင်း

4. S'ù-le [name of pagoda] ဆူးလေ

5. tăs'eh ten တစ်ဆယ်

Point 3: tones: à and á

1. Thămădá, Ban-dú-lá, Thamada, Bandoola, သမ္မတ၊ ဗန္ဒုလ၊
   Da-gá As for that ဒါက

2. A. Da-gá B. Da-gà ဒါက၊ ဒါကား

3. A. Thămădá B. Thămădà သမ္မတ၊ သမဒါး

Point 4: initial: th-

1. Thoùn, Thein-jì, Thămădá Three, Theingyi, Thamada သုံး၊ သိမ်ကြီး၊ သမ္မတ

2. Tthoùn, Tthein-jì, Tthămădá

3. thèh—tèh, sand—hut သဲ — ဘဲ
   thaun—taun, sandbank—mountain သောင် — တောင်
   ăthì—ătì fruit—music အသီး — အတီး

Diphthongs in the roman transcription:
pronounce ei as in *vein*, ai as in *Thailand*, ou as in *though*, au as in *Sauerkraut*.

LESSON 6

Review of numbers 1-9-0. Checking questions.
Phone numbers (including 0 and short 7).

Phone numbers

သမ္မတဟိုတယ်	၇၁၄၉၉	President Hotel	71499	Thămădá Ho-teh
စထရင်းဟိုတယ်	၈၁၅၃၃	Strand Hotel	81533	Săt'ărìn Ho-teh
အမျိုးသားပြတိုက်	၇၃၇၀၆	National Museum	73706	Ămyò-thà Pyá-daiq
ဗိုလ်ချုပ်ပြတိုက်	၅၀၆၀၀	Bogyoke Museum	50600	Bo-jouq Pyá-daiq
ဆူးလေဘုရား	၇၃၀၇၂	Sule Pagoda	73072	S'ù-le P'ăya

New words

တယ်လီဖုန်း	telephone	teh-li-p'oùn
ဘယ်လောက်လဲ	How much?	beh-lauq-lèh
သုည /သုန်ညာ့/	zero	thoun-nyá
ခွန်	seven	k'un

(an alternative form to ခုနစ် k'un-hniq: used in lists of numbers)

Example sentences

S1: သမ္မတဟိုတယ် တယ်လီဖုန်း နံပါတ် ဘယ်လောက်လဲ။	What's the phone number of the President Hotel?	Thămădá Ho-teh teh-li-p'oùn nan-baq beh-lauq-lèh?
S2: ခုနစ်–တစ်–လေး–ကိုး–ကိုး–ပါ။	It's seven one four nine nine.	K'un-hniq-tiq-lè-kò-kò-ba.
or:		
S2: ခွန်–တစ်–လေး–ကိုး–ကိုး–ပါ။	It's seven one four nine nine.	K'un-tiq-lè-kò-kò-ba.
S1: ခုနစ်–တစ်–လေး–ကိုး–ကိုး–လား။	Was that seven one four nine nine?	K'un-hniq-tiq-lè-kò-kò-là.
S2: ဟုတ်ကဲ့။ ခုနစ်–တစ်–လေး–ကိုး–ကိုး–ပါ။	Yes: seven one four nine nine.	Houq-kéh. K'un-hniq-tiq-lè-kò-kò-ba.

Models for the exercises

Ex. 1: use the phone list

S1: သမ္မတဟိုတယ် တယ်လီဖုန်းနံပါတ် ဘယ်လောက်လဲ။ — Thămădá Ho-teh teh-li-p'oùn nan-baq beh-lauq-lèh?

L/S2/L: ၇၁၄၉၉–ပါ။ — 71499-ba.

Diphthongs in the roman transcription:
pronounce ei as in *vein*, ai as in *Thailand*, ou as in *though*, au as in *Sauerkraut*.

Ex. 2

S1: သမ္မတဟိုတယ် တယ်လီဖုန်းနံပါတ်က ၇၁၄၉၉-လား။ — Thămădá Ho-teh teh-li-p'oùn nan-baq-ká 71499-là?

L/S2/L: ဟုတ်ကဲ့။ ၇၁၄၉၉-ပါ။ — Houq-kéh. 71499-ba.

Ex. 3

S1: သမ္မတဟိုတယ် တယ်လီဖုန်းနံပါတ် ဘယ်လောက်လဲ။ — Thămădá Ho-teh teh-li-p'oùn nan-baq beh-lauq-lèh?

L/S2/L: ၇၁၄၉၉-ပါ။ — 71499-ba.

S1: ၇၁၄၉၉-လား။ — 71499-là?

L/S2/L: ဟုတ်ကဲ့။ ၇၁၄၉၉-ပါ။ — Houq-kéh. 71499-ba.

Ex. 4: Prompt: Ask her the number of the National Museum.

L/S2: အမျိုးသားပြတိုက် တယ်လီဖုန်းနံပါတ် ဘယ်လောက်လဲ။ — Ămyò-thà Pyá-daiq teh-li-p'oùn nan-baq beh-lauq-lèh?

S1: ၇၃၇၃၆-ပါ။ — 73736-ba.

L/S2: ၇၃၇၃၆-လား။ — 73736-là?

S1: မဟုတ်ပါဘူး။ ၇၃၇၀၆-ပါ။ — Măhouq-pa-bù. 73706-ba.

In class: Ask telephone numbers of your own school/college/department/. . . .

L1: SOAS တယ်လီဖုန်းနံပါတ် ဘယ်လောက်လဲ။ — SOAS teh-li-p'oùn nan-baq beh-lauq-lèh?

L2: ၀၇၁ ၆၃၇ ၂၃၈၈-ပါ။ — 071-637-2388-ba.

Learners write them down. Then check them:

L1: SOAS တယ်လီဖုန်းနံပါတ်က ၀၇၁ ၆၃၇ ၂၃၈၈-လား။ — SOAS teh-li-p'oùn nan-baq-ká 071-637-2388-là?

L2: ဟုတ်ကဲ့။ ၀၇၁ ၆၃၇ ၂၃၈၈-လား-ပါ။ — Houq-kéh. 071-637-2388-ba.

Also ask Learners' own phone numbers:

L1: Sibylla တယ်လီဖုန်းနံပါတ် ဘယ်လောက်လဲ။ — Sibylla teh-li-p'oùn nan-baq beh-lauq-lèh?

and so on.

Also ask မှတ်ပုံတင်နံပါတ် (hmaq-poun-tin nan-baq) "I.D. number."

Notes

Pronunciation of loanwords. တယ်လီဖုန်း teh-li-p'oùn is a loanword from English, and so subject to the variations of pronunciation that we have pointed out for English loanwords above.

Grammar. Note that the standard formula for *is* sentences is still with us:

NOUN1+SUFFIX <is>	NOUN2	STC SFX
တယ်လီဖုန်းနံပါတ်	ဘယ်လောက်	-လဲ။
Teh-li-p'oùn nan-baq	beh-lauq	-lèh?
Telephone number <is>	how much	*question*

"What is the phone number?"

Diphthongs in the roman transcription:
pronounce ei as in *vein*, ai as in *Thailand*, ou as in *though*, au as in *Sauerkraut*.

		၇၁၄၉၉	–ပါ။
–		71499	-ba.
–	<is>	71499	*polite*

"[It is] 71499"

စကားပြောကြေးနန်း —

ညွှန်ကြားရေးမှူးချုပ် — ၁၅၀၁၁ လိုင်းခွဲ–၉၀
— ၁၁၂၉၉

ညွှန်ကြားရေးမှူး — ၁၅၀၁၁ လိုင်းခွဲ–၁၀၄
— ၁၅၂၀၄

ဒုတိယညွှန်ကြားရေးမှူး — ၁၅၀၁၁ လိုင်းခွဲ–၉၅
— ၁၄၅၂၂

ပြည်ထောင်စု ဆိုရှယ်လစ်သမ္မတ မြန်မာနိုင်ငံတော်
ပညာရေးဝန်ကြီးဌာန

အထက်တန်းပညာဦးစီးဌာန
(နိုင်ငံခြားပညာသင်)
ဝန်ကြီးများရုံး

From the letter heading of the Ministry of Education.
Notice the phone numbers and extensions.

Pronunciation Section for Lesson 6

Point 1: rhyme: -un

1.	k'un-hniq, k'un	seven [long and short forms]	ခုနစ်၊ ခွန်
2.	S'ăya Thàn T'ùn, Ù Tin T'ùn	[names of people]	ဆရာသန်းထွန်း၊ ဦးတင်ထွန်း
3.	Daw Kan Nyún, Ù Ci Nyún	[names of people]	ဒေါ်ကံညွန့်၊ ဦးကြည်ညွန့်
4.	Hùn măti-yá	No hooting	ဟွန်းမတီးရ
		["Horn-not-sound-may"]	
5.	cùn, coùn	island, moat	ကျွန်း၊ ကျိုး
6.	A. Da cùn-ba.	A. That's an island.	ဒါ ကျွန်းပါ။
	B. Da coùn-ba.	B. That's a moat.	ဒါ ကျိုးပါ။

Point 2: palatal nasal: ny-

1.	thoun-nyá	zero	သုည
2.	English: *minion, senior*; French: *mignon, seigneur*		
3.	thoun-nyá, nyan, nyaun-nyaun	zero, intelligence, miaow	သုည၊ ဉာဏ်၊ ညောင်ညောင်
4.	A. Na-deh. B. Nya-deh.	A. He's in pain. B. He's cheating.	နာတယ်၊ ညာတယ်
5.	A. Nìn-deh. B. Nyìn-deh.	A. He trod on it. B. He denied it.	နင်းတယ်၊ ငြင်းတယ်
6.	A. Ni-deh. B. Nyi-deh.	A. It's red. B. It's even.	နီတယ်၊ ညီတယ်

Point 3: final: -n and the next consonant

1.	Nan: Nam-baq	number	နံ — နံပါတ်

Diphthongs in the roman transcription:
pronounce ei as in *vein*, ai as in *Thailand*, ou as in *though*, au as in *Sauerkraut*.

27

2. Pàn-jan: Da pàn-jam-ba.   Park: That's a park.   ပန်းခြံ — ဒါပန်းခြံပါ
3. Yan: Yang-goun   Rangoon   ရန် — ရန်ကုန်
4. Păgan: Păgang-gá   Pagan: From Pagan   ပုဂံ — ပုဂံက
5. Ban: BaN-dú-lá   Bandoola   ဗန် — ဗန္ဓုလ
6. Màn: MàN-dălè   Mandalay   မန်း — မန္တလေး

LESSON 7

This [noun]: ဒီ-[noun]: di-[noun].
What road is this road? — It's Strand Road.

Rangoon roads

n°	script	English equivalent	pronunciation in roman [1]
100	ဗိုလ်ချုပ်လမ်း	Bogyoke Street	Bo-jouq Làn
200	အနော်ရထာလမ်း	Anawrahta Street	Ănaw-yăt'a Làn [2]
300	မဟာဗန္ဓုလလမ်း	Maha Bandoola Street	Măha Ban-dú-lá Làn
400	ကုန်သည်လမ်း	Merchant Street	Koun-dheh Làn
500	ကမ်းနားလမ်း	Strand Road	Kàn-nà Làn
600	ဗိုလ်အောင်ကျော်လမ်း	Bo Aung Kyaw Street	Bo Aun Jaw Làn
700	ပန်းဆိုးတန်း	Pansodan Street	Pàn-s'ò-dàn or Pàn-zò-dàn
800	ဆူးလေဘုရားလမ်း	Sule Pagoda Road	S'ù-le P'ăyà Làn
900	ရွှေဘုံသာလမ်း	Shwebontha Street	Shwe-boun-dha Làn
1000	[ရွှေတိဂုံ]ဘုရားလမ်း	Shwedagon Pagoda Rd	[Shwe-dăgoun] P'ăyà Làn

Rangoon road names with pronunciation shown in Burmese script

n°	script	English equivalent	pronunciation in script [1]
100	ဗိုလ်ချုပ်လမ်း	Bogyoke Street	/ဗိုလ်ဂျုတ်လန်း/
200	အနော်ရထာလမ်း	Anawrahta Street	/အနော်ယထာလန်း/ [2]
300	မဟာဗန္ဓုလလမ်း	Maha Bandoola Street	/မဟာဗန်ဒုလာလန်း/
400	ကုန်သည်လမ်း	Merchant Street	/ကုန်သုယ်လန်း/
500	ကမ်းနားလမ်း	Strand Road	as written
600	ဗိုလ်အောင်ကျော်လမ်း	Bo Aung Kyaw Street	/ဗိုအောင်ကျော်လန်း/
700	ပန်းဆိုးတန်း	Pansodan Street	/ပန်းဆိုးဒန်း/ or /ပန်းဇိဒန်း/
800	ဆူးလေဘုရားလမ်း	Sule Pagoda Road	/ဆူးလေဖယားလန်း/
900	ရွှေဘုံသာလမ်း	Shwebontha Street	/ရွှေဘုံသာလန်း/
1000	[ရွှေတိဂုံ]ဘုရားလမ်း	Shwedagon Pagoda Rd	/[ရွှေဒဂုန်]ဘုရားလန်း/

1. On "pronunciation in roman" and "pronunciation in script" see Appendix 3. The paucity of "as written" entries shows how many mismatches there are between sound and script.
2. Also pronounced /အနော်ရထာလန်း/ = Ănaw-răt'a Làn

Diphthongs in the roman transcription:
pronounce ei as in *vein,* ai as in *Thailand,* ou as in *though,* au as in *Sauerkraut.*

New words

လမ်း	road, street	làn
ဒီ–	this ...	di-
For example:		
ဒီဘုရား	this pagoda	di-p'ăyà
ဒီဟိုတယ်	this hotel	di-ho-teh
ဒီလမ်း	this road	di-làn

Maha Bandoola Park, Rangoon

Example sentences

S1: ဒီဘုရား ဘာဘုရားလဲ။	What pagoda is this? ("This pagoda <is> what pagoda?")	Di-p'ăyà ba-p'ăyà-lèh?
S2: ဆူးလေဘုရားပါ။	The Sule Pagoda.	S'ù-le P'ăyà-ba.
S1: ဒီလမ်းက ဘုရားလမ်းလား။	Is this road Pagoda Road? ("This road <is> Pagoda Road?")	Di-làn-gá P'ăyà Làn-là?
S2: ဟုတ်ကဲ့။ ဘုရားလမ်းပါ။	Yes. It is Pagoda Road.	Houq-kéh. P'ăyà Làn-ba.

Models for the Exercises

Ex. 1: Looking at the Rangoon map.

Prompt: S1 points to n° 7 and asks:

S1: ဒီဘုရား ဘာဘုရားလဲ။	Di p'ăyà ba p'ăyà-lèh?
L/S2: ဒီဘုရားက ဆူးလေဘုရားပါ။	Di p'ăyà-gá S'ù-le P'ăyà-ba.

Diphthongs in the roman transcription:
pronounce ei as in *vein,* ai as in *Thailand,* ou as in *though,* au as in *Sauerkraut.*

Ex. 2: Prompt: Point to road n° 100 and ask what road it is:

L/S2: ဒီလမ်း ဘာလမ်းလဲ။   Di làn ba làn-lèh?

S1: ဗိုလ်ချုပ်လမ်းပါ။   Bo-jouq Làn-ba.

L/S2: ဗိုလ်ချုပ်လမ်းလား။   Bo-jouq Làn-là?

S1: ဟုတ်ကဲ့။ ဗိုလ်ချုပ်လမ်းပါ။   Houq-kéh. Bo-jouq Làn-ba.

Ex. 3: Prompt: S2 points to road n° 500 and asks:

S2: ဒီလမ်း ဘာလမ်းလဲ။   Di làn ba làn-lèh?

L/S1: ကမ်းနားလမ်းပါ။   Kàn-nà Làn-ba.

S2: ကမ်းနားလမ်းလား။   Kàn-nà Làn-là?

L/S1: ဟုတ်ကဲ့။ ကမ်းနားလမ်းပါ။   Houq-kéh. Kàn-nà Làn-ba.

Ex. 4 For written answer: not on the tape.

The words in the following questions and answers have been split up and jumbled. Rearrange them to form meaningful sentences. There is a Key to this Exercise at the end of the Lesson. Don't forget that you may find it helpful to copy the words onto separate slips of paper and do your reordering by sliding the slips around.

Ex. 4. For written answer: not on the tape (script version).

S1: — လဲ — ဘာပြတိုက် — ဒီပြတိုက်   S2: — က — ပါ — ဗိုလ်ချုပ်ပြတိုက် — ဒီပြတိုက်

S1: — ပန်းခြံ — ဒီပန်းခြံ — လဲ — ဘာ   S2: — ပန်းခြံ — ဒီပန်းခြံ — ဗိုလ်ချုပ် — ပါ — က

S1: — ဒီ — ဘာ — လဲ — ဈေး — ဈေး   S2: — ဒီ — ပါ — က — ဈေး — ဈေး — သိမ်ကြီး

Ex. 4. For written answer: not on the tape (romanized version).

S1: — lèh — ba-pyá-daiq — di-pyá-daiq

    S2: — ká — pa — Bo-jouq-pyá-daiq — di-pyá-daiq

S1: — pàn-jan — di-pàn-jan — lèh — ba

    S2: — pàn-jan — di-pàn-jan — Bo-jouq — ba — gá

S1: — di — ba — lèh — zè — zè

    S2: — di — ba — gá — Thein-jì — zè — zè

In class: Exercises as above. Also use map of your own town and similar.

Notes

"This thing" and "this [thing]." ဒီ- di- "this ..." is used before a noun, as in the Examples above. Take care not to confuse this word with ဒါ da "this," which means "this [thing]" or "this [one]." Contrast:

ဒီလမ်း ဘာလမ်းလဲ။   What road is this road?   Di-làn ba-làn-lèh?

Burmese word order: This-road <is> what-road-*question*

ဒါ ဘာလမ်းလဲ။   What road is this?   Da ba-làn-lèh?

Burmese word order: This <is> what-road-*question*

English has only one word for both meanings of "this": Burmese has a separate word for each.

    Diphthongs in the roman transcription:
pronounce ei as in *vein,* ai as in *Thailand,* ou as in *though,* au as in *Sauerkraut.*

Hesitation: words for "um" and "erm." When you're speaking a foreign language, one of the things that makes you sound foreign, even if you have an almost perfect pronunciation, is the appearance of English sounds like "um" and "erm" in the gaps you leave while you're thinking of the next word. To make yourself sound more Burmese, try using the um-words that the Burmese use. The common ones are —

ဒီ …	this …	di …
ဟို …	that …	ho …
အင် …	um…	in …

The street names. ဗိုလ်ချုပ်လမ်း Bo-jouq Làn Bogyoke Street: the full name is ဗိုလ်ချုပ်အောင်ဆန်းလမ်း (Bo-jouq Aun S'àn Làn) Bogyoke Aung San Street, named in honour of General Aung San: see the note in Lesson 5.

အနော်ရထာလမ်း Ănaw-yăt'a Làn Anawrahta Street: King Anawrahta was a powerful king in the Kingdom of Pagan. He reigned from about 1044 to 1077 AD.

မဟာဗန္ဓုလလမ်း Măha Ban-dú-lá Làn Maha Bandoola Street: named after the Burmese general: see the note in Lesson 5.

ကုန်သည်လမ်း Koun-dheh Làn Merchant Street: from ကုန် koun "merchandise, wares" and –သည် -dheh "dealer."

ကမ်းနားလမ်း Kàn-nà Làn Strand Road: from ကမ်း kàn "coast, bank, strand" and –နား -nà "near, alongside." The road runs along the bank of Rangoon River.

ဗိုလ်အောင်ကျော်လမ်း Bo Aun Jaw Làn Bo Aung Kyaw Street: Bo Aung Kyaw was a student who died following injuries received when police violently broke up a demonstration against British rule in 1938.

ပန်းဆိုးတန်း Pàn-s'ò-dàn Pansodan: This is the only road name in the list that doesn't end in လမ်း làn "road." That's because the name means "Dyers' Row," and with တန်း tàn "row" in the name there is no need for လမ်း làn "road." Needless to say, the dyers have long since moved elsewhere. Pronunciation varies between /ပန်းဆိုးဒန်း/ Pàn-s'ò-dàn and /ပန်းဇိုးဒန်း/ Pàn-zò-dàn.

ဘုရားလမ်း P'ăyà Làn Shwedagon Pagoda Road: The full name is ရွှေတိဂုံ ဘုရားလမ်း Shwe-dăgoun P'ăyà Làn, but in everyday conversation people shorten the name to ဘုရားလမ်း P'ăyà Làn, and that is the form we use in the Exercises.

Keys to the Exercises

Key to Ex. 4. For written answer: not on the tape: script version
S1: — ဒီပြတိုက် — ဘာပြတိုက် — လဲ။ S2: — ဒီပြတိုက် — က — ဗိုလ်ချုပ်ပြတိုက် — ပါ။
S1: — ဒီပန်းခြံ — ဘာ — ပန်းခြံ — လဲ။ S2: — ဒီပန်းခြံ — က — ဗိုလ်ချုပ် — ပန်းခြံ — ပါ။
S1: — ဒီ — ဈေး — ဘာ — ဈေး — လဲ။ S2: — ဒီ — ဈေး — က — သိမ်ကြီး — ဈေး — ပါ။

Diphthongs in the roman transcription:	31
pronounce ei as in *vein*, ai as in *Thailand*, ou as in *though*, au as in *Sauerkraut*.	

Key to Ex. 4. For written answer: not on the tape: romanized version

    S1: — di-pyá-daiq — ba-pyá-daiq — lèh

        S2: — di-pyá-daiq — ká — Bo-jouq-pyá-daiq — pa

    S1: — di-pàn-jan — ba — pàn-jan — lèh

        S2: — di-pàn-jan — gá — Bo-jouq — pàn-jan — ba

    S1: — di — zè — ba — zè — lèh

        S2: — di — zè — gá — Thein-jì — zè — ba

Pronunciation Section for Lesson 7

Point 1: initials: **th-** and **dh-**

1.	English: *thing, this* (thing, dhis)		
2.	Koun-dheh Làn	Merchant Street	ကုန်သည်လမ်း
3.	Shwe-boun-dha Làn	[name of road]	ရွှေဘုံသာလမ်း
4.	A. Ămyò-thà B. Ămyò-dhà	national	အမျိုးသား

Point 2: initials: **my-** and **py-**

1.	Ămyò. Ămyò-thà (not Ămì-ò-thà)	national	အမျိုး၊ အမျိုးသား
	English: *miaow*		
2.	Myan-ma (not Mì-yan-ma)	Myanmar	မြန်မာ
3.	Me-myó, Maw-lămyain, Myiq-cì-nà	[town names]	မေမြို့၊ မော်လမြိုင်၊ မြစ်ကြီးနား
4.	pyá-daiq (not pì-yá-daiq)	museum	ပြတိုက်
5.	pyàw-ba (not pì-yàw-ba)	please speak	ပြောပါ

Point 3: tones: **a** and **à**

1.	thoun-nyá, thoùn-nyá	zero, three nights	သုည၊ သုံးည
2.	dăga-jì, dăgà-jì	main benefactor, main gate	ဒကာကြီး၊ တံခါးကြီး
3.	nan-byà, nàn-byà	bread, [kind of] noodles	နံပြား၊ နန်းပြား
4.	Da nan-byà-ba.	That's bread.	ဒါ နံပြားပါ။
	Da nàn-byà-ba.	That's noodles.	ဒါ နန်းပြားပါ။

LESSON 8

Numbers in round hundreds.
Weakening for 1, 2, 7.

၁၀၀	၂၀၀	၃၀၀	၄၀၀	၅၀၀	၆၀၀	၇၀၀	၈၀၀	၉၀၀	၁၀၀၀
100	200	300	400	500	600	700	800	900	1000

Diphthongs in the roman transcription:
pronounce ei as in *vein,* ai as in *Thailand,* ou as in *though,* au as in *Sauerkraut.*

New words

figure	script	English	pronunciation
–၀၀	–ရာ	hundred	-ya
၁၀၀၀	တစ်ထောင်	one thousand	tăt'aun

Example

သုံးရာ	three hundred	thoùn-ya
လေးရာ	four hundred	lè-ya
ငါးရာ	five hundred	ngà-ya
	and so on	

Note the unexpected pronunciations:

တစ်ရာ	/တယာ/	one hundred	tăya
နှစ်ရာ	/နယာ/	two hundred	hnăya
ခုနှစ်ရာ	/ခွန်နယာ/	seven hundred	k'un-năya

Models for the exercises

Ex. 1: 3 ⇒ 300
Prompt: Say 3
L/S2: သုံး   Thoùn.
S1/L: သုံးရာ   Thoùn-ya.

Ex. 2: 8 ⇒ 800
S1: ရှစ်   Shiq.
L/S2: ရှစ်ရာ   Shiq-ya.

Ex. 3: Add a hundred
S1: လေးရာ   Lè-ya.
L/S2: ငါးရာ   Ngà-ya.

Ex. 4: Prompt: What's the number under A?
(see the chart below)
L/S: လေးရာ   Lè-ya.

Chart for Ex. 4

	A	B	C	D	E	F	G	H
line 1:	၄၀၀	၃၀၀	၆၀၀	၅၀၀	၈၀၀	၁၀၀၀	၄၀၀	၆၀၀
line 2:	၅၀၀	၁၀၀	၂၀၀	၇၀၀	၁၀၀၀	၁၀၀	၇၀၀	၂၀၀

In class: Exercises as above.
Also with a book:
L1 holds some book and asks:

L1: စာမျက်နှာ နံပါတ် ဘယ်လောက်လဲ။   Sa-myeq-hna nan-baq beh-lauq-lèh?
L2: စာမျက်နှာ နံပါတ် ၄၀၀။   Sa-myeq-hna nan-baq lè-ya.

L1 opens at p.400 and shows it to L3, and asks:

L1: ဒါ စာမျက်နှာ နံပါတ် ၄၀၀-လား။   Sa-myeq-hna nan-baq lè-ya-là?
L3: ဟုတ်ကဲ့။ စာမျက်နှာ နံပါတ် ၄၀၀-ပါ။ Houq-kéh. Sa-myeq-hna nan-baq lè-ya-ba.

or No, as the case may be.

Vocabulary:
စာမျက်နှာ (sa-myeq-hna)   page

Diphthongs in the roman transcription:
pronounce ei as in *vein*, ai as in *Thailand*, ou as in *though*, au as in *Sauerkraut*.

33

Also with (easy!) additions:

L1: သုံးရာနဲ့ တစ်ရာ ပေါင်း ဘယ်လောက်လဲ။   Thoùn-ya-néh tăya-paùn beh-lauq-lèh?
L2: လေးရာ။   Lè-ya.
L3: သုံးရာနဲ့ တစ်ရာ ပေါင်း လေးရာလား။   Thoùn-ya-néh tăya-paùn lè-ya-là?
L2: ဟုတ်ကဲ့။ လေးရာပါ။   Houq-kéh, lè-ya-ba.
or No, as the case may be.

Vocabulary:

| [noun1]–နဲ့ [noun2] | [noun1] and [noun2] | [noun1]-néh [noun2] |
| [N°1]–နဲ့ [N°2] ပေါင်း | [N°1] and [N°2] added together | [N°1]-néh N°2] paùn |

Note

Spelling. တစ်ရာ /တယာ/ tăya "one hundred": you might expect the word written တစ်ရာ to be pronounced /တစ်ယာ/ tiq-ya, but, as you can see from the examples, it is pronounced /တယာ/ tăya. This is another example of weakening: see the note in Lesson 4. As noted there, texts printed before the mid-1980s will have the spelling တရာ။ After the spelling reform people changed to the longer version: တစ်ရာ။

The other two numbers that weaken (/နှစ်/ hniq ⇒ /နှ/ hnă and /ခုန်နှစ်/ k'un-hniq ⇒ /ခုန်န/ k'un-nă) are written with the longer form, and always have been; so no change in spelling practice was required for them. People write နှစ်ရာ and ခုနှစ်ရာ but read them as /နှယာ/ hnăya and /ခုန်နယာ/ k'un-năya.

Pronunciation Section for Lesson 8

Point 1: vowels: -e and -eh again

1.	tăs'e, tăs'eh	ghost, ten	တစ္ဆေ၊ တစ်ဆယ်
2.	lè-deh, lèh-deh	to be heavy, to exchange	လေးတယ်၊ လဲတယ်
3.	A. ămè—ămèh B. ămè—ămè C. ămèh—ămè D. ămèh—ămèh
	A. အမေး—အမဲ B. အမေး—အမေး C. အမဲ—အမေး D. အမဲ—အမဲ
	(ămè, ămèh	a question, beef	အမေး၊ အမဲ)
4.	lè: thoùn, lè, ngà	three, four, five	လေး ။ သုံးလေးငါး
5.	le: S'ù-le	[pagoda name]	လေ ။ ဆူးလေ
6.	shwe: Shwe-dăgoun	[pagoda name]	ရွှေ ။ ရွှေတိဂုံ
7.	shwe: Shwe-boun-dha	[road name]	ရွှေ ။ ရွှေဘုံသာ
8.	teh: ho-teh	hotel	တယ် ။ ဟိုတယ်
9.	teh: teh-li-p'oùn	telephone	တယ် ။ တယ်လီဖုန်း
10.	dheh: Koun-dheh	[road name]	သည် ။ ကုန်သည်
11.	lèh: ba-lèh?	what?	လဲ ။ ဘာလဲ
12.	kéh: houq-kéh	Yes	ကဲ့ ။ ဟုတ်ကဲ့

Point 2: vowels: -o and -aw again

1.	o-deh, aw-deh	to age, to shout	အိုတယ်၊ အော်တယ်
2.	A. ăp'aw—ăp'o B. ăp'o—ăp'o C. ăp'o—ăp'aw D. ăp'aw—ăp'aw
	A. အဖော်—အဖိုး B. အဖိုး—အဖိုး C. အဖိုး—အဖော် D. အဖော်—အဖော်
	(ăp'aw, ăp'o	companion, male	အဖော်၊ အဖိုး)

Diphthongs in the roman transcription:
pronounce ei as in *vein*, ai as in *Thailand*, ou as in *though*, au as in *Sauerkraut*.

3. bo: bo-jouq   general   ဗိုလ် ။ ဗိုလ်ချုပ်
4. bo: Bo Aun Jaw   [name of person]   ဗိုလ် ။ ဗိုလ်အောင်ကျော်
5. s'ò: Pàn-s'ò-dàn   [road name]   ဆိုး ။ ပန်းဆိုးတန်း
6. ho: ho-teh   hotel   ဟိုဗ် ။ ဟိုတယ်
7. kò: shiq, kò, tăs'eh   eight, nine, ten   ကိုး ။ ရှစ်ကိုးတစ်ဆယ်
8. myò: ămyò-thà   national   မျိုး ။ အမျိုးသား
9. naw: Ănaw-yăt'a   [king's name]   နော် ။ အနော်ရထာ
10. maw: Maw-lămyain   [town name]   မော် ။ မော်လမြိုင်
11. maw: Bămaw   [town name]   မော် ။ ဗန်းမော်
12. jaw: Bo Aun Jaw   [person's name]   ကျော် ။ ဗိုလ်အောင်ကျော်

Point 3: round-up of plain and aspirate

1. ăkoun, ăk'oun   all, jumping   အကုန် ၊ အခုံ
2. ătweq, ăt'weq   calculating, exit   အတွက် ၊ အထွက်
3. ăpaq, ăp'aq   week, reading   အပတ် ၊ အဖတ်
4. ăco, ăc'o   boiling, sweet   အကျို ၊ အချို
5. ăseiq, ăs'eiq   quarter, poison   အစိပ် ၊ အဆိပ်
6. Koun-dheh Làn,   Merchant St,   ကုန်သည်လမ်း
    Kàn-nà Làn, kò   Strand Rd, nine   ကမ်းနားလမ်း၊ ကိုး
    k'un-hniq, k'un   seven, seven [short form]   ခုနစ် ၊ ခွန်
7. ho-teh, tiq,   hotel, one,   ဟိုတယ် ၊ တစ်
    teh-li-p'oùn, tăt'aun   telephone, thousand   တယ်လီဖုန်း ၊ တစ်ထောင်
8. pàn-jan, Pàn-s'ò-dàn,   park, [road name],   ပန်းခြံ ၊ ပန်းဆိုးတန်း
    p'ăyà, teh-li-p'oùn   pagoda, telephone   ဘုရား ၊ တယ်လီဖုန်း

LESSON 9

Sentences without –ပါ -ba/-pa *"polite."*
What road is nº 500? — Strand Road.

Rangoon roads

nº	script	English equivalent	pronunciation in roman [1]
100	ဗိုလ်ချုပ်လမ်း	Bogyoke Street	Bo-jouq Làn
200	အနော်ရထာလမ်း	Anawrahta Street	Ănaw-yăt'a Làn [2]
300	မဟာဗန္ဓုလလမ်း	Maha Bandoola Street	Măha Ban-dú-lá Làn
400	ကုန်သည်လမ်း	Merchant Street	Koun-dheh Làn
500	ကမ်းနားလမ်း	Strand Road	Kàn-nà Làn
600	ဗိုလ်အောင်ကျော်လမ်း	Bo Aung Kyaw Street	Bo Aun Jaw Làn
700	ပန်းဆိုးတန်း	Pansodan Street	Pàn-s'ò-dàn or Pàn-zò-dàn
800	ဆူးလေဘုရားလမ်း	Sule Pagoda Road	S'ù-le P'ăyà Làn
900	ရွှေဘုံသာလမ်း	Shwebontha Street	Shwe-boun-dha Làn
1000	[ရွှေတိဂုံ]ဘုရားလမ်း	Shwedagon Pagoda Rd	[Shwe-dăgoun] P'ăyà Làn

Diphthongs in the roman transcription:
pronounce ei as in *vein,* ai as in *Thailand,* ou as in *though,* au as in *Sauerkraut.*

Rangoon road names with pronunciation shown in Burmese script

n°	script	English equivalent	pronunciation in script [1]
100	ဗိုလ်ချုပ်လမ်း	Bogyoke Street	/ဗိုဂျုက်လန်း/
200	အနော်ရထာလမ်း	Anawrahta Street	/အနော်ယထာလန်း/ [2]
300	မဟာဗန္ဓုလလမ်း	Maha Bandoola Street	/မဟာဗန်ဒုလ္လာလန်း/
400	ကုန်သည်လမ်း	Merchant Street	/ကုန်သုယ်လန်း/
500	ကမ်းနားလမ်း	Strand Road	as written
600	ဗိုလ်အောင်ကျော်လမ်း	Bo Aung Kyaw Street	/ဗိုအောင်ကျော်လန်း/
700	ပန်းဆိုးတန်း	Pansodan Street	/ပန်းဆိုးဒန်း/ or /ပန်းဇိုဒန်း/
800	ဆူးလေဘုရားလမ်း	Sule Pagoda Road	/ဆူးလေဖယားလန်း/
900	ရွှေဘုံသာလမ်း	Shwebontha Street	/ရွှေဘုံသာလန်း/
1000	[ရွှေတိဂုံ]ဘုရားလမ်း	Shwedagon Pagoda Rd	/[ရွှေဒဂုန်]ဘုရားလန်း/

1. On "pronunciation in roman" and "pronunciation in script" see Appendix 3. The paucity of "as written" entries shows how many mismatches there are between sound and script.
2. Also pronounced /အနော်ရထာလန်း/ = Ănaw-răt'a Làn

Example sentences

S1: နံပါတ် ၅၀၀ ဘာလမ်းလဲ။   What road is N° 500?   Nan-baq ngà-ya ba-làn-lèh?

S2: ကမ်းနားလမ်း။   Strand Road   Kàn-nà Làn.
    Note that a statement, like S2's answer to the question here, doesn't have to end in a –ပါ -ba/-pa meaning *"polite."* See the Note below.

Models for the Exercises

Ex. 1: Looking at the Rangoon street plan
    Prompt: Ask what road n° 600 is.
    L/S2: နံပါတ် ၆၀၀ ဘာလမ်းလဲ။   Nan-baq c'auq-ya ba làn-lèh?
    S1: ဗိုလ်အောင်ကျော်လမ်းပါ။   Bo Aun Caw Làn-ba.
    L: ဗိုလ်အောင်ကျော်လမ်းလား။   Bo Aun Caw Làn-là?
    S1: ဟုတ်ကဲ့။ ဗိုလ်အောင်ကျော်လမ်း။   Houq-kéh. Bo Aun Caw Làn-ba.

Ex. 2
    S1: နံပါတ် ၈၀၀ ဘာလမ်းလဲ။   Nan-baq shiq-ya ba làn-lèh?
    L/S2: ဆူးလေဘုရားလမ်း။   S'ù-le P'ăyà Làn-ba.

Ex. 3
    S1: ကုန်သည်လမ်း နံပါတ် ဘယ်လောက်လဲ။   Koun-dheh Làn nan-baq beh-lauq-lèh?
    L/S2: နံပါတ် ၄၀၀-ပါ။   Nan-baq lè-ya-ba.

In class: Exercises as above. Also use map of own town or other area.

Diphthongs in the roman transcription:
pronounce ei as in *vein*, ai as in *Thailand*, ou as in *though*, au as in *Sauerkraut*.

Notes

Degrees of politeness. Up to this point we have consistently ended statements with the suffix –ပါ -ba (or -pa). This suffix is a signal that the speaker is being polite to his listener. However, people don't use a –ပါ -ba/-pa at the end of every statement they make in a conversation: a –ပါ -ba/-pa here and there is enough to convey the message. Not using it at all means that the speaker is treating his listener as socially inferior to himself. If the speaker is an employer talking to a junior employee, or a parent talking to a child, then of course using no –ပါ -ba/-pa is entirely appropriate and correct. To use no –ပါ -ba/-pa when talking to (say) strangers of one's own age sounds uncouth and unfriendly. On the other hand using –ပါ -ba/-pa too frequently verges on the ingratiating. For this reason you need to get used to making statements without –ပါ -ba/-pa as well as with it.

Aye Khaing (Motor Vessel Owner), 99/101, 74662 Adamson Street, Botataung.	Aye Kyi, Daw—Daw Khin Latt, 63, Sanchaung 32757 Street, Sanchaung.
Aye Khin, Daw, 41/19, Shwe Taung Gone 30141 Yeiktha, Lewis Road.	Aye Kyi, Daw, Head of Division (2), Ministry of 30211 Education, 26, Short St., Sanchaung.
Aye Khin, Daw, 452, Lower Pazundaung Road. 81262	Aye Kyi, Dr. Daw, Room-12/292, Shwedagon 73615 Pagoda Road.
Aye Ko, 83, Padauk Pin Street, Kemmendine. 33988	
Aye Ko, 1063, Bazaar Street, Block (6) East, 50332 Thaketa.	Aye Kyi, Dr. Daw, Medical Supdt., Woman & 33660 Children Hospital, Hospitals, 2, Dagon Road, University Avenue.
Aye Ko, 430, Merchant Street 70274	Aye Kyi (Retd.), Room-15/271, East Yankin 51760
Aye Ko, 331/335, Pansodan Street (1st Floor). 73554	Aye Kyi, Secretary (Township People's Council, 55566 Thingangyun), Rangoon Division People's
Aye Ko, 105, Shwebontha Street (1st Floor). 77226	Council, 139/3, Yenatha Street, Thuwunna.
Aye Ko, 63, 13th Street.............................. 78904	
Aye Ko, 115, 27th Street 84738	**Aye Kyin, Daw,** 3-B, U Tun Nyein Street, 60183 Chawdwingone.
Aye Ko, 94, Shwebontha Street...................... 84927	Aye Kyin, Daw, 50, 30th Street 71478
Aye Ko Brother Myanaung Gold Shop, 25, 75883 D-Block, Theingyizay.	

Extract from the Rangoon telephone directory, containing some familiar street names.
(As you see, telephone directories are written in English)

Pronunciation Section for Lesson 9

1: voiced, plain and aspirate consonants

voiced:	g	d	b	j	z	ဂ	ဒ	ဎ	ဇ	ဩ	
plain:	k	t	p	c	s	က	တ	ပ	ကျ	စ	
aspirate:	k'	t'	p'	c'	s'	ခ	ထ	ဖ	ချ	ဆ	

2.   TTC   တီတီစီ

3.   BBS or PPS or PBS or BPS?   ဘီဘီအက်စ်—ပီပီအက်စ်—ပီဘီအက်စ်—ဘီပီအက်စ်

4.   PBI? BBI? PPI? BPI?   ပီဘီအိုင်—ဘီဘီအိုင်—ပီပီအိုင်—ဘီပီအိုင်

5.   RIT? RID?   အရ်အိုင်တီ—အရ်အိုင်ဒီ

6.   PED? BET? PET? BED?   ပီအီး:ဒီ—ဘီအီး:တီ—ပီအီး:တီ—ဘီအီး:ဒီ

Point 2: breathed nasal: h m-

1.   M word: ma.   HM word: hma.   မာ၊ မှာ

2.   Phases of ma: 1. m-   2. -a

     Phases of hma: 1. hm-   2. -m-   3. -a

Diphthongs in the roman transcription: pronounce ei as in *vein*, ai as in *Thailand*, ou as in *though*, au as in *Sauerkraut*.

3. A. ma-deh, hma-deh   B. hma-deh, ma-deh   C. ma-deh, ma-deh   D. hma-deh, hma-deh

    A. မတယ်၊ မှာတယ်   B. မှာတယ်၊ မတယ်   C. မတယ်၊ မတယ်   D. မှာတယ်၊ မှာတယ်

    (ma-deh, hma-deh   to be hard, to order   မတယ်၊ မှာတယ်)

4. ămaq, ăhmaq   minister, mark   အမတ်၊ အမှတ်

5. hmà-deh, hman-deh   to be wrong, to be right   မှားတယ်၊ မှန်တယ်

6. ăhmà-ăhman   right and wrong   အမှားအမှန်

Point 3: tones: **a** and **à** and **á**

1. A. Da than-ba.   That's iron.   ဒါ သံပါ။

    B. Da thàn-ba.   That's a louse.   ဒါ သန်းပါ။

2. A. Da s'è-youn-ba.   That's a hospital.   ဒါ ဆေးရုံပါ။

    B. Da s'è-yoùn-ba.   That's the medical office.   ဒါ ဆေးရုံးပါ။

3. A. ăcì—ăcí   B. ăcì—ăcì   C. ăcí—ăcì   D. ăcí—ăcí

    A. အကြီး–အကြည့်   B. အကြီး–အကြီး   C. အကြည့်–အကြီး   D. အကြည့်–အကြည့်

    (ăcì, ăcí   large, a look   အကြီး၊ အကြည့်)

4. A. Yá-ba-deh.   That's all right.   ရပါတယ်။

    B. Yà-ba-deh.   It's itching.   ယားပါတယ်။

LESSON 10

Numbers in round thousands.
Voicing for ထောင် -t'aun thousand and other words.

၁၀၀၀	၂၀၀၀	၃၀၀၀	၄၀၀၀	၅၀၀၀	၆၀၀၀	၇၀၀၀	၈၀၀၀	၉၀၀၀	၁၀၀၀၀
1000	2000	3000	4000	5000	6000	7000	8000	9000	10,000

New words

figure	script	English	pronunciation
–၀၀၀	–ထောင်	thousand	-t'aun
			(or -daun: see below)

Examples

ခြောက်ထောင်	six thousand	c'auq-t'aun
ရှစ်ထောင်	eight thousand	shiq-t'aun
	and so on	

Note weakening for 1, 2, 7 (as for the hundreds):

တစ်ထောင် /တထောင်/	one thousand	tăt'aun
နှစ်ထောင် /နှထောင်/	two thousand	hnăt'aun
ခုနစ်ထောင် /ခွန်နှ‌ထောင်/	seven thousand	k'un-năt'aun

Diphthongs in the roman transcription:
pronounce ei as in *vein*, ai as in *Thailand*, ou as in *though*, au as in *Sauerkraut*.

Note voicing for 3, 4, 5, 9 (see the Note below):

သုံးထောင်	/သုန်းဒေါင်/	three thousand	thoùn-daun
လေးထောင်	/လေးဒေါင်/	four thousand	lè-daun
ငါးထောင်	/ငါးဒေါင်/	five thousand	ngà-daun
ကိုးထောင်	/ကိုးဒေါင်/	nine thousand	kò-daun

Ten thousand and over

The following words are not practised in the Exercises, but are noted here for reference:

–သောင်း	10,000	-thaùn
–သိန်း	100,000	-theìn
–သန်း	1,000,000	-thàn

Examples:

နှစ်သောင်း	20,000	hnăthaùn
ခြောက်သိန်း	600,000	c'auq-theìn
ရှစ်သန်း	8,000,000	shiq-thàn

Models for the exercises

Ex. 1: 800 ⇒ 8000. Prompt: Say 800.

L/S2: ရှစ်ရာ။	Shiq-ya.
S1/L: ရှစ်ထောင်။	Shiq-t'aun.

Ex. 2: 600 ⇒ 6000

S1: ခြောက်ရာ။	C'auq-ya.
L/S2: ခြောက်ထောင်။	C'auq-t'aun.

Ex. 3: add a thousand

S1: လေးထောင်။	Lè-daun.
L/S2: ငါးထောင်။	Ngà-daun.

Ex. 4: Prompt: What's the number under A?
(see the chart below)

L/S: လေးထောင်	Lè-daun.

Chart for Ex. 4

	A	B	C	D	E	F	G	H
line 1:	၄၀၀၀	၃၀၀၀	၂၀၀၀	၅၀၀၀	၈၀၀၀	၇၀၀၀	၄၀၀၀	၆၀၀၀
line 2:	၅၀၀၀	၁၀၀၀	၉၀၀၀	၇၀၀၀	၆၀၀၀	၁၀၀၀	၃၀၀၀	၂၀၀၀

In class: Exercises as above.
Also with (easy!) additions:

L1: သုံးထောင်နဲ့ တစ်ထောင် ပေါင်း ဘယ်လောက်လဲ။
L2: လေးထောင်။
L3: သုံးထောင်နဲ့ တစ်ထောင် ပေါင်း လေးထောင်လား။
L2: ဟုတ်ကဲ့။ လေးထောင်ပါ။ or No, as the case may be.

Vocabulary:

[noun1]–နဲ့ [noun2]	[noun1] and [noun2]	[noun1]-néh [noun2]
[N°1]–နဲ့ [N°2] ပေါင်း	[N°1] and [N°2] added together	[N°1]-néh [N°2] paùn

Note

Voicing. The Burmese expressions for 3,000, 4,000, 5,000 and 9,000 are examples of a phenomenon we call "The Voicing Rule." This refers to the fact that, in Burmese, when two

Diphthongs in the roman transcription:
pronounce ei as in *vein*, ai as in *Thailand*, ou as in *though*, au as in *Sauerkraut*.

syllables are joined to make up a word, the consonant of the second syllable is "voiced." In the case of ေထာင် t'aun "thousand," voicing means that the sound of the consonant changes from /ထ/ to /ဒ/ (= from t' to d). Examples:

သုံး thoùn	+ ေထာင် t'aun	= /သုံးေဒါင်/ thoùn-daun		(not /သုံးေထာင်/ thoùn-t'aun)
ေလး lè	+ ေထာင် t'aun	= /ေလးေဒါင်/ lè-daun		(not /ေလးေထာင်/ lè-t'aun)

There are some exceptions. First, the voicing rule does not apply after a glottal stop (the sound written -q in the roman transcription, and –က် –စ် –တ် –ပ် and their like in the Burmese script); hence:

ေချာက် c'auq	+ /ေထာင်/ t'aun	= /ေချာက်ေထာင်/ c'auq-t'aun		(not /ေချာက်ေဒါင်/ c'auq-daun)
ရှစ် shiq	+ /ေထာင်/ t'aun	= /ရှစ်ေထာင်/ shiq-t'aun		(not /ရှစ်ေဒါင်/ shiq-daun)

Second, in many cases the voicing rule does not apply after a weakened syllable (after the vowel written ă in the roman transcription and by writing no vowel symbol in the script); hence

တစ် tiq	+ /ေထာင်/ t'aun	= /တေထာင်/ tăt'aun		(not /တေဒါင်/ tădaun)
နှစ် hniq	+ /ေထာင်/ t'aun	= /နှေထာင်/ hnăt'aun		(not /နှေဒါင်/ hnădaun)
ခုနှစ် k'un-hniq	+ /ေထာင်/ t'aun	= /ခုန်နှေထာင်/ k'un-năt'aun		(not /ခုန်နှေဒါင်/ k'un-nădaun)

Burmese script does not show the difference in pronunciation:
the /ေထာင်/ t'aun in ရှစ်ေထာင် shiq-t'aun and
the /ေဒါင်/ daun in ကိုးေထာင် kò-daun
are both written ေထာင်။

Thirdly, some speakers, on some occasions, fail to apply the voicing rule. So, in their speech, you will occasionally hear the pronunciation /ေလးေထာင်/ lè-t'aun as well as /ေလးေဒါင်/ lè-daun. Failure to voice is particularly common in Burmese spoken by Shans and Karens, but you will also find the rule ignored intermittently in the speech of native speaking Burmese, particularly young people, and particularly girls. Some speakers seem to adopt variable voicing as an affectation.

Finally, not all consonants are subject to the Voicing Rule: some are voiced already (for example: လ– l-, ဒ– d-, ယ– y-), and so can't be voiced again. The consonants that are subject to voicing are:

	/ က	ကျ	စ	ထ	ပ/
and	/ ခ	ချ	ဆ	ထ	ဖ/

and the voiced counterparts of both rows are:

	/ ဂ	ဂျ	ဇ	ဒ	ဗ/

Here is the same chart in the roman transcription:

voiceable consonants:	/k	c	s	t	p/
and	/k'	c'	s'	t'	p'/
voiced counterparts:	/g	j	z	d	b/

The chart is a concise way of stating that a word that begins with either a /က/ (k) or a /ခ/ (k') will be pronounced with a /ဂ/ (g) when it is in second (or later) position in a larger

Diphthongs in the roman transcription:
pronounce ei as in *vein*, ai as in *Thailand*, ou as in *though*, au as in *Sauerkraut*.

word (unless it is preceded by a glottal stop or a weak syllable); and likewise for the other four pairs of consonants listed.

It is because of the Voicing Rule that you find —
  –ပါ *"polite"* pronounced either /–ဗာ/ -ba or /–ပါ/ -pa (as noted in Lesson 1), and
  –က *"as for"* pronounced either /–ဂ့/ -gá or /–က့/ -ká (as noted in Lesson 4).

The Voicing Rule is complex to set out, but once you begin to get used to it you will be surprised how straightforward it is to use.

Pronunciation Section for Lesson 10

Point 1: breathed L: hl-
1. le, hle   wind, boat   လေ၊ လှေ
2. louq-teh, hlouq-teh   to do, to shake   လုပ်တယ်၊ လှုပ်တယ်
3. lá, hlá   moon, to be good-looking   လ၊ လှ
                                    (Hlá is common as a name)

Point 2: round-up of breathed nasals
1. chart:
   plain: ng-   n-   m-   ny-   င   န   မ   ည
   breathed: hng-   hn-   hm-   hny-   ငှ   နှ   မှ   ညှ
2. hngeq, hngà-   bird, to hire   ငှက်၊ ငှား
   hnyeìn-, hnyiq-   to put out, to wring out   ငြိမ်း၊ ညှစ်
3. hnè-deh, hnò-deh   to be slow, to wake up (sn)   နေးတယ်၊ နှိုးတယ်
4. hmà-deh, hman-deh   to be wrong, to be right   မှားတယ်၊ မှန်တယ်
5. nyiq-teh, hnyiq-teh   to be dirty, to wring out   ညစ်တယ်၊ ညှစ်တယ်
6. nya-deh, hnya-deh   to cheat, to spare   ညာတယ်၊ ညှာတယ်
7. hngà-deh, ăhngà-yin   to hire out, hire car (taxi)   ငှားတယ်၊ အငှားယာဉ်
8. hnaq hnyiq-teh   to blow one's nose   နှပ်ညှစ်တယ်

Point 3: round-up of tones: a and à and á
1. A. Da lu-ba.   That's a person.   ဒါ လူပါ။
   B. Da lù-ba.   That's millet.   ဒါ လူးပါ။
2. A. Nan-dhălà?   Does it smell?   နံသလား။
   B. Nàn-dhălà?   Did you sniff it?   နမ်းသလား။
   Note: -dhălà (sometimes pronounced -thălà) is a suffix you attach to verbs when you are asking a question. There is an explanation further on in *BISL*.
3. A. wa-zi. B. wa-zí   cotton-seed oil, cotton seed   ဝါဆီ၊ ဝါစေ့
4. A. Da Ù Tin-là?   Is that U Tin?   ဒါ ဦးတင်လား။
   — Măhouq-pa-bù. Da Ù Tín-ba.   — No, it's U Tint.   မဟုတ်ပါဘူး။ ဒါ ဦးတင့်ပါ။
   B. Da Ù Tín-là?   Is that U Tint?   ဒါ ဦးတင့်လား။
   — Măhouq-pa-bù. Ù Tin-ba.   — No, it's U Tin.   မဟုတ်ပါဘူး။ ဦးတင်ပါ။

Diphthongs in the roman transcription:
pronounce ei as in *vein*, ai as in *Thailand*, ou as in *though*, au as in *Sauerkraut*.

5. A. Beh-lauq cá-mălèh? How much will it cost? ဘယ်လောက် ကျမလဲ။
   — Ngà-daw-la cá-meh. — It'll cost five dollars. — ငါးဒေါ်လာ ကျမယ်။
   B. Beh-lauq ca-mălèh? How long will it take? ဘယ်လောက် ကြာမလဲ။
   — Ngà-măniq ca-meh. — It'll take five minutes. — ငါးမိနစ် ကြာမယ်။

   Note: The formula [verb]-mălèh? is used to ask questions about the future. [verb]-meh is the formula for the answer. More forthcoming in *BISL*.

6. A. ăt'ù. B. ăt'ú special, thumping အထူး၊ အထု

7. A. Màw-dhălà? Was he tired? မောသလား။
   — Mămàw-ba-bù. — He wasn't tired. — မမောပါဘူး။
   B. Máw-dhălà? Did he look up? မော့သလား။
   — Máw-ba-deh. — He did look up. — မော့ပါတယ်။

   Note: mă-[verb]-ba-bù is used to negate a verb. More in *BISL*. The parallel with mă-houq-ba-bù will not have escaped you.

8. A. Mè-t'à-ba-naw? Please do ask, won't you? မေးထားပါနော်။
   B. Mé-t'à-ba-naw? Please do forget it, won't you? မေ့ထားပါနော်။

9. A. Ku-pè-ba-naw? Please do help, won't you? ကူပေးပါနော်။
   B. Kù-pè-ba-naw? Please do copy it, won't you? ကူးပေးပါနော်။
   C. Kú-pè-ba-naw? Please do cure him, won't you? ကုပေးပါနော်။

10. A. Da than-là? Is that iron? ဒါ သံလား။
    — Houq-kéh. Da than-ba. — Yes, it is iron. ဟုတ်ကဲ့။ ဒါ သံပါ။
    B. Da thàn-là? Is that a louse? ဒါ သန်းလား။
    — Houq-kéh. Da thàn-ba. — Yes, it is a louse. ဟုတ်ကဲ့။ ဒါ သန်းပါ။
    C. Da Thán-là? Is that Thant [man's name]? ဒါ သန့်လား။
    — Houq-kéh. Da Thán-ba. — Yes, it is Thant. ဟုတ်ကဲ့။ ဒါ သန့်ပါ။

LESSON 11

Which [noun]. In [place]. In which [place]?
Which road is the Strand Hotel in/on? — In/on Strand Road.

Rangoon places and their streets

နေရာ	လမ်း	*place*	*street*
ဗိုလ်ချုပ်ပြတိုက်	ဗိုလ်ချုပ်ပြတိုက်လမ်း	Bogyoke Museum	Bogyoke Museum Road
ဗိုလ်ချုပ်ဈေး	ဗိုလ်ချုပ်လမ်း	Bogyoke Market	Bogyoke Street
သိမ်ကြီးဈေး	ဘုရားလမ်း	Theingyi Market	Shwedagon Pagoda Rd
ဆူးလေဘုရား	ဆူးလေဘုရားလမ်း	Sule Pagoda	Sule Pagoda Road
အမျိုးသားပြတိုက်	ပန်းဆိုးတန်း	National Museum	Pansodan
စထရင်းဟိုတယ်	ကမ်းနားလမ်း	Strand Hotel	Strand Road

Diphthongs in the roman transcription:
pronounce ei as in *vein*, ai as in *Thailand*, ou as in *though*, au as in *Sauerkraut*.

ne-ya	làn	*place*	*street*
Bo-jouq Pyá-daiq	Bo-jouq Pyá-daiq Làn	Bogyoke Museum	Bogyoke Museum Road
Bo-jouq Zè	Bo-jouq Làn	Bogyoke Market	Bogyoke Street
Thein-jì Zè	P'ăyà Làn	Theingyi Market	Shwedagon Pagoda Rd
S'ù-le P'ăyà	S'ù-le P'ăyà Làn	Sule Pagoda	Sule Pagoda Road
Ămyò-thà Pyá-daiq	Pàn-s'ò-dàn	National Museum	Pansodan
Săt'ărìn Ho-teh	Kàn-nà Làn	Strand Hotel	Strand Road

New words

[place]–မှာ	in/at/on [place]	[place]-hma
ဘယ် [noun]	which [noun]	beh [noun]
ဘယ် [place]–မှာလဲ	in which [place]?	beh [place]-hma-lèh?
Examples:		
ဘယ် ဈေးမှာလဲ	in which market?	beh zè-hma-lèh?
သိမ်ကြီးဈေးမှာ	in the Theingyi Market	Thein-jì Zè-hma
ဘယ် လမ်းမှာလဲ	in which road? on which road? *	beh làn-hma-lèh?
ဗိုလ်ချုပ်လမ်းမှာ	in/on Bogyoke Street *	Bo-jouq Làn-hma

* The phrase လမ်းမှာ reveals a difference between British and American English: British speakers say *"in Bogyoke Street"* where Americans say *"on Bogyoke Street."* We could use both options for every occurrence, as we have done up to this point, but the result is cumbersome, so from now on you will find just the British *in,* and American readers are asked to be tolerant of the writer's British habits.

The Strand Hotel, Rangoon

Example sentences

S1: စထရင်းဟိုတယ် �’ဘယ်လမ်းမှာလဲ။	Which road is the Strand Hotel in?	Săt'ărìn Ho-teh beh-làn-hma-lèh?
S2: ကမ်းနားလမ်းမှာပါ။	In Strand Road.	Kàn-nà Làn-hma-ba.
S1: စထရင်းဟိုတယ်က ကမ်းနားလမ်းမှာလား။	Is the Strand Hotel in Strand Road?	Săt'ărìn Ho-teh-gá Kàn-nà Làn-hma-là?
S2: ဟုတ်ကဲ့။ ကမ်းနားလမ်းမှာပါ။	Yes. It's in Strand Road.	Houq-kéh. Kàn-nà Làn-hma-ba.

Models for the Exercises

Ex. 1: Looking at the list of places and their roads
Prompt: Ask which road the Strand Hotel is in.

L/S2: စထရင်းဟိုတယ် ဘယ်လမ်းမှာလဲ။	Săt'ărìn Ho-teh beh làn-hma-lèh?
S1: ကမ်းနားလမ်းမှာပါ။	Kàn-nà Làn-hma-ba.
L/S2: အော်။ ကမ်းနားလမ်းမှာ။	Aw. Kàn-nà Làn-hma.

Ex. 2

S1: စထရင်းဟိုတယ်က ကမ်းနားလမ်းမှာလား။	Săt'ărìn Ho-teh-gá Kàn-nà Làn-hma-là?
L/S2: ဟုတ်ကဲ့။ ကမ်းနားလမ်းမှာပါ။	Houq-kéh. Kàn-nà Làn-hma-ba.
— or: မဟုတ်ပါဘူး။ ... as the case may be and sometimes a checking question.	Măhouq-pa-bù.

Ex. 3 For written answer: not on the tape.

The words in the following questions and answers have been split up and jumbled. Rearrange them to form meaningful sentences. There is a Key to this Exercise at the end of the Lesson. Don't forget that you may find it helpful to copy the words onto separate slips of paper and do your reordering by sliding the slips around.

S1: — ဘယ်လမ်း — ဈေး — လဲ — သိမ်ကြီး — မှာ

    S2: — ဘုရားလမ်း — ပါ — မှာ

S1: — မှာ — ပြတိုက် — ဘယ် — လဲ — လမ်း — အမျိုးသား

    S2: — မှာ — ပန်းဆိုးတန်း — ပါ

S1: — ဆူးလေဘုရား — မှာ — လား — ဗိုလ်အောင်ကျော်လမ်း — က

    S2: — ပါ — မှာ — ဆူးလေဘုရား — မဟုတ်ပါဘူး — လမ်း

Diphthongs in the roman transcription:
pronounce ei as in *vein*, ai as in *Thailand*, ou as in *though*, au as in *Sauerkraut*.

Ex. 3. Version in roman.

S1: — beh-làn — Zè — lèh — Thein-gyì — hma
    S2: — P'ăyà Làn — ba — hma
S1: — hma — pyá-daiq — beh — lèh — làn — Amyò-thà
    S2: — hma — Pàn-s'ò-dàn — ba
S1: — S'ù-le P'ăyà — hma — là — Bo Aun Jaw Làn — gá
    S2: — ba — hma — S'ù-le P'ăyà — măhouq-pa-bù — làn

In class: Exercises as above. Also use map (or knowledge) of your own town and the like; for example:

Odeon Cinema–က ဘယ်လမ်းမှာလဲ။ and so on.   Odeon Cinema-gá beh làn-hma-lèh?

Note

Grammar. The standard formula for *is* sentences is still valid for questions like "Which road is the Strand Hotel in?" and answers like "[It's] in Strand Road." Note that the NOUN2 slot now has a suffix.

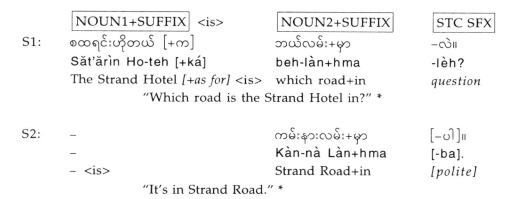

Brackets. In these examples –က -gá "as for" is bracketed to show that it may be omitted or inserted.

* On the difference between "in a road" and "on a road" see the Note in Lesson 11.

Unfilled suffix slots. NOUN2+SUFFIX. As you know from previous examples, the slot for a suffix after NOUN2 is not always filled. It is filled if the meaning of the sentence calls for it. In a sentence like —

NOUN1+SUFFIX <is>	NOUN2+SUFFIX	STC SFX
ဒါက	ကမ်းနားလမ်း	[–ပါ]။
Da-gá	Kàn-nà Làn	[-ba].
That <is>	Strand Road	[polite]

    "That is the Strand Road."

there is no call for a suffix on NOUN2; whereas in a sentence like —

Diphthongs in the roman transcription:
pronounce ei as in *vein*, ai as in *Thailand*, ou as in *though*, au as in *Sauerkraut*.

45

စထရင်းဟိုတယ်က   ကမ်းနားလမ်း+မှာ   [–ပါ]။

Săt'ărìn Ho-teh-gá   Kàn-nà Làn+hma   [-ba].

The Strand Hotel+*as for* <is>   Strand Road+in   *[polite]*

"The Strand Hotel is in Strand Road."

the meaning of the sentence requires one.

ဘယ် [noun] **beh** [noun] vs. ဘာ [noun] **ba** [noun]. You are familiar with ဘာ [noun] ba [noun] in questions like —

ဒါ ဘာလမ်းလဲ။   "What road is that?"   Da ba làn-lèh?

and in this Lesson you hear ဘယ် [noun] **beh** [noun] in questions like —

သမ္မတဟိုတယ်   "Which road is the   Thămădá Ho-teh

     ဘယ်လမ်းမှာလဲ။   President Hotel in?"   beh làn-hma-lèh?

As a general rule, you will find that the first (ဘာ– [noun] ba-[noun]) is like "what [noun]?" in English, and the second (ဘယ်– [noun] beh-[noun]) is more like "which [noun]?" This is a rough and ready rule, to which you find exceptions, but a comprehensive statement of the conditions under which you should use one or the other is beyond the scope of *BISL*.

Keys to the Exercises

Key to Ex. 3. For written answer: not on the tape.

S1:— သိမ်ကြီး — ဈေး — ဘယ်လမ်း — မှာ — လဲ။

     S2:— ဘုရားလမ်း — မှာ — ပါ။

S1:— အမျိုးသား — ပြုတိုက် — ဘယ် — လမ်း — မှာ — လဲ။

     S2:— ပန်းဆိုးတန်း — မှာ — ပါ။

S1:— ဆူးလေဘုရား — က — ဗိုလ်အောင်ကျော်လမ်း— မှာ— လား။

     S2:— မဟုတ်ပါဘူး။ — ဆူးလေဘုရား — လမ်း — မှာ— ပါ။

Key to Ex. 3. Version in roman.

S1: — Thein-gyì — Zè — beh-làn — hma — lèh

     S2: — P'ăyà Làn — hma — ba

S1: — Amyò-thà — pyá-daiq — beh — làn — hma — lèh

     S2: — Pàn-s'ò-dàn — hma — ba

S1: — S'ù-le P'ăyà — gá — Bo Aun Jaw Làn — hma — là

     S2: — măhouq-pa-bù. — S'ù-le P'ăyà — làn — hma — ba

Common phrases

This is a good point at which to start work on the Common Phrases Supplement — if you haven't already done so. You will find another reminder every other Lesson.

Diphthongs in the roman transcription:
pronounce ei as in *vein,* ai as in *Thailand,* ou as in *though,* au as in *Sauerkraut.*

LESSON 12

Numbers in round tens.
Voicing for ဆယ် (-s'eh) ten.

၁၀	၂၀	၃၀	၄၀	၅၀	၆၀	၇၀	၈၀	၉၀	၁၀၀
10	20	30	40	50	60	70	80	90	100

New words

–ဆယ်	ten, -ty	-s'eh (or -zeh: see below)

New numbers

တစ်ဆယ် /တဆယ်/	one ten (ten)	tăs'eh
နှစ်ဆယ် /နှဆယ်/	two tens (twenty)	hnăs'eh
သုံးဆယ် /သုန်းဇယ်/	three tens (thirty)	thoùn-zeh
လေးဆယ် /လေးဇယ်/	four tens (fourty)	lè-zeh
ငါးဆယ် /ငါးဇယ်/	five tens (fifty)	ngà-zeh
ခြောက်ဆယ်	six tens (sixty)	c'auq-s'eh
ခုနစ်ဆယ် /ခွန်နဆယ်/	seven tens (seventy)	k'un-năs'eh
ရှစ်ဆယ်	eight tens (eighty)	shiq-s'eh
ကိုးဆယ် /ကိုးဇယ်/	nine tens (ninety)	kò-zeh

Note weakening in 10, 20, 70 (as for the thousands),
and voicing in 30, 40, 50, 90 (as for the thousands).

Models for the exercises

Ex. 1: 8000 ⇒ 80
   Prompt: Say 8000

L/S2: ရှစ်ထောင်	Shiq-t'aun.
S1/L: ရှစ်ဆယ်	Shiq-s'eh.

Ex. 2: 6000 ⇒ 60

S1: ခြောက်ထောင်	C'auq-t'aun.
L/S2: ခြောက်ဆယ်	C'auq-s'eh.

Ex. 3: Times ten

S1: တစ်	Tiq.
L/S2: တစ်ဆယ်	Tăs'eh.

Ex. 4: Add ten

S1: ရှစ်ဆယ်	Shiq-s'eh.
L/S2: ကိုးဆယ်	Kò-zeh.

Diphthongs in the roman transcription:
pronounce ei as in *vein*, ai as in *Thailand*, ou as in *though*, au as in *Sauerkraut*.

Ex. 5: Prompt: What's the number under A? (see the chart below)
    L/S: လေးဆယ်   Lè-zeh.

Chart for Ex. 5

	A	B	C	D	E	F	G	H
line 1:	၅၀	၄၀	၃၀	၂၀	၈၀	၆၀	၇၀	၉၀
line 2:	၆၀	၅၀	၁၀	၇၀	၆၀	၃၀	၄၀	၂၀

In class: Exercises as above.

Also with page numbers and additions as in previous Lessons.

Note

Voicing. The Voicing Rule operates on –ဆယ် -s'eh "ten" just as it did on –ထောင် -t'aun "thousand." The voiced counterpart of /ဆ–/ s'- is /ဇ–/ z-. Examples:

သုံး thoùn + ဆယ် s'eh = /သုံးဇယ်/ thoùn-zeh (not /သုံးဆယ်/ thoùn-s'eh)
လေး lè + ဆယ် s'eh = /လေးဇယ်/ lè-zeh (not /လေးဆယ်/ lè-s'eh)

And the operation of the Voicing Rule is blocked in the same way as before: by a number ending in a glottal stop or a weak syllable.

Although the voicing rule may look hard to remember and apply, you will probably be surprised to find how little trouble it gives you. If you learn "fifty" as /ငါးဇယ်/ ngà-zeh and "sixty" as /ခြောက်ဆယ်/ c'auq-s'eh, you'll find you aren't thinking about the voicing rule at all.

LESSON 13

Names of some countries near Burma.
Please say that again.

New words

နိုင်ငံ	country	naing-ngan, nain-gan
ထပ်ပြောပါအုံး။	Please say that again.	T'aq-pyàw-ba-oùn.
ပြန်ပြောပါအုံး။	Please say that again.	Pyan-pyàw-ba-oùn.
ထပ်–[verb]	[verb] again	t'aq-[verb]
ပြန်–[verb]	[verb] again	pyan-[verb]
ပြော–	to say	pyàw-
[verb]–ပါ။	Please [verb]	[verb]-ba
[verb]–ပါအုံး။	Please [verb] more, further	[verb]-ba-oùn

The component elements of ပြန်ပြောပါအုံး are given here to satisfy curiosity only. They are not meant to be learned and used in other phrases — yet. Their turn will come when we meet sentences with verbs.

Diphthongs in the roman transcription:
pronounce ei as in *vein*, ai as in *Thailand*, ou as in *though*, au as in *Sauerkraut*.

Example sentences

S1: နံပါတ်(၂၀)က ဘာနိုင်ငံလဲ။	What country is n° 20?	Nan-baq-hnǎs'eh-gá ba naing-gan-lèh?
S2: ဘင်္ဂလားဒေ့ရှ်နိုင်ငံပါ။	Bangladesh.	Bin-gǎlà-désh Naing-gan-ba.
S1: ထပ်ပြောပါအုံး။	Could you please say that again?	T'aq-pyàw-ba-oùn.
S2: ဘင်္ဂလားဒေ့ရှ်နိုင်ငံ။	Bangladesh.	Bin-gǎlà-désh Naing-gan.
S1: နံပါတ်(၉၀)က ဂျပန်နိုင်ငံလား။	Is n° 90 Japan?	Nan-baq-kò-zeh-gá Jǎpan Naing-gan-là?
S2: ဟုတ်ကဲ့။ ဂျပန်နိုင်ငံပါ။	Yes. [It is] Japan.	Houq-kéh. Jǎpan Nain-gan-ba.

Models for the Exercises

Ex. 1: Looking at the Asia map (over the page)
Prompt: Ask what country n° 30 is.

L/S2: နံပါတ်(၃၀)က ဘာနိုင်ငံလဲ။	Nan-baq thoùn-zeh-gá ba nain-ngan-lèh?
S1: မြန်မာနိုင်ငံပါ။	Myan-ma Nain-ngan-ba.
L/S2: မြန်မာနိုင်ငံ။	Myan-ma Nain-ngan.

Ex. 2

S1: နံပါတ်(၈၀)က ဘာနိုင်ငံလဲ။	Nan-baq shiq-s'eh-gá ba nain-ngan-lèh?
L/S2: တရုပ်နိုင်ငံပါ။	Tǎyouq Nain-ngan-ba.
occasionally extended by:	
S1: ထပ်ပြောပါအုံး။	T'aq-pyàw-ba-oùn.
L/S2: တရုပ်နိုင်ငံ။	Tǎyouq Nain-ngan.

In class: Exercises as above. Also use map of the world, or of your own country with states, counties, Länder, and the like.

Note

Names of countries. The names of most countries in Burmese are taken from the English versions. Their pronunciation follows the principle noted in Lesson 1: either strongly Burmanized, or strongly Anglicized, or somewhere between the two.

Countries whose names differ markedly from the English include some of Burma's neighbours, and France, Sri Lanka and Burma itself. In several cases the official version of the name of the country (used in documents and formal announcements) is not the same as the colloquial version — like the difference between "The United States of America" and "America," or "The Netherlands" and "Holland": both versions are shown below

---

Diphthongs in the roman transcription:
pronounce ei as in *vein*, ai as in *Thailand*, ou as in *though*, au as in *Sauerkraut*.

country	official	transcription	colloquial	transcription
Burma	မြန်မာနိုင်ငံ	Myan-ma Nain-ngan or Myăma Nain-ngan	ဗမာပြည် /–ပျေ/	Băma-pye
Sri Lanka	သီရိလင်္ကာ /–လင်္ဂါ/	Thi-rí-lin-ga	သီဟိုဠ် /သီဟို/	Thi-ho
France	ပြင်သစ်နိုင်ငံ	Pyin-thiq Nain-ngan	ပြင်သစ်ပြည်	Pyin-thiq-pye
Thailand	ထိုင်းနိုင်ငံ	T'aìn Naing-ngan	ယိုးဒယားပြည်	Yò-dăyà-pye
China (PRC)	တရုပ်သမ္မတနိုင်ငံ /သမဒါ./	Tăyouq Thămădá Nain-ngan	တရုပ်ပြည်	Tăyouq-pye
India	အိန္ဒိယနိုင်ငံ	Ein-dí-yá Nain-ngan	ကုလားပြည်	Kălăbye

မြန်မာ **Myan-ma (or Myăma)** and ဗမာ **Băma: "Burmese."** These are two forms of the same word, which is used with two meanings: (a) "pertaining to (the whole country of) Burma (including all ethnic groups: Karen, Shan, Kachin, Burmese, and so on)," as in the following phrases (M/B stands for Myan-ma or Myăma or Băma)—

မြန်မာ (or ဗမာ) သမိုင်း	M/B thămaìn	Burmese history
မြန်မာ (or ဗမာ) စီးပွားရေး	M/B sì-pwà-yè	Burmese economics
မြန်မာ (or ဗမာ) ပြည်	M/B pye	the Burmese country (= Burma)
မြန်မာ (or ဗမာ) နိုင်ငံ	M/B nain-ngan	the Burmese country (= Burma)

and (b) "pertaining to the Burmese ethnic group (as distinct from the other ethnic groups)," as in —

မြန်မာ (or ဗမာ) စကား	M/B săgà	Burmese language
မြန်မာ (or ဗမာ) စာ	M/B-za	Burmese writing/literature/studies
မြန်မာ (or ဗမာ) စကားပုံ	M/B săgăboun	Burmese proverb
မြန်မာ (or ဗမာ) ဂီတ	M/B gi-tá	Burmese music
မြန်မာ (or ဗမာ) လူမျိုး	M/B lu-myò	the Burmese ethnic group

In general the form မြန်မာ Myan-ma is preferred in formal and official contexts, like the titles of boards and departments, newspaper articles, broadcasting, business and government correspondence and so on, while the form ဗမာ Băma is preferred in conversation, written dialogue, and personal letters.

A similar distinction is made with the name for the country: မြန်မာနိုင်ငံ Myan-ma Nain-ngan ("Burma-country") and ဗမာပြည် Băma-pye (also "Burma-country") both mean "Burma." The former is the version preferred in formal discourse, and the latter is used on conversation and chatty writing. However, people do occasionally use မြန်မာနိုင်ငံ Myan-ma Nain-ngan in conversation, and its use seems to be increasing. We have chosen it for your practice here because မြန်မာနိုင်ငံ Myan-ma Naing-ngan makes a better parallel with အိန္ဒိယနိုင်ငံ Ein-dí-yá Nain-ngan and the others.

The English name for the country, "Burma" (like French "Birmanie," German "Burma," Italian "Birmania" and so on) was clearly taken from the more colloquial form of the Burmese name. The earlier English spelling "Burmah" was probably meant to reflect the stress pattern of the Burmese word ဗမာ Băma, and it looks as if later on people who read the word without having heard it properly pronounced gave it its present pronunciation Bùr-mă (with the stress on *Bur-* instead of on *-mah*), and so eventually the "h" came to be dropped from the spelling.

Diphthongs in the roman transcription: pronounce ei as in *vein*, ai as in *Thailand*, ou as in *though*, au as in *Sauerkraut*.

Countries near Burma: map

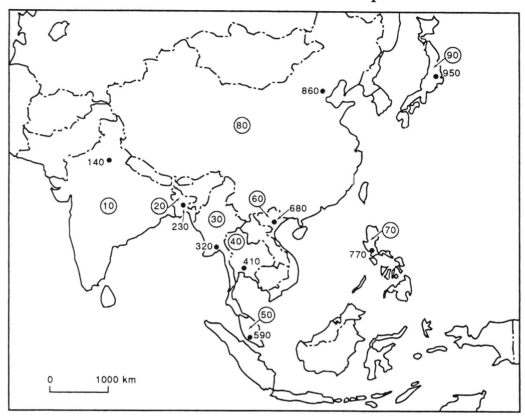

Key to countries

10.	အိန္ဒိယနိုင်ငံ	India	Ein-dì-yá Naing-ngan
20.	ဘင်္ဂလားဒေ့ရှ်နိုင်ငံ	Bangladesh	Bin-găla-désh Naing-ngan
30.	မြန်မာနိုင်ငံ	Burma/Myanmar*	Myan-ma Naing-ngan
40.	ထိုင်းနိုင်ငံ	Thailand	T'aìn Naing-ngan
50.	မလေးရှားနိုင်ငံ	Malaysia	Mălè-shà Naing-ngan
60.	ဗီယက်နမ်နိုင်ငံ	Vietnam	Bi-yeq-nan Naing-ngan
70.	ဖိလစ်ပိုင်နိုင်ငံ	Philippines	P'í-liq-pain Naing-ngan
80.	တရုပ်နိုင်ငံ	China	Tăyouq Naing-ngan
90.	ဂျပန်နိုင်ငံ	Japan	Jăpan Naing-ngan

Key to towns

140.	နယူးဒေလီ	New Delhi	Năyù De-li
230.	ဒက္ကား	Dacca	Deq-kà
320.	ရန်ကုန်	Rangoon/Yangon *	Yan-goun
410.	ဘန်ကောက်	Bangkok	Ban-kauq
590.	ကွာလာလမ်ပူ	Kuala Lumpur	Kwa-la Lan-pu
680.	ဟနွိုင်း	Hanoi	Hănwaìn
770.	မနီလာ	Manila	Măni-la
860.	ပီကင်း	Peking/Beijing	Pi-kìn
950.	တိုကျို	Tokyo	To-co

* For a note on the alternative forms of these names see the text for Lessons 13 and 15.

Diphthongs in the roman transcription:
pronounce ei as in *vein,* ai as in *Thailand,* ou as in *though,* au as in *Sauerkraut.*

51

Myanmar and Burma. In the past some English speakers have tried to disambiguate meanings (a) and (b) above by using "Burmese" for "pertaining to all Burma" and "Burman" for "pertaining to the Burmese ethnic group alone," but this convention has not been universally adopted. In June 1989 the State Law and Order Restoration Council launched a new solution. It announced that the formal version မြန်မာ Myan-ma (or Myăma) was to be used for the whole country, including all the races, and the informal name ဗမာ Băma was to be restricted to the Burmese ethnic group (as distinct from the other races). This innovation was to be reflected in English and other foreign languages also: the nation including all races was to be called "Myanmar," and the Burmese race was to become "Bamar." The names "Burma," "Burmese," and "Burman" were to be abandoned. The following is an extract from a press release.

> May 26: At the 40th State LORC Press Conference, the Information Committee spokesman said:
> -- "Measures are being taken for the correct use of Burmese expressions. For example, our country is officially called 'Pyi-daung-su Myanma Naing-Ngan' and is expressed in English as 'Union of Burma'. 'Burma' sounds like mentioning 'Bama'. In fact, it does not mean the Bama (Burmese nationals), one of the national racial groups of the Union only. It means 'Myanma', all the national racial groups who are resident in the Union such as Kachin, Kayah, Karen, Chin, Mon, Rakhine Bama, and Shan nationals. Therefore, to use 'Burma' is incorrect and 'Myanma' should be used instead. Accordingly, 'Union of Myanma' will be used in the future.

The change of name to Myanmar has not been adopted unanimously. At the time of writing (March 1994) Burmese government pronouncements and publications in English use "Myanmar" assiduously, while foreigners and expatriate Burmese fall into three groups: (1) opponents of the government continue to say "Burma" and "Burmese," flaunting them as a symbol of their defiance; (2) supporters of the government, and representatives of agencies with formal relationships with the Burmese government (such as the UN), have politely converted to "Myanmar"; and (3) others (like myself) continue to use "Burma" and "Burmese" on the grounds that this form is more familiar to most of their readers.

မြန်မာ Myan-ma and ဗမာ Băma are adjectives in Burmese, and you usually find them used to qualify something else, as in the examples listed above. This is why calling the country plain "Myanmar" sounds incomplete, and you will often find English language sources in Burma using "Myanmar Naing-ngan" (= "Burma state/country") instead.

Common phrases

To make sure you complete the Common Phrases Supplement by the end of Part 1, learn Section 2 at about this point.

Diphthongs in the roman transcription:
pronounce ei as in *vein*, ai as in *Thailand*, ou as in *though*, au as in *Sauerkraut*.

The official announcement of the change from "Burma" to "Myanmar"
published in the *Working People's Daily* of 19 June 1989

၁၃၅၁ ခုနှစ် နယုန်လဆုတ် ၁ ရက်၊ ၁၉၈၉ ခုနှစ် ဇွန်လ ၁၉ ရက်၊ တနင်္လာနေ့ (အတွဲ ၂၆၊ အမှတ် ၂၆၂)

စကားရပ်များ ပြောင်းလဲသတ်မှတ်သည့်ဥပဒေပြဋ္ဌာန်း

Union of Burma အစား Union of Myanmar ဟုပြောင်း

နိုင်ငံတော်ငြိမ်ဝပ်ပိပြားမှုတည်ဆောက်ရေးအဖွဲ့
စကားရပ်များ ပြောင်းလဲသတ်မှတ်သည့်ဥပဒေ

(နိုင်ငံတော်ငြိမ်ဝပ်ပိပြားမှုတည်ဆောက်ရေးအဖွဲ့ ဥပဒေအမှတ်၁၅/၈၉)

၁၃၅၁ ခုနှစ်၊ နယုန်လဆန်း ၁၅ရက်

(၁၉၈၉ ခုနှစ်၊ ဇွန်လ ၁၇ ရက်)

နိုင်ငံတော် ငြိမ်ဝပ်ပိပြားမှု တည်ဆောက်ရေး အဖွဲ့သည် အောက်ပါ ဥပဒေကို ပြဋ္ဌာန်း လိုက်သည်။

၁။ ဤဥပဒေကို စကားရပ်များပြောင်းလဲ သတ်မှတ်သည့် ဥပဒေဟု ခေါ်တွင်စေရမည်။

၂။ အင်္ဂလိပ်ဘာသာဖြင့် ပြဋ္ဌာန်းခဲ့သည့် တည်ဆဲဥပဒေများပါ"Union of Burma"ဆိုသည့် စကားရပ်အစား "Union of Myanmar" ဆိုသည့် စကားရပ်ကို လည်းကောင်း၊ "Burma" သို့မဟုတ် "Burman" သို့မဟုတ် "Burmese"ဆိုသည့် စကားရပ်အစား "Myanmar" ဆိုသည့် စကားရပ်ကိုလည်းကောင်း ထည့်သွင်းရမည်။

၃။ (က) အင်္ဂလိပ်ဘာသာဖြင့် လက်ရှိရေးသားသုံးစွဲလျက်ရှိသည့် ပြည်နယ်၊ တိုင်း၊ မြို့နယ်စု၊ မြို့နယ်၊ မြို့၊ ရပ်ကွက်၊ ကျေးရွာအုပ်စု၊ သို့မဟုတ် ကျေးရွာတစ်ခုခု၏အမည် အခေါ် အဝေါ်ကိုလည်းကောင်း၊ မြစ်၊ ချောင်း၊ တော၊ တောင်၊ သို့မဟုတ် ကျွန်းတစ်ခုခု၏ အမည်အခေါ်အဝေါ်ကို လည်းကောင်း မြန်မာအသံထွက်နှင့်ကိုက်ညီအောင် အင်္ဂလိပ် ဘာသာဖြင့် ပြင်ဆင်ရေးသားရန် လိုအပ်လျှင် အစိုးရအဖွဲ့က အမိန့်ကြော်ငြာစာ ထုတ်ပြန်၍ ပြင်ဆင် သတ်မှတ်နိုင်သည်။

(ခ) ပုဒ်မခွဲ(က)အရ အစိုးရအဖွဲ့က ထုတ်ပြန်သော အမိန့်ကြော်ငြာစာတွင် ပါရှိသည့် အမည်တစ်ခုခုသည် အင်္ဂလိပ်ဘာသာဖြင့် ပြဋ္ဌာန်းခဲ့သည့် တည်ဆဲဥပဒေတစ်ရပ်ရပ်တွင် ပါရှိနေလျှင် ယင်းအမည်ကို အဆိုပါ အမိန့်ကြော်ငြာစာတွင် အင်္ဂလိပ်ဘာသာဖြင့် ပြင်ဆင် ရေးသား ထားသည့်အတိုင်း ပြင်ဆင်ပြီးဖြစ်သည်ဟု မှတ်ယူရမည်။

ပုံ
စောမောင်
ဗိုလ်ချုပ်ကြီး
ဥက္ကဋ္ဌ
နိုင်ငံတော်ငြိမ်ဝပ်ပိပြားမှုတည်ဆောက်ရေးအဖွဲ့

Diphthongs in the roman transcription:
pronounce ei as in *vein,* ai as in *Thailand,* ou as in *though,* au as in *Sauerkraut.*

LESSON 14

Numbers in hundreds and tens.
Joining numbers with "and" or creaky tone.

New numbers

လေးရာနဲ့ ငါးဆယ်	450 ("400-and 50")	lè-ya-néh ngà-zeh
လေးရာ့ ငါးဆယ်	450 ("400-creak 50")	lè-yá ngà-zeh
လေးရာ ငါးဆယ်	450 ("400 50")	lè-ya ngà-zeh

Burmese has three ways of joining hundreds and tens. For example, when combining 400 and 50 to make 450:

1. the 400 and the 50 may be linked by –နဲ့ -néh "and/with" as in the first line above; or
2. the –နဲ့ -néh "and/ with" drops out, leaving only a creaky tone (–ရာ့ -yá in place of –ရာ -ya) to mark its place, as in the second line; or
3. the two numbers are just spoken in sequence, as in the third line.

Probably the second method is the one you'll hear most frequently, so we shall be using that most of the time; but you need to be aware of the other two methods, as you will hear them from time to time.

Models for the Exercises

Ex. 1: Change "and" to creaky
S1: တစ်ရာနဲ့ ကိုးဆယ်   Tăya-néh kò-zeh.
L/S2: တစ်ရာ့ ကိုးဆယ် [and writes 190]   Tăyá kò-zeh.
Check with Key at end of Lesson.

Ex. 2: Add ten
S1: တစ်ရာ့ လေးဆယ်   Tăyá lè-zeh.
L/S2: တစ်ရာ့ ငါးဆယ်   Tăyá ngà-zeh.

Ex. 3: Prompt: What's the number under A in the chart?
L/S2: လေးရာ လေးဆယ်။   Lè-ya lè-zeh.

Chart for Ex. 3

A	B	C	D	E	F	G	H	I	J
၄၄၀	၇၃၀	၆၇၀	၆၅၀	၃၆၀	၁၂၀	၂၈၀	၅၃၀	၈၆၀	၁၇၀

In class: Exercises as above. Also with page numbers and additions as in previous Lessons.

Keys to the Exercises

Key to Ex. 1

190	230	370	450	520	680	740	810	960
၁၉၀	၂၃၀	၃၇၀	၄၅၀	၅၂၀	၆၈၀	၇၄၀	၈၁၀	၉၆၀

Diphthongs in the roman transcription:
pronounce ei as in *vein*, ai as in *Thailand*, ou as in *though*, au as in *Sauerkraut*.

LESSON 15

Names of some towns in countries near Burma.
What town is nº 140? — New Delhi.

Names of towns

140.	နယူးဒေလီ	New Delhi	Năyù De-li
230.	ဒက္ကား /ဒက်ကား/	Dacca	Deq-kà
320.	ရန်ကုန်	Rangoon/Yangon *	Yan-goun
410.	ဘန်ကောက်	Bangkok	Ban-kauq
590.	ကွာလာလမ်ပူ	Kuala Lumpur	Kwa-la Lan-pu
680.	ဟနွိုင်း	Hanoi	Hănwaìn
770.	မနီလာ	Manila	Măni-la
860.	ပီကင်း	Peking/Beijing	Pi-kìn
950.	တိုကျို	Tokyo	To-co

* On the alternative forms of this name, see the Note below

New words

မြို့	town	myó

Example sentences

S1: နံပါတ်(၁၄၀)က ဘာမြို့လဲ။	What town is nº 140?	Nan-baq tăyá lè-zeh-gá ba myó-lèh?
S2: နယူးဒေလီပါ။	New Delhi.	Năyù De-li-ba.
S1: နံပါတ်(၉၅၀)က တိုကျိုလား။	Is nº 950 Tokyo?	Nan-baq kò-yá ngà-zeh-gá To-co-là?
S2: ဟုတ်ကဲ့။ တိုကျိုပါ။	Yes. [It is] Tokyo.	Houq-kéh. To-co-ba.

Models for the Exercises

Ex. 1: Looking at the Asia map
Prompt: Ask what town nº 410 is.

L/S2: နံပါတ်(၄၁၀)က ဘာမြို့လဲ။	Nan-baq lè-ya tăs'eh-gá ba myó-lèh?
sometimes extended by:	
S1: ၄၅၀–လား။	Lè-ya ngà-zeh-là?
L/S2: မဟုတ်ပါဘူး။ ၄၁၀–ပါ။	Măhouq-pa-bù. Lè-ya tăs'eh-ba.
S1: ဘန်ကောက်မြို့ပါ။	Ban-gauq-myó-ba.
L/S2: ထပ်ပြောပါအုံး။	T'aq-pyàw-ba-oùn.
S1: ဘန်ကောက်မြို့။	Ban-gauq-myó.
L/S2: အော်။ ဘန်ကောက်မြို့။	Aw. Ban-gauq-myó.

Ex. 2

S1: နံပါတ်(၇၇၀)က ဘာမြို့လဲ။	Nan-baq 770-gá ba myó-lèh?
L/S2: မနီလာမြို့ပါ။	Măni-la-myó-ba.
sometimes extended by:	
S1: ထပ်ပြောပါအုံး။	T'aq-pyàw-ba-oùn.

Diphthongs in the roman transcription:
pronounce ei as in *vein*, ai as in *Thailand*, ou as in *though*, au as in *Sauerkraut*.

L/S2: မနီလာမြို့ပါ။   Măni-la-myó-ba.

or by:

S1: မနီလာမြို့လား။   Măni-la-myó-là.

L/S2: ဟုတ်ကဲ့။ မနီလာမြို့ပါ။   Houq-kéh. Măni-la-myó-ba.

or: မဟုတ်ပါဘူး။ … as the case may be. Măhouq-pa-bù.

In class: Exercises as above. Also practise with map of world, your own country and so on.

Note

ရန်ကုန် **Yan-goun** **Rangoon/Yangon.** Western travellers first heard the names of some towns, rivers and mountains in Burma from non-standard speakers of Burmese (Mons, Arakanese, Indians, and others); so in some cases the forms that became established in English and other Western languages diverged to some degree from the standard Burmese pronunciation. "Rangoon" is one of these names. It became established in English as "Rangoon," though the Burmese ရန်ကုန် **Yan-goun** suggests a traditional romanization (see Appendix 3) more like "Yangon."

In 1989 the SLORC ruled that "Rangoon" should be replaced by "Yangon." A number of other geographical names in the same category were altered at the same time. See the note in Lesson 19. Western usage subsequent to this announcement has varied along the same lines as those described for "Burma" and "Myanmar." See the note in Lesson 13.

> Furthermore, measures are being taken for using words such as 'Yangon', 'Pyi', 'Sittwe', 'Mawlamyaing' and 'Pathein' in place of 'Rangoon', 'Prome', 'Akyab', 'Moulmein' and 'Bassein' respectively. These have been told to you, journalists in advance to have first hand knowledge."

From a press release announcing revised roman spellings for Yangon and other town names in Burma

မနီလာ **Măni-la** **Manila** vs. မနီလာမြို့. **Măni-la-myó** "Manila town" = **Manila.** When they refer to towns Burmese speakers may use the name alone, or the name followed by မြို့. **myó** "town." In the Exercises we use both forms.

တိုကျို **To-co** **Tokyo.** The Burmese sound system doesn't really include the sequence K+Y (k+y). Although Burmese speakers who are in the know can say it, most foreign words with this sequence get pronounced with a /ကျ/ **c-.** This correspondence is also reflected in Burmese script, where K+Y (က+ယ = ကျ) is the regular way of representing the sound /ကျ/ **c-.** Thus it is that you find words like —

Diphthongs in the roman transcription:
pronounce **ei** as in *vein,* **ai** as in *Thailand,* **ou** as in *though,* **au** as in *Sauerkraut.*

	script	standard pron.	informed pron.	English spelling
	တိုကျို	To-co	To-kyo	Tokyo
	ကျူဘာ	Cu-ba	Kyu-ba	Cuba
	ကျူ	cu	kyu	queue

T+Y (t+y) is also a sequence alien to the Burmese repertoire, so words pronounced in (British) English with T+Y are given the same treatment:

	script			
	ကျွတ်	cuq	tyub	tube
	ကျူရှင်	cu-shin	tyu-shin	tuition

Common phrases

To make sure you complete the Common Phrases Supplement by the end of Part 1, learn Section 3 at about this point.

LESSON 16

Numbers in tens and units.
No တစ် (tă) in 11-19.

New numbers

သုံးဆယ်နဲ့ ရှစ်	38 ("30-and 8")	thoùn-zeh-néh shiq
သုံးဆယ့် ရှစ်	38 ("30-creak 8")	thoùn-zéh shiq

Models for the Exercises

Ex. 1: change "and" to creaky
S1: သုံးဆယ်နဲ့ ရှစ်   Thoùn-zeh-néh shiq.
L/S2: သုံးဆယ့် ရှစ် [and writes 38]   Thoùn-zéh shiq.
Check with Key at end of Lesson

Ex. 2: add one
S1: ငါးဆယ့် လေး   Ngà-zéh lè.
L/S2: ငါးဆယ့် ငါး   Ngà-zéh ngà.

Ex. 3: Prompt: What's the number under A in the chart?
L/S2: ငါးဆယ့် လေး   Ngà-zéh lè.

Chart for Ex. 3

A	B	C	D	E	F	G	H	I
၁၄	၂၇	၆၂	၉၆	၈၁	၆၆	၇၂	၂၈	၁၅

In class: Exercises as above. Also practise with page numbers and additions as in previous Lessons.

Diphthongs in the roman transcription:
pronounce ei as in *vein*, ai as in *Thailand*, ou as in *though*, au as in *Sauerkraut*.

57

Notes

Joining with "and." In Lesson 14, on numbers from 110 to 990, you met hundreds and tens joined together either by –နဲ့ -néh "and" or by a creaky tone:

လေးရာနဲ့ ငါးဆယ်	450 ("400-and 50")	lè-ya-néh ngà-zeh
လေးရာ့ ငါးဆယ်	450 ("400-creak 50")	lè-yá ngà-zeh

Numbers containing tens and units (the range from 11 to 99) are made up in exactly the same way: see the examples above. In the earlier Lesson we chose the creaky-tone form as the standard, and we shall do the same for the 11 to 99 range: so in the Exercises we shall be using သုံးဆယ့် ရှစ် thoùn-zéh shiq for 38 unless there is some reason for using the "and" form.

In this range of numbers weakening and voicing work as before, but there are a couple of differences between these numbers and the hundreds and tens.

Weakening and voicing. In the hundreds and tens numbers there was a third option: to use neither "and" nor creaky tone:

လေးရာ ငါးဆယ်	450 ("400 50")	lè-ya ngà-zeh

That option is not used in the tens and units range.

Dropping တစ် tă "one." Second, within this range, for the numbers 11 to 19, you would expect to find

တစ်ဆယ့် တစ်	11 (" one 10-creak 1")	tă s'éh tiq
တစ်ဆယ့် နှစ်	12 (" one 10-creak 2")	tă s'éh hniq
တစ်ဆယ့် သုံး	13 (" one 10-creak 3")	tă s'éh thòun

and so on. People do sometimes say these numbers in this form, but far more often they drop the တစ် tiq and just say:

ဆယ့် တစ်	11 ("10-creak 1")	s'éh tiq
ဆယ့် နှစ်	12 ("10-creak 2")	s'éh hniq
ဆယ့် သုံး and so on.	13 ("10-creak 3")	s'éh thòun and so on.

Keys to the Exercises

Key to Ex. 1:

၃၈	၉၆	၂၅	၄၃	၇၂	၆၉	၅၁	၈၇	–	၁၄	၁၆	၁၉	၁၇	၁၂
38	96	25	43	72	69	51	87	—	14	16	19	17	12

Diphthongs in the roman transcription:
pronounce ei as in *vein*, ai as in *Thailand*, ou as in *though*, au as in *Sauerkraut*.

LESSON 17

Informal names for countries.
Which country is Manila in? — In the Philippines.

Towns and countries

မြို့	နိုင်ငံ	town	country
နယူးဒေလီ	အိန္ဒိယနိုင်ငံ	New Delhi	India
ဒက္ကား	ဘင်္ဂလားဒေ့ရှ်နိုင်ငံ	Dacca	Bangladesh
ရန်ကုန်	မြန်မာနိုင်ငံ	Rangoon/Yangon	Burma/Myanmar
ဘန်ကောက်	ထိုင်းနိုင်ငံ	Bangkok	Thailand
ကွာလာလမ်ပူ	မလေးရှားနိုင်ငံ	Kuala Lumpur	Malaysia
ဟနွိုင်း	ဗီယက်နမ်နိုင်ငံ	Hanoi	Vietnam
မနီလာ	ဖိလစ်ပိုင်နိုင်ငံ	Manila	Philippines
ပီကင်း	တရုပ်နိုင်ငံ	Peking/Beijing	China
တိုကျို	ဂျပန်နိုင်ငံ	Tokyo	Japan

myó	*naing-ngan*	*town*	*country*
Năyù De-li	Ein-dí-yá Naing-ngan	New Delhi	India
Deq-kà	Bin-gălà-désh Naing-ngan	Dacca	Bangladesh
Yan-goun	Myan-ma Naing-ngan	Rangoon/Yangon	Burma/Myanmar
Ban-kauq	T'aìn Naing-ngan	Bangkok	Thailand
Kwa-la Lan-pu	Mălè-shà Naing-ngan	Kuala Lumpur	Malaysia
Hănwaìn	Bi-yeq-nan Naing-ngan	Hanoi	Vietnam
Măni-la	P'í-liq-pain Naing-ngan	Manila	Philippines
Pi-kìn	Tăyouq Naing-ngan	Peking/Beijing	China
To-co	Jăpan Naing-ngan	Tokyo	Japan

Alternative names for countries

In informal conversations people often leave off the နိုင်ငံ naing-ngan "country" from the name of a country; so —

in place of:		they say:	
အိန္ဒိယနိုင်ငံ	Ein-dí-yá Naing-ngan	အိန္ဒိယ	Ein-dì-yá
မလေးရှားနိုင်ငံ	Mălè-shà Naing-ngan	မလေးရှား	Mălè-shà
ဂျပန်နိုင်ငံ	Jăpan Naing-ngan	ဂျပန်	Jăpan

and so on.

Sometimes people use ပြည် pye "country" in place of နိုင်ငံ naing-ngan "country"; so —

in place of:		you may hear:	
အိန္ဒိယနိုင်ငံ	Ein-dí-yá Naing-ngan	အိန္ဒိယပြည်	Ein-dí-yá-pye
မလေးရှားနိုင်ငံ	Mălè-shà Naing-ngan	မလေးရှားပြည်	Mălè-shà-pye
ဂျပန်နိုင်ငံ	Jăpan Naing-ngan	ဂျပန်ပြည်	Jăpan-pye

There are some exceptions to these options.

• China never loses the country word; so it is always

Diraphthongs in the roman transcription:
pronounce ei as in *vein*, ai as in *Thailand*, ou as in *though*, au as in *Sauerkraut*.

တရုပ်နိုင်ငံ Tăyouq Naing-ngan or တရုပ်ပြည် Tăyouq-pye

• Thailand has a different name altogether:

in place of: ထိုင်းနိုင်ငံ T'àin Naing-ngan
people say: ယိုးဒယားပြည် Yò-dăyà-pye
or: ယိုးဒယား Yò-dăyà

• and Burma both has a different name and always keeps the country word (this is why the SLORC's new name "Myanmar" sounds incomplete):

in place of: မြန်မာနိုင်ငံ Myan-ma Naing-ngan
people say: ဗမာပြည် Băma-pye

Example sentences

S1: မနီလာက ဘယ်နိုင်ငံမှာလဲ။	Which country is Manila in?	Măni-la-gá beh nain-gan-hma-lèh?
S2: ဖိလစ်ပိုင်မှာပါ။	In the Philippines.	P'í-liq-pain-hma-ba.
S1: မနီလာက ဖိလစ်ပိုင်မှာလား။	Is Manila in the Philippines?	Măni-la-gá P'í-liq-pain-hma-là?
S2: ဟုတ်ကဲ့။ ဖိလစ်ပိုင်မှာပါ။	Yes. It's in the Philippines.	Houq-kéh. P'í-liq-pain-hma-ba.

Models for the Exercises

Ex. 1: Looking at the list of towns and countries

Prompt: Ask which country Manila is in.

L/S2: မနီလာ ဘယ်နိုင်ငံမှာလဲ။ — Măni-la beh nain-ngan-hma-lèh?
S1: ဖိလစ်ပိုင်မှာပါ။ — P'í-liq-pain-hma-ba.
L/S2: အော်။ ဖိလစ်ပိုင်မှာ။ — Aw. P'í-liq-pain-hma.

Ex. 2

S1: မနီလာက ဖိလစ်ပိုင်မှာလား။ — Măni-la-gá P'í-liq-pain-hma-là?
L/S2: ဟုတ်ကဲ့။ ဖိလစ်ပိုင်မှာပါ။ — Houq-kéh. P'í-liq-pain-hma-ba.
— or: မဟုတ်ပါဘူး။ ... as the case may be — Măhouq-pa-bù.
and sometimes S1 asks a checking question.

Ex. 3 For written answer: not on the tape.

The words in the following questions and answers have been split up and jumbled. Rearrange them to form meaningful sentences. There is a Key to this Exercise at the end of the Lesson. Don't forget that you may find it helpful to copy the words onto separate slips of paper and do your reordering by sliding the slips around.

S1: – ဘယ်နိုင်ငံ – မနီလာမြို့ – လဲ – မှာ
S2: – ဖိလစ်ပိုင်နိုင်ငံ – ပါ – မှာ
S1: – မြို့ – မှာ – ဘန်ကောက် – ဘယ် – လဲ – နိုင်ငံ – က
S2: – မှာ – နိုင်ငံ – ထိုင်း – ပါ
S1: – ဒက္ကားမြို့ – မှာ – လား – အိန္ဒိယနိုင်ငံ – က
S2: – ပါ – မှာ – ဘင်္ဂလားဒေ့ရှ် – မဟုတ်ပါဘူး – နိုင်ငံ

Diphthongs in the roman transcription:
pronounce ei as in *vein,* ai as in *Thailand,* ou as in *though,* au as in *Sauerkraut.*

Ex. 3. For written answer: not on the tape.
> S1: — beh-nain-ngan — Mǎni-la myó — lèh — hma
>> S2: — P'í-liq-pain Nain-ngan — ba — hma
>
> S1: — myó — hma — Ban-kauq — beh — lèh — nain-ngan — ká
>> S2: — hma — nain-ngan — T'aìn — ba
>
> S1: — Deq-kà myó — hma — là — Ein-dí-yá nain-ngan — gá
>> S2: — ba — hma — Bin-gǎlà-désh — Mǎhouq-pa-bù. — nain-ngan

In class: Exercises as above. Also practise with map of world, your own country or other area.

Notes

သယ် [noun] (**beh** [noun]) vs. ဘာ [noun] (**ba** [noun]) again.

Notice that you use ဘာ [noun] (ba [noun]) when you are looking at a map or a street plan and asking questions like —

ဒါ ဘာနိုင်ငံလဲ။	What country is that?	Da ba-nain-ngan-lèh?
ဒါ ဘာမြို့လဲ။	What town is that?	Da ba-myó-lèh?
ဒါ ဘာလမ်းလဲ။	What road is that?	Da ba-làn-lèh?

But you use သယ် [noun] (beh [noun]) in questions like these:

ဘယ်နိုင်ငံမှာလဲ။	Which country is it in?	Beh-nain-ngan-hma-lèh?
ဘယ်မြို့မှာလဲ။	Which town is it in?	Beh-myó-hma-lèh?
ဘယ်လမ်းမှာလဲ။	Which road is it in?	Beh-làn-hma-lèh?

Keys to the Exercises

Key to Ex. 3. For written answer: not on the tape.
> S1:— မနီလာမြို့ — ဘယ်နိုင်ငံ — မှာ — လဲ။
>> S2:— ဖိလစ်ပိုင်နိုင်ငံ — မှာ — ပါ။
>
> S1:— ဘန်ကောက် — မြို့ — က — ဘယ် — နိုင်ငံ — မှာ — လဲ။
>> S2:— ထိုင်း — နိုင်ငံ — မှာ — ပါ။
>
> S1:— ဒက္ကားမြို့ — က — အိန္ဒိယနိုင်ငံ — မှာ— လား။
>> S2:— မဟုတ်ပါဘူး။ — ဘင်္ဂလားဒေ့ရှ် — နိုင်ငံ — မှာ — ပါ။

Key to Ex. 3. For written answer: not on the tape.
> S1: — Mǎni-la — myó — beh-nain-ngan — hma — lèh
>> S2: — P'í-liq-pain Nain-ngan — hma — ba
>
> S1: — Ban-kauq — myó — ká — beh — nain-ngan — hma — lèh
>> S2: — T'aìn — Nain-ngan — hma — ba
>
> S1: — Deq-kà-myó — gá — Ein-dí-yá nain-ngan — hma — là
>> S2: — Mǎhouq-pa-bù. — Bin-gǎlà-désh — nain-ngan — hma — ba

Common phrases

To make sure you complete the Common Phrases Supplement by the end of Part 1, learn Section 4 at about this point.

Diphthongs in the roman transcription:
pronounce ei as in *vein*, ai as in *Thailand*, ou as in *though*, au as in *Sauerkraut*.

LESSON 18

Numbers 1-9,999.
Omitting တစ် (tă) in 1000-1999.

New numbers

Three-figure numbers

ခြောက်ရာ သုံးဆယ့် ငါး	635	c'auq-yá thoùn-zéh ngà
လေးရာ ရှစ်ဆယ့် တစ်	481	lè-yá shiq-s'éh tiq
ခုနှစ်ရာ ကိုး	709	k'un-năyá kò
often: ခုနှစ်ရာနဲ့ ကိုး	709	k'un-năya-néh kò

In numbers with hundreds and tens and units, like the examples above, most people use the "creaky tone" method of connecting the three elements of the number. You may find a –နဲ့ -néh "and" between the elements here and there, particularly when the tens elements is 0 (as in 709 above), but we are going to use the creaky-tone form as standard.

In numbers in this range, all the rules you have learned for the other numbers continue to apply: weakening (for 1, 2, and 7 before –ရာ -ya and –ဆယ် -s'eh), voicing (for –ဆယ် -s'eh) and the dropping of တစ်– tă- (in the range 11 to 19).

Four-figure numbers

ရှစ်ထောင့် ခြောက်ရာ သုံးဆယ့် ငါး	8635	shiq-t'aún c'auq-yá thoùn-zéh ngà
နှစ်ထောင့် ကိုးရာ ခုနှစ်ဆယ့် သုံး	2973	hnăt'aún kò-yá k'un-năs'éh thoùn
သုံးထောင့် လေးရာ နှစ်ဆယ့် တစ်	3421	thoùn-daún lè-yá hnăs'éh tiq

Here too creaky tone is used for joining the elements, and weakening (as in 2973 in the example above), and voicing (as in 3421), apply as usual. However, there is one small irregularity: in numbers where there is just one thousand (rather than two or more), where you would expect (for example):

တစ်ထောင့် နှစ်ရာ ရှစ်ဆယ့် ခုနှစ်	1287	tăt'aún hnăyá shiq-s'éh k'un-hniq

people often drop the တစ် in တစ်ထောင့် and just say

ထောင့် နှစ်ရာ ရှစ်ဆယ့် ခုနှစ်	1287	t'aún hnăyá shiq-s'éh k'un-niq

You met a similar phenomenon in the numbers 11 to 19: instead of

တစ်ဆယ့် ခုနှစ်	17	tăs'éh k'un-hniq

people say just

ဆယ့် ခုနှစ်	17	s'éh k'un-hniq

Models for the Exercises

Ex. 1: Add one
S1: ခြောက်ရာ သုံးဆယ့် ငါး။ C'auq-yá thoùn-zéh ngà.
L/S2: ခြောက်ရာ သုံးဆယ့် ခြောက်။ C'auq-yá thoùn-zéh c'auq.
And writes down 636 or 636. Check with Key at end of Lesson.

Ex. 2: Add ten
S1: လေးရာ ခုနှစ်ဆယ့် နှစ်။ Lè-yá k'un-năs'éh hniq.
L/S2: လေးရာ ရှစ်ဆယ့် နှစ်။ Lè-yá shiq-s'éh hniq.

Diphthongs in the roman transcription:
pronounce ei as in *vein*, ai as in *Thailand*, ou as in *though*, au as in *Sauerkraut*.

And writes down ၄၈၂ or 482. Check with Key at end of Lesson.

Ex. 3: Add a hundred
    S1: သုံးရာ နှစ်ဆယ့် တစ်။   Thoùn-yá hnăs'éh tiq.
    L/S2: လေးရာ နှစ်ဆယ့် တစ်။   Lè-yá hnăs'éh tiq.
    And writes down ၄၂၁ or 421. Check with Key at end of Lesson.

Ex. 4: Prompt: What's the number under A in the chart?
    L/S2: သုံးရာ လေးဆယ့် တစ်။   Thoùn-yá lè-zéh tiq.

Chart for Ex. 4

A	B	C	D	E	F	G	H	I
၃၄၁	၆၁၆	၁၅၄	၈၇၉	၂၆၈	၉၂၃	၄၈၃	၇၃၇	၁၈၂

Ex. 5: Prompt: What's the number under A in the chart?
    L/S2: ကိုးထောင့် လေးရာ ခြောက်ဆယ့် ရှစ်။   Kò-daún lè-yá c'auq-s'éh shiq.

Chart for Ex. 5

A	B	C	D	E
၉၄၆၈	၃၁၇၈	၁၈၈၈	၁၈၉၀	၂၅၀၀

In class: Exercises as above. Also practise with page numbers, additions, and room numbers in internal directory, or students' hostel numbers (if they are three-figure numbers):
    L1: Professor Branestawm အခန်းနံပါတ် ဘယ်လောက်လဲ။
    L2 looks in directory and answers: အခန်းနံပါတ် ၂၅၉-ပါ။
    Ls write down the numbers. After asking five or six numbers, check them:
    L3: Professor Branestawm အခန်းနံပါတ်က ၂၅၇-လား။
    L4: မဟုတ်ပါဘူး။ နံပါတ်က ၂၅၇-ပါ။ or Yes, as the case may be.

Keys to the Exercises

Key to Ex. 1 in Lesson 18

၆၃၆	၁၉၇	၃၂၂	၈၄၉	၂၃၈	၅၈၃
636	197	322	849	238	583

Key to Ex. 2 in Lesson 18

၄၈၂	၁၉၅	၉၂၈	၆၇၄	၅၄၁
482	195	928	674	541

Key to Ex. 3 in Lesson 18

၄၂၁	၆၉၉	၇၃၈	၂၇၅
421	699	738	275

Diphthongs in the roman transcription:
pronounce ei as in vein, ai as in Thailand, ou as in though, au as in Sauerkraut.

Towns in Burma: Map

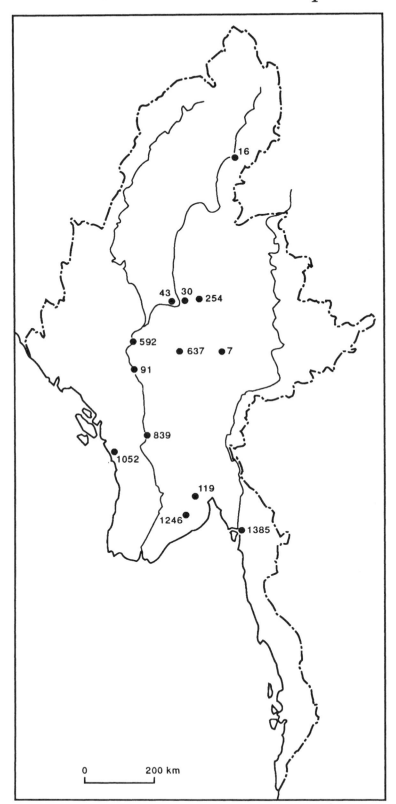

Diphthongs in the roman transcription:
pronounce ei as in *vein,* ai as in *Thailand,* ou as in *though,* au as in *Sauerkraut.*

LESSON 19

Names of towns in Burma: see map opposite

n°	script (with pron in script)	traditional romanization		revised traditional*	pronunciation (in roman)
၁၆	မြစ်ကြီးနား	Myitkyina	16	-	Myiq-cì-nà
၂၅၄	မေမြို့	Maymyo	254	-	Me-myó
၃၀	မန္တလေး /မန်းဒလေး/	Mandalay	30	-	Màn-dălè
၄၃	စစ်ကိုင်း /ဇဂိုင်း/	Sagaing	43	-	Săgaìn
၅၉၂	ပုဂံ /ဗဂန်/	Pagan	592	Bagan	Păgan
၆၃၇	သာစည် /သာဇီ/	Thazi	637	-	Tha-zi
၇	တောင်ကြီး /တောင်ဂျီး/	Taunggyi	7	-	Taun-jì
၈၃၉	ပြည် /ပျို့/ or /ပျေ/	Prome	839	Pyi /Pyay	Pye
၉၁	ရေနံချောင်း /ယေနန်ချောင်း/	Yenangyaung	91	-	Ye-nan-jaùn
၁၀၅၂	သံတွဲ /သန်ဒွဲ/	Sandoway	1052	Thandwe	Than-dwèh
၁၁၉	ပဲခူး /ဗဂိုး/	Pegu	119	Bago	Păgò
၁၂၄၆	ရန်ကုန် /ယန်ဂုန်/	Rangoon	1246	Yangon	Yan-goun
၁၃၈၅	မော်လမြိုင် /မော်လမျိုင်/	Moulmein	1385	Mawlamyine	Maw-lămyain

*See note in Lesson 19.

Example sentences

S1: နံပါတ်(၁၆)က ဘာမြို့လဲ။	What town is n° 16?	Nan-baq s'éh-c'auq-ká ba-myó-lèh?
S2: မြစ်ကြီးနားပါ။	Myitkyina.	Myiq-cì-nà-ba.
S1: နံပါတ်(၂၅၄)က မေမြို့လား။	Is n° 254 Maymyo?	Nan-baq hnăyá ngà-zéh lè-gá Me-myó-là?
S2: ဟုတ်ကဲ့။ မေမြို့ပါ။	Yes. [It is] Maymyo.	Houq-kéh. Me-myó-ba.

Models for the Exercises

Ex. 1: Looking at the Burma map
   Prompt: Ask what town n° 16 is.
   L/S2: နံပါတ်(၁၆)က ဘာမြို့လဲ။   Nan-baq-16-ká ba myó-lèh?
       occasionally extended by:
       S1: နံပါတ်(၁၆)လား။   Nan-baq-16-là?
       L: ဟုတ်ကဲ့။ နံပါတ်(၁၆)ပါ။   Houq-kéh. Nan-baq-16-pa.
       or — L: မဟုတ်ပါဘူး။ … as the case may be   Măhouq-pa-bù.
   S1: အော်။ နံပါတ်(၁၆)က မြစ်ကြီးနားပါ။   Aw. Nan-baq-16-ká Myiq-cì-nà-ba.
   L: အော်။ မြစ်ကြီးနား။   Aw. Myiq-cì-nà.

Diphthongs in the roman transcription:
pronounce ei as in *vein,* ai as in *Thailand,* ou as in *though,* au as in *Sauerkraut.*

Ex. 2

S1: နံပါတ်(၃၀)က ဘာမြို့လဲ။	Nan-baq-30-gá ba myó-lèh?
L/S2: မန္တလေးပါ။	Màn-dǎlè-ba.

occasionally extended by:

S1: ပြန်ပြောပါအုံး။	Pyan-pyàw-ba-oùn.
L/S2: မန္တလေး။	Màn-dǎlè.

or by:

S1: မန္တလေးလား။	Màn-dǎlè-là?
L/S2: ဟုတ်ကဲ့။ မန္တလေး။	Houq-kéh. Màn-dǎlè.
or — L: မဟုတ်ပါဘူး။ ...	Mǎhouq-pa-bù.

as the case may be

In class: Exercises as above. Also practise with another map of Burma, and have the Learners ask about other town names. They note them down and use them as dictation, to check how accurately they hear the sounds.

Notes

Established English names for Burmese towns. Some of the Western versions of Burmese place names are unexpectedly different from the current Burmese pronunciation. The following divergent names can be added to the list above:

name	traditional English	revised English	pronunciation
ပုသိမ် /ပသိမ်/	Bassein	Pathein	Pǎthein
သံလျင် /တညင်/	Syriam	Thanlyin	Tǎnyin
အင်းဝ or အဝ	Ava	-	Ìn-wá/ Ǎwá
သံလွင်	Salween	Thanlwin	Than-lwin
ဧရာဝတီ /အေယာဝဒီ/	Irrawaddy	Ayeyarwady	E-ya-wǎdi
စစ်တောင်း	Sittang	Sittoung	Siq-taùn
စစ်တွေ	Akyab	Sittwe	Siq-twe
တနသ်ာရီ /တနင်းသာယီ/	Tenasserim	Tanintharyi	Tǎnìn-tha-yi
ထားဝယ် /ဒဝယ်/	Tavoy	Dawei	Dǎweh
မြိတ် /ဗိတ်/	Mergui	Beik	Beiq
ကျိုင်းတုံ	Kengtung	-	Caìn-toun
လွယ်ကော်	Loikaw	-	Lweh-kaw

These discrepancies arose for several reasons:
• Some came about because Burmese pronunciation has changed since the days when the first travellers from the West went to Burma and noted the names of towns and rivers. These early versions became fixed in English and other Western languages and didn't change over time to match subsequent changes in Burmese pronunciation.
• Other discrepancies came about because Western travellers first learned the place name from people whose first language was not Burmese (such as the Mons), or who spoke a non-standard dialect of Burmese (such as the Arakanese), or perhaps from other foreign travellers (such as Portuguese or Armenians) and these versions of the names became

Diphthongs in the roman transcription:
pronounce ei as in *vein*, ai as in *Thailand*, ou as in *though*, au as in *Sauerkraut*.

established among speakers of English and other European languages. It is noticeable that most of the divergent names are for places along the coast or not far away. Places further inland have English names that correspond much more closely with contemporary Burmese pronunciation.

• A third category are names like Kengtung and Loikaw, where the original name of the place is in a non-Burmese language (in the case of these names, Shan and Karen respectively), and attempts by Burmese speakers to reproduce its sound in Burmese script produced a result that diverged markedly from similar attempts by English speakers using roman script. The latter form became the established form in English.

English equivalents and traditional romanization. In 1989 the State Law and Order Restoration Council decreed that international usage should abandon the established English equivalent "Rangoon" and use instead the Burmese name ရန်ကုန် in traditional romanization form: "Yangon." Corresponding changes were recommended for the other towns shown in the list above.

The intention seems to have been to try and cast off these reminders of Western intervention and use spellings that more accurately reflect the pronunciation in contemporary Burmese. At the same time many streets that had had foreign names since colonial days (Windsor Road, Mission Road, and many others) were renamed with Burmese names.

For a list of Nationalities, States, Divisions, Rivers, and Towns for which roman spellings were announced at the same time, see Appendix 6, Additional vocabulary.

Common phrases

To make sure you complete the Common Phrases Supplement by the end of Part 1, learn Section 5 at about this point.

LESSON 20

Where and here.
Where is Maymyo? — It's here.

New words

ဘယ်မှာလဲ	in/ at/ on which place? Where?	beh-hma-lèh?
ဒီမှာ	in/ at/ on this place. Here.	di-hma

In fast speech ဘယ်မှာ (beh-hma) is sometimes contracted to ဘမှာ (băhma) or ဘမာ (băma).

Example sentences

S1: ပုဂံ ဘယ်မှာလဲ။	Where is Pagan?	Păgan beh-hmalèh?
S2 (pointing): ပုဂံက ဒီမှာပါ။	Pagan is here.	Păgan-gá di-hma-ba.

Diphthongs in the roman transcription:
pronounce ei as in *vein,* ai as in *Thailand,* ou as in *though,* au as in *Sauerkraut.*

67

S1 (pointing): ပုဂံက ဒီမှာလား။	Is Pagan here?	Păgan-gá di-hma-là?
S2: ဟုတ်ကဲ့။ ဒီမှာပါ။	Yes. It's here.	Houq-kéh. Di-hma-ba.

Models for the Exercises

Ex. 1: Looking at the Burma map before Lesson 19
S1: မန္တလေး ဘယ်မှာလဲ။ — Màn-dălè beh-hma-lèh?
L/S2: ဒီမှာပါ။ (နံပါတ် ၃၀)။ — Di-hma-ba (Nan-baq-30).

Ex. 2: Looking at the Rangoon street plan before Lesson 9
Prompt: Ask where the Sule Pagoda is.
L/S2: ဆူးလေဘုရား ဘယ်မှာလဲ။ — S'ù-le P'ăyà beh-hma-lèh?
S1: ဒီမှာပါ။ (နံပါတ် ၇)။ — Di-hma-ba (Nan-baq-7).

Ex. 3: Looking at the Asia map before Lesson 13
S1: နံပါတ်(၁၀)က ဘာနိုင်ငံလဲ။ — Nan-baq-10-gá ba nain-ngan-lèh?
L/S2: အိန္ဒိယပါ။ — Ein-dí-yá-ba.

Ex. 4. For written answer: not on the tape.

The words in the following questions and answers have been split up and jumbled. Rearrange them to form meaningful sentences. There is a Key to this Exercise at the end of the Lesson. Don't forget that you may find it helpful to copy the words onto separate slips of paper and do your reordering by sliding the slips around.

Ex. 4 in Lesson 20 (script)
S1: — လဲ — မြစ်ကြီးနား — ဘယ်မှာ
    S2: — ပါ — ဒီမှာ
S1: — ဗိုလ်ချုပ် — လား — ဈေး — ဒီမှာ — က
    S2: — မှာ — ဟုတ်ကဲ့ — ပါ — ဒီ
S1: — က — ပန်းခြံ — ဒီ — လား — မှာ — မဟာဗန္ဓုလ
    S2: — ပါ — မဟုတ်ပါဘူး — မှာ — ဒီ

Ex. 4 in Lesson 20 (roman)
S1: — lèh — Myiq-kyì-nà — beh-hma
    S2: — ba — di-hma
S1: — Bo-jouq — là — zè — di-hma — gá
    S2: — hma — houq-kéh — ba — di
S1: — gá — Pàn-jan — di — là— hma — Măha Ban-dú-lá
    S2: — ba — măhouq-pa-bù — hma — di

In class: Exercises as above. Also practise with other maps: world, your own country, your own town, your own campus, or other area. Also map or similar with numbers on it: နံပါတ်– ၃၅ ဘယ်မှာလဲ။ — ဒီမှာပါ။

Notes

Where and here. You have met phrases like

| ဘယ်လမ်းမှာလဲ။ | beh-làn-hma-lèh? | in which road? |
| ဘယ်နိုင်ငံမှာလဲ။ | beh-nain-ngan-hma-lèh? | in which country? |

The new phrase introduced in this Lesson is like these, but it has a gap where the others had words for "road" and "country." You may find it helpful to think of the gap as being occupied by an invisible word meaning "place," like this:

| ဘယ်–[place]–မှာလဲ။ | in which [place]? = where? | beh-[place]-hma-lèh? |

Looking at it this way makes the new phrase match the earlier ones more neatly.

In the same way, ဒီမှာ di-hma "here" also seems to have lost a word for "place":

ဒီလမ်းမှာ	in this road	di-làn-hma
ဒီနိုင်ငံမှာ	in this country	di-nain-ngan-hma
ဒီ–[place]–မှာ	in this [place] = here.	di-[place]-hma

Grammar. The grammatical structure of the Example sentences in this Lesson follows the familiar formula:

	NOUN1+SUFFIX	\<is\>	NOUN2+SUFFIX	STC SFX
S1:	ပုဂံ [+က]		ဘယ်+မှာ	–လဲ။
	Păgan [+gá]		beh+hma	-lèh?
	Pagan[+as for]	\<is\>	which place+in	*question*
		"Where is Maymyo?"		
S2:	[ပုဂံ [+က]]		ဒီ+မှာ	[–ပါ]။
	[Păgan [+gá]]		di+hma	[-ba].
	[Pagan[+as for]]	\<is\>	this [place]+in	*[polite]*
		"[Maymyo is] here."		

The square brackets in S2's answer are there to show that NOUN1 (with or without its suffix) may be omitted.

Keys to the Exercises

Key to Ex. 4 in Lesson 20

S1: — မြစ်ကြီးနား — ဘယ်မှာ — လဲ။
      S2: — ဒီမှာ — ပါ။
S1: — ဗိုလ်ချုပ် — ဈေး — က ဒီမှာ — လား။
      S2: — ဟုတ်ကဲ့။ — ဒီ — မှာ — ပါ။
S1: — မဟာဗန္ဓုလ — ပန်းခြံ — က — ဒီ — မှာ — လား။
      S2: — မဟုတ်ပါဘူး။ — ဒီ — မှာ — ပါ။

Key to Ex. 4 in Lesson 20 (roman)

S1: — Myiq-kyì-nà — beh-hma — lèh
      S2: — di-hma — ba
S1: — Bo-jouq — zè — gá — di-hma — là
      S2: — houq-kéh — di — hma — ba
S1: — Măha Ban-dú-lá — Pàn-jan — gá — di — hma — là
      S2: — măhouq-pa-bù — di — hma — ba

Diphthongs in the roman transcription:
pronounce ei as in *vein,* ai as in *Thailand,* ou as in *though,* au as in *Sauerkraut.*

LESSON 20R

Review of material in Lessons 1 to 20.

The Exercises for the Review Lessons are not recorded on the same tape as the normal Lessons. To work through these Exercises you will need to load the separate Review tape.

Models for the Exercises

Note that where S asks the questions, L repeats the question as well as answering it; and where L asks the questions, she/he repeats S's answer.

Ex. 1: Looking at the Rangoon street plan before Lesson 1
Prompt: S1 points to n° 1 and asks:
S1/L: ဒါ ဘာလဲ။   Da ba-lèh?
L/S2: ပြတိုက်ပါ။   Pyá-daiq-pa.

Ex. 2
Prompt: Point to n° 7 and ask what it is.
L/S2: ဒါ ဘာလဲ ။   Da ba-lèh?
S1/L: ဆူးလေဘုရားပါ။   S'ù-le P'ăyà-ba.

Ex. 3: Looking at the Asia map before Lesson 13
Prompt: S1 points to n° 410 and asks:
S1/L: ဒါ ဘာမြို့လဲ။   Da ba myó-lèh?
L/S2: ဘန်ကောက်မြို့ပါ။   Ban-gauq-myó-ba.

Ex. 4
Prompt: Point to 140 and ask what town it is.
L/S2: ဒါ ဘာမြို့လဲ။   Da ba myó-lèh?
S1/L: နယူးဒေလီမြို့။   Năyù De-li-myó.

Ex. 5: Looking at the Burma map before Lesson 19
Prompt: S1 points to n° 1385 and asks:
S1/L: ဒါ ဘာမြို့လဲ။   Da ba myó-lèh?
L/S2: မော်လမြိုင်မြို့။   Maw-lămyain-myó.

Ex. 6
Prompt: Point to 30 and ask what town that is.
L/S2: ဒါ ဘာမြို့လဲ။   Da ba myó-lèh?
S1/L: မန္တလေးပါ။   Màn-dălè-ba.

Ex. 7: Looking at the list of phone numbers in Lesson 6
S1/L: သမ္မတဟိုတယ် တယ်လီဖုန်းနံပါတ်   Thămădá Ho-teh teh-li-p'oùn nan-baq
    ၇၁၄၉၉–လား။   71499-là?
L/S2: ဟုတ်ကဲ့။ ၇၁၄၉၉–ပါ။   Houq-kéh. 71499-ba.

Diphthongs in the roman transcription:
pronounce ei as in *vein*, ai as in *Thailand*, ou as in *though*, au as in *Sauerkraut*.

Ex. 8: Using the form below. Prompt: Ask if the number of the Strand Hotel is 81533.

L/S2: စထရင်းဟိုတယ် တယ်လီဖုန်းနံပါတ်က
ဓ၁၅၃၃–လား။

Săt'ărìn Ho-teh teh-li-p'oùn nan-baq-ká
81533-là?

S1/L: ဟုတ်ကဲ့။ ၈၁၅၃၃။

Houq-kéh. 81533.

Form for Ex. 8 in Lesson 20

Strand Hotel	....	Myanmar Travel	....
Sakhantha Hotel	....	UNDP	....
Inya Lake Hotel	....		

Ex. 9. Numbers. Use the form below.

Fill in the blanks in the form with the numbers you hear on the tape, and then compare your result with the Key at the end of the Lesson. You will probably need to pause the tape after hearing each number, so as to give yourself time to write it down.

A	B	C	D	E	F	G	H	I	J
…	…	…	…	…	…	…	…	…	…

K	L	M	N	O	P	Q	R	S	T
…	…	…	…	…	…	…	…	…	…

Ex. 10. Numbers. Use the chart below.

Prompt: Line 1. Read out the number under A.

L/S2: ခြောက်ဆယ်။

C'auq-s'eh.

Chart for Ex. 10

	A	B	C	D	E	F
Line 1	၆၀	၈၀	၃၀	၉၀	၁၀	၂၀
Line 2	၄၀၀	၈၀၀	၃၀၀	၇၀၀	၂၀၀	၁၀၀
Line 3	၆၀၀၀	၈၀၀၀	၁၀၀၀	၂၀၀၀	၃၀၀၀	၅၀၀၀
Line 4	၃၉	၄၁	၉၇	၂၆	၇၅	၁၁
Line 5	၄၅၆	၂၈၃	၉၆၂	၇၃၅	၃၂၁	၁၄၉
Line 6	၁၉၉၃	၁၉၈၈	၁၉၄၈	၁၈၂၆	၁၇၅၂	၁၂၈၂

The chart in roman

	A	B	C	D	E	F
Line 1	60	80	30	90	10	20
Line 2	400	800	300	700	200	100
Line 3	6000	8000	1000	2000	3000	5000
Line 4	39	41	97	26	75	11
Line 5	456	283	962	735	321	149
Line 6	1993	1988	1948	1826	1752	1282

Diphthongs in the roman transcription:
pronounce ei as in *vein,* ai as in *Thailand,* ou as in *though,* au as in *Sauerkraut.*

Keys to the Exercises

Key to Ex. 8 in Lesson 20R

Strand Hotel	81533
Sakhantha Hotel	82974
Inya Lake Hotel	50644
Myanmar Travel	78376
UNDP	82144

Key to Ex. 9 in Lsn 20R (English figures)

A	B	C	D	E	F	G	H	I	J
90	70	40	20	50	16	39	47	24	12

K	L	M	N	O	P	Q	R	S	T
250	440	356	111	999	1934	1960	1852	1685	1282

Key to Ex. 9 in Lsn 20R (Burmese figures)

A	B	C	D	E	F	G	H	I	J
၉၀	၇၀	၄၀	၂၀	၅၀	၁၆	၃၉	၄၇	၂၄	၁၂

K	L	M	N	O	P	Q	R	S	T
၂၅၀	၄၄၀	၃၅၆	၁၁၁	၉၉၉	၁၉၃၄	၁၉၆၀	၁၈၅၂	၁၆၈၅	၁၂၈၂

Common phrases

To make sure you complete the Common Phrases Supplement by the end of Part 1, learn Section 6 at about this point.

I must protest with all the vigour at my command against the suggestion that officers in Burma should learn Burmese. ... Burmese is far too difficult a language for an officer and a gentleman to acquire. ... I have administered this Province for twenty years without knowing a word of the language, and the natives have expressed themselves as in every way satisfied with my rule.

Colonel Bogle (mid 19th century), quoted in *Heaven-born in Burma: the Daily Round*, by Maurice Maybury. Castle Cary, Folio Hadspen, n.d. [1984], p. 129.

Diphthongs in the roman transcription:
pronounce ei as in *vein,* ai as in *Thailand,* ou as in *though,* au as in *Sauerkraut.*

OVERVIEW OF GRAMMAR FOR LESSONS 1 TO 20

Sentence structure (for *is* sentences) :

1. Basic formula

The grammatical structures of the sentences in Lessons 1 to 20 can be summarized as follows:

NOUN1+SUFFIX	\<is\>	NOUN2+SUFFIX		SENTENCE SUFFIX

> Note 1. In the examples below elements that may be omitted are shown in [...].
> Note 2. The symbols +- indicate that the suffix slot is not filled.

2. Questions and statements

Within this structure there are three types of sentence:

A. Statements, optionally marked by the sentence suffix –ပါ -pa:

NOUN1+SUFFIX	\<is\>	NOUN2+SUFFIX	SENTENCE SUFFIX
NOUN1+SUFFIX \<is\>		NOUN2+SUFFIX	[–ပါ -pa *"polite"*]

Examples:

ဒါ [+က]		ဆူးလေဘုရား+–	[–ပါ]။
Da [+gá]		S'ù-le P'ăyà+-	[-ba].
That [+*as for*] \<is\>		Sule Pagoda+-	*[polite]*

"That is the Sule Pagoda."

B. Yes or No questions, obligatorily marked by the sentence suffix –လား -là *"question"*:

NOUN1+SUFFIX	\<is\>	NOUN2+SUFFIX	SENTENCE SUFFIX
NOUN1+SUFFIX \<is\>		NOUN2+SUFFIX	–လား -là

Examples:

ဒါ [+က]		ဆူးလေဘုရား+–	လား။
Da [+gá]		S'ù-le P'ăyà+-	là?
That [+*as for*] \<is\>		Sule Pagoda+-	*question*

"Is that the Sule Pagoda?"

C. Information questions, obligatorily marked by the sentence suffix –လဲ -lèh *"question"* and including a question word (what? where? how much? and so on) in the NOUN2 position:

Diphthongs in the roman transcription:
pronounce ei as in *vein,* ai as in *Thailand,* ou as in *though,* au as in *Sauerkraut.*

NOUN1+SUFFIX <is>	NOUN2+SUFFIX	SENTENCE SUFFIX
NOUN1+SUFFIX <is>	ဘယ်/ဘာ beh-ba+SUFFIX	–လဲ -lèh

Examples:

ဒါ [+က]	ဘာဘုရား+–	လဲ။
Da [+gá]	ba p'ăyà+-	lèh?
That *[+as for]* <is>	what pagoda+-	*question*

"What pagoda is that?"

3. Further examples

Information question:

NOUN1+SUFFIX <is>	NOUN2+SUFFIX	SENTENCE SUFFIX
တယ်လီဖုန်း နံပါတ် [+က]	ဘယ်လောက်+–	–လဲ။
Teh-li-p'òun nan-baq [+ká]	beh-lauq+-	-lèh?
Telephone number *[+as for]* <is>	how much+-	*question*

"What is its phone number?"

Statement:

NOUN1+SUFFIX <is>	NOUN2+SUFFIX	SENTENCE SUFFIX
တယ်လီဖုန်း နံပါတ် [+က]	၇၁၄၉၉+–	[–ပါ။]
Teh-li-p'òun nan-baq [+ká]	71499+-	[-ba].
Telephone number *[+as for]* <is>	71499+-	*[polite]*

"The phone number is 71499."

Yes or No Question:

NOUN1+SUFFIX <is>	NOUN2+SUFFIX	SENTENCE SUFFIX
စထရင်းဟိုတယ် [+က]	ကမ်းနားလမ်း+မှာ	လား။
Săt'ărìn Ho-teh [+gá]	Kàn-nà Làn+hma	-là?
The Strand Hotel *[+as for]*<is>	Strand Road+in	*question*

"Is the Strand Hotel in Strand Road?"

Information Question:

NOUN1+SUFFIX <is>	NOUN2+SUFFIX	SENTENCE SUFFIX
တောင်ကြီး [+က]	ဘယ်+မှာ	–လဲ။
Taun-jì [+gá]	beh+hma	-lèh?
Taunggyi *[+as for]* <is>	which [place]+in	*question*

"Where is Taunggyi?"

4. Variation

In the answer to a question, NOUN1 may be omitted; for example:

Diphthongs in the roman transcription:
pronounce ei as in *vein,* ai as in *Thailand,* ou as in *though,* au as in *Sauerkraut.*

Question:

NOUN1+SUFFIX <is>	NOUN2+SUFFIX	SENTENCE SUFFIX
စထရင်းဟိုတယ် [+က]	ဘယ်လမ်း+မှာ	-လဲ။
Săt'ărin Ho-teh [+gá]	beh-làn+hma	-lèh?
The Strand Hotel *[+as for]* <is>	which road+in*	*question*

"Which road is the Strand Hotel in?"*

For a note on "on the road" vs. "in the road" see Lesson 11.

Answer:

NOUN1+SUFFIX <is>	NOUN2+SUFFIX	SENTENCE SUFFIX
–	ကမ်းနားလမ်း+မှာ	[-ပါ]။
–	Kàn-nà Làn+hma	[-ba].
– <is>	Strand Road+in*	*[polite]*

"In Strand Road."*

* For a note on "on the road" vs. "in the road" see Lesson 11.

OVERVIEW OF NUMBERS AND COUNTING FOR LESSONS 1 TO 20

1 Simple numbers

၁	၂	၃	၄	၅	၆	၇	၈	၉	(၀)
တစ်	နှစ်	သုံး	လေး	ငါး	ခြောက်	ခုနစ်	ရှစ်	ကိုး	(သုည)
/တစ်	နှစ်	သုန်း	လေး	ငါး	ချောက်	ခွန်နှစ်	ရှစ်	ကိုး	(သုန်ညာ့)/
tiq	hniq	thoùn	lè	ngà	c'auq	k'un-hniq	shiq	kò	(thoun-nyá)
one	two	three	four	five	six	seven	eight	nine	(zero)

-ဆယ်	-ရာ	-ထောင်
-s'eh	-ya	-t'aun
-tens	-hundreds	-thousands

2 Compound numbers

ရှစ်ဆယ်	ငါးရာ	ခြောက်ထောင်
shiq-s'eh	ngà-ya	c'auq-t'aun
eight-tens	five-hundreds	six-thousands
eighty	five hundred	six thousand

Diphthongs in the roman transcription:
pronounce ei as in *vein,* ai as in *Thailand,* ou as in *though,* au as in *Sauerkraut.*

3 Weakening: The following unit numbers weaken in compounds:

တစ်	နှစ်	ခုနှစ်
tiq	hniq	k'un-hniq
one	two	seven

Examples:

တစ်ဆယ်	နှစ်ရာ	ခုနှစ်ထောင်
/တဆယ်/	/နှယာ/	/ခွန်နထောင်/
tăs'eh	hnăya	k'un-năt'aun
ten	two hundred	seven thousand

4 Voicing: –ဆယ် -s'eh and –ထောင် -t'aun voice in a compound (–ရာ -ya can't be voiced anyway);

Examples:

သုံးဆယ်	ငါးဆယ်	ကိုးထောင်
/သုန်းဇယ်/	/ငါးဇယ်/	/ကိုးဒေါင်/
thoùn-zeh	ngà-zeh	kò-daun
thirty	fifty	nine thousand

But voicing doesn't operate after a glottal stop or a weak vowel; for example:

ခြောက်ဆယ်	ရှစ်ဆယ်	ခုနှစ်ထောင်
/ချောက်ဆယ်/	/ယှစ်ဆယ်/	/ခွန်နထောင်/
c'auq-s'eh	shiq-s'eh	k'un-năt'aun
sixty	eighty	seven thousand

5 Larger compound numbers

1. with "and"	2. with "creak"	3. with nothing
ကိုးရာနဲ့ ငါးဆယ်	ကိုးရာ ငါးဆယ်	ကိုးရာ ငါးဆယ်
kò-ya-néh ngà-zeh	kò-yá ngà-zeh	kò-ya ngà-zeh
900-and 50	900-creak 50	900 50

6 Quirks

- 11-19: in place of the expected

တစ်ဆယ့်တစ်	tăs'éh-tiq	11	တစ်ဆယ့်နှစ်	tăs'éh-hniq	12 and so on.

people usually omit the တစ် tă- "one" and just say:

ဆယ့်တစ်	tăs'éh-tiq	11	ဆယ့်နှစ်	tăs'éh-hniq	12 and so on.

but 10 remains unchanged:

တစ်ဆယ်	tăs'eh	10

- 1001-1999: as for 11-19: in place of the expected

တစ်ထောင့်တစ်ရာ	tăt'aún-tăya	1100	တစ်ထောင့်နှစ်ရာ	tăt'aún-hnăya 1200	and so on.

people usually omit the တစ် tă- "one" and just say:

ထောင့်တစ်ရာ	t'aún-tăya	1100	ထောင့်နှစ်ရာ	t'aún-hnăya	1200	and so on.

but 1000 remains unchanged:

တစ်ထောင်	tăt'aun	1000

Diphthongs in the roman transcription:
pronounce ei as in *vein,* ai as in *Thailand,* ou as in *though,* au as in *Sauerkraut.*

CUMULATED VOCABULARY FOR LESSONS 1 TO 20

This and That

script	English (roman)	pronunciation
ဒါ	this, that	da
ဒီ–[noun]	this [noun]	di-[noun]
ဒီမှာ	in this [place], here	di-hma

Examples

ဒါက ဟိုတယ်လား။	Is that a hotel?	Da-gá ho-teh-là?
ဒီဈေးက ဗိုလ်ချုပ်ဈေးပါ။	This market is Bogyoke Market.	Di zè-gá Bo-jouq Zè-ba.
စစ်ကိုင်းက ဒီမှာပါ။	Sagaing is here.	Săgaìn-gá di-hma-ba.

What and Which

ဘာ	what	ba
ဘာ–[noun]	what [noun]	ba-[noun]
ဘယ်–[noun]	which [noun]	beh-[noun]
ဘယ်မှာ	in which [place], where	beh-hma
ဘယ်လောက်	how much, what number	beh-lauq

Examples:

နံပါတ်(၁) ဘာလဲ။	What is n° 1?	Nan-baq-tiq ba-lèh?
ဒီဈေးက ဘာဈေးလဲ။	What market is this market?	Di zè-gá ba zè-lèh?
ဈေး ဘယ်လမ်းမှာလဲ။	Which road is the market in?	Zè beh làn-hma-lèh?
ကွာလာလမ်ပူ ဘယ်မှာလဲ။	Where is Kuala Lumpur?	Kwa-la Lan-pu beh-hma-lèh?
တယ်လီဖုန်းနံပါတ် ဘယ်လောက်လဲ။	What is the phone number?	Teh-li-p'oùn nan-baq beh-lauq-lèh?

Buildings and parks (Lesson 1)

ပြတိုက် /ပြ့ဒိုက်/	museum	pyá-daiq
ဘုရား /ဖယား/	lord, pagoda, Buddha image	p'ăyà
ပန်းခြံ /ပန်းဂျန်/	park, garden	pàn-jan
ဟိုတယ်	hotel [from English]	ho-teh
ဈေး /ဇေး/	market	zè

Diphthongs in the roman transcription:
pronounce ei as in *vein*, ai as in *Thailand*, ou as in *though*, au as in *Sauerkraut*.

Places in Rangoon (Lesson 5)

ဗိုလ်ချုပ်ပြတိုက်	/ဗို့ဂျုပ်ပျာ့ဒိုက်/	Bogyoke Museum	Bo-jouq Pyá-daiq
ရွှေတိဂုံဘုရား	/ရွှေဒဂုန်ဖယား/	Shwedagon Pagoda	Shwe-dăgoun P'ăyà
ဗိုလ်ချုပ်ပန်းခြံ	/ဗိုဂျုပ်ပန်းဂျန်/	Bogyoke Park	Bo-jouq Pàn-jan
သမ္မတဟိုတယ်	/သမဒၣ/	President Hotel	Thămădá Ho-teh
ဗိုလ်ချုပ်ဈေး	/ဗို့ဂျုပ်ဇေး/	Bogyoke Market	Bo-jouq Zè
သိမ်ကြီးဈေး	/သိန်ဂျီးဇေး/	Thein-gyi Market	Thein-jì-zè
ဆူးလေဘုရား	/ဖယား/	Sule Pagoda	S'ù-le P'ăya
မဟာဗန္ဓုလပန်းခြံ	/ဗန်ဒုလ္လာပန်းဂျန်/	Maha Bandoola Park	Măha Ban-dú-lá Pàn-jan
အမျိုးသားပြတိုက်	/ပျာ့ဒိုက်/	National Museum	Amyò-thà Pyá-daiq
စထရင်းဟိုတယ်		Strand Hotel	Săt'ărìn Ho-teh

Roads in Rangoon (Lessons 7 & 9)

လမ်း		road, street	làn
ဗိုလ်ချုပ်လမ်း	/ဗို့ဂျုပ်–/	Bogyoke Street	Bo-jouq Làn
အနော်ရထာလမ်း	/ယထာ or ရထာ/	Anawrahta Street	Ănaw-yăt'a (or -răt'à) Làn
မဟာဗန္ဓုလလမ်း	/ဗန်ဒုလ္လာ–/	Maha Bandoola Street	Măha Ban-dú-lá Làn
ကုန်သည်လမ်း	/–သယ်–/	Merchant Street	Koun-dheh Làn
ကမ်းနားလမ်း		Strand Road	Kàn-nà Làn
ဗိုလ်အောင်ကျော်လမ်း	/ဗို အောင်ကျော်–/	Bo Aung Kyaw Street	Bo Aun Jaw Làn
ပန်းဆိုးတန်း	/–ဆိုးဒန်း or –ဇိုးဒန်း/	Pansodan Street	Pàn-s'ò (or -zò) -dàn
ဆူးလေဘုရားလမ်း	/–ဖယား–/	Sule Pagoda Road	S'ù-le P'ăyà Làn
ရွှေဘုံသာလမ်း		Shwebontha Street	Shwe-boun-dha Làn
ဘုရားလမ်း	/–ဖယား–/	Shwedagon Pagoda Road	P'ăyà Làn

Countries in Asia (Lesson 13)

နိုင်ငံ		country, state	naing-ngan
အိန္ဒိယနိုင်ငံ	/အိန်ဒိယာ–/	India	Ein-dí-yá Naing-ngan
ဘင်္ဂလားဒေ့ရှ်နိုင်ငံ	/ဗင်ဂ–/	Bangladesh	Bin-gălà-désh Naing-ngan
မြန်မာနိုင်ငံ		Burma/Myanmar	Myan-ma Naing-ngan
ထိုင်းနိုင်ငံ		Thailand	T'aìn Naing-ngan
မလေးရှားနိုင်ငံ		Malaysia	Mălè-shà Naing-ngan
ဗီယက်နမ်နိုင်ငံ		Vietnam	Bi-yeq-nan Naing-ngan
ဖိလစ်ပိုင်နိုင်ငံ		Philippines	P'í-liq-pain Naing-ngan
တရုတ်နိုင်ငံ		China	Tăyouq Naing-ngan
ဂျပန်နိုင်ငံ		Japan	Jăpan Naing-ngan

Towns in Asia (Lesson 15)

မြို့		town	myó
နယူးဒေလီ		New Delhi	Năyù De-li
ဒက္ကား		Dacca	Deq-kà

Diphthongs in the roman transcription: pronounce ei as in *vein*, ai as in *Thailand*, ou as in *though*, au as in *Sauerkraut*.

ရန်ကုန်	Rangoon/Yangon	Yan-goun
ဘန်ကောက်	Bangkok	Ban-kauq
ကွာလာလမ်ပူ	Kuala Lumpur	Kwa-la Lan-pu
ဟန္နိုင်း	Hanoi	Hănwaìn
မနီလာ	Manila	Măni-la
ပီကင်း	Peking/Beijing	Pi-kìn
တိုကျို	Tokyo	To-co

Towns in Burma (Lesson 19)

မြစ်ကြီးနား	Myitkyina	Myiq-ci\-nà
မေမြို့	Maymyo	Me-myó
မန္တလေး /မန်းဒလေး/	Mandalay	Màn-dălè
စစ်ကိုင်း /ဇဂိုင်း/	Sagaing	Săgaìn
ပုဂံ /ဗဂန်/	Pagan (Bagan)	Păgan
သာစည် /သာဇီ/	Thazi	Tha-zi
တောင်ကြီး /-ဂျီး/	Taunggyi	Taun-jì
ပြည် /ပျေ/ပို/	Prome (Pyi/Pyay)	Pye
ရေနံချောင်း /ယေနန်ချောင်း/	Yenangyaung	Ye-nan-jaùn
သံတွဲ /-ဒွဲ/	Sandoway (Thandwe)	Than-dwèh
ပဲခူး /ဗဂိုး/	Pegu (Bago)	Păgò
ရန်ကုန် /ယန်ဂုန်/	Rangoon (Yangon)	Yan-goun
မော်လမြိုင်	Moulmein (Mawlamyine)	Maw-lămyain

Miscellaneous words

| နံပါတ် | number (Lesson 2) | nan-baq |
| တယ်လီဖုန်း | telephone (Lesson 6) | teh-li-p'oùn |

Phrases

ဟုတ်ကဲ့	It is so.	Houq-kéh (Lesson 3)
မဟုတ်ပါဘူး /-ဗူး/	It is not so.	Măhouq-pa-bù (Lesson 3)
အော်	Oh. (Lesson 5)	Aw. (Lesson 5)
ထပ်ပြောပါအုံး။ /-စာ-/	Please say that again.	T'aq-pyàw-ba-oùn. (Lesson 13)
ပြန်ပြောပါအုံး။ /-စာ-/	Please say that again.	Pyan-pyàw-ba-oùn. (Lesson 13)

Checking questions (Lesson 6)

| [noun]–လား။ | Did you say [noun]? | [noun]-là |
| | Was that [noun]? | |

Diphthongs in the roman transcription:
pronounce ei as in *vein,* ai as in *Thailand,* ou as in *though,* au as in *Sauerkraut.*

LESSON 21

Burmese personal names.
Who's that? — It's Tin Aye.

1	2	3	4
တင်အေး	သန်းဆွေ	စံသာအောင်	ခင်လှတင့်
Tin È	Thàn S'we	San Tha Aun	K'in Hlá Tín
Tin Aye	Than Swe	San Tha Aung	Khin Hla Tint
(boy)	(girl)	(boy)	(girl)

On romanization see note below.

New words

ဘယ်သူလဲ။	Who … ?	beh-dhu (bădhu)-lèh?

Examples

S1: ဒါ ဘယ်သူလဲ။   Who is that?   Da beh-dhu-lèh?
S2: ဒါက တင်အေးပါ။   That is Tin Aye.   Da-gá Tin È-ba.

Models for the Exercises

Ex. 1: Putting names to faces
    Prompt: First point to n° 1 and ask who he is.
    L/S2: ဒါ ဘယ်သူလဲ။   Da beh-dhu-lèh?
    S1: ဒါက တင်အေးပါ။   Da-gá Tin È-ba.
    L/S2: တင်အေး။   Tin È.

Diphthongs in the roman transcription:
pronounce ei as in *vein*, ai as in *Thailand*, ou as in *though*, au as in *Sauerkraut*.

Ex. 2: Prompt: S1 points to nº 1 and asks:

S1: ဒါ ဘယ်သူလဲ။   Da beh-dhu-lèh?

L/S2: ဒါက တင်အေးပါ။   Da-gá Tin È-ba.

In class: Exercises as above. Also use your own photographs, or photographs from newspapers and magazines.

Notes

Grammar. The grammatical structure of the Example sentences in this Lesson follows the familiar formula for *is* sentences:

	NOUN1+SUFFIX	<is>	NOUN2+SUFFIX	STC SFX
S1:	ဒါ		ဘယ်သူ	–လဲ။
	Da		beh-dhu	-lèh?
	That	<is>	who	*question*
	"Who is that?"			
S2:	[ဒါ]		တင်အေး	[–ပါ]။
	[Da]		Tin È	[-ba].
	[That]	<is>	Tin Aye	*[polite]*
	"[That is] Tin Aye."			

The square brackets in S2's answer are there to show that NOUN1 and –ပါ -ba (either or both) may be omitted.

Burmese personal names. Most Burmese names have two or three syllables — some have four, and some just one. Most of the syllables mean something desirable or lovable, like "beautiful," "victorious," "wealthy," "gold," "calm," "radiant," "million," "lovable," "little brother," "sweet," and so on. Generally the words for more macho attributes are used for boys' names, while parents choosing girls' names favour the gentler characteristics, but there are many names that are used for both boys and girls.

By tradition parents choose for their baby a name that both appeals to them and begins with letters appropriate to the weekday on which the baby was born. The names of the children thus bear no relation to the names of the parents: the children in the picture above could all be brothers and sisters despite their differing names. Likewise, there is no change of name on marriage: both men and women continue to be known by the name they used before marrying.

However, many Burmese have two names: a pet name, which is used by their family and close friends, and an official name (children call it their "school name" ကျောင်းနာမည်), which they use when filling in forms or being introduced to strangers. In addition, most writers and performers (actors, singers, dancers, musicians) also adopt a pen name or a stage name; so a writer, for example, may be known to his family by a pet name, to his readers by his pen name, and to the bureaucracy by his official name.

In the names of a few people (mainly educated townspeople), you will see the effects of contact with the West: some people have partly English names (like Dora Than Aye, or

---

Diphthongs in the roman transcription:
pronounce ei as in *vein*, ai as in *Thailand*, ou as in *though*, au as in *Sauerkraut*.

Kenneth Shein), which they may have been given by their parents, or by teachers at a mission school in pre-independence days, and some parents have perpetuated their own name in the names of their children (like the three brothers Min Thaw Kaung, Thant Thaw Kaung, and Myat Thaw Kaung, whose father's name is Thaw Kaung, who himself is the son of a man named Kaung). Again, some women, particularly if they have lived abroad, use an English first name and their husband's name as a surname (like Molly Ko, wife of a man called Ko).

Romanization. You saw from the note in Lesson 1 that Burmese place names are written here in both a "systematic" romanization and a "traditional" romanization. Personal names are treated in the same way. For the difference between the two methods see the section on script and transcription in Appendix 3. The first method gives you a guide to the way the names are pronounced, and the second lets you see how people romanize them in practice.

LESSON 22

Names with the prefixes U and Daw.
Who's that? — It's U Tin Aye.

1	2	3	4
ကြည်ကြည်မြ	လှရွှေ	မြစိန်	မောင်မောင်ကြီး
Ci Ci Myá	Hlá Shwe	Myá Sein	Maun Maun Jì
Kyi Kyi Mya	Hla Shwe	Mya Sein	Maung Maung Gyi

New words

ဦး	"Mr." — prefix to names of adult men	Ù
ဒေါ်	"Mrs./Miss/Ms." — prefix to names of adult women	Daw
	See the note below.	

Diphthongs in the roman transcription:
pronounce ei as in *vein,* ai as in *Thailand,* ou as in *though,* au as in *Sauerkraut.*

Examples

ဦးလှရွှေ	U Hla Shwe	Ù Hlá Shwe
ဒေါ်ကြည်ကြည်မြ	Daw Kyi Kyi Mya	Daw Ci Ci Myá

Models for the Exercises

Ex. 1: Putting names to faces
    Prompt: Ask about n° 1
    L/S2: နံပါတ်(၁) ဘယ်သူလဲ။   Nan-baq-tiq beh-dhu-lèh?
    S1: ဒါက ကြည်ကြည်မြပါ။   Da-gá Ci Ci Myá-ba.
    L/S2: ကြည်ကြည်မြ။   Ci Ci Myá.

Ex. 2: Prompt: Ask about n° 4
    L/S2: နံပါတ်(၄) ဘယ်သူလဲ။   Nan-baq-lè beh-dhu-lèh?
    S1: ဒါက ဦးမောင်မောင်ကြီးပါ။   Da-gá Ù Maun Maun Jì-ba.
    L/S2: ဦးမောင်မောင်ကြီး။   Ù Maun Maun Jì.

Ex. 3
    S1: နံပါတ်(၁) ဘယ်သူလဲ။   Nan-baq-tiq beh-dhu-lèh?
    L/S2: နံပါတ်(၁)က ဒေါ်ကြည်ကြည်မြပါ။   Nan-baq-tiq-ká Daw Ci Ci Myá-ba.

In class: Exercises as above. Also use your own photographs, or photographs from newspapers and magazines.

Notes

Prefixes to Burmese names. A child is usually addressed and referred to by his or her name as it stands. When you're using the name of an adult, and want to be polite and respectful, you need to add a prefix. Using an adult's name without a prefix sounds disrespectful: opponents of the régime in the early 1990s referred to U Ne Win as plain "Ne Win" to show the low regard in which they held him.

People use quite a range of prefixes to names, but by far the commonest prefixes are the two introduced here: ဦး Ù and ဒေါ် Daw (clearly derived from the words for "Uncle" and "Aunt"). These two are widely used for the names of adults you don't know intimately.

Among other prefixes, one common type is the Burmese equivalents of "General," "Major," and so on, which are used in place of ဦး Ù and ဒေါ် Daw. Another type is illustrated by titles like "Doctor" and "Teacher," which are used sometimes with and sometimes in place of ဦး Ù and ဒေါ် Daw. People also use other kin terms. Here is a list of some common prefixes to names for reference. You'll meet some of them in later Lessons.

ဦး Ù: originally "uncle"; used for men, respectful
ဒေါ် Daw: originally "aunt"; used for women, respectful

Diphthongs in the roman transcription:
pronounce ei as in *vein*, ai as in *Thailand*, ou as in *though*, au as in *Sauerkraut*.

ကို Ko: originally "older brother"; used for men with whom the speaker has a brotherly relationship; hence less distant and formal than U, and limited to people of roughly the same generation as the speaker, but also used by mature adults for referring to men of student age. Found more in conversation than in printing.

မ Má: originally "older sister"; used for women: same range as for ကို Ko.

မောင် Maun: originally "younger brother"; Used for boys of school age, or for young men if speaker is considerably older than they (say by 20 years) and is on affectionate terms.

(no prefix); used for small children, or someone older if you knew him/her as a small child, or if you feel towards him/her as you would if you had known him/her as a small child; more often used for women than for men.

င Ngă; used for men with whom speaker is on intimate terms (for example: younger sibling, old school friend, or child of close friends).

ဘိုး P'ò: originally "grandfather"; used for men: on same terms as င Ngă.

မိ Mí: originally "mother"; used for women: on same terms as င Ngă.

The following are some commonly encountered civil titles:

ဒေါက်တာ Dauq-ta "doctor"; used before U or Daw for medical doctors and Ph.D.s.

ဆရာ S'ăya "teacher (male)"; used with or without U for professional teachers and by extension for others with a skill or position of authority, such as a doctor, a high-ranking civil servant.

ဆရာမ S'ăya-má "teacher (female)"; used with or without Daw: as for ဆရာ S'ăya.

Military ranks are used before a name without U or Daw as in English. Frequently used titles include:

ဗိုလ်ချုပ်မှူး	senior general	Bo-jouq-hmù
ဗိုလ်ချုပ်ကြီး	general	Bo-jouq-cì
ဗိုလ်ချုပ်	major general	Bo-jouq
ဗိုလ်မှူးချုပ်	brigadier general	Bo-hmù-jouq
ဗိုလ်မှူးကြီး	colonel	Bo-hmù-jì
ဗိုလ်မှူး	major	Bo-hmù

Common phrases

To make sure you complete the Common Phrases Supplement by the end of Part 1, learn Section 7 at about this point.

Diphthongs in the roman transcription:
pronounce ei as in *vein*, ai as in *Thailand*, ou as in *though*, au as in *Sauerkraut*.

LESSON 23

Prices in dollars and pounds (unround numbers).
Weakening and voicing in prices.

Price lists

dollar	prices
1.	$3
2.	$43
3.	$156
4.	$1
5.	$2
6.	$7
7.	$97
8.	$82
9.	$361

sterling	prices
1.	£83
2.	£8
3.	£425
4.	£16
5.	£994
6.	£337
7.	£6841
8.	£1352
9.	£19

New words

ဒေါ်လာ	dollar	daw-la
ပေါင်	pound	paun
ဘယ်လောက်လဲ	how much? what price?	beh-lauq-lèh?
	["which-quantity-*question*"]	

Example prices

သုံးဒေါ်လာ	three dollars	thoùn-daw-la
ငါးဆယ့် ခြောက်ဒေါ်လာ	fifty-six dollars	ngà-zéh c'auq-daw-la
နှစ်ရာ ကိုးဆယ့် ရှစ်ပေါင်	298 pounds	hnăyá kò-zéh shiq-paun

Example sentences

S1: ဒါ ဘယ်လောက်လဲ။	How much is that?	Da beh-lauq-lèh?
S2: သုံးဒေါ်လာ။	$3.	Thòun-daw-la.
S1: နံပါတ်(၅)က နှစ်ဒေါ်လာလား။	Is n° 5 $2?	Nan-baq-ngà-gá hnădaw-la-là?
S2: ဟုတ်ကဲ့။ နှစ်ဒေါ်လာပါ။	Yes. It is $2.	Houq-kéh. Hnădaw-la-ba.
S1: နံပါတ်(၅)က သုံးဒေါ်လာလား။	Is n° 5 $3?	Nan-baq-ngà-gá thoùn-daw-la-là?
S2: မဟုတ်ပါဘူး။ နှစ်ဒေါ်လာပါ။	No. It's $2.	Măhouq-pa-bù. Hnădaw-la-ba.

Diphthongs in the roman transcription:
pronounce ei as in *vein,* ai as in *Thailand,* ou as in *though,* au as in *Sauerkraut.*

Models for the Exercises

Ex. 1 (using the dollar price list)

Prompt: Ask the price of nº 1.

L/S2: နံပါတ်(၁) ဘယ်လောက်လဲ။	Nan-baq-tiq beh-lauq-lèh?
S1/L: သုံးဒေါ်လာ။	Thoùn-daw-la.

Ex. 2 (using the sterling price list)

Prompt: Ask the price of nº 2.

L/S2: နံပါတ်(၂) ဘယ်လောက်လဲ။	Nan-baq-hniq beh-lauq-lèh?
S1/L: ရှစ်ပေါင်။	Shiq-paun.

Ex. 3

S1: နံပါတ်(၁) ဘယ်လောက်လဲ။	Nan-baq-tiq beh-lauq-lèh?
L/S2: ၃-ဒေါ်လာ။	Thoùn-daw-la.

In class: Exercises as above. Also use catalogues from stores, menus and so on — but prices must be in whole pounds or whole dollars, and with no round numbers. Use English for words not yet known; for example:

L1: *History of Burma* ဘယ်လောက်လဲ။	*History of Burma* beh-lauq-lèh?
L2: ၃၅-ဒေါ်လာ။	35-daw-la.
L1: Water pump ဘယ်လောက်လဲ။	Water pump beh-lauq-lèh?

and so on.

Notes

Weakening and voicing. Note that 1, 2 and 7 weaken before "dollars" and "pounds," in the same way as they do before "ten, " "hundred," "thousand" and so on. (see Lessons 8, 10, 12):

တစ်ဒေါ်လာ	/တဒေါ်လာ/	tădaw-la	one dollar
နှစ်ဒေါ်လာ	/နှဒေါ်လာ/	hnădaw-la	two dollars
နှစ်ပေါင်	/နှပေါင်/	hnăpaun	two pounds
ခုနစ်ပေါင်	/ခွန်နပေါင်/	k'un-năpaun	seven pounds

Weakening applies not only in unit numbers, like those above, but also in any larger number ending in 1, 2, or 7:

ဆယ့် တစ်ဒေါ်လာ	/ဆဲ့ တဒေါ်လာ/	s'éh tădaw-la	eleven dollars
ငါးဆယ့် နှစ်ဒေါ်လာ	/ငါးဲ့ နှဒေါ်လာ/	ngà-zéh hnădaw-la	fifty-two dollars
ရှစ်ဆယ့် ခုနစ်ဒေါ်လာ	/ယှစ်ဆဲ့ ခွန်နဒေါ်လာ/	shiq-s'éh k'un-nădaw-la	eighty-seven dollars

Note also that the word ပေါင် paun "pound(s)" obeys the Voicing Rule, like ဆယ် s'eh "ten" and ထောင် t'aun "thousand" (see Lessons 10 and 12):

သုံးပေါင်	/သုံးဘောင်/	thoùn-baun	three pounds
လေးပေါင်	/လေးဘောင်/	lè-baun	four pounds

Diphthongs in the roman transcription:
pronounce ei as in *vein,* ai as in *Thailand,* ou as in *though,* au as in *Sauerkraut.*

and it observes the same exceptions to the Voicing Rule:

နှစ်ပေါင်	/နှပေါင်/	hnăpaun	two pounds
ရှစ်ပေါင်	as written	shiq-paun	eight pounds

There is one small difference. Unlike ဆယ် s'eh "ten" and ထောင် t'aun "thousand" the word ပေါင် paun "pound(s)" *does* voice after တစ် /တ/ tă "one" although it has a weak vowel:

တစ်ပေါင်	/တဗောင်/	tăbaun	one pound

In this and analogous words, the တစ် /တ/ tă "one" often sounds voiced itself: it gets closer to a /ဒ/ dă than a /တ/ tă:

တစ်ပေါင်	/ဒဗောင်/	dăbaun	one pound

Notice how the Burmese spelling remains the same, whatever the changes in pronunciation.

The word ဒေါ်လာ daw-la would voice after 3, 4, 5 and similar numbers if it could, but it can't: its first consonant (/ဒ-/ d-) is a voiced one to start with.

LESSON 24

Names with the prefixes Ko and Ma.
Who is nº 1? — Nº 1 is Ko Khin Maung Aye.

1
ခင်မောင်အေး
K'in Maun È
Khin Maung Aye

2
သန်းသန်းဝင်း
Thàn Thàn Wìn
Than Than Win

3
ထွန်းကြည်
T'ùn Ci
Tun Kyi

4
စိန်ရီ
Sein Yi
Sein Yi

New words

ကို	prefix to names of young adult men	Ko
မ	prefix to names of young adult women	Má

Diphthongs in the roman transcription:
pronounce ei as in *vein*, ai as in *Thailand*, ou as in *though*, au as in *Sauerkraut*.

Note

In an earlier Lesson you met names used without prefixes for young children, and names used with the prefixes ဦး Ù and ဒေါ် Daw for adults you don't know well, whatever age they may be. When you get to know an adult well enough to have a warm and friendly relationship with him/her, particularly if she/he is of the same generation as yourself, the prefixes ဦး Ù and ဒေါ် Daw sound too distant and formal. In this case people often use ကို Ko and မ Má in place of ဦး Ù and ဒေါ် Daw.

The meaning of ကို Ko and မ Má is "older brother" and "older sister," and typically you would use these prefixes for the names of people who are as close to you as an older brother or sister might be, and who have the same age relationship to you. However, their usage has broadened with time. Older people use them for the names of young adults who fall between the "no prefix" and the "U/Daw" categories. Newspapers and broadcasters, for example, often use them before the names of university students.

Examples

ကိုထွန်းကြည်	Ko Tun Kyi	Ko T'ùn Ci
မသန်းသန်းဝင်း	Ma Than Than Win	Má Thàn Thàn Wìn

Models for the Exercises

Ex. 1: Putting names to faces
Prompt: Ask about n° 1
L/S2: နံပါတ်(၁) ဘယ်သူလဲ။   Nan-baq-tiq beh-dhu-lèh?
S1: ဒါက ခင်မောင်အေးပါ။   Da-gá K'in Maun È-ba.
L/S2: ခင်မောင်အေး။   K'in Maun È.

Ex. 2: Prompt: Ask about n° 4
L/S2: နံပါတ်(၄) ဘယ်သူလဲ။   Nan-baq-lè beh-dhu-lèh?
S1: ဒါက မစိန်ရီပါ။   Da-gá Má Sein Yi-ba.
L/S2: မစိန်ရီ။   Má Sein Yi.

Ex. 3
S1: နံပါတ်(၁) ဘယ်သူလဲ။   Nan-baq-tiq beh-dhu-lèh?
L/S2: ကိုခင်မောင်အေးပါ။   Ko K'in Maun È-ba.

In class: Exercises as above. Also use your own photographs, or photographs from newspapers and magazines.

Common phrases

To make sure you complete the Common Phrases Supplement by the end of Part 1, learn Section 8 at about this point.

Diphthongs in the roman transcription:
pronounce ei as in *vein*, ai as in *Thailand*, ou as in *though*, au as in *Sauerkraut*.

LESSON 25

Review of names and prefixes.
Who is nº 1? — That's Bo Ni. — Ah. U Bo Ni.

1
ဗိုလ်နီ
Bo Ni
Bo Ni

3
တင်မောင်
Tin Maun
Tin Maung

4
ခင်ချို
K'in C'o
Khin Cho

2
ကြည်ကြည်
Ci Ci
Kyi Kyi

5
အောင်ကျော်
Aun Caw
Aung Kyaw

6
သင်းသင်းဌေး
Thìn Thìn T'è
Thin Thin Htay

Model for the Exercise

Ex. 1. Imagine that an old lady, a relative of the people in the picture, is telling you their names. When you hear the name, you say "Ah," and repeat the name with the appropriate prefix.

Diphthongs in the roman transcription:
pronounce ei as in *vein,* ai as in *Thailand,* ou as in *though,* au as in *Sauerkraut.*

89

Prompt: Ask about n° 1
L/S2: နံပါတ်(၁) ဘယ်သူလဲ။   Nan-baq-tiq beh-dhu-lèh?
S1: ဒါက ဗိုလ်နီပါ။   Da-gá Bo Ni-ba.
L/S2: အာ။ ဦးဗိုလ်နီ။   A. Ù Bo Ni.

In class: Exercises as above. Also use your own photographs, or photographs from newspapers and magazines.

LESSON 26

Prices in pounds and pya.
Round and unround numbers, and ten.

Price lists

	sterling prices		pyà prices
1.	£5	1.	6 p.
2.	£64	2.	25 p.
3.	£831	3.	50 p.
4.	£50	4.	35 p.
5.	£640	5.	80 p.
6.	£800	6.	30 p.
7.	£5500	7.	39 p.
8.	£9980	8.	90 p.
9.	£20	9.	40 p.
10.	£10	10.	10 p.

New words

ပြား	pya [in Burmese currency]	pyà

This word is often used by Burmese abroad in place of —

ပဲနီ	penny [in British currency]	pèh-ní
ဆင့်	cent [in U.S. and other currencies]	s'ín

For a note on Burmese currency see Lesson 32.

Models for the Exercises

Ex. 1 (using Price List 1)
    Prompt: Ask the price of n° 1.
    L/S2: နံပါတ်(၁) ဘယ်လောက်လဲ။   Nan-baq-tiq beh-lauq-lèh?
    S1/L: ငါးပေါင်။   Ngà-baun.

Ex. 2 (using Price list 2). Answer without –ပါ (-ba).
    S1: နံပါတ်(၁) ဘယ်လောက်လဲ။   Nan-baq-tiq beh-lauq-lèh?
    L/S2: ခြောက်ပြား။   C'auq-pyà.

Diphthongs in the roman transcription:
pronounce ei as in *vein*, ai as in *Thailand*, ou as in *though*, au as in *Sauerkraut*.

Ex. 3 (using Price list 2)

S1: နံပါတ်(၁)က ခြောက်ပြားလား။   Nan-baq-tiq-ká c'auq-pyà-là?

L/S2: ဟုတ်ကဲ့။ ခြောက်ပြားပါ။   Houq-kéh. C'auq-pyà-ba.

In class: Exercises as above. Also use price lists with prices in whole pounds, dollars or pya (for example: £35 but not £35.50p.).

Notes

Round, unround numbers, and ten. Normally the number comes before the unit being counted; for example (with the unit ပေါင် paun "pounds"):

| ငါးပေါင် | ngà-baun | five pounds |
| ငါးဆယ့် ငါးပေါင် | ngà-zéh ngà-baun | £55 |

However, round numbers (any number ending in a 0)* are different. In round numbers, the number comes *after* the unit being counted:

ပေါင် ငါးဆယ်	paun ngà-zeh	£50
ပေါင် ငါးရာ	paun ngà-ya	£500
ပေါင် ငါးထောင်	paun ngà-daun	£5000
ပေါင် ငါးထောင့် ငါးရာ	paun ngà-daún ngà-ya	£5500
ပေါင် နှစ်ထောင့် လေးရာ ခြောက်ဆယ်	paun hnăt'aún lè-yá c'auq-s'eh	£2460

In effect, in Burmese you don't say "fifty pounds": you say "pounds five tens." The same goes for hundreds and for thousands, and for combinations of tens and hundreds and thousands — so long as the last figure is a 0.

In round number prices in everyday conversation people often omit the name of the currency unit if it is predictable. If you were in England and talking about the price of a cassette player, for example, in place of —

| ပေါင် သုံးဆယ် | paun thoùn-zeh | "pounds three tens" |

you might just say

| သုံးဆယ် | thoùn-zeh | "three tens" |

Your hearer would assume you meant £30. The same phrase in the US would be taken to mean $30. With unround numbers, however, people hardly ever omit the currency unit.

There is one exception to the round number rule. The number 10 has somehow got itself off the list of round numbers and is treated as an unround number. Instead of "pound one ten" (which you might have expected for a number ending in 0) Burmese says:

| ဆယ်ပေါင် | s'eh-baun | ten pounds |

as if ဆယ် s'eh were an unround number like 3 or 5 or 8.

* Do not confuse "round numbers" like 20, 300, 4000 and so on with "rounded numbers," which are approximations, and don't necessarily end in a 0:

    $30.85 is "rounded up" to $40.00

    £4.12 is "rounded down" to £5.00

    K74.95 is "rounded up" to K75

Here we are concerned with *round* numbers, not numbers *rounded* up or down.

Diphthongs in the roman transcription:
pronounce ei as in *vein,* ai as in *Thailand,* ou as in *though,* au as in *Sauerkraut.*

Common phrases

To make sure you complete the Common Phrases Supplement by the end of Part 1, learn Section 9 at about this point.

LESSON 27

Verbs in Which? questions.
Which road does he live in? — He lives in Bogyoke St.

Names and roads

The people named in this and subsequent lists in *BISL* bear no relation to individuals in real life, and any information provided about them (such as which road they live in) is entirely fictional and presented for the purpose of practice only. See the note in the Introduction, Section 2.

နာမည်	လမ်း	*name*	*road*
ဦးမြညွန့်	ဗိုလ်ချုပ်လမ်း	U Mya Nyunt	Bogyoke Street
ဗိုလ်မှူးဖေမြင့်	အနော်ရထာလမ်း	Major Pe Myint	Anawrahta Street
ကိုစံရွှေ	မဟာဗန္ဓုလလမ်း	Ko San Shwe	Maha Bandoola Street
ဦးချစ်စမ်း	ကုန်သည်လမ်း	U Chit San	Merchant Street
ဒေါ်အုံးကြည်	ကမ်းနားလမ်း	Daw Ohn Kyi	Strand Road
ဒေါက်တာဒေါ်မေစီဦး	ဗိုလ်အောင်ကျော်လမ်း	Dr. Daw May Si Oo	Bo Aung Kyaw Street
ဒေါ်မြမြရီ	ပန်းဆိုးတန်း	Daw Mya Mya Yi	Pansodan Street
မတင်တင်သန်း	ဆူးလေဘုရားလမ်း	Ma Tin Tin Than	Sule Pagoda Road
ဦးမောင်မောင်လွင်	ရွှေဘုံသာလမ်း	U Maung Maung Lwin	Shwebontha Street
ဒေါ်တင်ထွေး	ဘုရားလမ်း	Daw Tin Htway	Shwedagon Pagoda Rd.

nan-meh	*làn*	*name*	*road*
Ù Myá Nyún	Bo-jouq Làn	U Mya Nyunt	Bogyoke Street
Bo-hmù P'e Myín	Ănaw-yăt'a Làn	Major Pe Myint	Anawrahta Street
Ko San Shwe	Măha Ban-dú-lá Làn	Ko San Shwe	Maha Bandoola Street
Ù C'iq Sàn	Koun-dheh Làn	U Chit San	Merchant Street
Daw Oùn Ci	Kàn-nà Làn	Daw Ohn Kyi	Strand Road
Dr. Daw Me Si Ù	Bo Aun Jaw Làn	Dr. Daw May Si Oo	Bo Aung Kyaw Street
Daw Myá Myá Yi	Pàn-s'ò-dàn	Daw Mya Mya Yi	Pansodan Street
Má Tin Tin Thàn	S'ù-le P'ăyà Làn	Ma Tin Tin Than	Sule Pagoda Road
Ù Maun Maun Lwin	Shwe-boun-dha Làn	U Maung Maung Lwin	Shwebontha Street
Daw Tin T'wè	P'ăyà Làn	Daw Tin Htway	Shwedagon Pagoda Rd.

Diphthongs in the roman transcription:
pronounce ei as in *vein*, ai as in *Thailand*, ou as in *though*, au as in *Sauerkraut*.

New words

နေ–	to live	ne-
–တယ်	*verb suffix* (see note below on Tense)	-deh
–သ–	*variant form of* –တယ် -deh (see note on Weakening)	-dhă-
ဗိုလ်မှူး	Major (prefixed to a name)	Bo-hmù
ဒေါက်တာ	Doctor (prefixed to a name; from English)	Dauq-ta

Example sentences

S1: ဦးမြညွန့် �‌�‌ဘယ်လမ်းမှာ နေသလဲ။	Which road does U Mya Nyunt live in?	Ù Myá Nyún beh-làn-hma ne-dhălèh?
S2: ဦးမြညွန့် ဗိုလ်ချုပ်လမ်းမှာ နေပါတယ်။	U Mya Nyunt lives in Bogyoke Street.	Ù Myá Nyún Bo-jouq Làn-hma ne-ba-deh.
or:		
S2: ဗိုလ်ချုပ်လမ်းမှာ နေပါတယ်။	He lives in Bogyoke Street.	Bo-jouq Làn-hma ne-ba-deh.
or:		
S2: ဗိုလ်ချုပ်လမ်းမှာ။	In Bogyoke Street.	Bo-jouq Làn-hma

The three alternative answers for S2 are there to show that in response to a question like S1's, you may get a full answer, like S2's first version; or a minimal answer, like his third; or an answer of middling length, like his second. Choice of length is determined by the same factors as determine your choice in English.

A variation on the question above is:

S1: ဦးမြညွန့် ဘယ်မှာ နေသလဲ။	Where does U Mya Nyunt live?	Ù Myá Nyún beh-hma ne-dhălèh?

This shows that people may use plain ဘယ်မှာ beh-hma "in which [place]? where?" instead of —

ဘယ်လမ်းမှာ	"in which road?"	beh-làn-hma or
ဘယ်မြို့မှာ	"in which town?"	beh-myó-hma or
ဘယ်နိုင်ငံမှာ	"in which country?"	beh-nain-ngan-hma

and so on.

Models for the Exercises

Ex. 1: Names and addresses
Prompt: Ask which road U Mya Nyunt lives in.

L/S2: ဦးမြညွန့် ဘယ်လမ်းမှာ နေသလဲ။		Ù Myá Nyún beh làn-hma ne-dhălèh?
—or L/S2: ဦးမြညွန့် ဘယ်မှာ နေသလဲ။		Ù Myá Nyún beh-hma ne-dhălèh?
S1/L: ဗိုလ်ချုပ်လမ်းမှာ နေပါတယ်။		Bo-jouq Làn-hma ne-ba-deh.

Ex. 2

S1: ဦးမြညွန့် ဘယ်လမ်းမှာ နေသလဲ။		Ù Myá Nyún beh làn-hma ne-dhălèh?
L/S2: ဗိုလ်ချုပ်လမ်းမှာ နေပါတယ်။		Bo-jouq Làn-hma ne-ba-deh.

Diphthongs in the roman transcription:
pronounce ei as in *vein,* ai as in *Thailand,* ou as in *though,* au as in *Sauerkraut.*

In class: Exercises as above. Also use your own roads, or own towns. Explain using the person's name to mean "you" (anticipating practice on this point in Lesson 34):
L1: Mary ဘယ်လမ်းမှာ နေသလဲ။ = Which road do you (Mary) live in?

Notes

Grammar. This Lesson introduces a new formula for sentence structure. The formula for a Burmese sentence containing a verb is:

| NOUN | VERB+SUFFIX |

That is its most simplified form.
Often there are more nouns than one, so the formula expands to:

| NOUN1 | NOUN2 | NOUN3 | ... | VERB+SUFFIX |

As in *is* sentences, the nouns may have their own suffixes, so the formula must provide slots for those:

| NOUN1+SUFFIX | NOUN2+SUFFIX | NOUN3+SUFFIX | ... | VERB+SUFFIX |

And finally, there may be a sentence suffix crowning the whole structure:

| NOUN1+SUFFIX | NOUN2+SUFFIX | NOUN3+SUFFIX | ... | VERB+SUFFIX | STC SFX |

Examples:

NOUN1+SUFFIX	NOUN2+SUFFIX	VERB+SUFFIX	STC SFX
ဦးမြညွန့်	ဘယ်လမ်း+မှာ	နေ+သ–	လဲ။
Ù Myá Nyún	beh làn+hma	ne+dhă	-lèh?
U Mya Nyunt	which road+in	live+*pres/past**	*question*

"Which road does/did U Mya Nyunt live in?"

ဦးမြညွန့်+က	ဗိုလ်ချုပ်လမ်း+မှာ	နေ+တယ်။	–
Ù Myá Nyún+gá	Bo-jouq Làn+hma	ne+deh.	–
U Mya Nyunt	Bogyoke Street+in	live+*pres/past**	–

"U Mya Nyunt lives/lived in Bogyoke Street."

* As the suffix –တယ်/–သ (-deh/-dhă) indicates present or past time we "translate" it here as *"pres/past."*

Points to note
• Pronouns. Notice that in S2's second answer in the Example sentences, the middle-length one, there is no word in Burmese that corresponds to the "he" in the English. Burmese does have words corresponding to "he," "she," "it," "they" and their like, but in general they are only used when there is a danger that your listener might not be sure who you are talking about. When it is quite clear who you are talking about, as it is in these little exchanges, it is much more natural and common to leave them out.

Diphthongs in the roman transcription:
pronounce ei as in *vein*, ai as in *Thailand*, ou as in *though*, au as in *Sauerkraut*.

• Word order. In Burmese sentences the verb is placed after all the nouns. If there is a question word (who? where? how much? and so on) it usually comes after the other nouns, immediately before the verb. And the noun you are talking about usually comes before the noun which is news to your hearer. Consider the following two sentences:

A. ဦးမြညွန့်   ဗိုလ်ချုပ်လမ်း+မှာ   နေ+တယ်॥
    Ù Myá Nyún   Bo-jouq Làn+hma   ne+deh.
    U Mya Nyunt   Bogyoke Street+in   live+*pres/past*

B. ဗိုလ်ချုပ်လမ်း+မှာ   ဦးမြညွန့်   နေ+တယ်॥
    Bo-jouq Làn+hma   Ù Myá Nyún   ne+deh.
    Bogyoke Street+in   U Mya Nyunt   live+*pres/past*

Both mean:

"U Mya Nyunt lives/lived in Bogyoke Street."

but in sentence A NOUN1 is U Mya Nyunt, and in Sentence B NOUN1 is "in Bogyoke Street." The difference between the two (as a general rule) can be indicated by paraphrasing them as follows:

Sentence A: "We were talking about where U Mya Nyunt lives: well, I can tell you that it's in Bogyoke Street."

Sentence B: "We were talking about who lives in Bogyoke Street: well, I can tell you that it's U Mya Nyunt."

The paraphrases exaggerate the difference between the two sentences, but they help to point to the difference of focus between them.

• Tense. Verb suffix –တယ် -deh: is used with verbs when you are talking about events that take place regularly (like "I get up at six"), or situations that obtain now (like "He lives in Maymyo"), or events that took place in the past (like "I met him at a wedding reception"). So if you are translating a Burmese sentence ending in –တယ် -deh into a language like English, which makes finer distinctions in tense and aspect, you need to study the context to help you decide which of the several tenses available in English would be the most appropriate.

• Pronunciation. The suffix –တယ် -deh is extremely frequent and predictable, so it is often not pronounced very clearly. Particularly in fast speech it may sound like /–အယ်/ -eh, or it may be shortened so much as to be barely audible.

• Weakening. When the suffix –တယ် -deh is followed by –လဲ -lèh "question," it changes to –သ –dhă. Its vowel –ယ် -eh weakens, and the consonant တ– d- changes to သ– dh-. In short:

–တယ် + –လဲ ⟹ –သလဲ (-deh + -lèh ⟹ -dhălèh).

• Person. Verbs in many European languages change their form for different persons: "I *am*" vs. "you *are*" vs. "she *is*" and so on. One of the perks of learning Burmese is that you do not have to learn all that part of the grammar. Burmese verbs do not alter their form for person; so နေတယ် ne-deh is the same whether you are saying "he lives," "you live," "we live," or anyone else lives. Verbs in European languages also change their form for different tenses ("he takes," "he will take," "he took," "he has taken," and so on). As noted above, the form of the Burmese verb that means "live/s" may also mean "lived," so you don't have to learn different forms for present and past tenses either. Rejoice that you are exempted from learning so many pages of conjugations.

- VERB+SUFFIX. Unlike nouns, verbs in Burmese are nearly always used with a suffix of some kind after them. Besides –တယ် (-deh) there are about ten other suffixes that are used in this position in the sentence — though –တယ် (-deh) is by far the most commonly used member of the set. For that reason, when we list a verb in a vocabulary here, we write a hyphen after it, as a reminder that in connected speech you'll hardly ever find it in this naked state. When Burmese speakers quote a verb, as they do when you ask them, for example, "What's the Burmese for *to live*?", rather than just saying နေ– (ne-) you'll find they add the suffix –တယ် (-deh) and say နေတယ် (ne-deh).

- Polite suffix. In sentences without verbs (*is* sentences) the polite suffix –ပါ (-ba) comes, as you know, at the end of the sentence. Example:

ဒါက	ဦးမြညွန့်.	–ပါ။
Da-gá	Ù Myá Nyún	-ba.
That-as for	U Mya Nyunt	*polite*

       "That is U Mya Nyunt."

In sentences *with* verbs the polite suffix –ပါ (-ba) is incorporated into the verb. So (given appropriate social circumstances) the two sentences used above to illustrate the formula will have the polite suffix added, and will then take the form —

ဦးမြညွန့်.	ဘယ်လမ်း+မှာ	နေပါ+သ–	လဲ။
Ù Myá Nyún	beh làn+hma	ne-ba+dhă	-lèh?
U Mya Nyunt	which road+in	live-*polite*+*pres/past*	*question*

       "Which road does/did U Mya Nyunt live in?"

ဦးမြညွန့်.	ဗိုလ်ချုပ်လမ်း+မှာ	နေပါ+တယ်။	–
Ù Myá Nyún	Bo-jouq Làn+hma	ne-ba+deh.	–
U Mya Nyunt	Bogyoke Street+in	live-*polite*+*pres/past*	–

       "U Mya Nyunt lives/lived in Bogyoke Street."

In practice, people rarely use –ပါ -ba in questions, so in the Exercises we shall be practising questions *without* the polite suffix; but in statements, particularly in the circumstances you are likely to find yourself in when you first start using Burmese, people do use –ပါ -ba frequently, so when you are practising statements, we shall treat the polite suffix as the norm. This is why, in the Example sentences above, there is a –ပါ -ba in the answer but not in the question.

His (Mr. Judson's) anxiety to preach the unsearchable riches of Christ to the Burmans, had induced him to apply more closely to the study of the language than an eastern climate would allow. This circumstance, together with the want of exercise and a proper diet, reduced him to an alarming state of debility and nervous affection.

From: *An Account of the American Baptist Mission to the Burman Empire*, by Ann H. Judson, 1823, London, Butterworth, p. 61

Diphthongs in the roman transcription:
pronounce ei as in *vein*, ai as in *Thailand*, ou as in *though*, au as in *Sauerkraut*.

LESSON 28

Prices in pounds combined with pence.
How much is nº 1? — It's six pounds 45 pence.

Price list

Prices in pounds and pence

1.	£6.45 p.		6.	£50.80 p.
2.	£9.99 p.		7.	£20.10 p.
3.	£45.40 p.		8.	£42.25 p.
4.	£77.60 p.		9.	£13.68 p.
5.	£134.75 p.		10.	£10.20 p.

Examples of prices in two denominations

ရှစ်ဆယ့် ခြောက်ပေါင် လေးဆယ့် ငါးပြား	£86.45	shiq-s'éh c'auq-paun lè-zéh ngà-byà
ပေါင်ရှစ်ဆယ် လေးဆယ့်ငါးပြား	£80.45	paun shiq-s'eh lè-zéh ngà-byà
ပေါင်ရှစ်ဆယ် ပြားလေးဆယ်	£80.40	paun shiq-s'eh pyà lè-zeh
ရှစ်ဆယ့် ခြောက်ပေါင် ပြားလေးဆယ်	£86.40	shiq-s'éh c'auq-paun pyà lè-zeh
ရှစ်ဆယ့် ခြောက်ပေါင် ဆယ်ပြား	£86.10	shiq-s'éh c'auq-paun s'eh-byà
ဆယ်ပေါင် ဆယ်ပြား	£10.10	s'eh-baun s'eh-byà
ဆယ်ပေါင် ပြားလေးဆယ်	£10.40	s'eh-baun pyà lè-zeh
ပေါင်ရှစ်ဆယ် ဆယ်ပြား	£80.10	paun shiq-s'eh s'eh-byà

Round numbers and Ten. Note that the Round Number Rule applies to both pounds and pence independently. And that 10 is treated as an unround number with both denominations.

Joining with –နဲ့ -néh "and." In any price in two denominations you may find a –နဲ့ -néh "and" suffixed to any component but the last (compare the use of –နဲ့ -néh "and" in two-figure and three-figure numbers: Lessons 14 and 16); for example:

Burmese	Price	Transcription
ပေါင်ရှစ်ဆယ်နဲ့ လေးဆယ့်ငါးပြား	£80.45	paun shiq-s'eh-néh lè-zéh ngà-byà
ရှစ်ဆယ်နဲ့ ခြောက်ပေါင် ပြားလေးဆယ်	£86.40	shiq-s'éh-néh c'auq-paun pyà lè-zeh
ရှစ်ဆယ့် ခြောက်ပေါင်နဲ့ ပြားလေးဆယ်	£86.40	shiq-s'éh c'auq-paun-néh pyà lè-zeh
ရှစ်ဆယ်နဲ့ ခြောက်ပေါင်နဲ့ ပြားလေးဆယ်	£86.40	shiq-s'éh-néh c'auq-paun-néh pyà lè-zeh

In the Exercises we shall be using the version without the –နဲ့ -néh "and."

Models for the Exercises

Ex. 1: Prices
S1: နံပါတ်(၁)က ခြောက်ပေါင်
လေးဆယ့် ငါးပြားလား။

L/S2: ဟုတ်ကဲ့။ ခြောက်ပေါင်
လေးဆယ့် ငါးပြားပါ။

Nan-baq-tiq-ká c'auq-paun
lè-zéh ngà-byà-là?

Houq-kéh. C'auq-paun
lè-zéh ngà-byà-ba.

Dipthongs in the roman transcription:
pronounce ei as in *vein*, ai as in *Thailand*, ou as in *though*, au as in *Sauerkraut*.

In class: Exercises as above. Also use menu, price list, catalogue.

Common phrases

To make sure you complete the Common Phrases Supplement by the end of Part 1, learn Section 10 at about this point.

LESSON 29

Verbs in *Yes/No* questions.
Does he live in Bogyoke St? — Yes, he does/ No, he doesn't.

Names and addresses

နာမည်နဲ့ လိပ်စာ	*name and* *address*	*nan-meh-néh* *leiq-sa*

ဦးမြည့်နွန့်
  ၈၈ ဗိုလ်ချုပ်လမ်း
	U Mya Nyunt
	  88 Bogyoke Street
		Ù Myá Nyún
		  88 Bo-jouq Làn

ဗိုလ်မှူးဖေမြင့်
  ၁၂၆ အနော်ရထာလမ်း
	Major Pe Myint
	  126 Anawrahta Street
		Bo-hmù P'e Mýin
		  126 Ănaw-yăt'a Làn

ကိုစံရွှေ
  ၃၅ မဟာဗန္ဓုလလမ်း
	Ko San Shwe
	  35 Maha Bandoola St
		Ko San Shwe
		  35 Măha Ban-dú-lá Làn

ဦးချစ်စမ်း
  ၂၇၃ ကုန်သည်လမ်း
	U Chit San
	  273 Merchant Street
		Ù C'iq Sàn
		  273 Koun-dheh Làn

ဒေါ်အုံးကြည်
  ၂၇ ကမ်းနားလမ်း
	Daw Ohn Kyi
	  27 Strand Road
		Daw Oùn Ci
		  27 Kàn-nà Làn

ဒေါက်တာဒေါ်မေစီဦး
  ၃ ဗိုလ်အောင်ကျော်လမ်း
	Dr. Daw May Si Oo
	  3 Bo Aung Kyaw Street
		Dr. Daw Me Si Ù
		  3 Bo Aun Jaw Làn

ဒေါ်မြမြရီ
  ၃၉၀ ပန်းဆိုးတန်း
	Daw Mya Mya Yi
	  390 Pansodan Street
		Daw Myá Myá Yi
		  390 Pàn-s'ò-dàn

မတင်တင်သန်း
  ၂၈၇ ဆူးလေဘုရားလမ်း
	Ma Tin Tin Than
	  287 Sule Pagoda Road
		Má Tin Tin Thàn
		  287 S'ù-le P'ăyà Làn

ဦးမောင်မောင်လွင်
  ၁၄ ရွှေဘုံသာလမ်း
	U Maung Maung Lwin
	  14 Shwebontha Street
		Ù Maun Maun Lwin
		  14 Shwe-boun-dha Làn

ဒေါ်တင်ထွေး
  ၇၂ ဘုရားလမ်း
	Daw Tin Htway
	  72 Shwedagon Pagoda Rd
		Daw Tin T'wè
		  72 P'ăyà Làn

New words

မ–	not (prefix for verbs)	mă–
–ဘူး	*verb suffix: "negative"* [1]	-bù
အိမ်	house	ein
အိမ်နံပါတ်	house number	ein-nan-baq
လိပ်စာ	address	leiq-sa

Diphthongs in the roman transcription:
pronounce ei as in *vein,* ai as in *Thailand,* ou as in *though,* au as in *Sauerkraut.*

1. This suffix is in the same class as –တယ် (-teh/-deh), in that it is attached to a verb at the end of a sentence. It differs from –တယ် (-teh/-deh) in that it is only used with verbs that are negated (that is, when they have the prefix မ– (mǎ-) "not" in front of them), and although it is mostly used about the present and the past, it can (unlike တယ် (-teh/-deh)) also be used about the future ("will not [verb]").

Addresses

Many addresses in Burma take the form shown in the list above.
Variants include the following words:

အမှတ်	number	ăhmaq

[An alternative word for နံပါတ် (nan-baq), common in writing, and sometimes used in speech.]

ရပ် or ရပ်ကွက်	quarter, neighbourhood, ward	yaq or yaq-kweq
မြို့နယ်	township	myó-neh

Examples:

ဒေါ်ကြည်အေး၊ (၁၄) သီတာလမ်း၊ ရေအေးကွင်းရပ်၊ တောင်ကြီးမြို့။
ဦးဘရှင်၊ အိမ်အမှတ် (၇) ဗဟိုရ်စည်ဈေးလမ်း၊ လမ်းမတော်မြို့နယ်၊ ရန်ကုန်မြို့။
ဒေါ်သိန်းဆွေ၊ အိမ်အမှတ် (၁၆) အောင်ဇေယျလမ်း၊ (၄)ရပ်ကွက်၊ သုံးခွမြို့။
ဦးကျင်စိန်၊ (၁၀၅) ကွင်းကျောင်းလမ်း၊ အလုံမြို့နယ်၊ ရန်ကုန်မြို့။
မအေးအေးဝင်း၊ အမှတ် (၆၄) ၇၅–လမ်း၊ စိတ္တရမဟီရပ် မန္တလေးမြို့။

Daw Kyi Aye, 14 Thida Road, Ye-e-gwin Qr, Taung-gyi.
U Ba Shin, 7 Baho-si Zay Street, Lanmadaw Township, Rangoon.
Daw Thain Swe, 16 Aung-zay-ya Road, Quarter 4, Thongwa.
U Kyin Sein, 105 Kwin-gyaung Street, Ahlone Township, Rangoon.
Ma Aye Aye Winn, 64, 75th Street, Seittaramahi Quarter, Mandalay.

Daw Ci È, 14 Thi-da Làn, Ye-è-gwìn Yaq, Taun-jì Myó.
Ù Bá Shin, Ein-ăhmaq-7 Băho-si Zè Làn, Làn-mădaw Myó-neh, Yan-gon Myó.
Daw Thèin S'we, Ein-ăhmaq-16 Aun-ze-yá Làn, 4 Yaq-kweq, Thòun-gwá Myó.
Ù Cin Sein, 105 Kwìn-jaùn Làn, Ăloun Myó-neh, Yan-gon Myó.
Má È È Wìn, Ăhmaq-64, 75 Làn, Seiq-tărá-măhi Yaq, Màn-dălè Myó.

Example sentences

S1: ကိုစံရွှေ မဟာဗန္ဓုလလမ်းမှာ နေသလား။	Does Ko San Shwe live in Maha Bandoola St?	Ko San Shwe Măha Ban-dú-lá Làn-hma ne-dhălà?
S2: ဟုတ်ကဲ့။ နေပါတယ်။	Yes. He does.	Houq-kéh. Ne-ba-deh.
S1: ကိုစံရွှေ ကုန်သည်လမ်းမှာ နေသလား။	Does Ko San Shwe live in Merchant Street?	Ko San Shwe Koun-dheh Làn-hma ne-dhălà?
S2: မနေပါဘူး။ မဟာဗန္ဓုလ လမ်းမှာ နေပါတယ်။	No. He lives in Maha Bandoola Street.	Măne-ba-bù. Măha Ban-dú-lá Làn-hma ne-ba-deh.

Diphthongs in the roman transcription:
pronounce ei as in *vein*, ai as in *Thailand*, ou as in *though*, au as in *Sauerkraut*.

For answers of varying fullness, see the Note below.

Notice that in verb sentences the answer "No" is not မဟုတ်ပါဘူး (măhouq-pa-bù) as it was in "is" sentences. To answer "No" to verb sentence questions you re-use the verb of the question and say, in effect, "Does not [verb]."

Models for the Exercises

Ex. 1: Names and addresses
S1: ကိုစံရွှေ မဟာဗန္ဓုလလမ်းမှာ နေသလား။   Ko San Shwe Măha Ban-dú-lá Làn-hma ne-dhălà?

L/S2: ဟုတ်ကဲ့။ နေပါတယ်။   Houq-kéh. Ne-ba-deh.

or L/S2: မနေပါဘူး။ … as the case may be.   Măne-ba-bù.

Ex. 2: Prompt: Ask if Ko San Shwe lives in Merchant Street.
L/S2: ကိုစံရွှေ ကုန်သည်လမ်းမှာ နေသလား။   Ko San Shwe Koun-dheh Làn-hma ne-dhălà?

S1: မနေပါဘူး။ —   Măne-ba-bù. —
မဟာဗန္ဓုလလမ်းမှာ နေပါတယ်။   Măha Ban-dú-lá Làn-hma ne-ba-deh.

Ex. 3
S1: ဗိုလ်မှူးဖေမြင့် ဘယ်မှာ နေသလဲ။   Bo-hmù P'e Myín beh-hma ne-dhălèh?
L/S2: အိမ်နံပါတ်–၁၂၆ အနော်ရထာလမ်းမှာ   Ein nan-baq-126 Ănaw-yăt'a Làn-hma
နေပါတယ်။   ne-ba-deh.

Ex. 4
L/S2: ဦးမြညွန့် ဘယ်မြို့မှာ နေသလဲ။   Ù Myá Nyún beh-myó-hma ne-dhălèh?
— or L/S2: ဦးမြညွန့် ဘယ်မှာ နေသလဲ။   Ù Myá Nyún beh-hma ne-dhălèh?
S1: မြစ်ကြီးနားမှာ နေပါတယ်။   Myiq-cì-nà-hma ne-ba-deh.
L: writes down the answer (in script or transcription or English).

Form for Ex. 4
The Key is at the end of the Lesson.

နာမည်	nan-meh	town
ဦးမြညွန့်	Ù Myá Nyún	…
ဗိုလ်မှူးဖေမြင့်	Bo-hmù P'e Myín	…
ကိုစံရွှေ	Ko San Shwe	…
ဦးချစ်စမ်း	Ù C'iq Sàn	…
ဒေါ်အုံးကြည်	Daw Oùn Ci	…
ဒေါက်တာဒေါ်မေစီဦး	Dauq-ta Daw Me Si Ù	…
ဒေါ်မြမြရီ	Daw Myá Myá Yi	…
မတင်တင်သန်း	Má Tin Tin Thàn	…
ဦးမောင်မောင်လွင်	Ù Maun Maun Lwin	…
ဒေါ်တင်ထွေး	Daw Tin T'wè	…

Diphthongs in the roman transcription:
pronounce ei as in *vein*, ai as in *Thailand*, ou as in *though*, au as in *Sauerkraut*.

Ex. 5 For written answer: not on the tape.

The words in the following questions and answers have been split up and jumbled. Rearrange them to form meaningful sentences. There is a Key to this Exercise at the end of the Lesson. Don't forget that you may find it helpful to copy the words onto separate slips of paper and do your reordering by sliding the slips around.

S1: – နေသလဲ – ဘယ်လမ်းမှာ – ကိုစံရွှေ
S2: – နေပါတယ် – မဟာဗန္ဓုလလမ်းမှာ
S1: – နေသ – ကမ်းနားလမ်းမှာ – လား – ဒေါ်အုံးကြည်
S2: – နေပါ – ကမ်းနား – တယ် – လမ်းမှာ – ဟုတ်ကဲ့
S1: – မှာ – ဒေါ်မြမြရီ – သ – ဗိုလ်အောင်ကျော်လမ်း – နေ – လား
S2: – ဘူး – မနေပါ – တယ် – နေပါ – ပန်းဆိုးတန်းမှာ

Ex. 5 in Lesson 29 (roman)

S1: — ne-dhălèh — beh-làn-hma — Ko San Shwe
S2: — ne-ba-deh — Măha Ban-dú-lá Làn-hma
S1: — ne-dhă — Kàn-nà Làn-hma — là — Daw Oùn Ci
S2: — ne-ba — Kàn-nà — deh — Làn-hma — Houq-kéh
S1: — hma — Daw Myá Myá Yi — dhă — Bo Aun Jaw Làn — ne — là
S2: — bù — Măne-ba — deh — ne-ba — Pàn-s'ò-dàn-hma

In class: Exercises as above. Also use your own roads, or own towns, or own addresses, as for Lesson 27. Ask around for roads and other details, and compile a list. Then check the list to see if everyone got the names and roads right.

Notes

Grammar. The structure of the new sentences in this Lesson is the same as in the preceding Lesson:

NOUN1+SUFFIX	NOUN2+SUFFIX	VERB+SUFFIX	STC SFX
ကိုစံရွှေ	မဟာဗန္ဓုလလမ်း+မှာ	နေ+သ–	–လား။
Ko San Shwe	Măha Ban-dú-lá Làn+hma	ne+dhă	-là?
Ko San Shwe	Maha Bandoola Street+in	live+*pres/past*	*question*

"Does/did Ko San Shwe live in Maha Bandoola Street?"

ကိုစံရွှေ	မဟာဗန္ဓုလလမ်း+မှာ	နေပါ+တယ်။	–
Ko San Shwe	Măha Ban-dú-lá Làn+hma	ne-ba+deh.	–
Ko San Shwe	Maha Bandoola Street+in	live-*polite+pres/past*	–

"Ko San Shwe lives/lived in Maha Bandoola Street."

ကိုစံရွှေ	ကမ်းနားလမ်း+မှာ	မနေပါ+ဘူး။	–
Ko San Shwe	Kàn-nà Làn+hma	măne-ba+bù.	–
Ko San Shwe	Strand Road+in	not-live-*polite+neg.*	–

"Ko San Shwe does/did not live in Strand Road."

Notice that the verb is negated by the prefix မ– mă- "not," and that the verb suffix for a negated verb is not –တယ် -deh as before, but –ဘူး -bù.

Length of answer. For clarity in the Example sentences above, only one of the possible options is shown. In practice you will find people using other options as under:

Question:

S1: ကိုစံရွှေ မဟာဗန္ဓုလလမ်းမှာ နေသလား။	Does Ko San Shwe live in Maha Bandoola St?	Ko San Shwe Măha Ban-dú-lá Làn-hma ne-dhălà?

Answer Yes:

S2: ကိုစံရွှေ မဟာဗန္ဓုလလမ်းမှာ နေပါတယ်။	Ko San Shwe does live in Maha Bandoola St.	Ko San Shwe Măha Ban-dú-lá Làn-hma ne-ba-deh.
S2: မဟာဗန္ဓုလလမ်းမှာ နေပါတယ်။	He does live in Maha Bandoola Street.	Măha Ban-dú-lá Làn-hma ne-ba-deh.
S2: နေပါတယ်။	He does.	Ne-ba-deh.

Any of the above answers may be preceded by ဟုတ်ကဲ့ houq-kéh, so for the *Yes* answer there is a further set of options:

S2: ဟုတ်ကဲ့။ ကိုစံရွှေ မဟာဗန္ဓုလ လမ်းမှာ နေပါတယ်။	Yes. Ko San Shwe does live in Maha Bandoola Street.	Houq-kéh. Ko San Shwe Măha Ban-dú-lá Làn-hma ne-ba-deh.
S2: ဟုတ်ကဲ့။ မဟာဗန္ဓုလလမ်းမှာ နေပါတယ်။	Yes. He does live in Maha Bandoola Street.	Houq-kéh. Măha Ban-dú-lá Làn-hma ne-ba-deh.
S2: ဟုတ်ကဲ့။ နေပါတယ်။	Yes. He does.	Houq-kéh. Ne-ba-deh.

Finally a short answer may be just —

S2: ဟုတ်ကဲ့။	Yes.	Houq-kéh.

Answer No:

S2: ကိုစံရွှေ ကမ်းနားလမ်းမှာ မနေပါဘူး။	Ko San Shwe doesn't live in Strand Road.	Ko San Shwe Kàn-nà Làn-hma măne-ba-bù.
S2: ကမ်းနားလမ်းမှာ မနေပါဘူး။	He doesn't live in Strand Road.	Kàn-nà Làn-hma măne-ba-bù.
S2: မနေပါဘူး။	He doesn't.	Măne-ba-bù.

Each of these *No* answers would of course be followed by the correct street (မဟာဗန္ဓုလလမ်းမှာ နေပါတယ် Măha Ban-dú-lá Làn-hma ne-ba-deh), if the person answering knows it.

Diphthongs in the roman transcription: pronounce ei as in *vein,* ai as in *Thailand,* ou as in *though,* au as in *Sauerkraut.*

Keys to the Exercises

Key to Ex. 4 (script)

နာမည်	မြို့	*name*	*town*
ဦးမြညွန့်	မြစ်ကြီးနား	U Mya Nyunt	Myitkyina
ဗိုလ်မှူးဖေမြင့်	မေမြို့	Major Pe Myint	Maymyo
ကိုစံရွှေ	မန္တလေး	Ko San Shwe	Mandalay
ဦးချစ်စမ်း	စစ်ကိုင်း	U Chit San	Sagaing
ဒေါ်အုံးကြည်	ပုဂံ	Daw Ohn Kyi	Pagan = Bagan
ဒေါက်တာဒေါ်မေစီဦး	သာစည်	Dr. Daw Me Si Oo	Thazi
ဒေါ်မြမြရီ	တောင်ကြီး	Daw Mya Mya Yi	Taunggyi
မတင်တင်သန်း	ပြည်	Ma Tin Tin Than	Prome = Pyi/Pyay
ဦးမောင်မောင်လွင်	ရေနံချောင်း	U Maung Maung Lwin	Yenangyaung
ဒေါ်တင်ထွေး	သံတွဲ	Daw Tin Htway	Sandoway = Thandwe

Key to Ex. 4 (transcription)

nan-meh	*myó*	*name*	*town*
Ù Myá Nyún	Myiq-cì-nà	U Mya Nyunt	Myitkyina
Bo-hmù P'e Myín	Me-myó	Major Pe Myint	Maymyo
Ko San Shwe	Màn-dằlè	Ko San Shwe	Mandalay
Ù C'iq Sàn	Sằgaìn	U Chit San	Sagaing
Daw Oùn Ci	Pằgan	Daw Ohn Kyi	Pagan = Bagan
Dr. Daw Me Si Ù	Tha-zi	Dr. Daw Me Si Oo	Thazi
Daw Myá Myá Yi	Taun-jì	Daw Mya Mya Yi	Taunggyi
Má Tin Tin Thàn	Pye	Ma Tin Tin Than	Prome = Pyi /Pyay
Ù Maun Maun Lwin	Ye-nan-jaùn	U Maung Maung Lwin	Yenangyaung
Daw Tin T'wè	Than-dwèh	Daw Tin Htway	Sandoway = Thandwe

Key to Ex. 5 in Lesson 29

S1: — ကိုစံရွှေ — ဘယ်လမ်းမှာ — နေသလဲ။
    S2: — မဟာဗန္ဓုလလမ်းမှာ — နေပါတယ်။
S1: — ဒေါ်အုံးကြည် — ကမ်းနားလမ်းမှာ — နေသ — လား။
    S2: — ဟုတ်ကဲ့။ — ကမ်းနား — လမ်းမှာ — နေပါ — တယ်။
S1: — ဒေါ်မြမြရီ — ဗိုလ်အောင်ကျော်လမ်း — မှာ — နေ — သ — လား။
    S2: — မနေပါ — ဘူး။ ပန်းဆိုးတန်းမှာ နေပါ — တယ်။

Key to Ex. 5 in Lesson 29 (roman)

S1: — Ko San Shwe — beh-làn-hma — ne-dhằlèh
    S2: — Mằha Ban-dú-lá Làn-hma — ne-ba-deh
S1: — Daw Oùn Ci — Kàn-nà Làn-hma — ne-dhă — là
    S2: — Houq-kéh — Kàn-nà — Làn-hma — ne-ba — deh
S1: — Daw Myá Myá Yi — Bo Aun Jaw Làn — hma — ne — dhă — là
    S2: — Mằne-ba — bù — Pàn-s'ò-dàn-hma — ne-ba — deh

Diphthongs in the roman transcription:
pronounce ei as in *vein*, ai as in *Thailand*, ou as in *though*, au as in *Sauerkraut*.

LESSON 30

Counting: practice with numbered streets.
Where does U Sein Myint live? — He lives at 180, 84th St.

Numbered streets

Written	Spoken	English	transcription
Unround numbers			
၈၄-လမ်း	ရှစ်ဆယ့် လေး-လမ်း	84th Street	Shiq-s'éh lè-Làn
၇၅-လမ်း	ခုနစ်ဆယ့် ငါး-လမ်း	75th Street	Shiq-s'éh ngà-Làn
၃၂-လမ်း	သုံးဆယ့် နှစ်လမ်း	32nd Street	Thoùn-zéh hnăLàn
Round numbers			
၃၀-လမ်း	လမ်းသုံးဆယ်	30th Street	Làn Thoùn-zeh
၄၀-လမ်း	လမ်းလေးဆယ်	40th Street	Làn Lè-zeh
၂၀-လမ်း	လမ်းနှစ်ဆယ်	20th Street	Làn Hnăs'eh
Ten			
၁၀-လမ်း	ဆယ်လမ်း	10th Street	S'eh Làn

Some of the street names in both Rangoon and Mandalay are numbers: 32nd Street, 20th Street and so on. Like all objects that are counted, numbered streets too are subject to the Round Number Rule, including the exceptional status (honorary unround) of 10. See the examples above.

Although the *spoken* forms of the names of numbered streets follow the rules given above, the *written* forms (as seen on signposts) all keep to the same order (number followed by unit) whether they are round numbers or not. Hence the two columns in the examples above.

Names and addresses

ဦးစိန်မြင့်	အမှတ်–၁၈၀။ ၈၄-လမ်း	U Sein Myint	N° 180, 84th Street
ဦးအောင်သိန်း	အမှတ်–၁၆၀။ ၇၅-လမ်း	U Aung Thein	N° 160, 75th Street
Dr. ဦးခင်မောင်ညွန့်	အမှတ်–၁၃၄။ ၄၂-လမ်း	Dr. U Khin Maung Nyunt	N° 134, 42nd Street
ဒေါ်လှိုင်လှိုင်ချို	အမှတ်–၁၂။ ၃၀-လမ်း	Daw Hlaing Hlaing Cho	N° 12, 30th Street
ဒေါ်ကြည်ကြည်လှ	အမှတ်–၄၉။ ၈၀-လမ်း	Daw Kyi Kyi Hla	N° 49, 80th Street
ဒေါ်ခင်လေး	အမှတ်–၆၈။ ၁၀-လမ်း	Daw Khin Lay	N° 68, 10th Street

Ù Sein Myín	Ăhmaq Tăyá shiq-s'eh, Shiq-s'éh lè Làn
Ù Aun Theìn	Ăhmaq Tăyá c'auq-s'eh, K'un-năs'éh ngà Làn
Dauq-ta Ù K'in Maun Nyún	Ăhmaq Tăyá thoùn-zéh lè, Lè-zéh hnă-Làn
Daw Hlain Hlain C'o	Ăhmaq S'éh-hniq, Làn Thoùn-zeh
Daw Ci Ci Hlá	Ăhmaq Lè-zéh kò, Làn Shiq-s'eh
Daw K'in Lè	Ăhmaq C'auq-s'éh shiq, S'eh Làn

Diphthongs in the roman transcription:
pronounce ei as in *vein*, ai as in *Thailand*, ou as in *though*, au as in *Sauerkraut*.

Example addresses

ဦးစိန်မြင့် ဘယ်မှာ နေသလဲ။

Where does U Sein Myint live?

Ù Sein Myín beh-hma ne-dhălèh?

အမှတ် တရာ့ ရှစ်ဆယ်၊ ရှစ်ဆယ့် လေးလမ်းမှာ နေပါတယ်။

He lives at Nº 180, 84th Street.

Ăhmaq Tăyá shiq-s'eh, Shiq-s'éh lè Làn-hma ne-ba-deh.

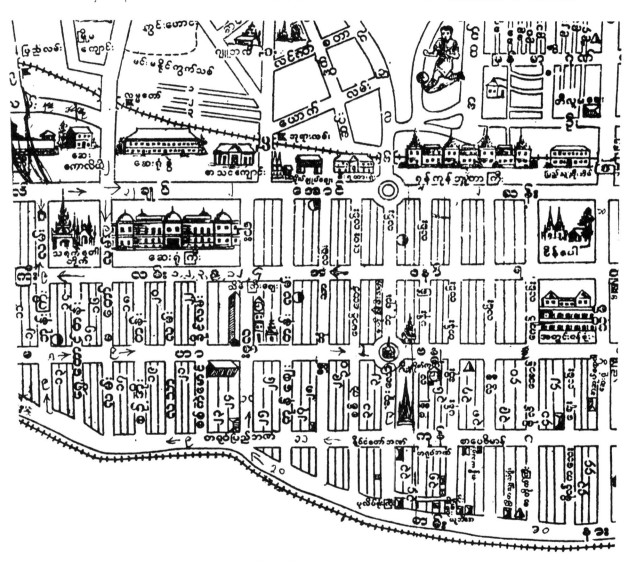

Part of a street plan of
Rangoon (Yangon), showing numbered streets

Models for the Exercises

Ex. 1: Using the list below.
Prompt: What's the street at A?
L/S2: သုံးဆယ့် သုံးလမ်း။

Thoùn-zéh thoùn Làn.

Diphthongs in the roman transcription:
pronounce ei as in *vein,* ai as in *Thailand,* ou as in *though,* au as in *Sauerkraut.*

List for Ex. 1

A	33rd Street	E	30th Street
B	42nd Street	F	10th Street
C	85th Street	G	16th Street
D	80th Street	H	70th Street

Ex. 2. Using the list of names and addresses above.

S1: ဦးစိန်မြင့် ဘယ်မှာ နေသလဲ။   Ù Sein Myín beh-hma ne-dhălèh?

L/S2: အမှတ် တရာ ရှစ်ဆယ်၊   Ăhmaq tăyá shiq-s'eh,

    ရှစ်ဆယ့် လေးလမ်းမှာ နေပါတယ်။   shiq-s'éh lè Làn-hma ne-ba-deh.

In class: Exercises as above.

For prices: also use menus, price lists, catalogues and the like.

For addresses: also use Learners' own addresses, or addresses from a local directory.

Common phrases

To make sure you complete the Common Phrases Supplement by the end of Part 1, learn Section 11 at about this point.

LESSON 31

Who comes from where.
What country does he come from? — He comes from India.

Names and countries

နာမည်	နိုင်ငံ	name	country
ဒေါက်တာ ဆင်း	အိန္ဒိယနိုင်ငံ	Dr. Singh	India
မစ္စတာ ရာမန်	ဘင်္ဂလားဒေ့ရှ်နိုင်ငံ	Mr. Rahman	Bangladesh
ဦးတင်လှိုင်	မြန်မာနိုင်ငံ	U Tin Hlaing	Burma/Myanmar
မစ္စတာ တွန်ချန်	ထိုင်းနိုင်ငံ	Mr. Tongchan	Thailand
မစ္စတာ မိုဟာမက်	မလေးရှားနိုင်ငံ	Mr. Mohamed	Malaysia
မစ္စတာ ဖမ်မန်ဒီယမ်	ဗီယက်နမ်နိုင်ငံ	Mr. Pham Man Diem	Vietnam
မစ္စက် ခရုဇ်	ဖိလစ်ပိုင်နိုင်ငံ	Mrs. Cruz	Philippines
မစ္စတာ ထွန်	တရုပ်နိုင်ငံ	Mr. Tung	China
မစ္စတာ ဆူကာမိုတို	ဂျပန်နိုင်ငံ	Mr. Tsukamoto	Japan

nan-meh	nain-gan	name	road
Dauq-ta S'ìn	Ein-dí-yá Nain-gan	Dr. Singh	India
Myiq-săta Ra-man	Bin-gălà-désh Nain-gan	Mr. Rahman	Bangladesh
Ù Tin Hlain	Myan-ma Nain-gan	U Tin Hlaing	Burma/Myanmar
Myiq-săta Tun C'an	T'aìn Nain-gan	Mr. Tongchan	Thailand
Myiq-săta Mo-ha-meq	Mălè-shà Nain-gan	Mr. Mohamed Amir	Malaysia
Myiq-săta P'an-man-di-yan	Bi-yeq-nan Nain-gan	Mr. Pham Man Diem	Vietnam
Myiq-seq K'ărú	P'í-liq-pain Nain-gan	Mr. Cruz	Philippines
Myiq-săta T'un	Tăyouq Nain-gan	Mr. Tung	China
Myiq-săta S'u-ka-mo-to	Jăpan Nain-gan	Mr. Tsukamoto	Japan

Diphthongs in the roman transcription:
pronounce ei as in *vein,* ai as in *Thailand,* ou as in *though,* au as in *Sauerkraut.*

New words

လာ–	to come	la-
–က	from	-gá

Examples:

ထိုင်းနိုင်ငံက	from Thailand	T'aìn-nain-ngan-gá
မန္တလေးက	from Mandalay	Màn-dălè-gá
ဘယ်နိုင်ငံကလဲ	from which country?	ɔeh nain-ngan-gá-lèh
ဘယ်မြို့ကလဲ	from which town?	beh myó-gá-lèh
ဘယ်ကလဲ	from which [place]?	beh-gá-lèh
	= from where?	
မစ္စတာ /မျစ်စတာ/	Mr. (for foreign names)	Myiq-săta
မစ္စက် /မျစ်စက်/	Mrs. (for foreign names)	Myiq-seq

Example sentences

S1: ဒေါက်တာဆင်း ဘယ်နိုင်ငံက လာသလဲ။	Which country does Dr. Singh come from?	Dauq-ta S'ìn beh-nain-gan-gá la-dhălèh?
S1: အိန္ဒိယနိုင်ငံက လာပါတယ်။	He comes from India.	Ein-dí-yá-nain-gan-gá la-ba-deh.
S1: ဒေါက်တာဆင်းက အိန္ဒိယ နိုင်ငံက လာသလား။	Does Dr. Singh come from India?	Dauq-ta S'ìn-gá Ein-dí-yá-nain-gan-gá la-dhălà?
S1: ဟုတ်ကဲ့။ အိန္ဒိယနိုင်ငံက လာပါတယ်။	Yes. He does come from India.	Houq-kéh. Ein-dí-yá-nain-gan-gá la-ba-deh.
S1: ဒေါက်တာဆင်းက ပါကစ္စ– တန် နိုင်ငံက လာသလား။	Does Dr. Singh come from Pakistan?	Dr. S'ìn-gá Pa-kiq-sătan-nain-gan-gá la-dhălà?
S1: မလာပါဘူး။ အိန္ဒိယနိုင်ငံက လာပါတယ်။	No. He comes from India.	Măla-ba-bù. Ein-dí-yá-nain-gan-gá la-ba-deh.

Alternative answers

As mentioned in Lessons 27 and 29, you can choose fuller or terser answers to these questions; for example:

Question:

ဒေါက်တာဆင်း ဘယ်နိုင်ငံက လာသလဲ။	Which country does Dr. Singh come from?	Dauq-ta S'ìn beh-nain-gan-gá la-dhălèh?

Answer options:

1. ဒေါက်တာဆင်း အိန္ဒိယနိုင်ငံက လာပါတယ်။	Dr. Singh does come from India.	Dauq-ta S'ìn Ein-dí-yá-nain-gan-gá la-ba-deh.

Diphthongs in the roman transcription:
pronounce ei as in *vein*, ai as in *Thailand*, ou as in *though*, au as in *Sauerkraut*.

107

2. အိန္ဒိယနိုင်ငံက လာပါတယ်။	He comes from India.	Ein-dí-yá-nain-gan-gá la-ba-deh.
3. အိန္ဒိယနိုင်ငံက။	From India.	Ein-dí-yá-nain-gan-gá.

The *Yes* and *No* answers have a corresponding range of options. See the note on "Length of answer" in Lesson 30. As before, the choice between the three options is determined by the same factors as determine your choice in English.

Models for the Exercises

Ex. 1: Using the list of countries of origin

S1: ဒေါက်တာဆင်း ဘယ်နိုင်ငံက လာသလဲ။ — Dauq-ta S'ìn beh nain-ngan-gá la-dhălèh?

L/S2: အိန္ဒိယနိုင်ငံက လာပါတယ်။ — Ein-dí-yá Nain-ngan-gá la-ba-deh.

Ex. 2: Prompt: Ask which country Mr. Shamsuddin comes from.

L/S2: Mr. Shamsuddin ဘယ်နိုင်ငံက လာသလဲ။ — Mr. Shamsuddin beh nain-ngan-gá la-dhălèh?

S1: ဘင်္ဂလားဒေ့ရှ်နိုင်ငံက လာပါတယ်။ — Bin-gălà-désh Nain-ngan-gá la-ba-deh.

L: Writes down: ဘင်္ဂလားဒေ့ရှ်နိုင်ငံ or Bin-gălà-désh or Bangladesh.

Check with Key at end of Lesson.

Form for Ex. 2

Mr. Shamsuddin	…	Mr. Ibanez	…
Mr. Mehta	…	Mr. Abdullah	…
U Zaw Win	…	Mr. Somchai	…
Mr. Nguyen	…	Mrs. Chang	…
Mr. Matsufuji	…		

Ex. 3 For written answer: not on the tape.

The words in the following questions and answers have been split up and jumbled. Rearrange them to form meaningful sentences. There is a Key to this Exercise at the end of the Lesson. Don't forget that you may find it helpful to copy the words onto separate slips of paper and do your reordering by sliding the slips around.

Ex. 4 in Lesson 31 (script)

S1: – လာသလဲ – ဘယ်နိုင်ငံက – ဒေါက်တာဆင်း
S2: – လာပါတယ် – အိန္ဒိယနိုင်ငံက
S1: – မစ္စတာရာမန်က – လာသလား – ဘင်္ဂလားဒေ့ရှ်နိုင်ငံက
S2: – တယ် – က – လာပါ – ဘင်္ဂလားဒေ့ရှ်နိုင်ငံ – ဟုတ်ကဲ့
S1: – လာသ – မစ္စတာတွန်ချမ်က – က – လား – ဗီယက်နမ်နိုင်ငံ
S2: – မလာပါ – တယ် – လာပါ – ဘူး – ထိုင်းနိုင်ငံက
S1: – လာသ – က – က – လဲ – ဘယ် – မစ္စတာမိုဟာမက်
S2: – တယ် – ပါ – လာ – က – မလေးရှားနိုင်ငံ

Diphthongs in the roman transcription:
pronounce ei as in *vein,* ai as in *Thailand,* ou as in *though,* au as in *Sauerkraut.*

Ex. 4 in Lesson 31 (roman)

S1: — la-dhǎlèh — beh nain-gan-gá — Dauq-ta S'ìn
  S2: — la-ba-deh — Ein-dí-yá nain-gan-gá

S1: — Myiq-sǎta Ra-man-gá — la-dhǎlà — Bin-gǎlà-désh nain-gan-gá
  S2: — deh — gá — la-ba — Bin-gǎlà-désh nain-gan — Houq-kéh

S1: — la-dhǎ — Myiq-sǎta Tun C'an-gá — gá — là — Bi-yeq-nan nain-gan·
  S2: — Mǎla-ba — deh — la-ba — bù — T'aìn-nain-gan-gá

S1: — la-dhǎ — ká — gá — lèh — beh — Myiq-sǎta Mo-ha-meq
  S2: — deh— ba — la — gá — Mǎlè-shà nain-gan

In class: Exercises as above. Also use Learners' own countries or towns, people you know, people in the news, and so on.

Notes

Grammar. The sentences in this Lesson are examples of the same verb sentence formula as those in Lessons 27 and 29.

NOUN1+SUFFIX	NOUN2+SUFFIX	VERB+SUFFIX	STC SFX
ဒေါက်တာဆင်း	ဘယ်နိုင်ငံ+က	လာ+သ–	လဲ။
Dauq-ta S'ìn	beh nain-ngan+gá	la+dhǎ	-lèh?
Dr. Singh	which country+from	come+*pres/past*	*question*

"Which country does/did Dr. Singh come from?"

ဒေါက်တာဆင်း	အိန္ဒိယနိုင်ငံ+က	လာပါ+တယ်။	–
Dauq-ta S'ìn	Ein-dí-yá nain-ngan+gá	la-ba+deh.	–
Dr. Singh	India+from	come-*polite*+*pres/past*	–

"Dr. Singh comes/came from India."

The formula applies in the same way to the *Yes/No* questions and answers.

Keys to the Exercises

Key to Ex. 2 in Lesson 31

Mr. Shamsuddin	ဘင်္ဂလားဒေ့ရှ်နိုင်ငံ	Bangladesh
Mr. Mehta	အိန္ဒိယနိုင်ငံ	India
U Zaw Win	မြန်မာနိုင်ငံ	Burma
Mr. Nguyen	ဗီယက်နမ်နိုင်ငံ	Vietnam
Mr. Matsufuji	ဂျပန်	Japan
Mr. Ibanez	ဖိလစ်ပိုင်	Philippines
Mr. Abdullah	မလေးရှားနိုင်ငံ	Malaysia
Mr. Somchai	ထိုင်းနိုင်ငံ	Thailand
Mrs. Chang	တရုပ်နိုင်ငံ	China

Diphthongs in the roman transcription:
pronounce ei as in *vein*, ai as in *Thailand*, ou as in *though*, au as in *Sauerkraut*.

Key to Ex. 4 in Lesson 31 (script)

S1: — ဒေါက်တာဆင်း — ဘယ်နိုင်ငံက — လာသလဲ။

S2: — အိန္ဒိယနိုင်ငံက — လာပါတယ်။

S1: — မစ္စတာရာမန်က — ဘင်္ဂလားဒေ့ရ်နိုင်ငံက — လာသလား။

S2: — ဟုတ်ကဲ့။ — ဘင်္ဂလားဒေ့ရ်နိုင်ငံ — က — လာပါ — တယ်။

S1: — မစ္စတာတွန်ချမ်က — ဗီယက်နမ်နိုင်ငံ — က — လာသ — လား။

S2: — မလာပါ — ဘူး။ — ထိုင်းနိုင်ငံက — လာပါ — တယ်။

S1: — မစ္စတာမိုဟာမက် — က — ဘယ် — က — လာသ — လဲ။

S2: — မလေးရှားနိုင်ငံ — က — လာ — ပါ — တယ်။

Key to Ex. 4 in Lesson 31 (roman)

S1: — Dauq-ta S'ìn — beh nain-gan-gá — la-dhălèh

S2: — Ein-dí-yá nain-gan-gá — la-ba-deh

S1: — Myiq-săta Ra-man-gá — Bin-gălà-désh nain-gan-gá — la-dhălà

S2: — Houq-kéh — Bin-gălà-désh nain-gan — gá — la-ba — deh

S1: — Myiq-săta Tun C'an-gá — Bi-yeq-nan nain-gan — gá la-dhă — là

S2: — Măla-ba — bù — T'aìn-nain-gan-gá — la-ba — deh

S1: — Myiq-săta Mo-ha-meq — ká beh — gá — la-dhă — lèh

S2: — Mălè-shà nain-gan — gá — la — ba — deh

LESSON 32

Prices in Burmese currency. Round, unround, and ten.
How much is nº 1? — It's three kyats.

Price list

Prices in kyat

1...........K3		6............K90
2...........K6		7...........K120
3..........K14		8..........K500
4..........K28		9..........K225
5...........K7		10...........K10

New words

ကျပ်	kyat	caq
ပြား	pya	pyà
ငွေ	silver, money	ngwe
ဗမာငွေ	Burmese currency	Băma ngwe

Kyat and pya. These are the two units of Burmese currency. The kyat (ကျပ် caq) is divided into 100 pya (ပြား pyà). In 1991 the official rate of exchange was about $1 = K6 and £1 = K10. Unofficial rates, offered in illegal street deals, were about ten times the official rates. As you can imagine, with a value (unofficial) of a hundredth of a UK penny, there is not much call for the pya — even single kyat are sometimes ignored in giving change — but pya are still needed for one or two purposes: see Lesson 38.

110 | Diphthongs in the roman transcription: pronounce ei as in *vein,* ai as in *Thailand,* ou as in *though,* au as in *Sauerkraut.*

Prices in kyat

Unround numbers of kyat

ခြောက်ကျပ်	c'auq-caq	K6
နှစ်ကျပ် /နှကျပ်/	hnăcaq	K2
ဆယ့်ငါးကျပ်	s'éh-ngà-jaq	K15
တရာ့ နှစ်ဆယ့် လေးကျပ်	tăyá hnăs'éh lè-jaq	K124

Round numbers of kyat (see the note under "Quirks" below)

(ဗမာငွေ) သုံးဆယ် /-ဇယ်/	(Băma ngwe) thoùn-zeh	K30
(ဗမာငွေ) ရှစ်ရာ	(Băma ngwe) shiq-ya	K800
(ဗမာငွေ) ခုနစ်ရာ ကိုးဆယ် /-ဇယ်/	(Băma ngwe) k'un-năya kò-zeh	K790

Ten kyat

(ဗမာငွေ) တစ်ဆယ် /တဆယ်/	(Băma ngwe) tăs'eh	K10

Kyat and pya

သုံးကျပ် ပြားလေးဆယ်	thoùn-jaq pyà-lè-zeh	K3/40

Photograph of a one kyat note (actual size)
with a portrait of General Aung San

Models for the Exercises

Ex. 1: Asking prices in Burmese currency

Prompt: Ask how much n° 1 is.

L/S2: နံပါတ်(၁) ဘယ်လောက်လဲ။ — Nan-baq-tiq beh-lauq-lèh?

S1/L: သုံးကျပ်။ — Thoùn-jaq.

Diphthongs in the roman transcription:
pronounce ei as in *vein,* ai as in *Thailand,* ou as in *though,* au as in *Sauerkraut.*

Ex. 2

S1: နံပါတ်(၁)က လေးကျပ်လား။   Nan-baq-tiq-ká lè-jaq-là?

L/S2: မဟုတ်ပါဘူး။ သုံးကျပ်ပါ။   Măhouq-pa-bù. Thoùn-jaq-pa.

In class: Exercises as above. Also use menus, price lists, catalogues in Burmese currency. The book lists published in ရုမဝ are good for this exercise.

Notes

"And" forms. As with other numbers, people sometimes use the "and" form for numbers over 100; for example:

တရာနဲ့ နှစ်ဆယ့် လေးကျပ်	tăya-néh hnăs'éh lè-jaq	"a hundred and 24 kyats"
ခုနစ်ရာနဲ့ ကိုးဆယ်	k'un-năya-néh kò-zeh	"seven hundred and 90"

Quirks.

You are by now familiar with the standard rules for counting. You have practised unrounded numbers, rounded numbers, and ten, with dollars, pounds and pennies/pya. The main unit of Burmese currency, the kyat, is subject to two exceptions to the normal rules.

1. Round numbers. On the basis of all other counting expressions you would be justified in expecting (for example) —

ကျပ် သုံးဆယ်	caq thoùn-zeh	K30

You will hear expressions of this kind from time to time; but in practice, this is not the way people express prices in Burmese currency. Instead they just say —

သုံးဆယ်	thoùn-zeh	"thirty"

Occasionally they may say —

ငွေ သုံးဆယ်	ngwe thoùn-zeh	"money: thirty"

or perhaps more often (particularly in contexts where some other currency might be assumed) —

ဗမာငွေ သုံးဆယ်	Băma-ngwe thoùn-zeh	"Burmese currency: thirty"

2. Ten kyats. Again by analogy with all you've learned in practising with dollars, pounds and pya (and what you will later find with any other unit: cupfuls, tons, minutes, miles, jars, …) you would expect K10 to be —

ဆယ်ကျပ်	s'eh-caq	ten kyats

Although 10 ends in a 0 and is therefore a round number in mathematics, in speech it is treated as an *unround* number. In Burmese currency this rule is altered too. Ten behaves like a regular round number and what people actually say is —

တစ်ဆယ်	tăs'eh	"one ten"

or occasionally —

ငွေ တစ်ဆယ်	ngwe tăs'eh	"money: one ten"

or

ဗမာငွေ တစ်ဆယ်	Băma-ngwe tăs'eh	"Burmese currency: one ten"

Diphthongs in the roman transcription: pronounce ei as in *vein*, ai as in *Thailand*, ou as in *though*, au as in *Sauerkraut*.

Currency notes

There were several demonetizations in the 1970s and 80s, in which the higher denomination notes were made valueless and new denominations were introduced. At the time of writing (early 1994) the currency notes in circulation were the following:

name of note	value	value in Burmese
တစ်ကျပ်တန်*	K1/-	တစ်ကျပ်
ငါးကျပ်တန်	K5/-	ငါးကျပ်
တစ်ဆယ်တန်	K10/-	တစ်ဆယ်
ဆယ့်ငါးကျပ်တန်	K15/-	ဆယ့်ငါးကျပ်
လေးဆယ့်ငါးကျပ်တန်	K45/-	လေးဆယ့်ငါးကျပ်
ကိုးဆယ်တန်	K90/-	ကိုးဆယ်

* –တန် -tan = "worth, value"

The names of the notes are sometimes preceded by ငွေစက္ကူ ngwe-seq-ku "currency note" ["money-paper"]; for example:

ငွေစက္ကူတစ်ဆယ်တန် ngwe-seq-ku tăs'eh-dan "currency note for the value of ten kyats"

> Stop press: Just as these pages were going to press, the Minister of Finance announced the issue of new notes in denominations of K500, K100, K50, K20 and 50 pya. The older denominations were to remain in circulation.

Common phrases

To make sure you complete the Common Phrases Supplement by the end of Part 1, learn Section 12 at about this point.

From a 90/- note, showing traditional turban. The originals are printed in colour. Note that although people *write* ကိုးဆယ်ကျပ် (kò-zeh caq), in speech they say ကျပ်ကိုးဆယ် (caq kò-zeh)or more often just ကိုးဆယ် (kò-zeh).

Diphthongs in the roman transcription:
pronounce ei as in *vein,* ai as in *Thailand,* ou as in *though,* au as in *Sauerkraut.*

113

LESSON 33

Clock times (hours). Who came when.
What time did she come? — She came at 3.00.

Names and times

နာမည်	အချိန်	*name*	*time*	*nan-meh*
မချိုချို	၃း၀၀	Ma Cho Cho	3.00	Má C'o C'o
ကိုသိန်းနိုင်	၄း၀၀	Ko Thein Naing	4.00	Ko Theìn Nain
ဒေါ်ညွန့်ညွန့်မြင့်	၅း၀၀	Daw Nyunt Nyunt Myint	5.00	Daw Nyún Nyún Myín
ဦးမြင့်ဦး	၆း၀၀	U Myint U	6.00	Ù Myín Ù
ဆရာမအေမီသန်း	၇း၀၀	Sayama Amy Than	7.00	Săya-má E-mi Thàn
ကိုစိုးနိုင်	၈း၀၀	Ko Soe Naing	8.00	Ko Sò Nain
မရင်ရင်ကြည်	၉း၀၀	Ma Yin Yin Kyi	9.00	Má Yin Yin Ci
ဦးခင်ထွန်း	၁၀း၀၀	U Khin Tun	10.00	Ù K'in T'ùn
ဒေါ်ခင်ခင်ထွေး	၁၁း၀၀	Daw Khin Khin Htwe	11.00	Daw K'in K'in T'wè
ကိုသောင်းကြည်	၁၂း၀၀	Ko Thaung Kyi	12.00	Ko Thaùn Ci
ဒေါ်ခင်ခင်ဝတီအေး	၁း၀၀	Daw Khin Khin Waddy E	1.00	Daw K'in K'in Wădi È
ဗိုလ်မှူးသိန်းလှအောင်	၂း၀၀	Major Thein Hla Aung	2.00	Bo-hmù Theìn Hlá Aun

New words

အချိန်	time	ăc'ein
ဘယ်အချိန်	at what time ... ?	beh-ăc'ein ... ?
နာရီ	hour	na-yi

Example sentences

S1: မချိုချို ဘယ်အချိန် လာသလဲ။	What time did Ma Cho Cho come?	Má C'o C'o beh-ăc'ein la-dhălèh?
S2: ၃–နာရီမှာ လာပါတယ်။	She came at 3 o'clock.	Thoùn-na-yi-hma la-ba-deh.
S1: ဦးမြင့်ဦး ၅–နာရီမှာ လာသလား။	Did U Myint U come at 5 o'clock?	Ù Myín Ù ngà-na-yi-hma la-dhălà?
S2: မလာပါဘူး။ ၆–နာရီမှာ လာပါတယ်။	No. He came at 6 o'clock.	Măla-ba-bù. C'auq-na-yi-hma la-ba-deh.

Notes

A number with နာရီ na-yi gives the time on the hour. The numbers 1, 2, 7, 11, and 12 weaken as for number+ကျပ် caq and the like (တစ်+နာရီ = /တနာရီ/).

Diphthongs in the roman transcription:
pronounce ei as in *vein,* ai as in *Thailand,* ou as in *though,* au as in *Sauerkraut.*

In a sentence, the time phrase is often followed by –မှာ -hma, but people may also omit the
–မှာ -hma. So you hear both —

    ၃–နာရီမှာ လာပါတယ်။   She came at 3 o'clock.   Thoùn-na-yi-hma la-ba-deh.

and —

    ၃–နာရီ လာပါတယ်။   She came at 3 o'clock.   Thoùn-na-yi la-ba-deh.

For consistency in the exercises we retain the –မှာ -hma.

Models for the Exercises

Ex. 1: Times. Prompt: Ask about မချိုချို

    L/S2: မချိုချို ဘယ်အချိန် လာသလဲ။   Má C'o C'o beh ăc'ein la-dhălèh?
    S1: ၃–နာရီမှာ လာပါတယ်။   Thoùn-na-yi-hma la-ba-deh.
    L/S2: ၃–နာရီ။   Thoùn-na-yi.

Ex. 2

    S1: မချိုချို ဘယ်အချိန် လာသလဲ။   Má C'o C'o beh ăc'ein la-dhălèh?
    L/S2: ၃–နာရီမှာ လာပါတယ်။   Thoùn-na-yi-hma la-ba-deh.

In class: exercises as above. Also deliverymen, visitors, Learners' times of arrival at school.

LESSON 34

Going to [place]. Who went where.
Which town did she go to? — She went to Maymyo.

Names and towns

နာမည်	မြို့	name	town
မစောမြသန်း	မေမြို့	Ma Saw Mya Than	Maymyo
ကိုတင်မောင်ဝင်း	ရေနံချောင်း /–ချောင်း/	Ko Tin Maung Win	Yenangyaung
ကိုဘသန်း	တောင်ကြီး /–ကြီး/	Ko Ba Than	Taunggyi
မခင်မူ	မန္တလေး /မန်း:ဒလေး:/	Ma Khin Mu	Mandalay
ကိုအောင်ကျော်ခိုင်	သာစည် /–ဇီ/	Ko Aung Kyaw Khaing	Thazi
ကိုသောင်းတင်	သံတွဲ /–ဒွဲ/	Ko Thaung Tin	Sandoway/Thandwe
မခင်အေးငွေ	စစ်ကိုင်း /ဇဂိုင်း/	Ma Khin Aye Ngwe	Sagaing
မဝေဝခိုင်	မြစ်ကြီးနား:	Ma We We Khine	Myitkyina
ကိုအောင်မြင့်	ပြည် /ပျေ/ or /ပို့/	Ko Aung Myint	Prome/Pyay

Diphthongs in the roman transcription:
pronounce ei as in *vein*, ai as in *Thailand*, ou as in *though*, au as in *Sauerkraut*.

nan-meh	*myó*	*name*	*town*
Má Sàw Myá Thàn	Me-myó	Ma Saw Mya Than	Maymyo
Ko Tin Maun Wìn	Ye-nan-jaùn	Ko Tin Maung Win	Yenangyaung
Ko Bá Thàn	Taun-jì	Ko Ba Than	Taunggyi
Má K'in Mu	Màn-dălè	Ma Khin Mu	Mandalay
Ko Aun Caw K'ain	Tha-zi	Ko Aung Kyaw Khaing	Thazi
Ko Thaùn Tin	Than-dwèh	Ko Thaung Tin	Sandoway/Thandwe
Má K'in È Ngwe	Săgaìn	Ma Khin Aye Ngwe	Sagaing
Má We We K'ain	Myiq-cì-nà	Ma We We Khine	Myitkyina
Ko Aun Myín	Pye	Ko Aung Myint	Prome/Pyay

New words

သွား–	to go	thwà-
[place]–	[no suffix: may mean] to [place] —	

Examples (note no suffix after the destination: Japan, Mandalay, which country and so on):

ဂျပန်နိုင်ငံ သွားတယ်။	She went to Japan.	Jăpan-nain-ngan thwà-deh.
မန္တလေး သွားသလား။	Did he go to Mandalay?	Màn-dălè thwà-dhălà?
ပြတိုက် လာသလား။	Did he come to the museum?	Pyá-daiq la-dhălà?
အင်္ဂလန် လာပါတယ်။	She came to England.	In-gălan la-ba-deh.
ဘယ်နိုင်ငံ သွားသလဲ။	To which country did he go?	Beh nain-ngan thwà-dhă-lèh?
ဘယ်မြို့ သွားသလဲ။	To which town did she go?	Beh myó thwà-dhă-lèh?
ဘယ် သွားသလဲ။	To which [place] did she go? Where did she go?	Beh thwà-dhă-lèh?

Names of countries

ဂျာမနီ	Germany	Ja-măni
ရတ်ရှား or ရုရှား	Russia	Raq-shà or Rú-shà
အင်္ဂလန်	England	In-gălan
ပြင်သစ်ပြည်	France	Pyin-thiq-pye
အမေရိက (အမေရိကန်)	America	Ăme-rí-ká (sts Ăme-rí-kan)
စင်္ကာပူ	Singapore	Sin-ga-pu
သြစတြေးလျ	Australia	Àw-sătrè-lyá
အိုင်ယာလန်	Ireland	Ain-ya-lan
ကိုရီးယား	Korea	Ko-rì-yà

Example sentences

S1: မစောမြသန်း ဘယ်မြို့ သွားသလဲ။	Which town did Ma Saw Mya Than go to?	Má Sàw Myá Thàn beh-myó thwà-dhălèh?
S1: မေမြို့ သွားပါတယ်။	She went to Maymyo.	Me-myó thwà-ba-deh.

Diphthongs in the roman transcription:
pronounce ei as in *vein*, ai as in *Thailand*, ou as in *though*, au as in *Sauerkraut*.

ကိုတင်မောင်ဝင်း ရေနံချောင်း သွားသလား။	Did Ko Tin Maung Win go to Yenangyaung?	Ko Tin Maung Wìn Ye-nan-jaùn thwà-dhălà?
S1: ဟုတ်ကဲ့။ ရေနံချောင်း သွားပါတယ်။	Yes. He did go to Yenangyaung.	Houq-kéh. Ye-nan-jaùn thwà-ba-deh.
S1: ကိုဘသန်း ရေနံချောင်း သွားသလား။	Did Ko Ba Than go to Yenangyaung?	Ko Bá Thàn Ye-nan-jaùn thwà-dhălà?
S1: မသွားပါဘူး။ တောင်ကြီး သွားပါတယ်။	No. He went to Taunggyi.	Măthwà-ba-bù. Taun-jì thwà-ba-deh.

You also find no suffix, with the meaning "to," used with the verb လာ– la- "to come":

S1: မခင်မူ အင်္ဂလန် လာသလား။	Did Ma Khin Mu come to England?	Má K'in Mu In-gălan la-dhălà?
S1: မလာပါဘူး။ ဂျာမနီ သွားပါတယ်။	No. She went to Germany.	Măla-ba-bù. Ja-măni thwà-ba-deh.

As mentioned in earlier Lessons (27, 29, 31) you can choose fuller or terser answers to these questions; for example:

Question:

မစောမြသန်း �’ ဘယ်မြို့ သွားသလဲ။	Which town did Ma Saw Mya Than go to?	Má Sàw Myá Thàn beh-myó thwà-dhălèh?

Answer options:

1. မစောမြသန်း မေမြို့ သွားပါတယ်။	Ma Saw Mya Than went to Maymyo.	Má Sàw Myá Thàn Me-myó thwà-ba-deh.
2. မေမြို့ သွားပါတယ်။	She went to Maymyo.	Me-myó thwà-ba-deh.
3. မေမြို့။	To Maymyo.	Me-myó.

The *Yes* and *No* answers have a corresponding range of options. See the note in Lesson 30. As before, the choice between the three options is determined by the same factors as determine your choice in English.

Models for the Exercises

Ex. 1: Where did they go?
  S1: မစောမြသန်း ဘယ်မြို့ သွားသလဲ။   Má Sàw Myá Thàn beh myó thwà-dhălèh?
  — or S1: မစောမြသန်း ဘယ် သွားသလဲ။   Má Sàw Myá Thàn beh thwà-dhălèh?
  L/S2: မေမြို့ သွားပါတယ်။   Me-myó thwà-ba-deh.

Diphthongs in the roman transcription:
pronounce ei as in *vein*, ai as in *Thailand*, ou as in *though*, au as in *Sauerkraut*.

117

Ex. 2: Prompt: Ask which country Ma Saw Mya Than went to.

L/S2: မစောမြသန်း ဘယ်နိုင်ငံ သွားသလဲ။	Má Sàw Myá Thàn beh nain-ngan thwà-dhălèh?
S1: ဂျာမနီ သွားပါတယ်။	Ja-măni thwà-ba-deh.
L/S2: ဂျာမနီ။	Ja-măni.

and writes down on form: ဂျာမနီ or Ja-măni or Germany.
Check answers against Key at end of Lesson.

Form for Ex. 2

မစောမြသန်း	...	Má Sàw Myá Thàn
ကိုတင်မောင်ဝင်း	...	Ko Tin Maun Wìn
ကိုဘသန်း	...	Ko Bá Thàn
မခင်မူ	...	Má K'in Mu
ကိုအောင်ကျော်ခိုင်	...	Ko Aun Caw K'ain
ကိုသောင်းတင်	...	Ko Thaùn Tin
မခင်အေးငွေ	...	Má K'in È Ngwe
မဝေဝေခိုင်	...	Má We We K'ain
ကိုအောင်မြင့်	...	Ko Aun Myín

Ex. 3: Prompt: Ask where Ko Ba Than went to.

L/S2: ကိုဘသန်း ဘယ်သွားသလဲ။	Ko Bá Thàn beh thwà-dhălèh?
S1: ပန်းခြံ သွားပါတယ်။	Pàn-jan thwà-ba-deh.
L/S2: ဘယ်ပန်းခြံ သွားသလဲ။	Beh pàn-jan thwà-dhălèh?
S1: ဗိုလ်ချုပ်ပန်းခြံ။	Bo-jouq Pàn-jan.

L/S2: ဗိုလ်ချုပ်ပန်းခြံ။ and notes ဗိုလ်ချုပ်ပန်းခြံ or Bo-jouq Pàn-jan or Bogyok Park on the form.

Form for Ex. 3 in Lesson 34
Check answers against Key at end of Lesson

နာမည်		*name*	နေရာ / *place*
မစောမြသန်း	Ma Saw Mya Than	Má Sàw Myá Thàn	...
ကိုတင်မောင်ဝင်း	Ko Tin Maung Win	Ko Tin Maun Wìn	...
ကိုဘသန်း	Ko Ba Than	Ko Bá Thàn	...
မခင်မူ	Ma Khin Mu	Má K'in Mu	...
ကိုအောင်ကျော်ခိုင်	Ko Aung Kyaw Khaing	Ko Aun Caw K'ain	...
ကိုသောင်းတင်	Ko Thaung Tin	Ko Thaùn Tin	...
မခင်အေးငွေ	Ma Khin Aye Ngwe	Má K'in È Ngwe	...
မဝေဝေခိုင်	Ma We We Khine	Má We We K'ain	...
ကိုအောင်မြင့်	Ko Aung Myint	Ko Aun Myín	...

Ex. 4: Prompt: Imagine you're at the Shwedagon Pagoda.

S1: မစောမြသန်းက ရွှေတိဂုံဘုရား လာသလား။	Má Sàw Myá Thàn-gá Shwe-dăgoun P'ăyà la-dhălà?
L/S2: မလာပါဘူး။ ရွှေတိဂုံဘုရား သွားပါတယ်။	Măla-ba-bù. S'ù-le P'ăyà thwà-ba-deh.

— or Yes, as the case may be.

Diphthongs in the roman transcription:
pronounce ei as in *vein,* ai as in *Thailand,* ou as in *though,* au as in *Sauerkraut*.

List for Ex. 4

မစောမြသန်း	ဆူးလေဘုရား	Ma Saw Mya Than	Sule Pagoda
ကိုတင်မောင်ဝင်း	မဟာဗန္ဒုလပန်းခြံ	Ko Tin Maung Win	Maha Bandoola Park
ကိုဘသန်း	ဗိုလ်ချုပ်ပန်းခြံ	Ko Ba Than	Bogyoke Park
မခင်မူ	ရွှေတိဂုံဘုရား	Ma Khin Mu	Shwedagon Pagoda
ကိုအောင်ကျော်ခိုင်	ဗိုလ်ချုပ်ဈေး	Ko Aung Kyaw Khaing	Bogyoke Market
ကိုသောင်းတင်	ဗိုလ်ချုပ်ပြတိုက်	Ko Thaung Tin	Bogyoke Museum
မခင်အေးငွေ	အမျိုးသားပြတိုက်	Ma Khin Aye Ngwe	National Museum
မဝေဝေခိုင်	သမ္မတဟိုတယ်	Ma We We Khine	President Hotel
ကိုအောင်မြင့်	သိမ်ကြီးဈေး	Ko Aung Myint	Thein-gyi Market

Ex. 5 For written answer: not on the tape.

The words in the following questions and answers have been split up and jumbled. Rearrange them to form meaningful sentences. There is a Key to this Exercise at the end of the Lesson. Don't forget that you may find it helpful to copy the words onto separate slips of paper and do your reordering by sliding the slips around.

S1: — ကိုဘသန်း — သွားသလဲ — ဘယ်မြို့

S2: — တယ် — သွားပါ — တောင်ကြီး

S1: — သွားသ — ကိုဘသန်း — လား — မြစ်ကြီးနား

S2: — သွားပါ — ဘူး — မသွားပါ — တယ် — တောင်ကြီး

S1: — ဘယ် — သ — မခင်မူ — လဲ — သွား

S2: — သွား — ထိုင်းနိုင်ငံ — တယ် — ပါ

Ex. 5 in Lesson 34

S1: — Ko Bá Thàn — thwà-dhǎlèh — beh-myó

S2: — deh — thwà-ba — Taun-jì

S1: — thwà-dhǎ — Ko Bá Thàn — là — Myiq-cì-nà

S2: — thwà-ba — bù — mǎthwà-ba — deh — Taun-jì

S1: — beh — dhǎ — Má K'in Mu — lèh — thwà

S2: — thwà — T'aìn-nain-gan — deh — ba

In class: Exercises as above. You can also do exercises with places the Learners went to if you first establish that you are talking about last summer, or some other specified period. Or use restaurant names, to talk about where Learners went at lunch time.

Notes

To [place]

ဘယ်မြို့ သွားသလဲ။	Beh myó thwà-dhǎlèh?	"Which town did she go to?"
ဘယ် သွားသလဲ။	Beh thwà-dhǎlèh?	"Where did she go to?"
မေမြို့ သွားပါတယ်။	Me-myó thwà-ba-deh.	"She went to Maymyo"
ဗမာပြည် လာသလား။	Bǎma-pye la-dhǎlà?	"Did she come to Burma"

Note that Burmese needs no element corresponding to English "to." In sentences with words like သွား– thwà- "go," and လာ– la- "come" —

ဘယ်မြို့ (beh myó) means "to which town?"

ဘယ် (beh) means "where to?" and

မေမြို့ (Me-myó) means "to Maymyo"

ဗမာပြည် (Bǎma-pye) means "to Burma"

Diphthongs in the roman transcription:
pronounce ei as in *vein,* ai as in *Thailand,* ou as in *though,* au as in *Sauerkraut.*

Burmese does have a suffix that corresponds to "to" in "to [place]." It is –ကို (-ko/-go). So sometimes you will find people saying

ဘယ် မြို့ကို သွားသလဲ။   Beh myó-go thwà-dhălèh?   "Which town did she go to?"
မေမြို့ကို သွားပါတယ်။   Me-myó-go thwà-ba-deh.   "She went to Maymyo."

but it is normal to do without the suffix when the destination [မေမြို့ (Me-myó) or ဘယ်မြို့ (Beh myó)] comes immediately before the verb [သွား– (thwà-)] — as it does in these sentences.

Later on you will meet sentences where there is some word or phrase (such as "last year" or "with her boyfriend") that comes between the destination and the verb, and you will find that people use the suffix more often then.

France. The Burmese name for France is one of those that diverge markedly from the English pronunciation of the name. It evidently came into Burmese, not from the English word "France" but from the French word "Français." That may not sound very convincing until you hear its pronunciation in the dialect of Arakan, on the west coast of Burma. There the Burmese word ပြင်သစ် (Pyin-thiq) (following regular rules of correspondence between the two dialects) is pronounced something like Prawn-thaiq, and in earlier times would have been Prawn-saiq. Now does it look more likely?

You may remember that the names of Burma and China, unlike the names of other countries, never (or hardly ever) drop the နိုင်ငံ (naing-ngan) or the ပြည် (pye) from their names. France is in the same class. It is always ပြင်သစ်နိုင်ငံ (Pyin-thiq Naing-ngan) or ပြင်သစ်ပြည် (Pyin-thiq-pye), never (or hardly ever) plain ပြင်သစ် (Pyin-thiq).

Grammar. The sentences in this Lesson are examples of the same verb sentence formula as those in the preceding Lessons.

NOUN1+SUFFIX	NOUN2+SUFFIX	VERB+SUFFIX	STC SFX
မစောမြသန်း	ဘယ်မြို့	သွား+သ–	–လဲ။
Ma Sàw Myá Thàn	beh myó	thwà+dhă	-lèh?
Ma Saw Mya Than	which town	go+*pres/past*	*question*

"Which town did Ma Saw Mya Than go to?"

မစောမြသန်း	မေမြို့	သွား+တယ်။	
Ma Sàw Myá Thàn	Me-myó	thwà+deh	–
Ma Saw Mya Than	Maymyo	go+*pres/past*	–

"Ma Saw Mya Than went to Maymyo."

The formula applies in the same way to the *Yes/No* questions and answers. The polite suffix is omitted in these examples: see the note in Lesson 27.

Diphthongs in the roman transcription:
pronounce ei as in *vein*, ai as in *Thailand*, ou as in *though*, au as in *Sauerkraut*.

Keys to the Exercises

Key to Ex. 2 in Lesson 34

နာမည်	နေရာ	*name*	*place*
မစောမြသန်း	ဂျာမနီ	Ma Saw Mya Than	Germany
ကိုတင်မောင်ဝင်း	ရတ်ရှား	Ko Tin Maung Win	Russia
ကိုဘသန်း	အင်္ဂလန်	Ko Ba Than	England
မခင်မူ	ပြင်သစ်ပြည်	Ma Khin Mu	France
ကိုအောင်ကျော်ခိုင်	အမေရိက	Ko Aung Kyaw Khaing	America
ကိုသောင်းတင်	စင်္ကာပူ	Ko Thaung Tin	Singapore
မခင်အေးငွေ	သြစတြေးလျ	Ma Khin Aye Ngwe	Australia
မဝေဝေခိုင်	အိုင်ယာလန်	Ma We We Khine	Ireland
ကိုအောင်မြင့်	ကိုရီးယား	Ko Aung Myint	Korea

nan-meh	*neya*
Má Sàw Myá Thàn	Ja-măni
Ko Tin Maun Wìn	Raq-shà or Rú-shà
Ko Bá Thàn	In-gălan
Má K'in Mu	Pyin-thiq-pye
Ko Aun Caw K'ain	Ăme-rí-ká (sts Ăme-rí-kan)
Ko Thaùn Tin	Sin-ga-pu
Má K'in È Ngwe	Àw-sătrè-lyá
Má We We K'ain	Ain-ya-lan
Ko Aun Myín	Ko-rì-yà

Key to Ex. 3 in Lesson 34

နာမည်	နေရာ	*name*	*place*
မစောမြသန်း	ဗိုလ်ချုပ်ပြတိုက်	Ma Saw Mya Than	Bogyoke Museum
ကိုတင်မောင်ဝင်း	ရွှေတိဂုံ ဘုရား	Ko Tin Maung Win	Shwedagon Pagoda
ကိုဘသန်း	ဗိုလ်ချုပ်ပန်းခြံ	Ko Ba Than	Bogyoke Park
မခင်မူ	သမ္မတဟိုတယ်	Ma Khin Mu	President Hotel
ကိုအောင်ကျော်ခိုင်	ဗိုလ်ချုပ်ဈေး	Ko Aung Kyaw Khaing	Bogyoke Market
ကိုသောင်းတင်	သိမ်ကြီးဈေး	Ko Thaung Tin	Thein-gyi Market
မခင်အေးငွေ	ဆူးလေဘုရား	Ma Khin Aye Ngwe	Sule Pagoda
မဝေဝေခိုင်	မဟာဗန္ဓုလပန်းခြံ	Ma We We Khine	Maha Bandoola Park
ကိုအောင်မြင့်	အမျိုးသားပြတိုက်	Ko Aung Myint	National Museum

Má Sàw Myá Thàn	Bo-jouq Pyá-daiq
Ko Tin Maun Wìn	Shwe-dăgoun P'ăyà
Ko Bá Thàn	Bo-jouq Pàn-jan
Má K'in Mu	Thămădá Ho-teh
Ko Aun Caw K'ain	Bo-jouq Zè
Ko Thaùn Tin	Thein-jì Zè
Má K'in È Ngwe	S'ù-le P'ăyà
Má We We K'ain	Măha Ban-dú-lá Pàn-jan
Ko Aun Myín	Ămyò-thà Pyá-daiq

Diphthongs in the roman transcription:
pronounce ei as in *vein,* ai as in *Thailand,* ou as in *though,* au as in *Sauerkraut.*

Key to Ex. 5 in Lesson 34 (script)

> S1: — ကိုဘသန်း — ဘယ်မြို့ — သွားသလဲ။
>> S2: — တောင်ကြီး — သွားပါ — တယ်။
> S1: — ကိုဘသန်း — မြစ်ကြီးနား — သွားသ — လား။
>> S2: — မသွားပါ — ဘူး။ — တောင်ကြီး — သွားပါ — တယ်။
> S1: — မခင်မူ — ဘယ် — သွား — သ — လဲ။
>> S2: — ထိုင်းနိုင်ငံ — သွား — ပါ — တယ်။

Key to Ex. 5 in Lesson 34 (roman)

> S1: — Ko Bá Thàn — beh-myó — thwà-dhǎlèh?
>> S2: — Taun-jì — thwà-ba — deh.
> S1: — Ko Bá Thàn — Myiq-cì-nà — thwà-dhǎ — là?
>> S2: — Mǎthwà-ba — bù. — Taun-jì — thwà-ba — deh.
> S1: — Má K'in Mu — beh — thwà — dhǎ — lèh?
>> S2: — T'aìn-nain-gan — thwà — ba — deh.

Common phrases

To make sure you complete the Common Phrases Supplement by the end of Part 1, learn Section 13 at about this point.

LESSON 35

More practice with going to.
Where did she go to? — She went to the library.

Names and places

နာမည်	နေရာ	name	place
မသန်းရွှေ	စာကြည့်တိုက်	Ma Than Shwe	library
ကိုသော်ဇင်	စားသောက်ခန်း	Ko Thaw Zin	eating room, canteen
မအုံးခင်	အိမ်သာ	Ma Ohn Khin	toilet
ကိုဘညွန့်	အပြင်	Ko Ba Nyunt	outside, out
ဦးလှရွှေ	ကုန်တိုက်	U Hla Shwe	department store
ကိုလှဖေ	သံတမန်ကုန်တိုက်	Ko Hla Pe	Diplomatic Store

nan-meh	ne-ya	name	place
Má Thàn Shwe	sa-cí-daiq	Ma Than Shwe	library
Ko Thaw Zin	sà-thauq-k'àn	Ko Thaw Zin	eating room, canteen
Má Oùn K'in	ein-dha	Ma Ohn Khin	toilet
Ko Bá Nyún	ǎpyin	Ko Ba Nyunt	outside, out
Ù Hla Shwe	koun-daiq	Ko Hla Shwe	department store
Ko Hlá P'e	Than-dǎman Koun-daiq	Ko Hla Pe	Diplomatic Store

122

Diphthongs in the roman transcription:
pronounce ei as in *vein,* ai as in *Thailand,* ou as in *though,* au as in *Sauerkraut.*

New words

Burmese	Meaning	Transcription
အိမ်သာ /–သွာ/	toilet	ein-dha
အိမ်	house	ein
–သွာ	pleasant	-dha
စာကြည့်တိုက် /–ကျို့ဒိုက်/	library	sa-cí-daiq
စာ	text, writing	sa
ကြည့် /ကျို့–/	look at, study	cí-
တိုက်	building	taiq
စားသောက်ခန်း 1	eating room, canteen	sà-thauq-k'àn
စား–	to eat	sà-
သောက်–	to drink	thauq-
အခန်း 1	room	ăk'àn
ကုန်တိုက် /–ဒိုက်/	department store	koun-daiq
ကုန်	goods, merchandise	koun
တိုက်	building	taiq
သံတမန်ကုန်တိုက် /–ဒမန်/	Diplomatic Store	Than-dăman Koun-daiq
သံတမန်	diplomatic	Than-dăman
အပြင်	outside, out	àpyin

1. The word အခန်း (ăk'àn) "room" contains the prefix အ–။ When the word is attached to other elements to form a compound word, the prefix is omitted: စားသောက်ခန်း (sà-thauq-k'àn) "eating and drinking room"; but when the word occurs on its own, the prefix is retained: ဘယ် အခန်းမှာလဲ (Beh-ăk'àn-hma-lèh?) "In which room?" The prefix has no meaning, but it is quite frequent, and you will find it comes and goes in this way in many other words: see, for example, Dialogues 1.4:

Burmese	Meaning	Transcription
အလုံး	round object	ăloùn
but: ငါးလုံး	five round objects	ngà-loùn
အရည်	juice	ăye
but: လက်ဖက်ရည်	tea ["tea-juice"]	lăp'eq-ye

Example sentences

Burmese	Meaning	Transcription
ကိုသော်ဇင် ဘယ် သွားသလဲ။	Where has Ko Thaw Zin gone?	Ko Thaw Zin beh thwà-dhălèh?
စားသောက်ခန်း သွားပါတယ်။	He went to the canteen.	Sà-thauq-k'àn thwà-ba-deh.

Models for the Exercises

Ex. 1: Where did they go?
Prompt: Ask where Ma Than Shwe went.

L/S2: မသန်းရွှေ ဘယ် သွားသလဲ။		Má Thàn Shwe beh thwà-dhălèh?
S1: စာကြည့်တိုက် သွားပါတယ်။		Sa-cí-daiq thwà-ba-deh.
L/S2: စာကြည့်တိုက်လား။		Sa-cí-daiq-là?
S1: ဟုတ်ကဲ့ပါ။		Houq-kéh-ba.

Diphthongs in the roman transcription:
pronounce ei as in *vein*, ai as in *Thailand*, ou as in *though*, au as in *Sauerkraut*.

Ex. 2

S1: မသန်းရွှေ ဘယ်သွားသလဲ။   Má Thàn Shwe beh thwà-dhǎlèh?
L/S2: စာကြည့်တိုက် သွားပါတယ်။   Sa-cí-daiq thwà-ba-deh.

In class: Exercises as above. Also ask times (on the hour only) and destinations of members of the class — using English if appropriate; for example: MacDonald's သွားပါတယ်။

LESSON 36

Asking people's names.
What's your name? — It's Aung San.

Names

Person nº 1	Matthew	Person nº 7	...
Person nº 2	Martha	Person nº 8	...
Person nº 3	Mark	Person nº 9	...
Person nº 4	Luke	Person nº 10	...
Person nº 5	Mary	Person nº 11	...
Person nº 6	John	Person nº 12	...

New words

နာမည် /နန်မယ် or နာမျို/ [1]	name	nan-meh (na-myi) [1]
ဘယ်လို	how, in what way	beh-lo
ခေါ်–	to call, be called	k'aw–
[name]–လို့	"[name]" [2]	[name]-ló
[name]–တဲ့	it's called "[name]" [3]	[name]-téh

1. Pronounced /နန်မယ်/ (nan-meh) in colloquial, but /နာမျို/ (na-myi) in reading style.
2. The suffix –လို့ (-ló) is like a spoken end-of-quotation mark. It shows that what precedes is a citation or reported speech. Don't confuse this –လို့ (-ló) "end-of-quote" with the –လို (-lo) in ဘယ်လို (beh-lo) "how." To a Burmese ear they are as far apart as *lock* and *log* to an English speaker.
3. The suffix –တဲ့ (-téh) has the same meaning as –လို့ ခေါ်ပါတယ် (-ló k'aw-ba-deh) (see below). It means "It is called '...'," or in other contexts it means "They said '...'."

Example sentences

S1: နာမည် ဘယ်လို ခေါ်သလဲ။   What is your name?   Nan-meh beh-lo k'aw-dhǎlèh?

S2: အောင်ဆန်းလို့ ခေါ်ပါတယ်။   It is Aung San.   Aun S'an-ló k'aw-ba-deh.

124

Diphthongs in the roman transcription:
pronounce ei as in *vein,* ai as in *Thailand,* ou as in *though,* au as in *Sauerkraut.*

Variations:

S2: အောင်ဆန်းပါ॥	Aung San.	Aung S'àn-ba.
S2: အောင်ဆန်းတဲ့॥	It's Aung San.	Aung S'àn-déh.

Notice that Burmese doesn't need a word corresponding to the English "your." It is enough to say just "Name how called?"

Notice also that when you are telling someone your own name, you often omit ဦး (Ù) or ဒေါ် (Daw) and other prefixes.

Models for the Exercises

Ex. 1: Asking names. Prompt: Imagine you are person n° 1:

S1: နာမည် ဘယ်လို ခေါ်သလဲ॥	Nan-meh beh-lo k'aw-dhălèh?
L/S2male: [Matthew]လို့ ခေါ်ပါတယ်॥	Matthew-ló k'aw-ba-deh.
S1: Matthew–လား॥	Matthew-là?
L/S2: ဟုတ်ကဲ့॥ Matthew–ပါ॥	Houq-kéh. Matthew-ba.

Ex. 2 in Lesson 36. You ask the names of Persons 7-12 above and fill in the blanks. Check answers against Key at end of Lesson. Prompt: Ask Person n° 7 his name:

L/S2: နာမည် ဘယ်လို ခေါ်သလဲ॥	Nan-meh beh-lo k'aw-dhălèh?
S1: ဦးစိန်လွင်လို့ ခေါ်ပါတယ်॥	Ù Sein Lwin-ló k'aw-ba-deh.
L/S2: ဦးစိန်လွင်လား॥	Ù Sein Lwin-là?
S1: ဟုတ်ကဲ့॥ ဦးစိန်လွင်ပါ॥	Houq-kéh. Ù Sein Lwin-ba.

In class: Exercises as above. Also ask names of members of class, of friends or of well-known people in photographs.

Notes

Grammar. The sentences in this Lesson are examples of the familiar verb sentence formula as those in Lessons 27 and 29 and 31.

NOUN1+SUFFIX	NOUN2+SUFFIX	VERB+SUFFIX	STC SFX
နာမည်	ဘယ်+လို	ခေါ်+သ–	လဲ॥
Nan-meh	beh+lo	k'aw+dhă	-lèh?
Name	which+way	call+*pres/past*	*question*

"What is your name?"

[နာမည်+က]	အောင်ဆန်း+လို့	ခေါ်ပါ+တယ်॥	–
[nan-meh+gá]	Aun S'àn+ló	k'aw-ba+deh.	–
[My name]	Aung San+*quote*	call-*polite+pres/past*	–

"My name is Aung San."

The formula applies in the same way to the *Yes/No* questions and answers.

Diphthongs in the roman transcription:
pronounce ei as in *vein*, ai as in *Thailand*, ou as in *though*, au as in *Sauerkraut*.

125

Keys to the Exercises

Key to Ex. 2 in Lesson 36

Person n° 7	ဦးစိန်လွင်	U Sein Lwin	Ù Sein Lwin
Person n° 8	ဦးတင်အောင်	U Tin Aung	Ù Tin Aun
Person n° 9	ဒေါ်စီစီဝင်း	Daw Si Si Win	Daw Si Si Wìn
Person n° 10	ဒေါ်ခင်မာလေး	Daw Khin Ma Lay	Daw K'in Ma Lè
Person n° 11	ဦးကိုကိုကြီး	U Ko Ko Gyi	Ù Ko Ko Jì
Person n° 12	ဒေါ်မြမြသိန်း	Daw Mya Mya Thein	Daw Myá Myá Thèin

Common phrases

To make sure you complete the Common Phrases Supplement by the end of Part 1, learn Section 14 at about this point.

LESSON 37

Clock times: hours and minutes. Where did he go and when?
What time did Ma San San Hlaing go? — She went at 7.45.

Names, places and times

နာမည်		name		နေရာ place	အချိန် time
မစန်စန်လှိုင်		Ma San San Hlaing	Má San San Hlain	…	…
ဦးဝင်းမြင့်		U Win Myint	Ù Wìn Myín	…	…
ကိုလှဝင်း		Ko Hla Win	Ko Hlá Wìn	…	…
ဦးအောင်သာ		U Aung Tha	Ù Aun Tha	…	…
ဒေါ်အေးကြည်		Daw Aye Kyi	Daw È Ci	…	…
ဒေါ်ရီရီခင်		Daw Yi Yi Khin	Daw Yi Yi K'in	…	…
ဒေါက်တာမြသိန်း		Dr. Mya Thein	Dauq-ta Myá Thèin	…	…
ဆရာမ ဒေါ်စန်းနု		Sayama Daw San Nu	Sǎya-má Daw Sàn Nú	…	…
ဗိုလ်မှူးကြီးသန်းတင်		Colonel Than Tin	Bo-hmù-jì Thàn Tin	…	…
ဒေါက်တာဒေါ်မြင့်ကြူ॥		Dr. Daw Myint Kyu	Dauq-ta Daw Myín Cu	…	…

New words

| မိနစ် /မိနစ်–မင်းနစ်–မနစ်/ 1 | minute | mí-niq / mìn-niq / mǎniq [1] |
| -ခွဲ | - and a half | -gwèh, sometimes -k'wèh |

Examples:

| တစ်နာရီခွဲ | 1.30 ["one hour and a half"] | tǎna-yi-gwèh or tǎna-yi-k'wèh |
| သုံးနာရီခွဲ | 3.30 ["three hours and a half"] | thoùn-na-yi-gwèh or -k'wèh |

1. The pronunciation of the first syllable varies with the speed of the speaker.

Diphthongs in the roman transcription:
pronounce ei as in *vein*, ai as in *Thailand*, ou as in *though*, au as in *Sauerkraut*.

Example sentences

S1: မစံစံလှိုင် ဘယ်အချိန်
သွားသလဲ။

What time did Ma San San Hlaing go?

Má San San Hlain beh-ăc'ein thwà-dhălèh?

S2: ၇-နာရီ ၄၅-မိနစ်မှာ
သွားပါတယ်။

She went at 7.45.

K'un-năna-yi lè-zéh ngà-măniq-hma thwà-ba-deh.

S1: ကိုလှဝင်း ဘယ်အချိန်
သွားသလဲ။

What time did Ko Hla Win go?

Ko Hlá Wìn beh-ăc'ein thwà-dhălèh?

S2: ၃-နာရီ မိနစ်-၃၀-မှာ
သွားပါတယ်။

He went at 3.30.

Thoùn-na-yi mí-niq-thoùn-zeh -hma thwà-ba-deh.

Variant:
S2: ၃-နာရီခွဲမှာ သွားပါတယ်။

He went at half past three.

Thoùn-na-yi-gwèh-hma thwà-ba-deh.

There are equivalents in Burmese of English expressions like "a quarter to four," "ten to three" and so on:

လေးနာရီ မတ်တင်း | 3.45 ("four hours a quarter short") | lè-na-yi maq-tìn

သုံးနာရီ ထိုးဖို့ ၁၀-မိနစ်အလို | 2.50 ("three-hours to-strike 10-minutes lacking") | thoùn-na-yi t'ò-bó s'eh-măniq ălo

However, the expression of time in hours and minutes as in the first examples above is very common, and we use them as standard in *BISL*.

Notes

The Round Number Rule applies to minutes in the same way as it does to units of currency: Round numbers (20, 30, 40, 50 …) come *after* the unit being counted:

မိနစ် သုံးဆယ် | 30 minutes | mí-niq thoùn-zeh
မိနစ် ငါးဆယ် | 50 minutes | mí-niq ngà-zeh

Otherwise the number comes *before* the unit:

ငါးမိနစ် | 5 minutes | ngà-mí-niq
နှစ်ဆယ့် ငါးမိနစ် | 55 minutes | hnăs'éh ngà-mí-niq

The exception, as with other counted units, is ဆယ် s'eh "ten," which, despite ending in 0 like a round number, is treated like an unround number:

ဆယ်မိနစ် | 10 minutes | s'eh mí-niq

Diphthongs in the roman transcription:
pronounce ei as in *vein*, ai as in *Thailand*, ou as in *though*, au as in *Sauerkraut*.

Models for the Exercises

Ex. 1: Prompt: Ask where Ma San San Hlaing went to.

L/S2: မစံစံလှိုင် ဘယ်သွားသလဲ။   Má San San Hlain beh thwà-dhălèh?

S1: စားသောက်ခန်း သွားပါတယ်။   Sà-thauq-k'àn thwà-ba-deh.

Prompt: Ask when she went.

L/S2: ဘယ်အချိန် သွားသလဲ။   Beh ăc'ein thwà-dhălèh?

S1: ၇-နာရီ ၄၅-မိနစ်မှာ သွားပါတယ်။   7-na-yi 45-măniq-hma thwà-ba-deh.

L/S2: ၇-နာရီ ၄၅-မိနစ်။ and fill in blank   7-na-yi 45-măniq.

Then check answers against Key at end of Lesson.

Ex. 2

S1: ဒေါ်အေးကြည် ဘယ်အချိန် သွားသလဲ။   Daw È Ci beh ăc'ein thwà-dhălèh?

L/S2: ၄-နာရီ ၁၅-မိနစ်မှာ သွားပါတယ်။   4-na-yi 15-măniq-hma thwà-ba-deh.

S1: ၄-နာရီ ၁၅-မိနစ်မှာလား။   4-na-yi 15-măniq-hma-là?

L/S2: ဟုတ်ကဲ့။ ၄-နာရီ ၁၅-မိနစ်မှာပါ။   Houq-kéh. 4-na-yi 15-măniq-hma-ba.

In class: Exercises as above. Also times and destinations of class.

Keys to the Exercises

Key to Ex. 1 in Lesson 37

နာမည်	နေရာ	အချိန်
မစံစံလှိုင်	စားသောက်ခန်း	၇:၄၅
ဦးဝင်းမြင့်	သမ္မတဟိုတယ်	၂:၃၅
ကိုလှဝင်း	အမျိုးသားပြတိုက်	၃:၃၀
ဦးအောင်သာ	သံတမန်ကုန်တိုက်	၆:၂၅
ဒေါ်အေးကြည်	အပြင်	၄:၁၅
ဒေါ်ရီရီခင်	အိမ်သာ	၁:၁၀
ဒေါက်တာမြသိန်း	ဗိုလ်ချုပ်ဈေး	၁၁:၅၅
ဆရာမ ဒေါ်စန်းနု	စာကြည့်တိုက်	၁၂:၂၀
ဗိုလ်မှူးကြီးသန်းတင်	သိမ်ဖြူလမ်း	၈:၅၀
ဒေါက်တာဒေါ်မြင့်ကြူ	ကုန်တိုက်	၁၀:၄၀

name	*place*	*time*
Ma San San Hlaing	canteen	7.45
U Win Myint	President Hotel	2.35
Ko Hla Win	National Museum	3.30
U Aung Tha	Diplomatic Store	6.25
Daw Aye Kyi	out	4.15
Daw Yi Yi Khin	toilet	1.10
Dr. Mya Thein	Bogyoke Market	11.55
Sayama Daw San Nu	library	12.20
Colonel Than Tin	Theinbyu Road	8.50
Dr. Daw Myint Kyu	department store	10.40

Diphthongs in the roman transcription:
pronounce ei as in *vein*, ai as in *Thailand*, ou as in *though*, au as in *Sauerkraut*.

nan-meh	*ne-ya*	*ăc'ein*
Má San San Hlain	sà-thauq-k'àn	7.45
Ù Wìn Myín	Thămădá Ho-teh	2.35
Ko Hlá Wìn	Ămyò-dhà Pyá-daiq	3.30
Ù Aun Tha	Than-dăman Koun-daiq	6.25
Daw È Ci	ăpyin	4.15
Daw Yi Yi K'in	ein-dha	1.10
Dauq-ta Myá Thein	Bo-jouq Zè	11.55
Săya-má Daw Sàn Nú	sa-cí-daiq	12.20
Bo-hmù-jì Thàn Tin	Thein-byu Làn	8.50
Dauq-ta Daw Myín Cu	koun-daiq	10.40

LESSON 38

Burmese currency: parts of a kyat.
How much is this? — K1/50.

New words

–ခွဲ	- and a half	-k'wèh

You met this word in connection with telling the time (Lesson 37); it is also used for sums of money (and with other categories of measure) for example:

နှစ်ကျပ်ခွဲ	two kyats and a half, K2.50	hnăcaq-k'wèh
လေးကျပ်ခွဲ	four kyats and a half, K4.50	lè-jaq-k'wèh

Note that –ခွဲ k'wèh always follows a full number and means "*and* a half": it does *not* mean "half a kyat."

Models for the Exercises

Ex. 1: add a half
S1: သုံးကျပ်။   Thoùn-jaq.
L/S2: သုံးကျပ်ခွဲ။   Thoùn-jaq-k'wèh.

Ex. 2: Prompt: Pick up the hat and ask how much it is.
L: ဒါ ဘယ်လောက်လဲ။   Beh-lauq-lèh?
S1/L: ၄၅–ကျပ်။   45-jaq.
L: writes down the price.

Diphthongs in the roman transcription:
pronounce ei as in *vein,* ai as in *Thailand,* ou as in *though,* au as in *Sauerkraut.*

129

Form for Ex. 2

item	*price*	*item*	*price*
h a t	၄၅/– or 45/–	soap	...
T-shirt	...	toilet paper	...
rubber sandals	...	comb	...
battery	...	carved figure	...
film	...	key-ring	...
pen	...	fan	...
postcard	...	Coca-cola	...
glue	...	Vimto	...
envelope	...	banana	...

In class: Exercises as above. Also use price lists (such as book lists from ရန်ကုန်), or make up your own price list, to include fraction prices with half a kyat. Also receipts from Burma.

Note

Fractions of the kyat. The kyat is notionally divided into 100 pya, but at the time of writing (summer 1991) prices have risen so high that there are very few items for which you have to pay a price that includes pya: almost everything is priced in whole kyat. Exceptions include single envelopes (K1.50 each), stamps for internal postage (-/15 pya at the Post Office, -/30 pya elsewhere), local calls from a payphone (-/50), and small quantitites of foodstuffs. Because pya prices are so rare, we don't use prices involving less than half a kyat in the exercises.

Abbreviated forms for writing fractions of a kyat: for example: for 3 kyats and 50 pyas —

script:	၃/၅၀ or ၃–၅၀ or ၃.၅၀
also:	၃/၅ပါး or ၃ိ–၅ပါး or ၃ိ.၅ပါး (mostly in handwriting)
roman:	3/50 or K3/50 or K 3.50 or 3.50 K

Certain sums involving pya have their own names:

name	*meaning*	*pron.*	*value*	*expressed in pya*
တစ်မတ်	a quarter	tămaq	-/25 pya	နှစ်ဆယ့် ငါးပြား
ငါးမူး	"five mu"*	ngà-mù	-/50 pya	ပြားငါးဆယ်
သုံးမတ်	three quarters	thoùn-maq	-/75 pya	ခုနစ်ဆယ့် ငါးပြား
ငါးမတ်	five quarters	ngà-maq	1/25 pya	တစ်ကျပ် နှစ်ဆယ့် ငါးပြား
–ခွဲ	and a half	-k'wèh	+/50 pya	–နဲ့ ပြားငါးဆယ်

* The *mu* is a measure now obsolete. At one time it was a tenth of unit; hence five *mu* = half a kyat. It survives only in this phrase.

Diphthongs in the roman transcription:
pronounce ei as in *vein*, ai as in *Thailand*, ou as in *though*, au as in *Sauerkraut*.

Here are the pya coins in circulation in 1991.

shape	value	name of coin	shape	value	name of coin
	တစ်ပြား: tăbyà 1 pya	ပြား:စေ့ pyà-zí 1 pya coin		ငါး:ပြား: ngà-byà 5 pya	ငါး:ပြား:စေ့ ngà-byà-zí 5 pya coin
	ဆယ်ပြား: s'eh-byà 10 pya	ဆယ်ပြား:စေ့ s'eh-byà-zí 10 pya coin		နှစ်ဆယ့်ငါး:ပြား: hnăs'éh-ngà-byà 25 pya	မတ်စေ့ maq-sí quarter coin
	ပြား:ငါး:ဆယ် pyà ngà-zeh 50 pya	ငါး:မူး:စေ့ ngà-mù-zí 5 mu coin		တစ်ကျပ် tăjaq 1 kyat	ကျပ်စေ့* caq-sí kyat coin

* K1/- coins are rare: kyat notes are the norm.

Keys to the Exercises

Key to Ex. 2 in Lesson 38: see the price list in Lesson 39.

Common phrases

To make sure you complete the Common Phrases Supplement by the end of Part 1, learn Section 15 at about this point.

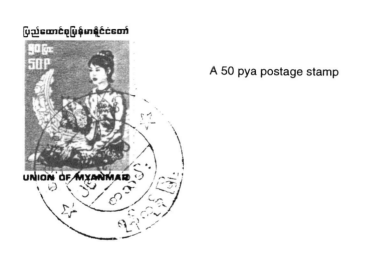

A 50 pya postage stamp

Diphthongs in the roman transcription:
pronounce ei as in *vein*, ai as in *Thailand*, ou as in *though*, au as in *Sauerkraut*.

LESSON 39

Paying a price. Who paid what.
How much did you pay for that? — I paid K45.

Goods and prices

item	ဈေး	price	item	ဈေး	price
hat	၄၅/–	45.00	soap	၁၅/–	15.00
T-shirt	၁၀၀/–	100.00	toilet paper	၁၆/–	16.00
rubber sandals	၄၀/–	40.00	comb	၁၀/–	10.00
battery	၇/၅၀	7.50	carved figure	၇၅/–	75.00
film	၂၀၀/–	200.00	key-ring	၈/–	8.00
pen	၁၀/–	10.00	fan	၃/၅၀	3.50
postcard	၅/–	5.00	Coca-cola	၄၅/–	45.00
glue	၆/–	6.00	Vimto	၂၀/–	20.00
envelope	၁/၅၀	1.50	banana	၁/၅၀	1.50

New words

အဲဒါ	that (nearer you than me)	èh-da
ပေးရ–	to pay ("to have to give")	pè-yá-
ဘယ်လောက် ... လဲ။	how much? what price?	beh-lauq ... -lèh?

Example sentences

S1: အဲဒါ ဘယ်လောက် ပေးရသလဲ။ | How much did you pay for that? | È-da beh-lauq pè-yá-dhălèh?

S1: ၄၅–ကျပ် ပေးရပါတယ်။ | I paid K45/-. | Lè-zéh ngà-jaq pè-yá-ba-deh.

S1: အဲဒါ ၄၅/– ပေးရသလား။ | Did you pay K45/- for that? | È-da lè-zéh ngà-jaq pè-yá-dhălà?

S1: ဟုတ်ကဲ့။ ၄၅/– ပေးရပါတယ်။ | Yes. I paid K45/- for it. | Houq-kéh. Lè-zéh ngà-jaq pè-yá-ba-deh.

S1: အဲဒါ ၅၅/– ပေးရသလား။ | Did you pay K55/- for that? | È-da ngà-zéh ngà-jaq pè-yá-dhălà?

S1: မပေးရပါဘူး။ ၄၅/– ပေးရပါတယ်။ | No. I paid K45/- for it. | Măpè-yá-ba-bù. Lè-zéh ngà-jaq pè-yá-ba-deh.

As mentioned in earlier Lessons you can choose fuller or terser answers to these questions. For examples see Lessons 27, 29, 31, 34.

You and I. Note that although the English translations in the Example sentences have to have words for "you" and "I," in Burmese it is normal to leave them out, provided it is clear from the context who you are talking about. If someone asks you a question without specifying who he asking about, the assumption is that he is asking about you. And when you answer that question, you can only be talking about yourself. There *are* words in

Diphthongs in the roman transcription:
pronounce ei as in *vein*, ai as in *Thailand*, ou as in *though*, au as in *Sauerkraut*.

Burmese that correspond to "you" and "I," but they tend to be used only when your listener might not be able to tell who you are referring to. We noted the same for "he" and "she" in Lesson 27.

When you do have to use a word for "you" there are many options to choose from. One common one is the person's name: if you were talking to U Ba and wanted to ask "How much did you pay?" (and couldn't omit the word for "you") you would say in effect "How much did U Ba pay?" (ဦးဘ ဘယ်လောက် ပေးရသလဲ = Ù Bá beh-lauq pè-yá-dhăleh?) — the same form of words as if you were asking someone else about U Ba rather than speaking to him directly.

A second option is to use a kin term; so your question to U Ba would come out as "How much did Uncle pay?", or "How much did Brother pay?", or "How much did Son pay?", depending on your relative ages. You use kin terms (a) when you don't know the person's name, and are thus prevented from using that; or (b) when you know the person so well that you feel as close to him as you would to an uncle or brother or son.

A third option is to use a title: "How much did Minister pay?", "How much did Teacher pay?", "How much did Ambassador pay?", and so on.

A fourth option is to use the word မိတ်ဆွေ (meiq-s'we) "friend": "How much did Friend pay?"

And lastly, if you are talking to persons of your own age and rank, or to juniors, you can use ခင်ဗျား (k'in-byà) "you" (for male speakers) or ရှင် (shin) "you" (for female speakers). Burmese speakers often present these two words to foreign learners as the Burmese equivalent for "you," but you should bear in mind that their application is restricted: it would be disrespectful to use them to address people older than yourself, or people who should be treated with respect.

Notice that although ခင်ဗျား (k'in-byà) and ရှင် (shin), meaning "you," are not for use with seniors, the opposite applies to the two very similar words that are used as polite tags at the end of a sentences, namely ခင်ဗျာ (k'in-bya) (note the different tone) and ရှင် (shin). These two are conspicuously courteous and respectful, and their use when speaking to seniors is encouraged and admired. For more on the polite tags, see the Common Phrases Supplement.

Models for the Exercises

Ex. 1: How much did you pay for that?
S1: အဲဒါ ဘယ်လောက် ပေးရသလဲ။   È-da beh-lauq pè-yá-dhăleh?
L/S2: ၄၅-ကျပ် ပေးရပါတယ်။   45-jaq pè-yá-ba-deh.

Ex. 2 For written answer: not on the tape.
The words in the following questions and answers have been split up and jumbled. Rearrange them to form meaningful sentences. There is a Key to this Exercise at the end of the Lesson. Don't forget that you may find it helpful to copy the words onto separate slips of paper and do your reordering by sliding the slips around.

Diphthongs in the roman transcription:
pronounce ei as in *vein*, ai as in *Thailand*, ou as in *though*, au as in *Sauerkraut*.

Ex. 2 in Lesson 39 (script)

S1: — ပေးရ — ဘယ်လောက် — အဲဒါ — သလဲ
    S2: — တယ် — ပေးရ — တစ်ရာ — ပါ
S1: — ခေါ် — နာမည် — သလဲ — ဘယ်လို
    S2: — ခေါ် — လို့ — ပါတယ် — ခင်မောင်ဝင်း
S1: — သွား — ကုန်တိုက် — သံတမန် — မပြိုး — လား — သ
    S2: — ဘူး — တယ် — စာကြည့်တိုက် — သွားပါ — မသွားပါ
S1: — သလဲ — အချိန် — သွား — ဘယ်
    S2: — လေး — သုံးဆယ် — နာရီ — မိနစ် — တယ် — သွားပါ — မှာ

Ex. 2 in Lesson 39 (roman)

S1: — pè-yá — beh-lauq — è-da — dhǎlèh
    S2: — deh — pè-yá — tǎya — ba
S1: — k'aw — nan-meh — dhǎlèh — beh-lo
    S2: — k'aw — ló — ba-deh — K'in Maun Wìn
S1: — thwà — Koun-daiq — Than-dǎman — Má Pyoùn — là — dhǎ
    S2: — bù — deh — sa-cí-daiq — thwà-ba — mǎthwà-ba
S1: — dhǎlèh — ǎc'ein — thwà — beh
    S2: — lè — thoùn-zeh — na-yi — mí-niq — deh — thwà-ba — hma

In class: Exercises as above. Also Learners ask each other how much their belongings cost:
    L1 points to [thing]* and asks: အဲဒါ ဘယ်လောက် ပေးရသလဲ။   L2: ဒေါ်လာ ၂၀။
All Learners make a list of the prices stated, and then ask round the group checking their accuracy.
    * [thing] = watch, spectacles, camera, pen, hat, umbrella, briefcase, ring, calculator, tape recorder, file, trousers, shirt, shoes, handbag, earrings, necklace, bangle, ...

Keys to the Exercises

Key to Ex. 2 in Lesson 39 (script)

S1: — အဲဒါ — ဘယ်လောက် — ပေးရ — သလဲ။
    S2: — တစ်ရာ — ပေးရ — ပါ — တယ်။
S1: — နာမည် — ဘယ်လို — ခေါ် — သလဲ။
    S2: — ခင်မောင်ဝင်း — လို့ — ခေါ် — ပါတယ်။
S1: — မပြိုး — သံတမန် — ကုန်တိုက် — သွား — သ — လား။
    S2: — မသွားပါ — ဘူး။ — စာကြည့်တိုက် — သွားပါ — တယ်။
S1: — ဘယ် — အချိန် — သွား — သလဲ။
    S2: — လေး — နာရီ — မိနစ် — သုံးဆယ် — မှာ — သွားပါ — တယ်။

Key to Ex. 2 in Lesson 39 (roman)

S1: — È-da — beh-lauq — pè-yá — dhǎlèh?
    S2: — Tǎya — pè-yá — ba — deh.
S1: — Nan-meh — beh-lo — k'aw — dhǎlèh?
    S2: — K'in Maun Wìn — ló — k'aw — ba-deh.
S1: — Má Pyoùn — Than-dǎman — Koun-daiq — thwà — dhǎ — là?
    S2: — Mǎthwà-ba — bù. — Sa-cí-daiq — thwà-ba — deh.
S1: — Beh — ǎc'ein — thwà — dhǎlèh?
    S2: — Lè — na-yi — mí-niq — thoùn-zeh — hma — thwà-ba — deh.

Diphthongs in the roman transcription:
pronounce ei as in *vein*, ai as in *Thailand*, ou as in *though*, au as in *Sauerkraut*.

LESSON 40

Asking for words.
What's that called in Burmese?
— It's called စာအိတ် (sa-eiq)

Things

article	*price*	*article*	*price*
ဘောပင်	၁၀/-	bàw-pin	10/-
ပို့စကဒ်	၆/-	pó-săkaq	6/-
စာအိတ်	၁/၅၀	sa-eiq	1/50
စာရွက်	၁၈/-	sa-yweq	18/-
ဆယ်လိုတိပ်	၁၂/-	s'eh-lo-teiq	12/-
မြေပုံ	၁၇/-	mye-boun	17/-
ဖလင်	၄၅၀/-	p'ălin	450/-
တိပ်ခွေ	၃၂၀/-	teiq-k'we	320/-
ကော်ဖီမှုန့်	၂၁၀/-	kaw-p'i-hmoún	210/-
နို့မှုန့်	၁၉၅/-	nó-hmoún	195/-
ဘီစကွတ်	၈/၅၀	bi-săkuq (bi-săkiq)	8/50

New words

အဲဒါ	that [nearer you than me]	èh-da
ဗမာလို	in Burmese ["Burmese-way"]	Băma-lo
Names of things:		
ဘောပင်	ballpoint pen [from English]	bàw-pin
ပို့စကဒ် /-စကတ်/	postcard [from English]	pó-săkaq
စာအိတ်	envelope ["letter-bag"]	sa-eiq
စာရွက်	writing paper, pad ["paper-sheet"]	sa-yweq
ဆယ်လိုတိပ်	sellotape (Scotchtape) [from English]	s'eh-lo-teiq
မြေပုံ /-ပုန်/	map ["earth picture"]	mye-boun
ဖလင်	film [from English]	p'ălin
တိပ်ခွေ	tape ["tape-reel"]	teiq-k'we
ကော်ဖီမှုန့်	instant or ground coffee ["coffee-powder"]	kaw-p'i-hmoún
နို့မှုန့်	milk powder ["milk-powder"]	nó-hmoún
ဘီစကွတ်	biscuit [= cookie; from English]	bi-săkuq (bi-săkiq)

Example sentences

S1: အဲဒါ ဗမာလို ဘယ်လို ခေါ်သလဲ။	What's that called in Burmese?	È-da Băma-lo beh-lo k'aw-dhălèh?
S2: "စာအိတ်"လို့ ခေါ်ပါတယ်။	It's called "sa-eiq."	"Sa-eiq"-ló k'aw-ba-deh.
S1: ဒီဘောပင် ဘယ်လောက် ပေးရသလဲ။	How much did you pay for this ballpoint pen?	Di bàw-pin beh-lauq pè-yá-dhălèh?
S2: ၁၀/- ပေးရပါတယ်။	I paid 10 kyats.	Tăs'eh pè-yá-ba-deh.

Diphthongs in the roman transcription:
pronounce ei as in *vein,* ai as in *Thailand,* ou as in *though,* au as in *Sauerkraut.*

Coconuts and bananas for sale at a market stall

Exercises

Ex. 1: Asking what things are called. Prompt: Point to an envelope and ask what it's called.

L/S2: အဲဒါ ဗမာလို ဘယ်လို ခေါ်သလဲ॥	È-da Băma-lo beh-lo k'aw-dhălèh?
S1: "စာအိတ်"လို့ ခေါ်ပါတယ်॥	"Sa-eiq"-ló k'aw-ba-deh.
L/S2: "စာအိတ်"လား॥	"Sa-eiq"-là?
S1: ဟုတ်ကဲ့॥	Houq-kéh.

Ex. 2: Prompt: S1 points to his ballpoint pen and asks:

S1: ဒီဘောပင် ဘယ်လောက် ပေးရသလဲ॥	Di bàw-pin beh-lauq pè-dhălèh?
L/S2: ဒီဘောပင်လား॥	Di bàw-pin-là?
S1: ဟုတ်ကဲ့॥	Houq-kéh.
L/S2: ၁၀/– ပေးရပါတယ်॥	Tăs'eh pè-yá-ba-deh.

Ex. 3 [new prices]. Prompt: Ask S1 about her bag of biscuits:

L/S2: ဒီဘီစကွတ် ဘယ်လောက် ပေးရသလဲ॥	Di bi-săkuq beh-lauq pè-yá-dhălèh?
S1: ၅/ ၂၅ ပေးရပါတယ်॥	Ngà-jaq hnăs'éh ngàbyà pè-yá-ba-deh.
L/S2: ၅/ ၂၅လား॥	Ngà-jaq hnăs'éh ngàbyà-là?
S1: ဟုတ်ကဲ့ပါ॥	Houq-kéh-ba.

L notes price on list, and checks answers with Key at end of Lesson.

---

136 |

Blank form for Ex. 3

biscuits	...	postcard	...
ballpoint pen	...	envelope	...
instant coffee	...	writing paper	...
map	...	sellotape (Scotchtape)	...
milk powder	...	tape	...
film	...		

In class: Exercises as above. Also Learners ask Teacher the names for things they often want to refer to. They make notes, and at intervals the teacher goes round checking memory, or gets Learners to ask each other. Also if any Learner knows another language — German, for example — the teacher can get Learners to ask အဲဒါ ဂျာမန်လို ဘယ်လို ခေါ်သလဲ။ and then do a check-up.

Notes

Grammar. The sentences in this Lesson are examples of the same familiar verb sentence formula as those in Lessons 27, 29, 31 and 36, though there is an extra noun in these examples.

N1+SFX	N2+SFX	N3+SFX	VERB+SFX	STC SFX
အဲဒါ	ဗမာ+လို	ဘယ်+လို	ခေါ်+သ–	လဲ။
È-da	Băma+lo	beh+lo	k'aw+dhă	-lèh?
That	Burmese+way	which+way	call+*pres/past*	*question*

"What is that called in Burmese?"

[ဒါ+က]	[ဗမာ+လို]	စအိတ်+လို့	ခေါ်ပါ+တယ်။	–
[Da+gá]	[Băma+lo]	sa-eiq+ló	k'aw-ba+deh.	–
[That]	[Burmese+way]	sa-eiq+*quote*	call-*polite+pres/past*	–

"[In Burmese] [that] is called 'sa-eiq'."

Common phrases

To make sure you complete the Common Phrases Supplement by the end of Part 1, learn Section 16 at about this point.

Diphthongs in the roman transcription:
pronounce ei as in *vein,* ai as in *Thailand,* ou as in *though,* au as in *Sauerkraut.*

Keys to the Exercises

Key to Ex. 3 in Lesson 40

ဘီစကွတ်	၅/၂၅	biscuits	5/25	bi-săkuq
ဘောပင်	၈/၅၀	ballpoint pen	8/50	bàw-pin
ကော်ဖီမှုန့်	၁၇၅/–	instant coffee	175/–	kaw-p'i-hmoún
မြေပုံ	၂၀/–	map	20/–	mye-boun
နို့မှုန့်	၁၆၂/–	milk powder	162/–	nó-hmoún
ဖလင်	၄၀၀/–	film	400/–	p'ălin
ပို့စကဒ်	၄/၅၀	postcard	4/50	pó-săkaq
စာအိတ်	၀/၇၅	envelope	0/75	sa-eiq
စာရွက်	၁၅/–	writing paper	15/–	sa-yweq
ဆယ်လိုတိပ်	၁၀/–	sellotape (Scotchtape)	10/–	s'eh-lo-teiq
တိပ်ခွေ	၂၉၀/–	tape	290/–	teiq-k'we

LESSON 41

Buying things. Who bought what.
What did he buy? — He bought a map and some sellotape.

Names and purchases

နာမည်	နေရာ	ပစ္စည်း
ဒေါ်ခင်ဆွေ	အနော်ရထာလမ်း	...
မမေမေခင်	ဗိုလ်အောင်ကျော်လမ်း	...
ဒေါ်ခင်ဆွေမြင့်	မဟာဗန္ဓုလလမ်း	...
ကိုရိုးတင့်	သံတမန်ကုန်တိုက်	...+...
ဗိုလ်မှူးကြီးဟန်တင်	ဗိုလ်ချုပ်လမ်း	...+...
ဒေါ်ဌေးဌေး	ဗိုလ်ချုပ်ဈေး	...+...
ဒေါက်တာဦးဝင်း	သိမ်ကြီးဈေး	...+...

name	place	article
Daw Khin Swe	Anawrahta Street	...
Ma May May Khin	Bo Aung Gyaw Street	...
Daw Khin Swe Myint	Maha Bandula Street	...
Ko Yoe Tint	Diplomatic Store	...+...
Colonel Han Tin	Bogyoke Street	...+...
Daw Htay Htay	Bogyoke Market	...+...
Dr. U Win	Theingyi Market	...+...

Diphthongs in the roman transcription:
pronounce ei as in *vein*, ai as in *Thailand*, ou as in *though*, au as in *Sauerkraut*.

nan-meh	*ne-ya*	*pyiq-sì*
Daw K'in S'we	Ănaw-yăt'a Làn	...
Má Me Me K'in	Bo Aun Jaw Làn	...
Daw K'in S'we Myín	Măha Ban-dú-lá Làn	...
Ko Yò Tín	Than-dăman Koun-daiq	... + ...
Bo-hmù-jì Han Tin	Bo-jouq Làn	... + ...
Daw T'è T'è	Bo-jouq Zè	... + ...
Dauq-ta Ù Wìn	Thein-jì Zè	... + ...

New words

ဝယ်–	to buy	weh-
[noun1]–နဲ့ [noun2]	[noun1] and [noun2]	[noun1]-néh [noun2]

    Examples:

ကိုတင်နဲ့ မလှ	Ko Tin and Ma Hla	Ko Tin-néh Má Hlá
ဖလင်နဲ့ တိပ်ခွေ	film and tape	p'ălin-néh teiq-k'we

In a string of nouns longer than two, –နဲ့ (-néh) is placed between the second-last and last; for example:

ဦးဝင်း၊ ဦးတင်နဲ့ ဦးကောင်း	U Win, U Tin and U Kaung	Ù Wìn, Ù Tin-néh Ù Kaùn

Note that –နဲ့ (-néh) is used to link two *nouns*. In English you can use "and" to link two verbs or clauses as well as two nouns: "He went to the market *and* bought some milk powder." Burmese –နဲ့ (-néh) is not used in this function. In Burmese you use other suffixes to link verbs.

Example sentences

S1: ကိုရိုးတင့် �’ဘာ ဝယ်သလဲ။	What did Ko Yo Tint buy?	Ko Yò Tín ba weh-dhălèh?
S2: ကော်ဖီမှုန့်နဲ့ နို့မှုန့် ဝယ်ပါတယ်။	He bought instant coffee and milk powder.	Kaw-p'i-hmóun-néh nó-hmoún weh-ba-deh.

Models for the Exercises

Ex. 1: What they bought. Prompt: Ask what Daw Khin Swe bought.

L/S2: ဒေါ်ခင်ဆွေ ’ဘာ ဝယ်သလဲ။	Daw K'in S'we ba weh-dhălèh?
S1: ဖလင် ဝယ်ပါတယ်။	P'ălin weh-ba-deh.
L/S2: ဖလင် and notes it in the blank.	P'ălin.

Check answers with Key at end of Lesson.

Ex. 2

S1: ဒေါက်တာဦးဝင်း ’ဘာ ဝယ်သလဲ။	Dauq-ta Ù Wìn ba weh-dhălèh?
L/S2: စာရွက်နဲ့ စာအိတ် ဝယ်ပါတယ်။	Sa-yweq-néh sa-eiq weh-ba-deh.
S1: စာရွက်နဲ့ စာအိတ် ဘယ်မှာ ဝယ်သလဲ။	Sa-yweq-néh sa-eiq beh-hma weh-dhălèh?
L/S2: သိမ်ကြီးဈေးမှာ ဝယ်ပါတယ်။	Thein-jì Zè-hma weh-ba-deh.

Diphthongs in the roman transcription:
pronounce ei as in *vein*, ai as in *Thailand*, ou as in *though*, au as in *Sauerkraut*.

Ex. 3

S1: ဒေါ်ခင်ဆွေက အနော်ရထာလမ်းမှာ ဖလင် ဝယ်ပါတယ်။	Daw K'in S'we-gá Ănaw-yăt'a Làn-hma p'ălin weh-ba-deh.
L/S2: ဟုတ်ကဲ့။ ဝယ်ပါတယ်။	Houq-kéh. Weh-ba-deh.
S1: မမေမေခင်က ဗိုလ်ချုပ်ဈေးမှာ တိပ်ခွေ ဝယ်ပါတယ်။	Má Me Me K'in-gá Bo-jouq Zè-hma teiq-k'we weh-ba-deh.
L/S2: မဟုတ်ပါဘူး။ ဗိုလ်အောင်ကျော်လမ်းမှာ ဝယ်ပါတယ်။	Măhouq-pa-bù. Bo Aun Jaw Làn-hma weh-ba-deh.

Ex. 4 in Lesson 41. For written answer: not on the tape.

The words in the following questions and answers have been split up and jumbled. Rearrange them to form meaningful sentences. There is a Key to this Exercise at the end of the Lesson. Don't forget that you may find it helpful to copy the words onto separate slips of paper and do your reordering by sliding the slips around.

S1: — ဝယ်သလဲ — ဘာ — ဒေါ်ဌေးဌေး — ဗိုလ်ချုပ်ဈေး — က — မှာ
S2: — ဘောပင်နဲ့ — တယ် — ဝယ်ပါ — ပို့စကဒ်
S1: — လား — သံတမန်ကုန်တိုက် — နဲ့ — နို့မှုန့် — ကော်ဖီမှုန့် — ဝယ်သ — မှာ
S2:— ဝယ်ပါ — ပါဘူး — ဘီစကွတ် — မဝယ် — တယ်
S1: — ဗမာ — ဘယ် — အဲဒါ — လို — လို — သလဲ — ခေါ်
S2: — တယ် — လို့ — ခေါ်ပါ — တိပ်ခွေ

Ex. 4 in Lesson 41 (roman)

S1: — weh-dhălèh — ba — Daw T'è T'è — Bo-jouq Zè — gá — hma
S2: — bàw-pin-néh — deh — weh-ba — pó-săkaq
S1: — là — Than-dăman Koun-daiq — néh — kaw-p'i-hmóun — nó-hmoún — weh-dhă — hma
S2: — weh-ba — ba-bù — bi-săkuq — măweh — deh
S1: — Băma — beh — è-da — lo — lo — dhălèh — k'aw
S2: — deh — ló — k'aw-ba — teiq-k'we

In class: Exercises as above. Also Learners ask each other what they bought and all try and remember. Then have check-up questions. Or Learners make up purchases. Or play Granny went to market:

L1: ဒေါ်ဒေါ် ဈေး သွားတယ်။ [thing1] ဝယ်တယ်။
L1: ဒေါ်ဒေါ် ဈေး သွားတယ်။ [thing1]–နဲ့ [thing2]ဝယ်တယ်။
L1: ဒေါ်ဒေါ် ဈေး သွားတယ်။ [thing1], [thing2]–နဲ့ [thing3] ဝယ်တယ်။

and so on till the list is too long to remember.

Diphthongs in the roman transcription:
pronounce ei as in *vein*, ai as in *Thailand*, ou as in *though*, au as in *Sauerkraut*.

Keys to the Exercises

Key to Ex. 1 in Lesson 41 (script)

နာမည်	နေရာ	ပစ္စည်း
ဒေါ်ခင်ဆွေ	အနော်ရထာလမ်း	ဖလင်
မမေမေခင်	ဗိုလ်အောင်ကျော်လမ်း	တိပ်ခွေ
ဒေါ်ခင်ဆွေမြင့်	မဟာဗန္ဓုလလမ်း	ဘီစကွတ်
ကိုရိုးတင့်	သံတမန်ကုန်တိုက်	ကော်ဖီမှုန့် + နို့မှုန့်
ဗိုလ်မှူးကြီးဟန်တင်	ဗိုလ်ချုပ်လမ်း	မြေပုံ + ဆယ်လိုတိပ်
ဒေါ်ဌေးဌေး	ဗိုလ်ချုပ်ဈေး	ဘောပင် + ပို့စကဒ်
ဒေါက်တာဦးဝင်း	သိမ်ကြီးဈေး	စာရွက် + စာအိတ်

name	*place*	*article*
Daw Khin Swe	Anawrahta Street	film
Ma May May Khin	Bo Aung Gyaw Street	tape
Daw Khin Swe Myint	Maha Bandula Street	biscuit, cookie
Ko Yoe Tint	Diplomatic Store	instant coffee + milk powder
Colonel Han Tin	Bogyoke Street	map + sellotape (Scotchtape)
Daw Htay Htay	Bogyoke Market	ballpoint pen + postcard
Dr. U Win	Theingyi Market	writing paper + envelope

nan-meh	*ne-ya*	*pyiq-sì*
Daw K'in S'we	Ănaw-yăt'a Làn	p'ălin
Má Me Me K'in	Bo Aun Jaw Làn	teiq-k'we
Daw K'in S'we Myín	Măha Ban-dú-lá Làn	bi-săkuq
Ko Yò Tín	Than-dăman Koun-daiq	kaw-p'i-hmoún-néh nó-hmoún
Bo-hmù-jì Han Tin	Bo-jouq Làn	mye-poun-néh s'eh-lo-teiq
Daw T'è T'è	Bo-jouq Zè	bàw-pin-néh pó-săkaq
Dauq-ta Ù Wìn	Thein-jì Zè	sa-yweq-néh sa-eiq

Key to Ex. 4 in Lesson 41

S1: — ဒေါ်ဌေးဌေး — က — ဗိုလ်ချုပ်ဈေး — မှာ — ဘာ — ဝယ်သလဲ။

   S2: — ဘောပင်နဲ့ — ပို့စကဒ် — ဝယ်ပါ — တယ်။

S1: — သံတမန်ကုန်တိုက် — မှာ — ကော်ဖီမှုန့် — နဲ့ — နို့မှုန့် — ဝယ်သ — လား။

   S2: — မဝယ် — ပါဘူး။ — ဘီစကွတ် — ဝယ်ပါ — တယ်။

S1: — အဲဒါ — ဗမာ — လို — ဘယ် — လို — ခေါ် — သလဲ။

   S2: — တိပ်ခွေ — လို့ — ခေါ်ပါ — တယ်။

Key to Ex. 4 in Lesson 41 (roman)

S1: — Daw T'è T'è — gá — Bo-jouq Zè — hma — ba — weh-dhălèh?

   S2: — Bàw-pin-néh — pó-săkaq — weh-ba — deh.

S1: — Than-dăman Koun-daiq — hma — kaw-p'i-hmoún — néh — nó-hmoún — weh-dhă — là.

   S2: — Măweh — ba-bù — Bi-săkuq — weh-ba — deh.

S1: — È-da — Băma — lo beh — lo — k'aw — dhălèh?

   S2: — teiq-k'we — ló — k'aw-ba — deh.

Dithongs in the roman transcription:
pronounce ei as in *vein*, ai as in *Thailand*, ou as in *though*, au as in *Sauerkraut*.

LESSON 41R

This Lesson gives you a run-through of almost all the words and structures you've practised up to this point. The exercises for this Lesson are on the Review Tape, which is on a separate cassette from the regular Lessons. Each Exercise is split into an A section and a B section: in one you ask the questions, and in the other you give the answers. Where there's a choice between answers of different lengths, aim for the middle-length answer. If you want to remind yourself of the difference between long, middling and short answers, you'll find some notes in the Example Sentences for Lessons 27 and the Notes for Lesson 29.

1. What is it and where?

Look at the street plan of Rangoon that comes before Lesson 1 in the text.
In Ex. 1A you answer S1's questions.
In Ex. 1B you ask the questions. Follow the prompt on the tape.

2. Towns of Burma

Look at the Burma map before Lesson 19. For Ex. 2A answer S1's questions.
In Ex. 2B you ask the questions: follow the prompt on the tape, and fill in the blanks when you hear the answer. Write your answers in Burmese script, or the romanization, or give the traditional English equivalents. At the end of the Exercise check that your answers tally with the Key at the end of the Lesson.

၈၇၆	...	၁၂၄၆	...
၆၁	...	၇	...
၁၀၅၂	...	၁၇၈၂	...
၁၁၆	...		

3. Who are they?

The list below gives details of some imaginary foreign residents of Rangoon. For Ex. 3A use the information to answer S1's questions.

n°	name	comes from	address	phone n°
1.	Mr. Amin	Malaysia	234 Strand Road	79447
2.	Mrs. Li	China	88 Anawrahta Street	82063
3.	Mr. Varma	India	300 Shwebontha Street	30418

In Ex. 3B you ask the questions. Follow the prompt on the tape and use the answers you hear to fill in the blanks.

Diphthongs in the roman transcription:
pronounce ei as in *vein*, ai as in *Thailand*, ou as in *though*, au as in *Sauerkraut*.

n°	name	comes from	address	phone n°
4.	…	…	…	…
5.	…	…	…	…
6.	…	…	…	…

4. Where are they?

For this Exercise you have to imagine you are working in a school or college. In Ex. 4A S1 is asking about some of your colleagues. Some have come in and gone out again, and some have arrived and gone to other parts of the building. Use the information below to answer the questions.

n°	1	2	3
name script	ဦးတင်အောင်	ဒေါ်ခင်မာမာ	ဦးအောင်ခင်
name trad roman	U Tin Aung	Daw Khin Ma Ma	U Aung Khin
name sys roman	Ù Tin Aun	Daw K'in Ma Ma	Ù Aun K'in
location	library	outside	Aung San Museum
time of coming/going	9.00	12.30	10.15

In Ex. 4B you ask the questions and record the information in the blanks.

n°	4	5	6
name script	ဒေါ်ခင်သန်းမြင့်	ဦးသောင်းအေး	ဒေါ်မြတ်ကြည်
name trad roman	Daw Khin Than Myint	U Thaung Aye	Daw Myat Kyi
name sys roman	Daw K'in Thàn Myín	Ù Thaùn È	Daw Myaq Ci
location	…	…	…
time of coming/going	…	…	…

5. What did they buy?

The notes below show who bought what and how much they paid for their purchases. Use the notes to answer S1's questions as usual.

n°	1	2	3
name script	ကိုကျော်မင်း	မခင်နီနီ	ကိုစောလွင်
name trad roman	Ko Kyaw Min	Ma Khin Ni Ni	Ko Saw Lwin
name sys roman	Ko Caw Mìn	Má K'in Ni Ni	Ko Sàw Lwin
bought	instant coffee	writing paper	tape
paid	K35/-	K12/50	K26/-

In Ex. 5B you ask the questions and fill in the blanks

n°	4	5	6
name script	မစိန်စိန်မြင့်	ကိုသန်း	…
name trad roman	Ma Sein Sein Myint	Ko Than	…
name sys roman	Má Sein Sein Myín	Ko Thàn	…
bought	…	…	envelope
paid	…	…	…

Diphthongs in the roman transcription:
pronounce ei as in *vein,* ai as in *Thailand,* ou as in *though,* au as in *Sauerkraut.*

6. What's it called?

In this Exercise, we start with you asking the questions for a change. Fill in the blanks when you hear the answer, and when you've finished check your results with the Key.

English	Burmese	bought at	paid
L asks questions			
၁။ pencil	...	...	...
၂။ ivory carving	...	...	...
၃။ bowl	...	...	...

In Ex. 6B, S1 asks you about some of your belongings, so you don't need to find out what the object is called in Burmese. Just answer the questions.

၄။ h a t	—	Washington	$25
၅။ battery	—	London	£1.50
၆။ calendar	—	Bangkok	450 baht

7. Jumbled sentences

For written answer: not on the tape.

The words in the following questions and answers have been split up and jumbled. Rearrange them to form meaningful sentences, and check your answer with the Key. Don't forget that you may find it helpful to copy the words onto separate slips of paper and do your reordering by sliding the slips around.

Ex. 7. Jumbled version (script)

1. S1:— လာသ — Mr. Schwarz — လဲ — ဘယ်နိုင်ငံက
   S2:— က — ဂျာမနီနိုင်ငံ — တယ် — လာပါ
2. S1:— နေသ — လမ်းမှာ — လဲ — ဘယ်
   S2:— ရွှေဘုံသာလမ်း — တယ် — နေပါ — မှာ
3. S1:— သ — ဘယ် — လဲ — သွား
   S2:— ပါ — သွား — ဈေး — တယ်
4. S1:— ဘယ်ဈေး — လဲ — သ — သွား
   S2:— သွား — ဈေး — တယ် — ဗိုလ်ချုပ် — ပါ
5. S1:— လဲ — ဘယ် — သွား — အချိန် — သ
   S2:— မှာ — ပါ — သွား — တယ် — ဆယ်နာရီ
6. S1:— သ — ဝယ် — ဘာ — လဲ
   S2:— ဝယ် — တယ် — ဘီစကွတ် — ပါ
7. S1:— ပေးရ — လဲ — ဘယ်လောက် — သ
   S2:— ကျပ် — တယ် — ပေးရ — ရှစ် — ပါ

Ex. 7. Jumbled version (roman)

1. S1: — la-dhă — Mr. Schwarz — lèh — beh-nain-ngan-gá
   S2: — gá — Ja-măni nain-ngan — deh — la-ba
2. S1: — ne-dhă — làn-hma — lèh — beh
   S2: — Shwe-boun-dha-Làn — deh — ne-ba — hma
3. S1: — dhă — beh — lèh — thwà
   S2: — ba — thwà — zè — deh

Diphthongs in the roman transcription:
pronounce ei as in *vein*, ai as in *Thailand*, ou as in *though*, au as in *Sauerkraut*.

4. S1: — beh-zè — lèh — dhă — thwà
   S2: — thwà — Zè — deh — Bo-jouq — ba
5. S1: — lèh — beh — thwà — ăc'ein — dhă
   S2: — hma — ba — thwà — deh — s'eh-na-yi
6. S1: — dhă — weh — ba — lèh
   S2: — weh — deh — bi-să-kuq — ba
7. S1: — pè-yá — lèh — beh-lauq — dhă
   S2: — caq — deh — pè-yá — shiq — ba

Keys to the Exercises in Lesson 41R

Key to Ex. 2B in Lesson 41R

၈၃၉	ပြည် /ပျို/ or /ပျေ/	Prome (Pyi/Pyay)	Pye
၉၁	ရေနံချောင်း /ယေနန်ကျောင်း/	Yenangyaung	Ye-nan-jaùn
၁၀၅၂	သံတွဲ	Sandoway (Thandwe)	Than-dwèh
၁၁၉	ပဲခူး /ဗဂိုး/	Pegu (Bago)	Păgò
၁၂၄၆	ရန်ကုန် /ယန်ဂန်/	Rangoon (Yangon)	Yan-goun
၇	တောင်ကြီး /တောင်ဂျိုး/	Taunggyi	Taun-jì
၁၃၈၅	မော်လမြိုင်	Moulmein (Mawlamyine)	Maw-lămyain

Key to Ex. 3B in Lesson 41R

4.	Mr. Tanong	ထိုင်းနိုင်ငံ	၇၆–ကုန်သည်လမ်း	၃၃၂၀၁
5.	Mrs. Husain	ဘင်္ဂလားဒေ့ရှ်နိုင်ငံ	၄၅၀–မဟာဗန္ဓုလလမ်း	၃၅၃၇၈
6.	Mr. Yoshida	ဂျပန်နိုင်ငံ	၁၉–ဗိုလ်အောင်ကျော်လမ်း	၅၂၆၉၈

4.	Mr. Tanong	T'aìn Nain-ngan	76 Koun-dheh Làn	33201
5.	Mrs. Husain	Bin-gălà-désh Nain-ngan	450 Măha Ban-dú-lá Làn	35378
6.	Mr. Yoshida	Jăpan Nain-ngan	19 Bo Aun Jaw Làn	52698

4.	Mr. Tanong	Thailand	76 Strand Road	33201
5.	Mrs. Husain	Bangladesh	450 Maha Bandoola Street	35378
6.	Mr. Yoshida	Japan	19 Bo Aung Gyaw Street	52698

Key to Ex. 4B in Lesson 41R

n°	4	5	6
name script	ဒေါ်ခင်သန်းမြင့်	ဦးသောင်းအေး	ဒေါ်မြတ်ကြည်
name trad roman	Daw Khin Than Myint	U Thaung Aye	Daw Myat Kyi
name sys roman	Daw K'in Thàn Myín	Ù Thaùn È	Daw Myaq Ci
location	canteen	President Hotel	toilet
time of coming/going	1.10	2.45	3.00

Diphthongs in the roman transcription:
pronounce ei as in *vein,* ai as in *Thailand,* ou as in *though,* au as in *Sauerkraut.*

Key to Ex. 5B in Lesson 41R

n°	4	5	6
name script	မစိန်စိန်မြင့်	ကိုသန်း	မနန်းဦး
name trad rom	Ma Sein Sein Myint	Ko Than	Ma Nan Oo
name sys roman	Má Sein Sein Myín	Ko Thàn	Má Nàn Ù
bought	milk powder	map	envelope
paid	K30/-	K8/50	K1/20

Key to Ex. 6A in Lesson 41R

၁॥	pencil	ခဲတံ (k'èh-dan)	Merchant Street	K4/-
၂॥	ivory carving	ဆင်စွယ်ရုပ် (s'in-zweh-youq)	Strand Hotel	K250/-
၃॥	bowl	ခွက် (k'weq)	Diplomatic Store	K145/-

Key to Ex. 7 in Lesson R41 (script)

1. S1: – Mr. Schwarz – ဘယ်နိုင်ငံက – လာသ – လဲ॥
   S2: – ဂျာမန်နိုင်ငံ – က – လာပါ – တယ်॥
2. S1: – ဘယ် – လမ်းမှာ – နေသ – လဲ॥
   S2: – ရွှေဘုံသာလမ်း – မှာ – နေပါ – တယ်॥
3. S1: – ဘယ် – သွား – သ – လဲ॥
   S2: – ဈေး – သွား – ပါ – တယ်॥
4. S1: – ဘယ်ဈေး – သွား – သ – လဲ॥
   S2: – ဘိုလ်ချုပ် – ဈေး – သွား – ပါ – တယ်॥
5. S1: – ဘယ် – အချိန် – သွား – သ – လဲ॥
   S2: – ဆယ်နာရီ – မှာ – သွား – ပါ – တယ်॥
6. S1: – ဘာ – ဝယ် – သ – လဲ॥
   S2: – ဘီစကွတ် – ဝယ် – ပါ – တယ်॥
7. S1: – ဘယ်လောက် – ပေးရ – သ – လဲ॥
   S2: – ရှစ် – ကျပ် – ပေးရ – ပါ – တယ်॥

Key to Ex. 7 in Lesson R41 (roman)

1. S1: — Mr. Schwarz — beh-nain-ngan — gá — la-dhă — lèh?
   S2: — Ja-măni nain-ngan — gá — la-ba — deh.
2. S1: — Beh — làn-hma — ne-dhă — lèh?
   S2: — Shwe-boun-dha-Làn — hma — ne-ba — deh.
3. S1: — Beh — thwà-dhă — lèh?
   S2: — Zè — thwà — ba — deh.
4. S1: — Beh-zè — thwà — dhă — lèh?
   S2: — Bo-jouq — Zè — thwà — ba — deh.
5. S1: — Beh — ăc'ein — thwà — dhă — lèh?
   S2: — S'eh-na-yi — hma — thwà — ba — deh.
6. S1: — Ba — weh — dhă — lèh?
   S2: — Bi-să-kuq — weh — ba — deh.
7. S1: — Beh-lauq — pè-yá — dhă — lèh?
   S2: Shiq — caq — pè-yá — ba — deh.

Diphthongs in the roman transcription:
pronounce ei as in *vein,* ai as in *Thailand,* ou as in *though,* au as in *Sauerkraut.*

Common phrases

To make sure you complete the Common Phrases Supplement by the end of Part 1, learn Section 17 at about this point.

LESSON 42

Want to [verb]: [verb]–ချင်–॥ [verb]-jin-.
Where did he want to go? — He wanted to go to Peking.

Unfulfilled aspirations

Table 1

name	went to	wanted to go to	lives in	wanted to live in
ဒေါ်ခင်ခင်ကြီး*	ဒက္ကား	ပီကင်း	မြစ်ကြီးနား	ရန်ကုန်
ဒေါ်ခင်ခင်လတ်*	ဘန်ကောက်	တိုကျို	ပဲခူး	စစ်ကိုင်း
ဒေါ်ခင်ခင်လေး*	ဟန္နွိုင်း	မနီလာ	ရေနံချောင်း	မန္တလေး

name	went to	wanted to go to	lives in	wanted to live in
Daw Khin Khin Gyi*	Dacca	Peking	Myitkyina	Rangoon
Daw Khin Khin Latt*	Bangkok	Tokyo	Pegu	Sagaing
Daw Khin Khin Lay*	Hanoi	Manila	Yenangyaung	Mandalay

name	went to	wanted to go to	lives in	wanted to live in
Daw K'in K'in Jì	Deq-kà	Pi-kìn	Myiq-cì-nà	Yan-goun
Daw K'in K'in Laq	Ban-kauq	To-co	Băgò	Săgaìn
Daw K'in K'in Lè	Hănwaìn	Măni-la	Ye-nan-jaùn	Màn-dălè

* If it strikes you as flippant to list three ladies with such similar names, it may seem downright perverse when you learn that the three final elements in the names, –ကြီး –လတ် –လေး (-jì, -laq, -lè), mean "senior," "middling" and "junior" respectively. In fact the names are taken as they stand from the telephone directory listing of the members of staff of the Ministry of Cooperative. By coincidence, all three ladies worked at the time in the same ministry. It is possible that their normal names were plain Khin Khin, but when three different Khin Khins came to work in the same organization they (or their colleagues) added the final syllables to help distinguish one from the other.

Diphthongs in the roman transcription:
pronounce ei as in *vein*, ai as in *Thailand*, ou as in *though*, au as in *Sauerkraut*.

Table 2

name	wants to come at	wants to buy
ဒေါ်ခင်ခင်ကြီး	၃း၁၅	နို့မှုန့်
ဒေါ်ခင်ခင်လတ်	၇း၄၀	မြေပုံ
ဒေါ်ခင်ခင်လေး	၂း၃၀	စာအိတ်နဲ့ စာရွက်

name	wants to come at	wants to buy
Daw Khin Khin Gyi	3.15	milk powder
Daw Khin Khin Latt	7.40	map
Daw Khin Khin Lay	2.30	envelopes and writing paper

name	wants to come at	wants to buy
Daw K'in K'in Jì	3.15	nó-hmoún
Daw K'in K'in Laq	7.40	mye-boun
Daw K'in K'in Lè	2.30	sa-eiq-néh sa-yweq

New words

–ချင်–	-jin- / -c'in-	to want to

Example sentences

သွားပါတယ်	[he] went	thwà-ba-deh
သွားချင်ပါတယ်	[he] wanted to go	thwà-jin-ba-deh

ဒီမှာ နေသလား	does [he] live here?	di-hma ne-dhălà?
ဒီမှာ နေချင်သလား	does he want to live here?	di-hma ne-jin-dhălà?

လန်ဒန် မလာပါဘူး	[He] didn't come to London.	Lan-dan mălа-ba-bù
လန်ဒန် မလာချင်ပါဘူး	[He] didn't want to come to London.	Lan-dan mălа-jin-ba-bù

S1: ဦးဘ ပုဂံ သွားချင်သလား။	Does U Ba want to go to Pagan?	Ù Bá Păgan thwà-jin-dhălà?
S2: ဟုတ်ကဲ့။ သွားချင်ပါတယ်။	Yes. He does.	Houq-kéh. Thwà-jin-ba-deh.
or:		
S2: မသွားချင်ပါဘူး။ – တောင်ကြီး သွားချင်ပါတယ်။	No. He wants to go to Taunggyi.	Măthwà-jin-ba-bù. — Taun-jì thwà-jin-ba-deh.
S1: ဒေါ်မေ ဘယ် သွားချင်သလဲ။	Where does Daw May want to go to?	Daw Me beh thwà-jin-dhălèh?
S2: ပုဂံ သွားချင်ပါတယ်။	She wants to go to Pagan.	Păgan thwà-jin-ba-deh.

Diphthongs in the roman transcription:
pronounce ei as in *vein*, ai as in *Thailand*, ou as in *though*, au as in *Sauerkraut*.

Models for the Exercises

Ex. 1: He went ⇒ He wants to go. Prompt: Sentence 1.

    S1: ပုဂံ သွားပါတယ်။   Păgan thwà-ba-deh.

    L/S2: ပုဂံ သွားချင်ပါတယ်။   Păgan thwà-jin-ba-deh.

    See Key at end of Lesson for translation.

Ex. 2

    S1: ဒေါ်ခင်ခင်ကြီး ဘယ် သွားသလဲ။   Daw K'in K'in Jì beh thwà-dhălèh?

    L/S2: ဒက္ကား သွားပါတယ်။   Deq-kà thwà-ba-deh.

Ex. 3

    S1: ဒက္ကား ဘယ်သူ သွားသလဲ။   Deq-kà beh-dhu thwà-dhălèh?

    L/S2: ဒေါ်ခင်ခင်ကြီး သွားပါတယ်။   Daw K'in K'in Jì thwà-ba-deh.

Ex. 4: Prompt: You're talking to U Kyaw Win. Ask him where he went.

    L/S2: ဘယ် သွားသလဲ။   Beh thwà-dhălèh?

    S1: ဒတ်ဘလင် သွားပါတယ်။   Daq-bălin thwà-ba-deh.

    L enters the information. Check answers with Key at end of Lesson.

Form for Ex. 4

name	went to	wanted to go to	lives in	wants to live in
ဦးကျော်ဝင်း	...	...	...	...
ဦးလှမောင်	...	...	...	...
ဦးချစ်ကိုကို	...	...	...	...

name	went to	wanted to go to	lives in	wants to live in
U Kyaw Win	...	...	...	...
U Hla Maung	...	...	...	...
U Chit Ko Ko	...	...	...	...

Ex. 5

    S1: ဒေါ်ခင်ခင်ကြီး ဘယ်အချိန် လာချင်သလဲ။ Daw K'in K'in Jì beh ăc'ein la-jin-dhălèh?

    L/S2: ၃:၁၅ လာချင်ပါတယ်။   Thoùn-na-yi s'éh-ngà măniq la-jin-ba-deh.

Ex. 6

The words in the following questions and answers have been split up and jumbled. Rearrange them to form meaningful sentences. There is a Key to this Exercise at the end of the Lesson. Don't forget that you may find it helpful to copy the words onto separate slips of paper and do your reordering by sliding the slips around.

Jumbled sentences (script)

S1: – ဒေါ်ခင်ခင်လတ် – ပီကင်း – သလား – က – သွား

    S2: – သွား – မသွား – ပါတယ် – ပါဘူး – ဘန်ကောက်

S1: – ချင် – သွား – ဘန်ကောက် – သလား

    S2: – တိုကျို – မသွားချင် – ပါတယ် – သွားချင် – ပါဘူး

Diphthongs in the roman transcription:
pronounce ei as in *vein,* ai as in *Thailand,* ou as in *though,* au as in *Sauerkraut.*

149

Jumbled sentences (roman)

> S1: — Daw K'in K'in Laq — Pi-kìn — dhǎlà — ká — thwà
>> S2: — thwà — mǎthwà — ba-deh — ba-bù — Ban-kauq
> S1: — jin — thwà — Ban-kauq — dhǎlà
>> S2: — To-co — mǎthwà-jin — ba-deh — thwà-jin — ba-bù

In class: Exercises as above. Also Learners ask each other where they went and where they live and where they want to go and where they want to live.

Notes

Grammar. The sentences in this Lesson are examples of the same verb sentence formula as those in Lessons 27, 29, 31, 36, and 40. The only difference is that the verb slot contains a verb with –ချင်– (-jin-) attached:

NOUN1+SUFFIX	NOUN2+SUFFIX	VERB+SUFFIX	STC SFX
ဦးဘ	ဘယ်	သွား–ချင်+သ–	လဲ။
Ù Bá	beh	thwà-jin+dhǎ	-lèh?
U Ba	where-to	go-want+*pres/past*	*question*
	"Where does U Ba want to go to?"		
ဦးဘ+က	ပုဂံ	သွား–ချင်–ပါ+တယ်။	–
Ù Bá+gá	Pǎgan	thwà-jin-ba+deh.	–
U Ba+*subject*	to Pagan	go-want-*polite+pres/past*	–
	"U Ba wants to go to Pagan."		

The formula applies in the same way to the *Yes/No* questions and answers.

Keys to the Exercises

Key to Ex. 1 in Lesson 42

1. She wants to go to Pagan.
2. Where does she want to go to?
3. Does she want to go to Maymyo?
4. She doesn't want to go to Sandoway.
5. She doesn't want to live in Bangkok.
6. She wants to live in Singapore.
7. Where does she want to live?
8. Does she want to live in London?
9. Where did she go?
10. Did she go to Australia?
11. She doesn't live in Malaysia.
12. She lives in Taunggyi.

Diphthongs in the roman transcription:
pronounce ei as in *vein*, ai as in *Thailand*, ou as in *though*, au as in *Sauerkraut*.

Key to Ex. 4 in Lesson 42

name	went to	wanted to go to	lives in	wants to live in
ဦးကျော်ဝင်း	ဒတ်ဘလင်	လန်ဒန်	မေမြို့	ပုဂံ
ဦးလှမောင်	ဘာလင်	ဝါရှင်တန်	ပြည်	သာစည်
ဦးချစ်ကိုကို	စင်္ကာပူ	ကင်ဘာရာ	သံတွဲ	တောင်ကြီး

U Kyaw Win	Dublin	London	Maymyo	Pagan
U Hla Maung	Berlin	Washington	Prome/Pyay	Thazi
U Chit Ko Ko	Singapore	Canberra	Sandoway	Taunggyi

Key to Ex. 6 in Lesson 42 (script)

S1: — ဒေါ်ခင်ခင်လတ် — က — ပီကင်း — သွား — သလား။

S2: — မသွား — ပါဘူး။ — ဘန်ကောက် — သွား — ပါတယ်။

S1: — ဘန်ကောက် — သွား — ချင် — သလား။

S2: — မသွားချင် — ပါဘူး။ — တိုကျို — သွားချင် — ပါတယ်။

Key to Ex. 6 in Lesson 42 (roman)

S1: — Daw K'in K'in Laq — ká — Pi-kìn — thwà — dhǎlà?

S2: — Mǎthwà — ba-bù. — Ban-kauq — thwà — ba-deh.

S1: — Ban-kauq — thwà — jin — dhǎlà?

S2: — Mǎthwà-jin — ba-bù. To-co — thwà-jin — ba-deh.

LESSON 43

Practice with want to [verb]. More verbs.
Where do you want to sit? Do you want the fan on?

More wanting to

List 1: seating plan

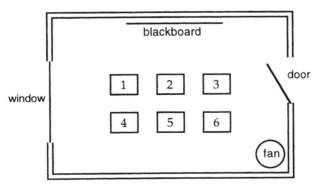

နာမည်	စားပွဲနံပါတ်	name	desk nº	name
ကိုသော်ကောင်း	၁	Ko Thaw Kaung	1	Ko Thaw Kaùn
မခင်ခင်အုံး	၂	Ma Khin Khin Ohn	2	Má K'in K'in Oùn
ကိုမောင်မောင်အေး	၃	Ko Maung Maung Aye	3	Ko Maun Maun È
မစမ်းမြိုင်	၄	Ma San Myaing	4	Má Sàn Myain
ကိုဝင်းမောင်	၅	Ko Win Maung	5	Ko Wìn Maun
မခင်နှင်းဦး	၆	Ma Khin Hnin Oo	6	Má K'in Hnìn Ù

Diphthongs in the roman transcription:
pronounce ei as in *vein*, ai as in *Thailand*, ou as in *though*, au as in *Sauerkraut*.

151

List 2: comfort needs

	ကိုသာကျော်	မစောနွဲ့ဦး	ကိုစိုးမင်း
မီး	ဖွင့်	ပိတ်	ပိတ်
ပန်ကာ	ပိတ်	ဖွင့်	ပိတ်
တံခါး	ပိတ်	ပိတ်	ဖွင့်
ပြတင်းပေါက်	ဖွင့်	ပိတ်	ဖွင့်

	Ko Tha Kyaw Ko Tha Jaw	Ma Saw Nwe Oo Má Sàw Nwéh Ù	Ko So Min Ko Sò Mìn	
mì	on	off	off	light
pan-ka	off	on	off	fan
dăgà	closed	closed	open	door
pădìn-bauq	open	closed	open	window

New words

ထိုင်–	to sit	t'ain–
စားပွဲ /စဗွဲ/	table, desk	săbwèh
ပိတ်–	to close, turn off	peiq–
ဖွင့်–	to open, turn on	p'wín
မီး	fire, light	mì
ပန်ကာ	fan	pan-ka
တံခါး /ဒဂါး/	door	dăgà
ပြတင်းပေါက် /ပဒင်းဘောက်/	window	pădìn-bauq

Example sentences

S1: ကိုသော်ကောင်း ဘယ်မှာ ထိုင်သလဲ။	Where does Ko Thaw Kaung sit?	Ko Thaw Kaùn beh-hma t'ain-dhălèh?
S2: စားပွဲနံပါတ်(၁)မှာ ထိုင်ပါတယ်။	He sits at desk n° 1.	Săbwèh nan-baq-tiq-hma t'ain-ba-deh.
S1: ဘယ်မှာ ထိုင်ချင်သလဲ။	Where do you want to sit?	Beh-hma t'ain-jin-dhălèh?
S2: စားပွဲနံပါတ်(၂)မှာ ထိုင်ချင်ပါတယ်။	I want to sit at desk n° 2.	Săbwèh nan-baq-hniq-hma t'ain-jin-ba-deh.
S1: မီး ဖွင့်ချင်သလား။	Do you want to turn on the light? (= Would you like the light on?)	Mì p'wín-jin-dhălà?
2: မဖွင့်ချင်ပါဘူး။ ပိတ်ချင်ပါတယ်။	No. I want to turn it off. (= No. I want it off.)	Măp'wín-jin-ba-bù. Peiq-c'in-ba-deh.

Diphthongs in the roman transcription:
pronounce ei as in *vein,* ai as in *Thailand,* ou as in *though,* au as in *Sauerkraut.*

Models for the Exercises

Ex. 1: Seating and comfort. List 1.

S1: ကိုသော်ကောင်း ဘယ်မှာ ထိုင်သလဲ။ Ko Thaw Kaùn beh-hma t'ain-dhălèh?

 စားပွဲနံပါတ်(၁)မှာ ထိုင်သလား။ Săbwèh nan-baq-tiq-hma t'ain-dhălà?

L/S2: ဟုတ်ကဲ့။ Houq-kéh.

 စားပွဲနံပါတ်(၁)မှာ ထိုင်ပါတယ်။ Săbwèh nan-baq-tiq-hma t'ain-ba-deh.

Ex. 2: List 1 revised.

Follow the prompt in asking the class where they *want to* sit, and make a note of the revised seating plan on the blank.

Prompt: Ask ကိုသော်ကောင်း where he wants to sit

L/S2: ကိုသော်ကောင်း ဘယ်မှာ ထိုင်ချင်သလဲ။ Ko Thaw Kaùn beh-hma t'ain-jin-dhălèh?

S1: စားပွဲနံပါတ်(၄)မှာ ထိုင်ချင်ပါတယ်။ Săbwèh nan-baq-lè-hma t'ain-jin-ba-deh.

Ex. 2: Blank for revised seating plan. Check answers with Key at end of Lesson.

ကိုသော်ကောင်း	Ko Thaw Kaung	Ko Thaw Kaùn	...
မခင်ခင်အုံး	Ma Khin Khin Ohn	Má K'in K'in Oùn	...
ကိုမောင်မောင်အေး	Ko Maung Maung Aye	Ko Maun Maun È	...
မစမ်းမြိုင်	Ma San Myaing	Má Sàn Myain	...
ကိုဝင်းမောင်	Ko Win Maung	Ko Wìn Maun	...
မခင်နှင်းဦး	Ma Khin Hnin Oo	Má K'in Hnìn Ù	...

Ex. 3: Use List 2 to answer S1's questions.

S1: ကိုသာကျော် မီး ဖွင့်ချင်သလား။ Ko Tha Jaw mì p'wín-jin-dhălà?

L/S2: ဟုတ်ကဲ့။ ဖွင့်ချင်ပါတယ်။ Houq-kéh. Mì p'wín-jin-ba-deh.

Ex. 4: Prompt: Ask Ma Ngwe Sein if she wants the lights on:

L/S2: မငွေစိန် မီး ဖွင့်ချင်သလား။ Má Ngwe Sein mì p'wín-jin-dhălà?

S1: မဖွင့်ချင်ပါဘူး။ ပိတ်ချင်ပါတယ်။ Măp'wín-jin-ba-bù. Peiq-c'in-ba-deh.

Blank for Ex. 4. Check answers with Key at end of Lesson.

	မငွေစိန်	ကိုဖေချစ်	
	Ma Ngwe Sein	Ko Pe Chit	
မီး	...	...	mì
ပန်ကာ	...	...	pan-ka
တံခါး	...	...	dăgà
ပြတင်းပေါက်	...	...	pădìn-bauq

Ex. 5 in Lesson 43. For written answer: not on the tape.

The words in the following questions and answers have been split up and jumbled. Rearrange them to form meaningful sentences. There is a Key to this Exercise at the end of the Lesson. Don't forget that you may find it helpful to copy the words onto separate slips of paper and do your reordering by sliding the slips around.

Diphthongs in the roman transcription:
pronounce ei as in *vein*, ai as in *Thailand*, ou as in *though*, au as in *Sauerkraut*.

S1: — ဘယ်မှာ — သလဲ — ထိုင်ချင် — ကိုမောင်မောင်အေး
S2: — ပါတယ် — ထိုင်ချင် — နံပါတ်(၁) — စားပွဲ — မှာ
S1: — မစောနဲ့ဦး — သလား — ချင် — ဖွင့် — ပြတင်းပေါက်
S2: — မဖွင့် — ပိတ် — ပါဘူး — ပါတယ် — ချင် — ချင်
S1: — ဘယ်သူ — သွား — သလဲ — ချင် — ပီကင်း
S2: — ပါတယ် — သွား — ဒေါ်ခင်ခင်ကြီး — ချင်

Ex. 5 in Lesson 43

S1: — beh-hma — dhălèh — t'ain-jin —Ko Maun Maun È
S2: — ba-deh — t'ain-jin — nan-baq(tiq) — săbwèh — hma
S1: — Má Sàw Nwéh Ù — dhălà — jin — p'wín — pădìn-bauq
S2: — măpw'ín — peiq — ba-bù — ba-deh — jin — c'in
S1: — beh-dhu — thwà — dhălèh — jin — Pi-kìn
S2: — ba-deh — thwà — Daw K'in K'in Jì — jin

In class: Exercises as above. Also Learners use the plan in the text to decide where they want to sit, and ask each other about that. Then check-up: Does Mary want to sit at Table 6? and so on. Also Learners say preferences for light, window, door, fan (radio, video, cassette, …), and then ask around: Does Mary want the window open? and so on.

Keys to the Exercises

Key to revised seating plan for Ex. 2 in Lesson 43

ကိုသော်ကောင်း	၄	Ko Thaw Kaung	4	Ko Thaw Kaùn
မခင်ခင်အုံး	၂	Ma Khin Khin Ohn	2	Má K'in K'in Oùn
ကိုမောင်မောင်အေး	၁	Ko Maung Maung Aye	1	Ko Maun Maun È
မစမ်းမြိုင်	၆	Ma San Myaing	6	Má Sàn Myain
ကိုဝင်းမောင်	၅	Ko Win Maung	5	Ko Wìn Maun
မခင်နှင်းဦး	၃	Ma Khin Hnin Oo	3	Má K'in Hnìn Ù

Key to Ex. 4 in Lesson 43

	မငွေစိန်	ကိုဖေချစ်	Ma Ngwe Sein	Ko Pe Chit
မီး	ပိတ်	ဖွင့်	off	on
ပန်ကာ	ပိတ်	ဖွင့်	off	on
တံခါး	ပိတ်	ဖွင့်	closed	open
ပြတင်းပေါက်	ဖွင့်	ပိတ်	open	closed

Key to Ex. 5 in Lesson 43

S1: — ကိုမောင်မောင်အေး — ဘယ်မှာ — ထိုင်ချင် — သလဲ။
S2: — စားပွဲ — နံပါတ်(၁) — မှာ — ထိုင်ချင် — ပါတယ်။
S1: — မစောနဲ့ဦး — ပြတင်းပေါက် — ဖွင့် — ချင် — သလား။
S2: — မဖွင့် — ချင် — ပါဘူး။ — ပိတ် — ချင် — ပါတယ်။
S1: — ပီကင်း — ဘယ်သူ — သွား — ချင် — သလဲ။
S2: — ဒေါ်ခင်ခင်ကြီး — သွား — ချင် — ပါတယ်။

Diphthongs in the roman transcription:
pronounce ei as in *vein*, ai as in *Thailand*, ou as in *though*, au as in *Sauerkraut*.

Key to Ex. 5 in Lesson 43

S1: —Ko Maun Maun È — beh-hma — t'ain-jin — dhălèh?
S2: — Săbwèh — nan-baq(tiq) — hma — t'ain-jin — ba-deh.
S1: — Má Sàw Nwéh Ù — pădìn-bauq — p'wín — jin — dhălà?
S2: — — Măpw'ín — jin — ba-bù. — Peiq — c'in — ba-deh.
S1: — Pi-kìn — beh-dhu — thwà — jin — dhălèh?
S2: — Daw K'in K'in Jì — thwà — jin — ba-deh.

Common phrases

To make sure you complete the Common Phrases Supplement by the end of Part 1, learn Section 18 at about this point.

LESSON 44

Going to [verb]: [verb]–မယ်။ [verb]-meh.
Where is he going to sit? — He's going to sit here.

Names and desks, roads, times, places, and things

name	is going to sit at desk	is going to live in road	is going to come at	is going to go to	is going to buy
ကိုကျော်အောင်	၃၀	ရွှေဘုံသာလမ်း	၃:၀၀	စာကြည့်တိုက်	ဘီစကွတ်
မညွန့်ညွန့်	၁၈	ဗိုလ်ချုပ်လမ်း	၁၀:၁၅	ကုန်တိုက်	ကော်ဖီမှုန့်
ကိုမောင်သိန်း	၂၄	ကမ်းနားလမ်း	၉:၄၀	ဈေး	နို့မှုန့်
မလှလှ	၁၀	ပန်းဆိုးတန်း	၂:၅၀	ဆူးလေဘုရား	တိပ်ခွေ

name	is going to sit at desk	is going to live in road	is going to come at	is going to go to	is going to buy
Ko Kyaw Aung	30	Shebontha Street	3.00	the library	biscuits
Ma Nyunt Nyunt	18	Bogyoke Street	10.15	dept store	instant coffee
Ko Maung Thein	24	Strand Road	9.40	market	milk powder
Ma Hla Hla	10	Pansodan	2.50	Sule Pagoda	tapes

name	is going to sit at desk	is going to live in road	is going to come at	is going to go to	is going to buy
Ko Caw Aun	30	Shwe-boun-dha Làn	3.00	sa-cí-daiq	bi-săkuq
Má Nyún Nyún	18	Bo-jouq Làn	10.15	koun-daiq	kaw-p'i-hmoún
Ko Maun Thein	24	Kàn-nà Làn	9.40	zè	nó-hmoún
Má Hlá Hlá	10	Pàn-s'ò-dàn	2.50	S'ù-le P'ăyà	teiq-k'we

Diphthongs in the roman transcription:
pronounce ei as in *vein*, ai as in *Thailand*, ou as in *though*, au as in *Sauerkraut*.

New words

–မယ်	*verb suffix: "future"*	-meh
[verb]–မယ်	is going to [verb]	[verb]-meh

–မယ် weakens to –မ– when followed by a question suffix:

[verb]–မယ် + –လား။ ⇒ [verb]–မလား။	[verb]-meh + -là ⇒ [verb]-mălà
[verb]–မယ် + –လဲ။ ⇒ [verb]–မလဲ။	[verb]-meh + -lèh ⇒ [verb]-mălèh

Example sentences

S1: ဘယ်အချိန် လာမလဲ။	What time are you going to come?	Beh-ăc'ein la-mălèh?
S2: ၁၀–နာရီမှာ လာမယ်။	I'm going to come at 10.	S'eh-na-yi-hma la-meh.
S1: ၆–နာရီမှာ လာမလား။	Are you going to come at 6?	C'auq-na-yi-hma la-mălà?
S2: မလာပါဘူး။ — ၁၀–နာရီမှာ လာမယ်။	I'm not. — I'm going to come at 10.	Măla-ba-bù. — S'eh-na-yi-hma la-meh.
S1: ၁၂–နာရီမှာ လာမလား။	Are you going to come at 12?	S'éh-hnăna-yi-hma la-mălà?
S2: ဟုတ်ကဲ့။ — ၁၂–နာရီမှာ လာမယ်။	Yes. — I'm going to come at 12.	Houq-kéh. — S'éh-hnăna-yi-hma la-meh.

Models for the Exercises

Ex. 1: Is going to …
        S1: ကိုကျော်အောင် ဘယ်မှာ ထိုင်မလဲ။   Ko Caw Aun beh-hma t'ain-mălèh?
        L/S2: စားပွဲ နံပါတ် (၃၀)မှာ ထိုင်မယ်။   Săbwèh nan-baq-30-hma t'ain-meh.

Ex. 2: Prompt: Ask Ko Maung Thein which desk he's going to sit at.
        L/S2: ဘယ်စားပွဲမှာ ထိုင်မလဲ။   Beh săbwèh-hma t'ain-mălèh?
        S1: စားပွဲနံပါတ် (၂၄)မှာ ထိုင်မယ်။   Săbwèh nan-baq-24-hma t'ain-meh.

In class: Exercises as above. Also where Learners are going to go, what they are going to buy, what time they are going to come, and so on.

Notes

Grammar. The sentences in this Lesson are examples of the same verb sentence formula as those in Lessons 27, 29, 31, 36, 40, and 42. The only difference is that the verb suffix is not –တယ် (-deh) but –မယ် (-meh) :

Diphthongs in the roman transcription:
pronounce ei as in *vein*, ai as in *Thailand*, ou as in *though*, au as in *Sauerkraut*.

NOUN1+SUFFIX	NOUN2+SUFFIX	VERB+SUFFIX	STC SFX

ဦးဘ	ဘယ်+မှာ	ထိုင်+မ–	လဲ။
Ù Bá	beh+hma	t'ain+mă	-lèh?
U Ba	where-at	sit+*future*	*question*

"Where is U Ba going to sit?"

ဦးဘ+က	ဒီ+မှာ	ထိုင်+မယ်။	–
Ù Bá+gá	di+hma	t'ain+meh.	–
U Ba+*subject*	here+at	sit+*future*	–

"U Ba is going to sit here."

The formula applies in the same way to the *Yes/No* questions and answers.

LESSON 45

Will have to [verb].
Where is he going to have to live?
— He'll have to live in Taunggyi.

Names and desks, towns, times, places, and prices

In script

name	*is going to have to sit at desk n°*	*is going to have to live in*	*is going to have to come at*
မမြင့်မြင့်ခင်	၄၈	မန်ချက်စတာ	၁၂း၀၀
ကိုအောင်ကြည်	၆၃	ဆစ်ဒနီ	၄း၄၅
မသောင်းခင်	၅၂	ဂျကာတာ	၁၁း၄၀
ကိုသက်လွင်	၇၁	မနီလာ	၅း၂၀

name	*is going to have to go to*	*is going to have to buy*	*is going to have to pay*
မမြင့်မြင့်ခင်	မြစ်ကြီးနား	စာအိတ်	၈၅/–
ကိုအောင်ကြည်	တောင်ကြီး	ဖလင်	၄/၅၀
မသောင်းခင်	မော်လမြိုင်	စာရွက်	၆၀/–
ကိုသက်လွင်	စစ်တွေ	ဘောပင်	၃/၂၅

Diphthongs in the roman transcription:
pronounce **ei** as in *vein*, **ai** as in *Thailand*, **ou** as in *though*, **au** as in *Sauerkraut*. | 157

In English

name	is going to have to sit at desk n°	is going to have to live in	is going to have to come at
Ma Myint Myint Khin	48	Manchester	12:00
Ko Aung Kyi	63	Sydney	4:45
Ma Thaung Khin	52	Jakarta	11:40
Ko Thet Lwin	71	Manila	5:20

name	is going to have to go to	is going to have to buy	is going to have to pay
Ma Myint Myint Khin	Myitkyina	envelopes	85/-
Ko Aung Kyi	Taunggyi	film	4/50
Ma Thaung Khin	Moulmein	writing paper	60/-
Ko Thet Lwin	Akyab/Sittwe	ballpoint pens	3/25

In romanized Burmese

name	is going to have to sit at desk n°	is going to have to live in	is going to have to come at
Má Myín Myín K'in	48	Man-c'eq-săta	12:00
Ko Aun Ci	63	Siq-dăni	4:45
Má Thaùn K'in	52	Jăka-ta	11:40
Ko Theq Lwin	71	Măni-la	5:20

name	is going to have to go to	is going to have to buy	is going to have to pay
Má Myín Myín K'in	Myiq-cì-nà	sa-eiq	85/-
Ko Aun Ci	Taun-jì	p'ălin	4/50
Má Thaùn K'in	Maw-lămyain	sa-yweq	60/-
Ko Theq Lwin	Siq-twe	bàw-pin	3/25

New words

[verb]-ရမယ်	is going to have to [verb] will have to [verb] should, ought to [verb]	[verb]-yá-meh

Suffix –ရ– (-yá-) is also used in [verb]–ရတယ် (-yá-deh) meaning "has to [verb], had to [verb]," but the combination [verb]–ရမယ် (-yá-meh) is more useful for our present purpose. You have met suffix –ရ– (-yá-) before, in the compound verb ပေးရ– (pè-yá-) "to pay," literally "have to give."

Diphthongs in the roman transcription:
pronounce ei as in *vein,* ai as in *Thailand,* ou as in *though,* au as in *Sauerkraut.*

Pronunciation. When people are speaking fast, the consonant sound –ရ– (-y-) in [verb]–ရ–
(-yá-) often suffers. This is most noticeable when the –ရ– (-yá-) follows a verb with the
rhyme –ာ (-a) or ဟ (-u). Be prepared to hear လာရမယ် (la-yá-meh) pronounced လာအမယ် (la-
á-meh), and ယူရမယ် (yu-yá-meh) pronounced ယူဝမယ် (yu-wá-meh).

Example sentences

�‌ဘောပင် ဝယ်မယ်။	I'm going to buy a ballpoint pen.	Bàw-pin weh-meh.
‌ဘောပင် ဝယ်ရမယ်။	I'm going to have to buy a ballpoint pen.	Bàw-pin weh-yá-meh.
	I have to buy a ballpoint pen.	

ဘယ်အချိန် လာမလဲ။	What time will they come?	Beh-ăc'ein la-mălèh?
ဘယ်အချိန် လာရမလဲ။	What time will they have to come?	Beh-ăc'ein la-yá-mălèh?
	What time should they come?	

| S1: ဘယ်မှာ ထိုင်ရမလဲ။ | Where do we have to sit? | Beh-hma t'ain-yá-mălèh? |
| | Where should we sit? | |

| S1: ဒီမှာ ထိုင်ရမလား။ | Should we sit here? | Di-hma t'ain-yá-mălà? |

| S2: ဟုတ်ကဲ့။ — | Yes. — | Houq-kéh. — |
| ဒီမှာ ထိုင်ရမယ်။ | You should sit here. | Di-hma t'ain-yá-meh. |

| S1: ဘယ်လောက် ပေးရမလဲ။ | How much would we have to pay? | Beh-lauq pè-yá-mălèh? |

| S1: ၁၀/– ပေးရမလား။ | Would we have to pay K10? | Tăs'eh pè-yá-mălà? |

| S2: မပေးရပါဘူး။ — | No. — | Măpè-yá-ba-bù. — |
| ၈/၅၀ ပေးရမယ်။ | You'd have to pay K8.50. | Shiq-caq-k'wèh pè-yá-meh. |

Exercises

Ex. 1: Is going to have to ...
　　S1: မမြင့်မြင့်ခင် ဘယ်မှာ ထိုင်ရမလဲ။　　　　Má Myín Myín K'in beh-hma t'ain-yá-mălèh?
　　L/S2: စားပွဲ နံပါတ်(၄၈)မှာ ထိုင်ရမယ်။　　　Săbwèh nan-baq-48-hma t'ain-yá-meh.

Ex. 2: Prompt: Ask မသောင်းခင် which desk she has to sit at.
　　L/S2: ဘယ်စားပွဲမှာ ထိုင်ရမလဲ။　　　　　　Beh săbwèh-hma t'ain-yá-mălèh?
　　S1: စားပွဲ နံပါတ်(၅၂)မှာ ထိုင်ရမယ်။　　　Săbwèh nan-baq-52-hma t'ain-yá-meh.

Ex. 3 in Lesson 45. For written answer: not on the tape.
　　The words in the following questions and answers have been split up and jumbled.
Rearrange them to form meaningful sentences. There is a Key to this Exercise at the end of
the Lesson. Don't forget that you may find it helpful to copy the words onto separate slips
of paper and do your reordering by sliding the slips around.

| Diphthongs in the roman transcription: | 159 |

pronounce ei as in *vein,* ai as in *Thailand,* ou as in *though,* au as in *Sauerkraut.*

S1: — မသောင်းခင် — မလဲ — နေရ — ဘယ်မှာ
  S2: — ရမယ် — မှာ — နေ — ဂျကာတာ
S1: — မလဲ — ဘယ် — ကိုချစ်ခိုင် — သွား
  S2: — မယ် — စာကြည့်တိုက် — သွား
S1: — မ — မသန်းနု — လား — စာကြည့်တိုက် — သွား
  S2: — ပါဘူး — မယ် — ကုန်တိုက် — သွား — မသွား

Ex. 3 in Lesson 45 (romanized version)
  S1: — Má Thaùn K'in — mălèh — ne-yá — beh-hma
    S2: — yá-meh — hma — ne — Jăka-ta
  S1: — mălèh — beh — Ko C'iq K'ain — thwà
    S2: — meh — sa-cí-daiq — thwà
  S1: — mă — Má Thàn Nú — là — sa-cí-daiq — thwà
    S2: — ba-bù — meh — koun-daiq — thwà — măthwà

In class: Exercises as above. Also Learners make up places they have to go to, times they have to go, what they'll have to buy, where they'll have to live, and how much they'll have to pay.

Notes

Grammar. The sentences in this Lesson are examples of the familiar verb sentence formula. For others see Lessons 27, 29, 31, 36, 40, 42, and 44. The difference from earlier examples is that the verb slot contains a verb with –ရ– (-yá-) attached, and the verb suffix is not –တယ် (-deh) but –မယ် (-meh):

NOUN1+SUFFIX	NOUN2+SUFFIX	VERB+SUFFIX	STC SFX
ဦးဘ	ဘယ်+လောက်	ပေး–ရ+မ–	လဲ॥
Ù Bá	beh+lauq	pè-yá+mă	-lèh?
U Ba	which+quantity	give-must+*future*	*question*

"How much will U Ba have to pay?"

ဦးဘ+က	သုံးဆယ်	ပေး–ရ+မယ်॥	–
Ù Bá+gá	thoùn-zeh	pè-yá+meh.	–
U Ba	thirty	give-must+*future*	–

"U Ba will have to pay K30."

The formula applies in the same way to the *Yes/No* questions and answers.

Keys to the Exercises

Key to Ex. 3 in Lesson 45
  S1: — မသောင်းခင် — ဘယ်မှာ — နေရ — မလဲ॥
    S2: — ဂျကာတာ — မှာ — နေ — ရမယ်॥
  S1: — ကိုချစ်ခိုင် — ဘယ် — သွား — မလဲ॥
    S2: — စာကြည့်တိုက် — သွား — မယ်॥

Diphthongs in the roman transcription:
pronounce ei as in *vein*, ai as in *Thailand*, ou as in *though*, au as in *Sauerkraut*.

S1: — မသန်းနဲ့ — စာကြည့်တိုက် — သွား — မ — လား။
S2: — မသွား — ပါဘူး။ — ကုန်တိုက် — သွား — မယ်။

Key to Ex. 3 in Lesson 45

S1: — Má Thàun K'in — beh-hma — ne-yá — mălèh?
    S2: — Jăka-ta — hma — ne — yá-meh.
S1: — Ko C'iq K'ain — beh — thwà — mălèh?
    S2: — Sa-cí-daiq — thwà — meh.
S1: — Má Thàn Nú — sa-cí-daiq — thwà — mă — là?
    S2: — Măthwà — ba-bù. — Koun-daiq — thwà — meh.

Common phrases

To make sure you complete the Common Phrases Supplement by the end of Part 1, learn Section 19 at about this point.

LESSON 46

Requests: Please [verb]. / Please don't [verb].
Should I sit here? — Yes, please do. / No, please don't.

Desks and comfort needs

List 1

နာမည်	name	nan-meh	*should I come at*	*should I sit at desk*
ဒေါ်မြမြစန်း	Daw Mya Mya San	Daw Myá Myá Sàn	၂:၃၀	၁၃
ဦးစိန်ရွှေး	U Sein Htay	Ù Sein T'è	၁၁:၄၅	၂၅
ဒေါ်ခင်ခင်ခ	Daw Khin Khin Kha	Daw K'in K'in K'á	၇:၁၀	၁၇
ဦးငွေရ	U Ngwe Ya	Ù Ngwe Yá	၄:၅၀	၃၀

List 2

နာမည်	ဒေါ်စိန်စိန်	ဦးကျော်စိန်	ဒေါ်ခင်သန်း
မီး	ဖွင့်	ပိတ်	...
ပန်ကာ	ဖွင့်	ပိတ်	...
ပြတင်းပေါက်	ပိတ်	ဖွင့်	...
တံခါး	ပိတ်	ဖွင့်	...

name	Daw Sein Sein	U Kyaw Sein	Daw Khin Than	
	Daw Sein Sein	Ù Caw Sein	Daw K'in Thàn	
light	on	off	...	mì
fan	on	off	...	pan-ka
window	closed	open	...	pădìn-bauq
door	closed	open	...	dăgà

Diphthongs in the roman transcription:
pronounce ei as in *vein,* ai as in *Thailand,* ou as in *though,* au as in *Sauerkraut.*

161

New words

[verb]–ပါ	"Please [verb]"	[verb]-ba
မ–[verb]–ပါနဲ့	"Please don't [verb]"	mă-[verb]-ba-néh

The –ပါ (-ba) is the familiar suffix conveying politeness. It can be omitted, and the verb alone still issues a command/request: ထိုင် (t'ain) "Sit!" However, the verb alone sounds peremptory, and should only be used when you are sure it would not cause offence (or when you are determined to cause offence), so for our exercises in *BISL* we retain [verb]–ပါ ([verb]-ba) as the standard form for requests and commands. The negated form is also used without –ပါ (-ba): မထိုင်နဲ့ (măt'ain-néh) "Don't sit down!", and the social perils are equally great.

We romanize –ပါ here as -ba, but it is subject to the Voicing Rule, and exempted after a syllable ending in a glottal stop. Before a glottal stop it is pronounced -pa.

Example sentences

S1: ဘယ်မှာ ထိုင်ရမလဲ။	Where should I sit? = Where would you like me to sit?	Beh-hma t'ain-yá-mălèh?
S2: ဒီမှာ ထိုင်ပါ။	Please sit here.	Di-hma t'ain-ba.
S1: ဒီမှာ ထိုင်ရမလား။	Should I sit here? = Would you like me to sit here?	Di-hma t'ain-yá-mălà?
S2: မထိုင်ပါနဲ့။ — ဒီမှာ ထိုင်ပါ။	Don't sit [there]. — Sit here.	Măt'ain-ba-néh. — Di-hma t'ain-ba.

Note that [verb]–ရမလား ([verb]-yá-mălà) means "Should I [verb]," but is also used where in English we would say "Would you like me to [verb]?"

Models for the Exercises

Ex. 1: What time should they ... Prompt: Daw Mya Mya Sein wants to know what time she has to come. What would she say?

L/S2: ဘယ်အချိန် လာရမလဲ။	Beh ăc'ein la-yá-mălèh?
S1: နှစ်နာရီခွဲမှာ လာပါ။	Hnăna-yi-gwèh-hma la-ba.

Ex. 2. Prompt: Here's Daw Khin Khin Kha.

S1: ဘယ်အချိန် လာရမလဲ။	Beh ăc'ein la-yá-mălèh?
L/S2: ၇း၁၀–မှာ လာပါ။	K'un-năna-yi s'eh-măniq-hma la-ba.

Ex. 3: Prompt: Ask Daw Sein Sein if she wants you to turn on the light.

L/S2: မီး ဖွင့်ရမလား။	Mì p'wín-yá-mălà?
S1: ဟုတ်ကဲ့။ ဖွင့်ပါ။	Houq-kéh. Pwín-ba.

Diphthongs in the roman transcription: <br> pronounce ei as in *vein*, ai as in *Thailand*, ou as in *though*, au as in *Sauerkraut*.

Ex. 4. Prompt: Imagine you are U Kyaw Sein.
S1: မီး ဖွင့်ရမလား။ Mì p'wín-yá-mălà?
L/S2: မဖွင့်ပါနဲ့။ Măp'wín-ba-néh.

Ex. 5. You ask Daw Khin Than how she wants things arranged. Note her answers on the blank form below, and compare them with the Key at the end of the Lesson.
    Prompt: Ask her if she wants you to turn on the light.
L/S2: မီး ဖွင့်ရမလား။ Mì p'wín-yá-mălà?
S1: ဟုတ်ကဲ့။ ဖွင့်ပါ။ Houq-kéh. P'wín-ba.

Blank for Ex. 5: Daw Khin Than's preferences
    light   ...
    fan   ...
    window   ...
    door   ...

In class: Exercises as above. Also Learners ask each other what they want open and closed, and respond with "Yes, do" or "No, don't." Also each makes a seating plan for the class: the others ask စားပွဲနံပါတ်-၅-မှာ ထိုင်ရမလား။ and the Learner who has the plan replies ဟုတ်ကဲ့၊ ထိုင်ပါ။ or မထိုင်ပါနဲ့ and so on.

Notes

Grammar. The sentences in this Lesson are examples of the familiar verb sentence formula. For others see Lessons 27, 29, 31, 36, 40, 42, 44, and 45. The intriguing difference from earlier examples is that, in the positive form, the verb suffix is not –တယ် (-**deh**) or –မယ် (-**meh**) but zero, null, empty (its position is shown here by the symbol ∅):

NOUN1+SUFFIX	NOUN2+SUFFIX	VERB+SUFFIX	STC SFX
ဦးဘ	ဒီ+မှာ	ထိုင်–ပါ+∅	–
U̇ Bá	di+hma	t'ain-ba+∅	–
U Ba	this [place]+at	sit-*polite*+ ∅	–

"U Ba please sit here."

ဦးဘ	ဒီ+မှာ	မထိုင်–ပါ+နဲ့	
U̇ Bá	di+hma	măt'ain-ba+néh	
U Ba	this [place]+at	not sit-*polite*+*néh*	

"U Ba please don't sit here."

Diphthongs in the roman transcription:
pronounce **ei** as in *vein*, **ai** as in *Thailand*, **ou** as in *though*, **au** as in *Sauerkraut*.

163

Keys to the Exercises

Key to Ex. 5

နာမည်	ဒေါ်ခင်သန်း			Daw Khin Than	
မီး	ဖွင့်	light	on		mì
ပန်ကာ	ပိတ်	fan	off		pan-ka
ပြတင်းပေါက်	ဖွင့်	window	open		pădìn-bauq
တံခါး	ပိတ်	door	closed		dăgà

LESSON 46R

Review of material in Lessons 1 to 46.

Like the earlier Review Lessons (20R and 41R), this Lesson gives you a run-through of most of the words and structures you've practised up to this point. The exercises for this Lesson are on the Review Tape, which is on a separate cassette from the regular Lessons. Each Exercise is split into an A section and a B section: in one you answer the questions, and in the other you ask them. Where there's a choice between answers of different lengths, aim for the middle-length answer. If you want to remind yourself of the difference between long, middling and short answers, you'll find some notes in the Example Sentences for Lessons 27 and the Notes for Lesson 29.

1. Personal details and travel plans

Imagine that S1 is some kind of clerk taking down details from people who are planning to travel abroad. In Ex. 1A you take the part of the travellers and answer S1's questions for them. In Ex. 1B you ask the questions, following the prompt on the tape, and use the answers to fill in the blanks in the lists below.

number	1	2	3	4
name script	ဦးထွန်းမင်း	ဒေါ်မြစိန်	...	...
name trad roman	U Tun Min	Daw Mya Sein	...	...
name sys roman	Ù T'ùn Mìn	Daw Myá Sein	...	...
address	23, Market St.	647, Pagoda Road		...	...
town	Thazi	Taunggyi	...	...
phone	Thazi 29	21304	...	...
wants to go to	New Delhi	Hanoi	...	...
will have to pay	£560	$424	...	...

2. Comfort requirements

Imagine people being ushered into a room full of numbered desks. They have to sit there while they fill in a form, and S1 is anxious to make sure they are as comfortable as they can be. In Ex. 1A you answer for the visitors. When S1 asks if she should do something, or if

Diphthongs in the roman transcription:
pronounce ei as in *vein*, ai as in *Thailand*, ou as in *though*, au as in *Sauerkraut*.

you'd like something done, ask her to do it — or not do it, according to the brief. In Ex. 2B you ask the questions, following the prompt, and fill in the blanks.

You will notice that S1 uses a few phrases you have not met in the Lessons to this point. You can ignore them. They come from the Common Phrases Supplement, and are put in to make the dialogue a little less stilted.

name script	ဒေါ်သန်းနု	ဦးမျိုးမင်း	ကိုလှထွန်း	အေးအေးမြင့်
name trad roman	Daw Than Nu	U Myo Min	Ko Hla Tun	Aye Aye Myint
name sys roman	Daw Thàn Nú	Ù Myò Mìn	Ko H̦lá T'ùn	È È Myín
wants to sit at nº	48	19	…	…
wants fan	on	off	…	…
wants light	off	on	…	…
wants window	open	closed	…	…
wants door	open	closed	…	…

3. Shopping plans

This is an Exercise on "going to [verb]." You have to imagine that a group of people have made plans to go shopping for specific items at specific times. S1 quizzes them about their intentions, and you speak their parts for them. In Ex. 3B you take a turn at the quizzing, and use the answers to fill in the blanks below.

name script	ခင်ခင်လင်း	ကိုညွန့်မောင်	ဦးအောင်သန်း	သန္တာဖြူ
name trad roman	Khin Khin Lin	Ko Nyunt Maung	U Aung Than	Than Dar Pyu
name sys roman	K'in K'in Lìn	Ko Nyún Maun	Ù Aun Thàn	Than-da P'yu
to go to	canteen	Diplomatic Store	…	…
to go at	3.30	4.10	…	…
to buy	milk powder	film	…	…
to pay	K34/-	$6.00	…	…

4. Shopping wants

This Exercise is to practice "wanting to [verb]." In Ex. 4A you answer questions about what the people in the lists want to do, and in Ex. 4B you do the asking.

name script	သန်းသန်းနု	ဦးမြင့်ဝေ	ကိုတင်ဦး	မမြတ်သီ
name trad roman	Than Than Nu	U Myint Wai	Ko Tin U	Ma Myat Thi
name sys roman	Thàn Thàn Nú	Ù Myín We	Ko Tin Ù	Má Myaq Thi
wants to go to	library	Theingyi Mkt	…	…
wants to go at	10.25	8.50	…	…
wants to buy	tape	biscuits	…	…

Diphthongs in the roman transcription:	165
pronounce ei as in *vein*, ai as in *Thailand*, ou as in *though*, au as in *Sauerkraut*.	

5. Translation

The following sentences illustrate the uses of the auxiliary verbs you have recently learned. Translate them into English.

1. S1: ထိုင်ချင်သလား။ S2: ဟုတ်ကဲ့။ ထိုင်ချင်ပါတယ်။
2. S1: ထိုင်ပါ။ S2: ဘယ်မှာ ထိုင်ရမလဲ။ ဒီမှာ ထိုင်ရမလား။
3. S1: ဒီမှာ မထိုင်ပါနဲ့။ ဒီမှာ ထိုင်ပါ။ S2: ဟုတ်ကဲ့။
4. S1: ပြတင်းပေါက် ဖွင့်ရမလား။ S2: မဖွင့်ပါနဲ့။ တံခါး ဖွင့်ပါ။
5. S1: ပန်ကာ ပိတ်ရမလား။ S2: ဟုတ်ကဲ့။ ပိတ်ပါ။ မဖွင့်ချင်ပါဘူး။
6. S1: မီး ဖွင့်ချင်သလား။ S2: ဟုတ်ကဲ့။ ဖွင့်ချင်ပါတယ်။ ဖွင့်ပါ။

7. S1: အပြင် သွားချင်သလား။ S2: ဟုတ်ကဲ့။ သွားချင်ပါတယ်။
8. S1: ကမ်းနားလမ်း သွားချင်သလား။ S2: မသွားချင်ပါဘူး။ ဈေး သွားမယ်။
9. S1: ဘယ်ဈေး သွားမလဲ။ S2: ဗိုလ်ချုပ်ဈေး သွားမယ်။
10. S1: နို့မှုန့် ဝယ်မလား။ S2: မဝယ်ပါဘူး။
11. S1: ဘာ ဝယ်မလဲ။ S2: ကော်ဖီမှုန့် ဝယ်မယ်။
12. S1: ဘယ်အချိန် သွားရမလဲ။ S2: ၈–နာရီမှာ သွားရမယ်။

1. S1: T'ain-jin-dhălà? S2: Houq-kéh. T'ain-jin-ba-deh.
2. S1: T'ain-ba. S2: Beh-hma t'ain-yá-mălèh? Di-hma t'ain-yá-mălà?
3. S1: Di-hma măt'ain-ba-néh. Di-hma t'ain-ba. S2: Houq-kéh.
4. S1: Pădìn-bauq p'wín-yá-mălà? S2: Măp'wín-ba-néh. Tăgà p'wín-ba.
5. S1: Pan-ka peiq-yá-mălà? S2: Houq-kéh. Peiq-pa. Măp'wín-jin-ba-bù.
6. S1: Mì p'wín-jin-dhălà? S2: Houq-kéh. P'wín-jin-ba-deh. P'wín-ba.

7. S1: Ăpyin thwà-jin-dhălà? S2: Houq-kéh. Thwà-jin-ba-deh.
8. S1: Kàn-nà Làn thwà-jin-dhălà? S2: Măthwà-jin-ba-bù. Zè thwà-meh.
9. S1: Beh zè thwà-mălèh? S2: Bo-jouq Zè thwà-meh.
10. S1: Nó-hmoún weh-mălà? S2: Măweh-ba-bù.
11. S1: Ba weh-mălèh? S2: Kaw-p'i-hmoún weh-meh.
12. S1: Beh-ăc'ein thwà-yá-mălèh? S2: Shiq-na-yi-hma thwà-yá-meh.

Keys to the Exercises in Lesson 46R

Key to Ex. 1

number	3	4
name script	ဝင်းကျော်	မသူဇာ
name trad roman	Win Kyaw	Ma Thuza
name sys roman	Wìn Caw	Má Thu-za

Diphthongs in the roman transcription:
pronounce ei as in *vein,* ai as in *Thailand,* ou as in *though,* au as in *Sauerkraut.*

address	91, 85th St.	101, 30th St.
town	Mandalay	Myitkyina
phone	23710	21043
wants to go to	Peking	Tokyo
will have to pay	K6500	$320

Key to Ex. 2 in Lesson 46R

name script	ကိုလှထွန်း	အေးအေးမြင့်
name trad roman	Ko Hla Tun	Aye Aye Myint
name sys roman	Ko Hlá T'ùn	È È Myín

wants to sit at n°	70	26
wants fan	on	off
wants light	on	off
wants window	closed	open
wants door	open	closed

Key to Ex. 3 in Lesson 46R

name script	ဦးအောင်သန်း	သန္တာဖြူ
name trad roman	U Aung Than	Than Dar Pyu
name sys roman	Ù Aun Thàn	Than-da P'yu

to go to	Bogyoke Market	National Museum
to go at	8.45	10.40
to buy	writing paper	postcard
to pay	K10/-	K3/-

Key to Ex. 4 in Lesson 46R

name script	ကိုတင်ဦး	မမြတ်သီ
name trad roman	Ko Tin U	Ma Myat Thi
name sys roman	Ko Tin Ù	Má Myaq Thi

wants to go to	President Hotel	Theingyi Market
wants to go at	5.20	12.15
wants to buy	envelopes	ball pen

Key to Ex. 5 in Lesson 46R: Translation into English

1. S1: Would you like to sit down?   S2: Yes. I would.
2. S1: Please do.   S2: Where should I sit? Should I sit here?
3. S1: Don't sit there. Sit here.   S2: Right.
4. S1: Should I open the window?   S2: No, don't. Please open the door.
5. S1: Should I turn off the fan?   S2: Yes, please do. I don't want it on.
6. S1: Would you like the light on?   S2: Yes, I would. Please turn it on.

Diphthongs in the roman transcription:
pronounce ei as in *vein*, ai as in *Thailand*, ou as in *though*, au as in *Sauerkraut*.

7. S1: Do you want to go out?   S2: Yes, I do.

8. S1: Would you like to go to Strand Road?   S2: No. I'm going to go to the market.

9. S1: Which market are you going to go to?   S2: I'm going to go to Bogyoke Market.

10. S1: Are you going to buy some milk powder?   S2: No.

11. S1: What are you going to buy?   S2: I'm going to buy instant coffee.

12. S1: What time will you have to go?   S2: I'll have to go at 8.00.

Common phrases

If you have kept up to schedule in learning the Common Phrases, you should have only one more to learn at this point: Section 20.

OVERVIEW OF GRAMMAR FOR PART 1

This Overview is arranged in the following sections:

1.	*Is* sentences
2.	Verb sentences
2.1	The verb phrase (verb + suffix)
2.1.1	The verb
2.1.2	The verb suffix
2.2	The noun phrase (noun + suffix)
2.2.1	The noun
2.2.2	The noun suffix
3.	The sentence suffix
3.1	Questions
3.2	Statements

1. *Is* sentences

The formula for the grammatical structures of *is* sentences is:

NOUN1+SUFFIX	\<is\>	NOUN2+SUFFIX	SENTENCE SUFFIX

Examples:

ဒါ [+က] *   ဆူးလေဘုရား:+–   [–ပါ]॥ *

Da [+gá] *   S'ù-le P'ăyà+–   [-ba]. *

That [+*as for*] \<is\>   Sule Pagoda+–   [*polite*]

"That is the Sule Pagoda."

* The brackets [...] are used to show elements that may be omitted.

This formula for *is* sentences is used in Statements, in *Yes/No* questions, and in Information questions. For more examples see the summary of grammar following Lesson 20.

Diphthongs in the roman transcription:
pronounce ei as in *vein*, ai as in *Thailand*, ou as in *though*, au as in *Sauerkraut*.

2. Verb sentences

Lesson 27, 29, 31, 36, 40, 42, 44, 45, and 46: The essential formula for the structure of a Burmese sentence containing a verb has two components:

| NOUN | VERB+SUFFIX |

That is its simplest form.

Often the NOUN has a suffix, so the formula expands to:

| NOUN+SUFFIX | VERB+SUFFIX |

Often there are more nouns than one, so the formula expands again to:

| NOUN1+SUFFIX | NOUN2+SUFFIX | ... | VERB+SUFFIX |

Sometimes the sentence has a sentence suffix, so the formula expands to:

| NOUN1+SUFFIX | NOUN2+SUFFIX | ... | VERB+SUFFIX | SENTENCE SUFFIX |

As with *is* sentences, the formula may be used for Statements, for *Yes/No* questions, and for Information questions.

Examples:

Note that the suffix slot is not always filled.

| NOUN1+SUFFIX | NOUN2+SUFFIX | VERB+SUFFIX | STC SFX |

(a1) Statement

ကိုစံရွှေ / မဟာဗန္ဓုလလမ်း+မှာ / နေပါ+တယ်။ / –
Ko San Shwe / Măha Ban-dú-lá Làn+hma / ne-ba+deh. / –
Ko San Shwe / Maha Bandoola Rd+in / live-*polite+pres/past* –

"Ko San Shwe lives/lived in Maha Bandoola Street."

(a2) Statement (with negated verb)

ကိုစံရွှေ / ကမ်းနားလမ်း+မှာ / မနေပါ+ဘူး။ / –
Ko San Shwe / Kàn-nà Làn+hma / măne-ba+bù. / –
Ko San Shwe / Strand Road+in / not-live-*polite+pres/past*

"Ko San Shwe does/did not live in Strand Road."

(b) Yes or No question: sentence suffix is –လား: -là *"question"*

ကိုစံရွှေ / မဟာဗန္ဓုလလမ်း+မှာ / နေ+သ– / –လား။
Ko San Shwe / Măha Ban-dú-lá Làn+hma / ne+dhă / -là?
Ko San Shwe / Maha Bandoola road+in / live+*pres/past* / *question*

"Does/did Ko San Shwe live in Maha Bandoola Street?"

(c) Information question: sentence suffix is –လဲ -lèh *"question"* **and the last NOUN is a question word (who? which? where? and so on)**

ကိုစံရွှေ / ဘယ်လမ်း+မှာ / နေ+သ– / လဲ။
Ko San Shwe / beh làn+hma / ne+dhă / -lèh?
Ko San Shwe / which road+in / live+*pres/past* / *question*

"Which road does/did Ko San Shwe live in?"

The next section takes a closer look at the structure of the verb phrase (VERB+SUFFIX) and the noun phrase (NOUN+SUFFIX).

Diphthongs in the roman transcription:
pronounce ei as in *vein,* ai as in *Thailand,* ou as in *though,* au as in *Sauerkraut.*

2.1 The verb phrase

The standard formula for the verb phrase is VERB+SUFFIX.

2.1.1 The occupant of the VERB slot in the verb phrase may be a single verb, or a verb with one or more associated elements. One is a prefix:

မ–[verb]–   mǎ-[verb]-   not [verb] (Lesson 29)

The others follow the verb, and are known (to some) as "auxiliary verbs." In Part 1 you meet three:

[verb]–ပါ–   [verb]-ba-   *polite* (Lesson 27)

[verb]–ချင်–   [verb]-jin-   want to [verb] (Lesson 42)

[verb]–ရ–   [verb]-yá-   have to [verb] (Lesson 45)

Examples of occupants of the VERB slot in the verb phrase:

Single verb:

နေ–   ne-   to live

သွား:–   thwà-   to go

Prefix and verb:

မ–နေ–   mǎ-ne-   not-live

မ–လာ–   mǎ-la-   not-come

Verb and additional element ("auxiliary verb"):

လာ–ပါ–   la-ba   come-*polite*

သွား:–ချင်–   thwà-jin-   go-want ["want to go"]

ပေး:–ရ–   pè-yá-   give-have to ["pay"]

Combinations of prefix and additional elements:

မ–သွား:–ချင်–   mǎ-thwà-jin-   not-go-want ["not want to go"]

သွား:–ချင်–ပါ–   thwà-jin-ba-   go-want-*polite* ["want to go"]

မ–ပေး:–ရ–   mǎ-pè-yá-   not-give-have to ["not have to give, not pay"]

မ–နေ–ချင်–ပါ   mǎ-ne-jin-ba-   not-live-want-*polite* ["not want to live"]

2.1.2 The occupant of the SUFFIX slot in the verb phrase may be one of:

–တယ်   -deh (-teh)   present or past, with positive verb

–သ–   -dhǎ (-thǎ)   [weakened form of preceding, used before certain sentence suffixes]

–မယ်   -meh   future, with positive verb

–မ–   -mǎ-   [weakened form of preceding, used before certain sentence suffixes]

–ဘူး:   -bù (-p'ù)   present, past or future, with negative verb

– Ø (symbol used to indicate no suffix)   requests/commands, with positive verb

–နဲ့,   -néh   requests/commands, with negative verb

Examples of verb phrases (VERB+SUFFIX)

နေ+တယ်   ne+deh   live+*pres/past*

   "he [or she/they/you/we/I] lives [or lived]"

လာ+မယ်   la+meh   come+*future*

   "he [or she/they/you/we/I] is going to come"

မနေ+ဘူး:   mǎne+bù   not-live+*negative*

   "he [or she/they/you/we/I] does [or did] not live"

လာပါ+တယ်   la-ba+deh   come-*polite*+*pres/past*

   "he [or she/they/you/we/I] come [or came]"

Diphthongs in the roman transcription:
pronounce ei as in *vein*, ai as in *Thailand*, ou as in *though*, au as in *Sauerkraut*.

လာချင်+တယ် la-jin+deh   come-want+*pres/past*

 "he [or she/they/you/we/I] wants [or wanted] to come"

လာရ+တယ် la-yá+deh   come-have to+*pres/past*

 "he [or she/they/you/we/I] has [or had] to come"

မသွားချင်+ဘူး măthwà-jin+bù not-go-want+*negative*

 "he [or she/they/you/we/I] does [or did] not want to go"

မလာပါ+ဘူး măla-ba+bù   not-come-*polite*+*negative*

 "he [or she/they/you/we/I] does [or did] not come"

Weakened form of verb suffix before a sentence suffix:

နေ+သ+လား ne+dhă+là   live+*pres/past*+*question*

 "does [or did] he [or she/they/you/we/I] live?"

နေ+မ+လား ne+mă+là   live+*future*+*question*

 "will he [or she/they/you/we/I] live?"

2.2 The noun phrase

The standard formula for the noun phrase is NOUN+SUFFIX.

2.2.1 The occupant of the NOUN slot in the noun phrase may be any noun. In the examples in the text and Exercises you have met noun slots filled with a name, a place, an object, a time, a sum of money, or a telephone number. You have also met noun slot occupants which are nouns strung together; for example:

  ဘောပင်နဲ့ စာရွက်   ကိုတင်နဲ့ မလှ

  bàw-pin-néh sa-yweq Ko Tin-néh Má Hlá

  Ball pen-and paper   Ko Tin-and Ma Hla

Longer strings are possible.

2.2.2 The occupant of the SUFFIX slot in the noun phrase may be nil, or a noun suffix. In Part 1 you meet:

NOUN+nil = object of verb

  NOUN+SUFFIX VERB+SUFFIX

  သုံးကျပ်+nil   ပေးရ+တယ်

  thoùn-jaq+nil   pè-yá+deh

  three kyats+nil   pay+*pres/past*

  "[He] paid three kyats."

NOUN+nil = destination (place to which someone goes)

  NOUN+SUFFIX VERB+SUFFIX

  ဈေး+nil   သွား+တယ်

  zè+nil   thwà+deh

  market+nil   go+*pres/past*

  "[He] went to the market."

NOUN+nil = subject of sentence

  NOUN+SUFFIX NOUN+SUFFIX VERB+SUFFIX

  ဦးဘ+nil   ဈေး+nil   သွား+တယ်

  Ù Bá+nil   zè+nil   thwà+deh

  U Ba+nil   market+nil   go+*pres/past*

  "U Ba went to the market."

Diphthongs in the roman transcription:
pronounce ei as in *vein*, ai as in *Thailand*, ou as in *though*, au as in *Sauerkraut*.

NOUN+က = subject of sentence (optional: see preceding example)

NOUN+SUFFIX	NOUN+SUFFIX	VERB+SUFFIX
ဦးဘ+က	ဈေး+nil	သွား+တယ်
Ù Bá+gá	zè+nil	thwà+deh
U Ba+*subject*	market+nil	go+*pres/past*

"U Ba went to the market."

NOUN+က = source (place from which someone comes)

NOUN+SUFFIX	VERB+SUFFIX
ထိုင်းနိုင်ငံ+က	လာ+တယ်
T'aìn-nain-ngan+gá	la+deh
Thailand-from	come+*pres/past*

"[He] comes from Thailand."

NOUN+မှာ = location (place at/in which someone lives)

NOUN+SUFFIX	VERB+SUFFIX
ထိုင်းနိုင်ငံ+မှာ	နေ+တယ်
T'aìn-nain-ngan+hma	ne+deh
Thailand-in	live+*pres/past*

"[He] lives in Thailand."

NOUN+လို့ = quotation (marks a word as a quoted name)

NOUN+SUFFIX	VERB+SUFFIX
ထိုင်းနိုင်ငံ+လို့	ခေါ်+တယ်
T'aìn-nain-ngan+ló	k'aw+deh
Thailand-*quoted*	call+*pres/past*

"[It] is called 'Thailand'."

3. The sentence suffix

Any sentence may carry a sentence suffix. In Part 1 you meet three:

–လား	-là	*question*
–လဲ	-lèh	*question*
–ပါ	-ba (-pa)	*polite*

3.1 Questions

Examples: (a) *is* sentences

SENTENCE		+	SENTENCE SUFFIX
ဒါ	နို့မှုန့်+–		–လား။
Da	nó-hmoún+–		-là?
That <is>	milk powder+–		-*question*

"Is that milk powder?"

ကော်ဖီမှုန့်	ဘယ်မှာ+–		–လဲ။
Kaw-p'i-hmoún	beh-hma+–		-lèh?
The instant coffee <is>	where+–		-*question*

"Where is the instant coffee?"

Diphthongs in the roman transcription:
pronounce ei as in *vein*, ai as in *Thailand*, ou as in *though*, au as in *Sauerkraut*.

(b) verb sentences

The verb suffixes –တယ် (-deh/-teh) and –မယ် (-meh) weaken to –သ (-dhă/-thă) and –မ (-mă) when they are followed by a question suffix.

SENTENCE			+	SENTENCE SUFFIX
ကိုညို	ဘောပင်	ဝယ်သ+		–လား။
Ko Nyo	bàw-pin	weh-dhă		-là?
Ko Nyo	ballpoint pen	buy+*pres/past*		-*question*

"Did Ko Nyo buy a ballpoint pen?"

မဝါ	ဘယ်အချိန်	လာမ+		–လဲ။
Má Wa	beh-ăc'ein	la-mă		-lèh?
Ma Wa	what time	come+*future*		-*question*

"What time is Ma Wa going to come?"

3.2 Statements

Example: *is* sentences

SENTENCE	+	SENTENCE SUFFIX

Examples:

ဒါ	နို့မှုန့်+–	–ပါ။
Da	nó-hmoún+–	-ba.
That <is>	milk powder+–	-*polite*

"That is milk powder."

The polite suffix –ပါ (-ba/-pa) is not normally attached to verb sentences. Instead the –ပါ (-ba/-pa) appears as an element following the verb and preceding the verb suffix:

ကိုညို	ဘောပင်	ဝယ်ပါတယ်။
Ko Nyo	bàw-pin	weh-ba-deh.
Ko Nyo	ballpoint pen	buy+*polite*+*pres/past*

"Ko Nyo bought a ballpoint pen."

In both *is* sentences and verb sentences, if you omit the polite suffix, you will sound less courteous, but the sentence will not be ungrammatical.

Diuphthongs in the roman transcription:
pronounce ei as in *vein*, ai as in *Thailand*, ou as in *though*, au as in *Sauerkraut*.

173

OVERVIEW OF NUMBERS AND COUNTING FOR PART 1

1. Numbers

1 Simple numbers

၁	၂	၃	၄	၅	၆	၇	၈	၉	(၀)
တစ်	နှစ်	သုံး	လေး	ငါး	ခြောက်	ခုနစ်	ရှစ်	ကိုး	(သုည)
/တစ်	နှစ်	သုန်း	လေး	ငါး	ချောက်	ခွန်နစ်	ရှစ်	ကိုး	(သုန်ညာ့)/
tiq	hniq	thoùn	lè	ngà	c'auq	k'un-hniq	shiq	kò	(thoun-nyá)
one	two	three	four	five	six	seven	eight	nine	(zero)

–ဆယ်	–ရာ	–ထောင်
-s'eh	-ya	-t'aun
-tens	-hundreds	-thousands

2 Compound numbers

ရှစ်ဆယ်	ငါးရာ	ခြောက်ထောင်
shiq-s'eh	ngà-ya	c'auq-t'aun
eight-tens	five-hundreds	six-thousands
eighty	five hundred	six thousand

3 Weakening: The following unit numbers weaken in compounds:

တစ်	နှစ်	ခုနစ်
tiq	hniq	k'un-hniq
one	two	seven

Examples:

တစ်ဆယ်	နှစ်ရာ	ခုနစ်ထောင်
/တဆယ်/	/နှယာ/	/ခွန်နထောင်/
tăs'eh	hnăya	k'un-năt'aun
ten	two hundred	seven thousand

4 Voicing: –ဆယ် -s'eh and –ထောင် -t'aun voice in a compound (–ရာ -ya can't be voiced anyway); for example:

သုံးဆယ်	ငါးဆယ်	ကိုးထောင်
/သုန်းဇယ်/	/ငါ ဇယ်/	/ကိုးဒေါင်/
thoùn-zeh	ngà-zeh	kò-daun
thirty	fifty	nine thousand

Diphthongs in the roman transcription:
pronounce ei as in *vein*, ai as in *Thailand*, ou as in *though*, au as in *Sauerkraut*.

But voicing doesn't operate after a glottal stop or a weak vowel; for example:

ခြောက်ဆယ်	ရှစ်ဆယ်	ခုနစ်ထောင်
/ချောက်ဆယ်/	/ယှစ်ဆယ်/	/ခွန်နထောင်/
c'auq-s'eh	shiq-s'eh	k'un-năt'aun
sixty	eighty	seven thousand

5 Larger compound numbers

1. with "and"	2. with "creak"	3. with nothing
ကိုးရာနဲ့ ငါးဆယ်	ကိုးရာ ငါးဆယ်	ကိုးရာ ငါးဆယ်
kò-ya-néh ngà-zeh	kò-yá ngà-zeh	kò-ya ngà-zeh
900-and 50	900-creak 50	900 50

6 Quirks

* 11-19: in place of the expected

တစ်ဆယ့်တစ်	tăs'éh-tiq	11	တစ်ဆယ့်နှစ်	tăs'éh-hniq	12 and so on.

people usually omit the တစ် tă- "one" and just say:

ဆယ့်တစ်	tăs'éh-tiq	11	ဆယ့်နှစ်	tăs'éh-hniq	12 and so on.

but 10 remains unchanged:

တစ်ဆယ်	tăs'eh	10

* 1001-1999: as for 11-19: in place of the expected

တစ်ထောင်တစ်ရာ	tăt'aún-tăya	1100	တစ်ထောင်နှစ်ရာ	tăt'aún-hnăya	1200	and so on.

people usually omit the တစ် tă- "one" and just say:

ထောင်တစ်ရာ	t'aún-tăya	1100	ထောင်နှစ်ရာ	t'aún-hnăya	1200	and so on.

but 1000 remains unchanged:

တစ်ထောင်	tăt'aun	1000

2. Counting

The rule is: NUMBER followed by UNIT (Lesson 23); for example:

သုံးဒေါ်လာ	thoùn-daw-la	three dollars
ငါးဆယ့် ခြောက်ဒေါ်လာ	ngà-zéh c'auq-daw-la	fifty-six dollars
နှစ်ရာ ကိုးဆယ့် ရှစ်ပေါင်	hnăyá kò-zéh shiq-paun	298 pounds

The weakening and voicing rules apply to units of currency, and other units, in the same way as they do in counting in tens, hundreds, thousands (Lesson 23); for example:

Examples of weakening:

တစ်ဒေါ်လာ	/တဒေါ်လာ/	tădaw-la	one dollar
နှစ်ဒေါ်လာ	/နဒေါ်လာ/	hnădaw-la	two dollars
နှစ်ပေါင်	/နပေါင်/	hnăpaun	two pounds
ခုနစ်ပေါင်	/ခွန်နပေါင်/	k'un-năpaun	seven pounds
ဆယ့် တစ်ဒေါ်လာ	/ဆဲ့ တဒေါ်လာ/	s'éh tădaw-la	eleven dollars
ငါးဆယ့် နှစ်ဒေါ်လာ	/ငါးဲ့ နဒေါ်လာ/	ngà-zéh hnădaw-la	fifty-two dollars
ရှစ်ဆယ့် ခုနစ်ဒေါ်လာ	/ယှစ်ဆဲ့ ခွန်နဒေါ်လာ/	shiq-s'éh k'un-nădaw-la	eighty-seven dollars

Diphthongs in the roman transcription:	175
pronounce ei as in *vein*, ai as in *Thailand*, ou as in *though*, au as in *Sauerkraut*.	

Examples of voicing and exceptions to voicing:

သုံးပေါင်	/သုံးဘောင်/	thoùn-baun	three pounds
လေးပေါင်	/လေးဘောင်/	lè-baun	four pounds
နှစ်ပေါင်	/နှပေါင်/	hnăpaun	two pounds
ရှစ်ပေါင်	as written	shiq-paun	eight pounds

Round numbers in counting come after the unit, not before (Lesson 26); for example:

ပေါင် ငါးဆယ်	paun ngà-zeh	£50
ပေါင် ငါးရာ	paun ngà-ya	£500
ပေါင် ငါးထောင်	paun ngà-daun	£5000
ပေါင် ငါးထောင့် ငါးရာ	paun ngà-daún ngà-ya	£5500
ပေါင် နှစ်ထောင့် လေးရာ ခြောက်ဆယ်	paun hnăt'aún lè-yá c'auq-s'eh	£2460

Except ten units:

| ဆယ်ပေါင် | s'eh-baun | ten pounds |
| ဆယ်ပြား | s'eh-byà | ten pya |

Two units of currency together (Lesson 30)

The larger denomination precedes the smaller, optionally with suffix –နဲ့ (-néh) after the first; for example:

သုံးကျပ်[နဲ့] ပြားလေးဆယ်	thoùn-jaq[-néh] pyà lè-zeh	K3/40
ပေါင်နှစ်ဆယ်[နဲ့] ဆယ့်ငါးပြား	paun hnăs'eh[-néh] s'éh-ngà-byà	£20.15
တရာ သုံးဆယ့် ငါးဒေါ်လာ[နဲ့] —	tăyá thoùn-zéh ngà-daw-la[-néh] —	
လေးဆယ့် ငါးဆင့်	lè-zéh ngà s'ín	$135.45

Quirks: Burmese currency (Lesson 32)

Unround numbers of kyat are regular:

ခြောက်ကျပ်	c'auq-caq	K6
နှစ်ကျပ်	hnăcaq	K2
ဆယ့်ငါးကျပ်	s'éh ngà-jaq	K15
တရာ နှစ်ဆယ့် လေးကျပ်	tăyá hnăs'éh lè-jaq	K124

Round numbers of kyat don't use the word ကျပ် caq. They use nothing or sometimes ငွေ ngwe or ဗမာငွေ Băma-ngwe:

(ဗမာငွေ) သုံးဆယ်	(Băma ngwe) thoùn-zeh	K30
(ဗမာငွေ) ရှစ်ရာ	(Băma ngwe) shiq-ya	K800
(ဗမာငွေ) ခုနှစ်ရာ ကိုးဆယ်	(Băma ngwe) k'un-năya kò-zeh	K790

Ten kyat follows the round number pattern

| (ဗမာငွေ) တစ်ဆယ် | (Băma ngwe) tăs'eh | K10 |

With other currencies and other units of measure ten is treated as an unround number:

| ဆယ်ပေါင် | s'eh-baun | £10 |

Diphthongs in the roman transcription:
pronounce ei as in *vein,* ai as in *Thailand,* ou as in *though,* au as in *Sauerkraut.*

CUMULATED VOCABULARY FOR PART 1

The Lesson numbers show where the items were introduced.

This and That

ဒါ	da	this, that
အဲဒါ	èh-da	that (nearer you) (Lesson 39)
ဒီ–[noun]	di-[noun]	this [noun]
ဒီမှာ	di-hma	in this [place], here

Examples:

ဒါ ဟိုတယ်လား။	Da ho-teh-là?	Is that a hotel?
ဒီဈေးက ဗိုလ်ချုပ်ဈေးပါ။	Di zè-gá Bo-jouq Zè-ba.	This market is Bogyoke Market.
စစ်ကိုင်းက ဒီမှာပါ။	Săgaìn-gá di-hma-ba.	Sagaing is here.

What and Which

ဘာ	ba what	
ဘာ–[noun]	ba-[noun]	what [noun]
�‌ဘယ်–[noun]	beh-[noun]	which [noun]
ဘယ်မှာ	beh-hma	in which [place], where
ဘယ်လောက်	beh-lauq	how much, what (number, price)
ဘယ်သူ	beh-dhu	who
ဘယ်လို	beh-lo	how, in what way (Lesson 36)

Examples:

နံပါတ်(၁) ဘာလဲ။	What is n° 1?	Nan-baq-tiq ba-lèh?
ဒီဈေးက ဘာဈေးလဲ။	What market is this market?	Di zè-gá ba zè-lèh?
ဈေး ဘယ်လမ်းမှာလဲ။	Which road is the market in?	Zè beh làn-hma-lèh?
ကွာလာလမ်ပူ ဘယ်မှာလဲ။	Where is Kuala Lumpur?	Kwa-la Lan-pu beh-hma-lèh?
တယ်လီဖုန်းနံပါတ် ဘယ်လောက်လဲ။	What is the phone number?	Teh-li-p'oùn nan-baq beh-lauq-lèh?

Personal names and prefixes (Lessons 21, 22, 24)

ဦး /အူး/ Ù for older men	ဒေါ် Daw for older women
ကို Ko for younger men	မ Má for younger women

Verbs and related noun suffixes

[place]–မှာ နေ–	[place]-hma ne-	to live in [place] (Lessons 27, 29, 30)
[place]–က လာ–	[place]-gá la-	to come from [place] (Lesson 31)
[place] သွား:–	[place] thwà-	to go to [place] (Lesson 34-35)
[place] လာ–	[place] la-	to come to [place] (Lesson 34)

Diphthongs in the roman transcription:
pronounce ei as in *vein,* ai as in *Thailand,* ou as in *though,* au as in *Sauerkraut.*

[time]–မှာ [verb]	[time]-hma [verb]	to [verb] at [time] (Lesson 33)
[price] ပေး ရ–	[price] pè-yá-	to pay [price] (Lesson 39)
[name]–လို့ ခေါ်–	[name]-ló k'aw-	to call, be called [name] (Lesson 36)
[name]–တဲ့ [no verb]	[name]-déh	it is called [name] (Lesson 36)
[thing] ဝယ်–	[thing] weh-	to buy [thing] (Lesson 41)
[place]–မှာ ထိုင်–	[place]-hma t'ain-	to sit in [place] (Lesson 43)
[thing] ပိတ်–	[thing] peiq-	to close, turn off [thing] (Lesson 43)
[thing] ဖွင့်–	[thing] p'wín-	to open, turn on [thing] (Lesson 43)

"auxiliary verbs"

[verb]–ပါ–	[verb]-ba-	to [verb] *(polite)* (Lesson 42)
[verb]–ချင်–	[verb]-jin-	to want to [verb] (Lesson 42)
[verb]–ရ–	[verb]-yá-	to have to [verb] (Lesson 45)

Pronouns

Words for "he," "she," "they" and so on are mostly omitted (Lesson 27), as are words for "you" and "I" (Lesson 39).

Currency words

ကျပ်	caq	kyat (Lesson 32)
ပြား	pyà	pya (or English penny) (Lesson 25)
ပေါင်	paun	pound (Lesson 23)
ဒေါ်လာ	daw-la	dollar (Lesson 23)
ပဲနီ	pèh-ní	penny (Lesson 26)
ဆင့်	s'ín	cent (Lesson 26)

Fractions of the kyat (Lesson 38)

မတ်	maq	quarter
ငါးမူး	ngà-mù	half
–ခွဲ	-k'wèh	and a half

Things to buy (Lesson 40)

ဘောပင်	bàw-pin	ballpoint pen [from English]
ပို့စကဒ် /–ကတ်/	pó-săkaq	postcard [from English]
စာအိတ်	sa-eiq	envelope ["letter-bag"]
စာရွက်	sa-yweq	writing paper ["paper-sheet"]
ဆယ်လိုတိပ်	s'eh-lo-teiq	sellotape/Scotchtape [from English]
မြေပုံ /–ပုံ/	mye-boun	map ["earth picture"]
ဖလင်	p'ălin	film [from English]
တိပ်ခွေ	teiq-k'we	tape ["tape-reel"]
ကော်ဖီမှုန့်	kaw-p'i-hmoún	instant coffee ["coffee-powder"]
နို့မှုန့်	nó-hmoún	milk powder ["milk-powder"]
ဘီစကွတ်	bi-săkuq	biscuit [= cookie; from English]

Things in a room (Lesson 43)

စားပွဲ /စပွဲ/	săbwèh	table, desk
မီး	mì	fire, light
ပန်ကာ	pan-ka	fan

Diphthongs in the roman transcription:
pronounce ei as in *vein,* ai as in *Thailand,* ou as in *though,* au as in *Sauerkraut.*

တံခါး	/ဒဂါး/	dăgà	door
ပြတင်းပေါက်	/ပဒင်းဘောက်/	pădìn-bauq	window

Indoor places (Lesson 35)

အိမ်သာ/	–သာ/	ein-dha	toilet
အိမ်		ein	house
သာ–		tha-	to be pleasant
စာကြည့်တိုက်	/–ကျိဒိုက်/	sa-cí-daiq	library
စာ		sa	text, writing
ကြည့်	/ကျိ/	cí-	to look at, study
တိုက်		taiq	building
စားသောက်ခန်း		sà-thauq-k'àn	eating room, canteen
စား–		sà-	to eat
သောက်–		thauq-	to drink
အခန်း		ăk'àn	room

Buildings and parks (Lesson 1)

ပြတိုက်	/ပြဒိုက်/	pyá-daiq	museum
ပြ–		pyá-	to show, exhibit
တိုက်		taiq	building
ဘုရား	/ဖယား/	p'ăyà	lord, pagoda, Buddha image
ပန်းခြံ	/–ဂျန်/	pàn-jan	park, garden
ပန်း		pàn	flower
ခြံ		c'an	enclosure, compound
ဟိုတယ်		ho-teh	hotel [from English]
ဈေး	/ဇေး/	zè	market
အပြင်		ăpyin	outside, out (Lesson 35)

Places in Rangoon (Lesson 5)

ဗိုလ်ချုပ်ပြတိုက်	/ဗိုဂျုပ်ပျာ့ဒိုက်/	Bo-jouq Pyá-daiq	Bogyoke Museum
ရွှေတိဂုံဘုရား	/ရွှေဒဂုန်ဖယား/	Shwe-dăgoun P'ăyà	Shwedagon Pagoda
ဗိုလ်ချုပ်ပန်းခြံ	/ဗိုဂျုပ်ပန်းဂျန်/	Bo-jouq Pàn-jan	Bogyoke Park
သမ္မတဟိုတယ်	/သမဒ၁/	Thămădá Ho-teh	President Hotel
ဗိုလ်ချုပ်ဈေး	/ဗိုဂျုပ်ဇေး/	Bo-jouq Zè	Bogyoke Market
သိမ်ကြီးဈေး	/သိန်ဂျီးဇေး/	Thein-jì-zè	Thein-gyi Market
ဆူးလေဘုရား	/–ဖယား/	S'ù-le P'ăya	Sule Pagoda
မဟာဗန္ဓုလပန်းခြံ	/ဗန်ဒုလ္လာ့ပန်းဂျန်/	Măha Ban-dú-lá Pàn-jan	Maha Bandoola Park
အမျိုးသားပြတိုက်	/–ပျာ့ဒိုက်/	Amyò-thà Pyá-daiq	National Museum
စထရင်းဟိုတယ်		Săt'ărìn Ho-teh	Strand Hotel

— from Lesson 35

ကုန်တိုက်	/–ဒိုက်/	koun-daiq	department store
ကုန်		koun	goods, merchandise
တိုက်		taiq	building
သံတမန်ကုန်တိုက်	/–ဒမန် –ဒိုက်/	than-dăman koun-daiq	Diplomatic Store
သံတမန်	/–ဒမန်/	than-dăman	diplomatic

Diphthongs in the roman transcription:	179
pronounce ei as in *vein*, ai as in *Thailand*, ou as in *though*, au as in *Sauerkraut*.	

Roads in Rangoon (Lessons 7 & 9)

လမ်း	làn	road, street
ဗိုလ်ချုပ်လမ်း /ဗိုချုပ်–/	Bo-jouq Làn	Bogyoke Street
အနော်ရထာလမ်း /ယထာ or ရထာ/	Ănaw-yăt'a Làn (yă or ră)	Anawrahta Street
မဟာဗန္ဓုလလမ်း /ဗန်ဒုလာ–/	Măha Ban-dú-lá Làn	Maha Bandoola Street
ကုန်သည်လမ်း /–သွယ်–/	Koun-dheh Làn	Merchant Street
ကမ်းနားလမ်း	Kàn-nà Làn	Strand Road
ဗိုလ်အောင်ကျော်လမ်း /ဗို အောင်ကျော်–/	Bo Aun Jaw Làn	Bo Aung Kyaw Street
ပန်းဆိုးတန်း /ဆိုး or ဇိုး/	Pàn-s'ò-dàn (s'ò or zò)	Pansodan Street
ဆူးလေဘုရားလမ်း /–ဖယား–/	S'ù-le P'ăyà Làn	Sule Pagoda Road
ရွှေဘုံသာလမ်း	Shwe-boun-dha Làn	Shwebontha Street
ဘုရားလမ်း /ဖယား–/	P'ăyà Làn	Shwedagon Pagoda Road

Countries in Asia (Lesson 13)

နိုင်ငံ	naing-ngan	country, state
အိန္ဒိယနိုင်ငံ /အိန်ဒီယာ–/	Ein-dí-yá Naing-ngan	India
ဘင်္ဂလားဒေ့ရှ်နိုင်ငံ /ဗင်ဂ–/	Bin-gălà-désh Naing-ngan	Bangladesh
မြန်မာနိုင်ငံ	Myan-ma Naing-ngan	Burma/Myanmar
ထိုင်းနိုင်ငံ	T'aìn Naing-ngan	Thailand
မလေးရှားနိုင်ငံ	Mălè-shà Naing-ngan	Malaysia
ဗီယက်နမ်နိုင်ငံ	Bi-yeq-nan Naing-ngan	Vietnam
ဖိလစ်ပိုင်နိုင်ငံ	P'í-liq-pain Naing-ngan	Philippines
တရုပ်နိုင်ငံ	Tăyouq Naing-ngan	China
ဂျပန်နိုင်ငံ	Jăpan Naing-ngan	Japan

More countries (Lesson 34)

ဂျာမနီ	Ja-măni	Germany
ရတ်ရှား	Raq-shà	Russia
အင်္ဂလန်နိုင်ငံ /အင်ဂလန်/	In-gălan Nain-ngan	England
ပြင်သစ်နိုင်ငံ	Pyin-thiq Nain-ngan	France
အမေရိကနိုင်ငံ	Ăme-rí-ká Nain-ngan	America
စင်္ကာပူ /စင်ဂါ/	Sin-ga-pu	Singapore
သြစတြေးလျနိုင်ငံ /အော့စတရေးလျာ/	Àw-sătrè-lyá	Australia
အိုင်ယာလန်	Ain-ya-lan	Ireland
ကိုရီးယား	Ko-rì-yà	Korea

Towns in Asia (Lesson 15)

မြို့	myó	town
နယူးဒေလီ	Năyù De-li	New Delhi
ဒက္ကား	Deq-kà	Dacca
ရန်ကုန် /ယန်ဂုန်/	Yan-goun	Rangoon/ Yangon
ဘန်ကောက်	Ban-kauq	Bangkok
ကွာလာလမ်ပူ	Kwa-la Lan-pu	Kuala Lumpur
ဟနွိုင်း	Hănwaìn	Hanoi
မနီလာ	Măni-la	Manila
ပီကင်း	Pi-kìn	Peking/Beijing
တိုကျို	To-co	Tokyo

Diphthongs in the roman transcription:
pronounce ei as in *vein*, ai as in *Thailand*, ou as in *though*, au as in *Sauerkraut*.

Towns in Burma (Lesson 19)

မြစ်ကြီးနား	Myiq-cì-nà	Myitkyina
မေမြို့	Me-myó	Maymyo
မန္တလေး /မန်းဒလေး/	Màn-dălè	Mandalay
စစ်ကိုင်း /ဇဂိုင်း/	Săgaìn	Sagaing
ပုဂံ /ပုဂန်/	Păgan	Pagan (Bagan)
သာစည် /သာဇီ/	Tha-zi	Thazi
တောင်ကြီး /–ဂျီး/	Taun-jì	Taunggyi
ပြည် /ပျေ/ or /ပို/	Pye	Prome (Pyi/Pyay)
ရေနံချောင်း /ယေနန်ချောင်း/	Ye-nan-jaùn	Yenangyaung
သံတွဲ /–ဒွဲ/	Than-dwèh	Sandoway (Thandwe)
ပဲခူး /ဗဂိုး/	Păgò	Pegu (Bago)
ရန်ကုန် /ယန်ဂုန်/	Yan-goun	Rangoon (Yangon)
မော်လမြိုင်	Maw-lămyain	Moulmein (Mawlamyine)

Phrases

ဟုတ်ကဲ့	Houq-kéh	It is so. (Lesson 3)
မဟုတ်ပါဘူး /–ဘူး/	Măhouq-pa-bù	It is not so. (Lesson 3)
အော်	Aw.	Oh. (Lesson 5)
ထပ်ပြောပါအုံး။ /–ဗာ–/	T'aq-pyàw-ba-oùn	Please say that again. (Lesson 13)
ပြန်ပြောပါအုံး။ /–ဗာ–/	Pyan-pyàw-ba-oùn	Please say that again. (Lesson 13)

Checking questions (Lesson 6)

[noun]–လား။	[noun]-là	Did you say [noun]?
		Was that [noun]?

Miscellaneous words

နံပါတ် /–ဗတ်/	nan-baq	number (Lesson 2)
အမှတ်	ăhmaq	number (Lesson 29)
အိမ်	ein	house (Lesson 29)
တယ်လီဖုန်း	teh-li-p'oùn	telephone (Lesson 6)
နာမည် /နန်မယ်//နာမို/	nan-meh	name (Lesson 27)
	Pronounced /နန်မယ်/ in colloquial, but /နာမို/ in reading style.	
လိပ်စာ	leiq-sa	address (Lesson 29)
ရပ် or ရပ်ကွက်	yaq or yaq-kweq	Quarter (in a town) (Lesson 29)
မြို့နယ်	myó-neh	township (Lesson 29)
အချိန်	ăc'ein	time (Lesson 33)
နေရာ	ne-ya	place (Lesson 35)
နာရီ	na-yi	hour (Lesson 33)
မိနစ် /မိနစ်–မင်းနစ်–မနစ်/	mí-niq, mìn-niq, măniq	minute (Lesson 37)

The pronunciation of the first syllable varies with the speed of the speaker.

–ခွဲ	-gwèh	- and a half (Lesson 37)

Examples:

တစ်နာရီခွဲ	tăna-yi-gwèh	1.30 ["one hour and a half"]
သုံးနာရီခွဲ	thoùn-na-yi-gwèh	3.30 ["three hours and a half"]
သုံးကျပ်ခွဲ	thoùn-jaq-k'wèh	K3.50 ["three kyats and a half"]
ဗမာလို	Băma-lo	in Burmese ["Burmese-way"] (Lesson 40)

Diphthongs in the roman transcription:
pronounce ei as in *vein,* ai as in *Thailand,* ou as in *though,* au as in *Sauerkraut.*

COMMON PHRASES SUPPLEMENT

CLASSROOM GREETINGS AND HANDY PHRASES

Most teachers and students like to be able to use Burmese for classroom interaction: "Sorry I'm late," "Would you like the window open?", "Don't look at the book now," and so on. What you need to say will vary according to the size of the class, the structure of the lesson, the layout and facilities of the room, the personalities of the teacher and the students, and other factors, and it would be out of place to try and cover all possible needs in this course. Your teacher will coach you in the language your situation requires. However, ways of saying Hallo and How are you and Goodbye are needed in almost all classroom situations, so Section 1 below presents a few phrases and notes that may be helpful. At the end of the supplement there are lists of some phrases that teachers may wish to use in class. These phrases are set out for reference only, and are not practised on the tape.

In Section 2 you will find a small set of phrases that are not limited to the classroom context. They are phrases of high frequency that you will need for the dialogues in *BISL* Part 2. You may also find a use for them in the classroom situation. They don't fit naturally into the drills and exercises of the regular Lessons of *BISL* Groundwork, so they are set out here apart from the Lessons.

The Common Phrases Supplement is self-contained: it doesn't assume any prior knowledge of the *BISL* material, and its oral exercises are on a separate tape, so you can start working on it as soon or as late as you like, and study it at your own pace — but make sure you know the phrases before you start work on the Dialogues. We recommend that you start work on the phrases when you have reached Lesson 11 in Part 1 (where the Pronunciation Sections end), and thereafter take them at a rate of about one to every two Part 1 Lessons.

CONTENTS

Section 1. Classroom greetings

1. Greeting
S1: မင်္ဂလာပါ။   Good morning/afternoon (opening).   Min-gǎla-ba.
S2: မင်္ဂလာပါ။   Good morning/afternoon (response).   Min-gǎla-ba.

2. Greeting Teacher
S1: မင်္ဂလာပါ ဆရာ။   Good morning/afternoon, Teacher.   Min-gǎla-ba S'ǎya.
Teacher: မင်္ဂလာပါ။   Good morning/afternoon (response).   Min-gǎla-ba.

3. How are you?
S1: နေကောင်းရဲ့လား။   How are you?   Ne-kaùn-yéh-là?
S2: နေကောင်းပါတယ်။   I'm fine.   Ne-kaùn-ba-deh.

4. And how are *you*?

Teacher: Tom–ကော၊
နေကောင်းရဲ့လား။

Tom: နေကောင်းပါတယ် ဆရာ။

How about you (Tom):
    Are you all right?

I'm fine, Teacher.

Tom-gàw:
    ne-kaùn-yéh-là?

Ne-kaùn-ba-deh, S'ăya.

5. Goodbye

S1: သွားပါအုံးမယ်။

S2: ကောင်းပါပြီ။

Goodbye (initiating).

Goodbye (response).

Thwà-ba-oùn-meh.

Kaùn-ba-bi.

6. See you later

S1: တွေ့သေးတာပေါ့။

S2: ဟုတ်ကဲ့။
    တွေ့သေးတာပေါ့။

See you later/next time.

Yes. Right.
    See you later/next time.

Twé-dhè-da-báw.

Houq-kéh.
    Twé-dhè-da-báw.

Section 2. Handy phrases

7. Is this all right?

S1: ရတယ်နော်။

S2: ရပါတယ်။

This is all right, isn't it?

Yes, it is.

Yá-deh-naw?

Yá-ba-deh.

8. Just a moment

S1: ခဏလေးနော်။

S2: ရပါတယ်။

or S2: ကိစ္စ မရှိပါဘူး။

Just a moment, OK?

That's all right.

No problem.

K'ăná-lè-naw?

Yá-ba-deh.

Keiq-sá măshí-ba-bù.

9. Thank you

S1: ကျေးဇူး တင်ပါတယ်။

S2: ရပါတယ်။

or S2: ကိစ္စ မရှိပါဘူး။

Thank you.

That's all right.

No problem.

Cè-zù tin-ba-deh.

Yá-ba-deh.

Keiq-sá măshí-ba-bù.

10. Polite tags

M: ...... ခင်ဗျာ။

F: ...... ရှင်။

...... [Monsieur/Madame]

...... [Monsieur/Madame]

...... K'in-bya.

...... Shin.

11. Goodbye (less formal version)

S1: သွားမယ်နော်။

S2: ကောင်းပါပြီ။

Goodbye (initiating).

Goodbye (responding).

Thwà-meh-naw?

Kaùn-ba-bi.

12. No you can't

S1: ရတယ်နော်။

S2: မရဘူး။

S1: ကောင်းပါပြီ။

This is all right, isn't it?

No, it isn't.

Very well. Fine. OK.

Yá-deh-naw?

Măyá-bù.

Kaùn-ba-bi.

13. Sorry

S1: ဆောရီးပဲ။

S2: ရပါတယ်။

or: S2: ကိစ္စ မရှိပါဘူး။

Sorry!

That's all right.

It doesn't matter.

S'àw-rì-bèh.

Yá-ba-deh.

Keiq-sá măshí-ba-bù.

14. There: got it
S1: ခဏလေးနော်။   Just a moment, OK?   K'ăná-lè-naw?
Then, after some activity
S1: ကဲ။ ရပြီ။   There. Got it.   Kèh. Yá-bi.
or S1: ကဲ။ ပြီးပြီ။   There. That's done.   Kèh. Pì-bi.

15. Have you finished?
S1: ပြီးပြီလား။   Have you finished?   Pì-bi-là?
S2: ပြီးပြီ။   Yes, I have.   Pì-bi.
or S2: မပြီးသေးပါဘူး။   No, not yet.   Măpì-dhè-ba-bù.

16. All set?
S1: ရပြီလား။   All set? Ready?   Yá-bi-là?
S2: ရပြီ။   Yes, I am.   Yá-bi.
or S2: မရသေးပါဘူး။   No, not yet.   Măyá-dhè-ba-bù.

17. Is that all?
S1: ဒါပဲလား။   Is that all? Is that the lot?   Da-bèh-là?
S2: ဒါပါပဲ။   That's it.   Da-ba-bèh.
or S2: ရှိပါသေးတယ်။   There's more.   Shí-ba-dhè-deh.

18. Do you understand?
S1: နား လည်သလား။   Do you understand?   Nà leh-dhă-là?
S2: နား လည်ပါတယ်။   Yes, I do.   Nà leh-ba-deh.
or S2: နား မလည်ပါဘူး။   No, I don't.   Nà măleh-ba-bù.

19. May I leave now?
S1: ခွင့် ပြုပါအုံး။   May I leave now?   K'wín pyú-ba-oùn.
S2: ဟုတ်ကဲ့။ or ကောင်းပါပြီ။   Certainly.   Houq-kéh or Kaùn-ba-bi.

20. I enjoyed talking to you.
S1: စကား ပြောလို့ ကောင်းပါတယ်။   I enjoyed talking to you.   Săgà pyàw-ló kaùn-ba-deh.
S2: ဟုတ်ကဲ့။   I agree.   Houq-kéh.
or S2: ကောင်းပါတယ်။   Me too.   Kaùn-ba-deh.

Section 3. Reference Section

Teacher instructions
Teacher comments
Question and answer

SECTION 1. CLASSROOM GREETINGS

First read through the text for each exchange, then listen to the tape.

1. Greeting

S1: မင်္ဂလာပါ။	Good morning/afternoon (opening)	Min-găla-ba.
S2: မင်္ဂလာပါ။	Good morning/afternoon (response)	Min-găla-ba.

Notes

မင်္ဂလာ (min-găla) means something like "auspiciousness, good omens," and the greeting မင်္ဂလာပါ (Min-găla-ba) was deliberately coined in the 1930s for use in the school classroom (for a concise account see ရဲဘော်ထွန်းမြင့် [ရေး] မြန်မာ့ယဉ်ကျေးမှု။ 1991, Rangoon, Ministry of Information, pp. 47-48). It is not in widespread use as a greeting outside the classroom, except occasionally to foreigners and on loudspeaker announcements on trains and planes. You will also find it written as a welcome in places like a stand for drinking-water, or an entrance to a garden or a motor launch. If you have a teacher and classmates, it is an appropriate greeting to use with them.

Outside schools Burmese has no single equivalent for the conventional greetings phrases of English and other cultures: the words used depend on the circumstances of the meeting and the relationship between the speakers; for example:

ဘယ် သွားမလဲ။	Where are you going?	Beh thwà-mălèh?
ဘယ်က ပြန်လာတာလဲ။	Where have you been?	Beh-gá pyan-la-da-lèh?
ထမင်း စားပြီးပြီလား။	Have you had a meal?	T'ămìn sà-pì-bi-là?
ပြန်ရောက်ပြီလား။	You're back, I see.	Pyan-yauq-pi-là?
ရောက်နေတာ ကြာပြီလား။	Have you been here long?	Yauq-ne-da ca-bi-là?
အစောကြီး ထနေပါလား။	*You're up early!*	Ăsàw-jì t'á-ne-ba-là.

=====

2. Greeting Teacher

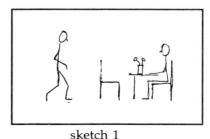

sketch 1

Speaker 1   Speaker 2
(student)   (teacher)

S1: မင်္ဂလာပါ ဆရာ။   Good morning/afternoon, (male) Teacher   Min-găla-ba S'ăya.

or:

S1: မင်္ဂလာပါ ဆရာမ။   Good morning/afternoon, (female) Teacher   Min-găla-ba S'ăya-má.

Teacher: မင်္ဂလာပါ။   Good morning/afternoon (response)   Min-găla-ba.

Notes

ဆရာ (S'ăya) means a teacher, or specifically a male teacher, and ဆရာမ (S'ăya-má) means a female teacher. When addressing a teacher it is polite to add this tag to what you say, both greetings and other remarks — in fact it would sound rather curt to omit it. The teacher would not normally add a tag to his or her greeting.

ဆရာ (S'ăya) and ဆရာမ (S'ăya-má) are also used when speaking to other people with some knowledge or skill or authority; for example: by a patient to a doctor or nurse, by a clerk to his office senior, a musician to the leader of his troupe, a batman to his officer, a taximan to his passenger.

Other titles are used as tags in the same way, as appropriate to the person addressed; for example:

ဗိုလ်ချုပ်ကြီး	Bo-jouq-cì	General
ဝန်ကြီး	Wun-jì	Minister
သံအမတ်ကြီး	Than-Ămaq-cì	Ambassador
ဘုရား	P'ăyà	"Your Reverence"
		[for monks, like the English "Father" for priests]

and so on.

---

3. How are you?

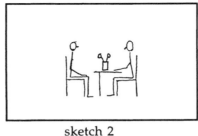

sketch 2

Speaker 1   Speaker 2

S1: နေကောင်းရဲ့လား။   How are you?   Ne-kaùn-yéh-là?

S2: နေကောင်းပါတယ်။   I'm fine.   Ne-kaùn-ba-deh.

Notes

The standard greeting to use when you meet someone you know. Here we have in mind the teacher and student meeting for the day's class.

နေ– (ne-) "to be (in a certain state)" and ကောင်း– (kaùn-) "to be good" are used together in နေကောင်း– (ne-kaùn-) "being/state is good" to mean something like "to be in good health, be well." So a more literal translation of the question would be "Is your state good?" or "Are you well?"

–ရဲ့လား (-yéh-là) and –ပါတယ် (-ba-deh) are grammatical suffixes attached to verbs. The first marks a question and the second marks a statement.

Variants

နေကောင်းလား။	How are you?	Ne kaùn-là?
နေကောင်းတယ်နော်။	You're well, I hope?	Ne kaùn-deh-naw?

The first of these is slightly more casual than the standard form; and the second, depending on the circumstances, can be either a shade more concerned ("You really are all right, are you?"), or a shade more dismissive (implying "I don't want to spend too long on this topic").

Either the question, or the answer, may be followed by a polite tag where appropriate:

Teacher: နေကောင်းရဲ့လား။	How are you?	Ne-kaùn-yéh-là?
S2: နေကောင်းပါတယ် ဆရာမ။	I'm fine, Teacher.	Ne-kaùn-ba-deh, S'ăya-má.

4. And how are *you*?

Version 1: Tom begins

Tom: နေကောင်းရဲ့လား ဆရာ။	How are you, Teacher?	Ne-kaùn-yéh-là, S'ăya?
Teacher: နေကောင်းပါတယ်။	I'm fine.	Ne-kaùn-ba-deh.
Tom–ကော၊	How about you (Tom):	Tom-gàw:
နေကောင်းရဲ့လား။	Are you all right?	ne-kaùn-yéh-là?
Tom: နေကောင်းပါတယ် ဆရာ။	I'm fine, Teacher.	Ne-kaùn-ba-deh, S'ăya.

Version 2: Teacher begins

Teacher: နေကောင်းရဲ့လား။	How are you?	Ne-kaùn-yéh-là?
Tom: နေကောင်းပါတယ် ဆရာ။	I'm fine, Teacher.	Ne-kaùn-ba-deh, S'ăya.
ဆရာကော၊	How about you (Teacher):	S'ăya-gàw:
နေကောင်းရဲ့လား။	Are you all right?	ne-kaùn-yéh-là?
Teacher: နေကောင်းပါတယ်။	I'm fine.	Ne-kaùn-ba-deh.

Notes

The standard riposte to "How are you?" A common way of saying "you" is to use the person's name; hence the "Tom" in line 3 of Version 1. If the person is a teacher, it is normal to use ဆရာ or ဆရာမ (S'ăya or S'ăya-má) for "you," as in Version 2.

The suffix –ကော (-gàw) is attached to a noun and implies that the last question asked is to be repeated with reference to the new noun; for example: in an exchange where the Teacher is addressing Tom, and Tom's sister is called Lucy:

Teacher: နေကောင်းရဲ့လား။	Are you (Tom) all right?	Ne-kaùn-yéh-là?
Tom: နေကောင်းပါတယ်။	Yes.	Ne-kaùn-ba-deh.
Teacher: Lucy-ကော၊	How about Lucy:	Lucy-gàw:
နေကောင်းရဲ့လား။	is she all right?	ne-kaùn-yéh-là?
Tom: နေကောင်းပါတယ်။	Yes, she is.	Ne-kaùn-ba-deh.

Once your listener has heard [noun]–ကော ([noun]-gàw) he knows the new subject and knows the question that will follow, so the question is often left unspoken:

Teacher: နေကောင်းရဲ့လား။	Are you (Tom) all right?	Ne-kaùn-yéh-là?
Tom: နေကောင်းပါတယ်။	Yes.	Ne-kaùn-ba-deh.
Teacher: Lucy-ကော။	How about Lucy?	Lucy-gàw?
Tom: နေကောင်းပါတယ်။	She's fine.	Ne-kaùn-ba-deh.

Variant. –ကော (-gàw) is sometimes written and pronounced –ရော (-yàw):

Teacher: နေကောင်းပါတယ်။	I'm fine.	Ne-kaùn-ba-deh.
Tom-ရော၊	How about you (Tom):	Tom-yàw:
နေကောင်းရဲ့လား။	Are you all right?	ne-kaùn-yéh-là?

---

5. Goodbye

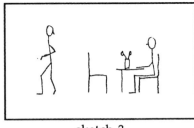

sketch 3

	Speaker 1	Speaker 2
S1: သွားပါအုံးမယ်။	Goodbye (initiating)	Thwà-ba-oùn-meh.
S2: ကောင်းပါပြီ။	Goodbye (response)	Kaùn-ba-bi.

188

Notes

သွား– (thwà-) means "to go," and သွားပါအုံးမယ် (Thwà-ba-oùn-meh) means something like "I'll be getting along now." It is often used where English speakers would say "goodbye" — but notice that S1's phrase has to be used by the person who is leaving, not the person who is staying behind.

ကောင်း– (kaun-) means "to be good," and the response ကောင်းပါပြီ (Kaùn-ba-bi) means "That's fine, OK, All right," and the like.

Variants

There are many variants of the သွားပါအုံးမယ် (Thwà-ba-oùn-meh) phrase, each at a slightly different position on the scale of deference or brusqueness. Here are some possibilities:

သွားမယ်။	Thwà-meh.
သွားအုံးမယ်။	Thwà-oùn-meh.
သွားပါအုံးမယ်။	Thwà-ba-oùn-meh.
သွားတော့မယ်။	Thwà-dáw-meh.
သွားပါတော့မယ်။	Thwà-ba-dáw-meh.
သွားလိုက်မယ်။	Thwà-laiq-meh.
သွားလိုက်ပါမယ်။	Thwà-laiq-pa-meh.
သွားလိုက်အုံးမယ်။	Thwà-laiq-oùn-meh.
သွားလိုက်ပါအုံးမယ်။	Thwà-laiq-pa-oùn-meh.
သွားပြီ။	Thwà-bi.

In any of these, if the departing speaker is going to go home he may use ပြန်– (pyan-) "to go back, go home" in place of သွား– (thwà-) "go" (yielding ပြန်ပါအုံးမယ် Pyan-ba-oùn-meh, and so on), and any variant may be followed by –နော် (-naw), which means something like "I hope that's all right by you?."

Finally, either the statement or the response may be followed by a polite tag:

S1: သွားပါအုံးမယ် ဆရာ။	Goodbye, Teacher.	Thwà-ba-oùn-meh, S'ăya.
Teacher: ကောင်းပါပြီ။	Goodbye.	Kaùn-ba-bi.

As you will have noticed, the Goodbye exchange is normally initiated by the person leaving and responded to by the person staying behind. If the person leaving fails to initiate the exchange, clearly it would be inappropriate for the person staying behind to try and initiate the exchange him/herself with သွားပါအုံးမယ် (Thwà-ba-oùn-meh) because "I'll be getting along now" can only be said by the leaver. In this contingency the person staying behind usually prompts the exchange by saying —

သွားတော့မလား။	Are you about to go?	Thwà-dáw-mălà?
or: ပြန်တော့မလား။	Are you about to go home?	Pyan-dáw-mălà?

The response from the leaver will then usually be ဟုတ်ကဲ့ (Houq-kéh) followed by one of the intiating phrases; for example:

S1: သွားတော့မလား။	Are you just off?	Thwà-dáw-mălà?
S2: ဟုတ်ကဲ့။ သွားပါအုံးမယ်။	Yes. Goodbye.	Houq-kéh.Thwà-ba-oùn-meh.
S1: ကောင်းပါပြီ။	Goodbye.	Kaùn-ba-bi.

6. See you later

S1: တွေ့သေးတာပေါ့။	See you later/next time.	Twé-dhè-da-báw.
S2: ဟုတ်ကဲ့။	Yes. Right.	Houq-kéh.
တွေ့သေးတာပေါ့။	See you later/next time.	Twé-dhè-da-báw.

Notes

တွေ့-	to meet, see, notice	twé-
-သေး-	again, further, more	-dhè-
-တာပေါ့	[grammatical suffixes]	-da-báw

Put together in တွေ့သေးတာပေါ့ (twé-dhè-da-báw) these elements mean something like "We'll surely meet again."

Variants

တွေ့မယ်နော်။	See you later/next time.	Twé-meh-naw.
တွေ့အုံးမယ်နော်။	See you later/next time.	Twé-oùn-meh-naw.

There is almost no difference in meaning or level of courtesy between any of the variants.

SECTION 2. HANDY PHRASES

7. Is this all right?

S1: ရတယ်နော်။	This is all right, isn't it?	Yá-deh-naw?
S2: ရပါတယ်။	Yes, it is.	Yá-ba-deh.

Variant

ရတယ် (Yá-deh) is a shorter, more familiar variant for ရပါတယ် (Yá-ba-deh).

Notes

You use ရတယ်နော် (Yá-deh-naw?) when you're about to do something and want to check that the person affected has no objections. For example, if you wanted to have a closer look at something on a bazaar stall, you could make as if to pick it up and then ask the stall-holder ရတယ်နော် (Yá-deh-naw?) to see if he minded. Or if you wanted to sit down on an unoccupied chair but wanted to make sure it wasn't needed by the people sitting nearby, you could use the phrase to them. Or you could go to the light switch in the classroom and ask the question before switching on, to make sure no one objected. Or you could set up your camera to take a photograph and use this question to check that photography was allowed.

ရတယ် (yá-deh) or ရပါတယ် (yá-ba-deh) is a verb phrase meaning "it is all right, it is acceptable, it is permitted"; and the suffix –နော် (-naw) indicates a request for agreement.

---

8. Just a moment

S1: ခဏလေးနော်။	Just a moment, OK?	K'ăná-lè-naw?
S2: ရပါတယ်။	That's all right.	Yá-ba-deh.
or		
S2: ကိစ္စ မရှိပါဘူး။	No problem.	Keiq-sá măshí-ba-bù.

Variants

S1: ခဏ။	One moment.	K'ăná.
S1: ခဏ စောင့်နေပါ။	Please wait a moment.	K'ăna saún-ne-ba.
S1: ခဏနော်။	One moment, OK?	K'ăná-naw?.
S1: ခဏ စောင့်နေပါနော်။	Just wait a moment, will you?	K'ăna saún-ne-ba-naw?

In any of these versions the word ခဏ (k'ăná) "moment" may be replaced by ခဏလေး (k'ăná-lè) "a small moment."

Notes

ခဏလေး (K'ăná-lè) doesn't always need a response. Sometimes you just wait. But if a response seems called for, you can use either of the alternatives above.

ခဏ	moment	k'ăná
စောင့်နေ–	to wait	saún-ne-
[noun]–လေး	small [noun]	[noun]-lè
–နော်	[request for agreement]	-naw
ကိစ္စ	business, important matter	keiq-sá
မရှိပါဘူး။	there is not	măshí-ba-bù.

The last two elements put together yield ကိစ္စ မရှိပါဘူး (keiq-sá măshí-ba-bù), which means something like "There is no serious business involved," and it is used where English speakers would use "No problem."

---

9. Thank you

S1: ကျေးဇူး တင်ပါတယ်။	Thank you.	Cè-zù tin-ba-deh.
S2: ရပါတယ်။	That's all right.	Yá-ba-deh.
or		
S2: ကိစ္စ မရှိပါဘူး။	No problem.	Keiq-sá măshí-ba-bù.

191

Variant

S1: ကျေးဇူးပဲ။   Thanks.   Cè-zù-bèh.

Notes

As you see, the response to ကျေးဇူး တင်ပါတယ် (cè-zù tin-ba-deh) is the same as the response to ခဏလေးနော် (k'ăná-lè-naw?).

In earlier times in Burma ကျေးဇူး တင်ပါတယ် (cè-zù tin-ba-deh) was used to express serious debts of gratitude, like your obligation to someone who has saved your life, or to your parents for bringing you up. Contact with Westerners, who say "Thank you" when someone opens the door for them or gives them change in a shop, has brought ကျေးဇူး တင်ပါတယ် (cè-zù tin-ba-deh) into wider currency, but predictably the change has not spread uniformly through Burmese society. At one extreme there are people who use it for trivial assistance, like Westerners, and at the other, particularly in the countryside far from towns, there are people who have not yet devalued the phrase so far. So don't be surprised if someone simply smiles to express his gratitude and doesn't actually say the words ကျေးဇူး တင်ပါတယ် (cè-zù tin-ba-deh).

ကျေးဇူး (cè-zù) means "service, favour," and တင်ပါတယ် (tin-ba-deh) means (among other things) "I am aware of, I appreciate"; so together they mean "I am grateful." ကျေးဇူးပဲ (cè-zù-bèh) is just a shortened form of the standard phrase, with the emphatic suffix –ပဲ (-bèh).

================================

10. Polite tags

Listen to the following exchanges on the tape. M and F indicate Male and Female speakers respectively. Then read the notes below.

M: ရတယ်နော်။   You don't mind, do you?   Yá-deh-naw?
M: ရပါတယ် ခင်ဗျာ။   No. Go ahead.   Yá-ba-deh K'in-bya.

M: ရတယ်နော်။   You don't mind, do you?   Yá-deh-naw?
F: ရပါတယ် ရှင်။   No. Go ahead.   Yá-ba-deh Shin.

F: ခဏလေးနော်။   Just a moment, OK?   K'ăná-lè-naw?
M: ကိစ္စ မရှိပါဘူး ခင်ဗျာ။   No problem.   Keiq-sá măshí-ba-bù K'in-bya.

F: ကျေးဇူး တင်ပါတယ် ရှင်။   Thank you.   Cè-zù tin-ba-deh Shin.
M: ရပါတယ် ခင်ဗျာ။   That's all right.   Yá-ba-deh K'in-bya.

M: ကျေးဇူး တင်ပါတယ် ခင်ဗျာ။   Thank you.   Cè-zù tin-ba-deh K'in-bya.
M: ကိစ္စ မရှိပါဘူး ခင်ဗျာ။   No problem.   Keiq-sá măshí-ba-bù K'in-bya.

Notes

ခင်ဗျာ and ရှင် (K'in-bya and Shin) are polite tags. The nearest English has to them are the words *Sir* and *Madam*, but *Sir* and *Madam* are different in several important respects.

1. Scope. In England *Sir* and *Madam* are restricted to a limited number of situations, such as a shopkeeper talking to a customer, or a soldier talking to an officer. ခင်ဗျာ and ရှင် (K'in-bya and Shin), on the other hand, are used far more widely: you use them when you're talking to a stranger you stop in the street to ask the way, or to a shopkeeper, or to friends and acquaintances, and you'll hear them used by a lecturer to his or her audience, and by radio and television announcers to their listeners.

2. Reciprocity. It is unusual for both parties to a conversation in English to use *Sir/Madam:* the shopkeeper may use them to customers, but customers don't use them to shopkeepers. In Burmese it is not uncommon for both parties to use ခင်ဗျာ and ရှင် (K'in-bya and Shin) to each other. In this respect ခင်ဗျာ and ရှင် (K'in-bya and Shin) are more like the French words *Monsieur* and *Madame.*

3. Gender differences. In English you choose *Sir* when you're speaking to a man, and *Madam* when you're speaking to a woman. You may have noticed when you listened to the tape, and you can see from the placing of M and F in the text above, that in Burmese you do the opposite: a male speaker always uses ခင်ဗျာ (K'in-bya), whether he's speaking to a man or a woman; and a female speaker always uses ရှင် (Shin), irrespective of the gender of her hearer.

Precisely because they are polite tags and indicate a degree of deference, ခင်ဗျာ and ရှင် (K'in-bya and Shin) are used between speakers of equal age and status, or by junior to senior, but not by senior to junior. So an adult would not use them to a child.

Finally, it is not customary to use ခင်ဗျာ and ရှင် (K'in-bya and Shin) with a question ending in –နော် (-naw).

---

11. Goodbye (less formal version)

S1: သွားမယ်နော်။	Goodbye (initiating)	Thwà-meh-naw?
S2: ကောင်းပါပြီ။	Goodbye (responding)	Kaùn-ba-bi.

Variant

S1: ပြန်မယ်နော်။	Goodbye (initiating)	Pyan-meh-naw?

This variant is used if you are heading for home.

Notes

သွား– (thwà-) means "to go," and သွားမယ် (Thwà-meh) means "I'm going to go," "I'm about to go," so သွားမယ်နော် (Thwà-meh-naw) means "I'm going to go, if that's all right with you." It is an informal request for S2's agreement to S1's leaving, and is often used where English speakers would say "goodbye." In Section 1 you learned a phrase for "Goodbye" that is appropriate to the classroom: သွားပါအုံးမယ် (Thwà-ba-oùn-meh). The shorter version presented here is less formal, and is more appropriate for taking leave of people like shopkeepers, taxi drivers, and same-age friends.

If the departing speaker is going to go home he may use the variant noted above, which has the verb ပြန်– (pyan-) "to go back, go home" in place of သွား– (thwà-) "go."

12. No you can't

S1: ရတယ်နော်။	This is all right, isn't it?	Yá-deh-naw?
S2: မရဘူး။	No, it isn't.	Măyá-bù.
S1: ကောင်းပါပြီ။	Very well. Fine. OK	Kaùn-ba-bi.

Notes

မရဘူး (Măyá-bù) is the *No* answer to S1's question (see Phrase 7). ကောင်းပါပြီ (Kaùn-ba-bi) is a way of showing that you understand and accept the prohibition.

13. Sorry

S1: ဆောရီးပဲ။	Sorry!	S'àw-rì-bèh.
S2: ရပါတယ်။	That's all right. No problem.	Yá-ba-deh.
or: ကိစ္စ မရှိပါဘူး။	It doesn't matter.	Keiq-sá măshí-ba-bù.

Variants

S1: ဆောရီးနော်။	Sorry!	S'àw-rì-naw.
or: ဆောရီးပဲနော်။	Sorry!	S'àw-rì-bèh-naw.

The variants only add a request for acknowledgment to the original phrase. Here you can think of the suffix –နော် (-naw) as meaning something like "You do accept my apology, don't you?"

Notes

A way of apologizing for minor offences, such as bumping into someone, knocking over a glass, breaking something. It is also used to apologize for not being able to help: "Sorry I don't know the answer," "Sorry I can't understand," and the like.

ဆောရီး (S'àw-rì) is from the English word *sorry*, and –ဝဲ (-bèh) is an emphatic suffix. You have already met S2's responses in an earlier exchange.

There are other ways of saying sorry for minor offences, such as:

S1: မတော်လို့နော်။	"It was unintentional."	Mătaw-ló-naw.
S1: စိတ် မရှိနဲ့နော်။	"Please don't be annoyed."	Seiq măshí-néh-naw.
S1: တောင်းပန်ပါတယ်။	"I ask forgiveness."	Taùn-ban-ba-deh.
S1: ကန်တော့၊ ကန်တော့။	"I make obeisance."	Gădáw gădáw.

We choose ဆောရီးဝဲ (S'àw-rì-bèh) in preference to these because it is in widespread use and is easy to remember.

---

14. There: got it

S1: ခဏလေးနော်။	Just a moment, OK?	K'ăná-lè-naw?
S2: ရပါတယ်။	That's all right.	Yá-ba-deh.
or		
S2: ကိစ္စ မရှိပါဘူး။	No problem.	Keiq-sá măshí-ba-bù.
Then, after some activity		
S1: ကဲ။ ရပြီ။	There. Got it.	Kèh. Yá-bi.
or		
S1: ကဲ။ ပြီးပြီ။	There. That's done.	Kèh. Pì-bi.
S2: ကောင်းပါပြီ။	OK. Fine.	Kaùn-ba-bi.

S2's responses are marked with a bar to show that no response is necessary. When you're asked to wait you can just wait, without saying anything. If you feel the need to fill the gap, you can use the responses given above.

Notes

Imagine you are digging around among all the belongings in your bag trying to find a pen. You say ခဏလေးနော် (K'ăná-lè-naw?) to ask your hearer to bear with you, and you use ကဲ။ ရပြီ (Kèh. Yá-bi) to announce that you've found it. You might do the same if you were wiping your spectacles before reading something, or rearranging your desktop before taking notes, or adjusting the settings on a camera before taking a photograph. There's not a lot of difference between ရပြီ (Yá-bi) and ပြီးပြီ (Pì-bi), but on the whole the first is more common when you've found or obtained something, and the second when you have completed some task.

ကဲ (kèh) is a word people use when they want to leave one topic or activity and turn to the next, so it's like "Right, Well, OK, Now, There, Now then." For this reason you'll often hear it before phrases with meanings like "I'm ready now," "Let's go then," "Let's start then," "The other thing to decide is … ." ရပြီ (yá-bi) means "I've got it" or "That's OK now," and ပြီးပြီ (pì-bi) means "I've finished" or "That's over."

═══════════════════════

15. Have you finished?

S1: ပြီးပြီလား။	Have you finished?	Pì-bi-là?
S2: ပြီးပြီ။	Yes, I have.	Pì-bi.
or		
S2: မပြီးသေးပါဘူး။	No, not yet.	Măpì-dhè-ba-bù.

Notes

ပြီး– (pì-) is a verb meaning "to finish," and all the phrases in this exchange include it. The question means "finished now?" (without specifying who is doing the finishing), the *Yes* answer means "finished now," and the *No* answer means "not finished yet."

Both the answers may include or omit the suffix –ပါ (-ba):

	ပြီးပြီ။	Pì-bi.	မပြီးသေးဘူး။	Măpì-dhè-bù.
or	ပြီးပါပြီ။	Pì-ba-bi.	မပြီးသေးပါဘူး။	Măpì-dhè-ba-bù.

You use –ပါ (-ba) when you want to make the answer sound more polite or more deliberate. As a standard for practice we shall be using the version shown above: a –ပါ (-ba) in the *No* answer, but no –ပါ (-ba) in the *Yes* answer.

In many situations the *No* answer will be followed by some activity and then:

ကဲ။ ပြီးပြီ။	There. That's done.	Kèh. Pì-bi.

═══════════════════════

16. All set?

S1: ရပြီလား။	All set? Ready?	Yá-bi-là?
S2: ရပြီ။	Yes, I am.	Yá-bi.
or		
S2: မရသေးပါဘူး။	No, not yet.	Măyá-dhè-ba-bù.

Notes

This is the question you would use when you had been waiting for someone to find a pencil to write with, or to spruce themselves up before you took a photograph, or to change a film before they took a photograph. It is the same as the previous exchange, except that the verb is not ပြီး- (pì-) "to finish," but ရ- (yá-) "to get, succeed, manage."

As in the previous exchange either of the answers may include the suffix –ပါ (-ba) to indicate politeness:

	ရပြီ။	Yá-bi.	မရသေးဘူး။	Măyá-dhè-bù.
or	ရပါပြီ။	Yá-ba-bi.	မရသေးပါဘူး။	Măyá-dhè-ba-bù.

Again as with the preceding exchange, we shall be using the version shown above: a –ပါ (-ba) in the *No* answer, but no –ပါ (-ba) in the *Yes* answer.

Again like the previous exchange the *No* answer is often followed, after a pause, by:

ကဲ။ ရပြီ။	There. Got it.	Kèh. Yá-bi.

You may have noticed the similarities between A and B below:

A.	S1: ရတယ်နော်။	This is all right, isn't it?	Yá-deh-naw?
	S2: ရပါတယ်။	Yes, it is.	Yá-ba-deh.
	or S2: မရဘူး။	No, it isn't.	Măyá-bù.

B.	S1: ရပြီလား။	All set? Ready?	Yá-bi-là?
	S2: ရပြီ။	Yes, I am.	Yá-bi.
	or S2: မရသေးပါဘူး။	No, not yet.	Măyá-dhè-ba-bù.

The difference is that the exchanges in A are to do with situations that are in force more or less permanently (it is/is not acceptable to take a photograph here, to sit here, to pick up one of these); while the exchanges in B are to do with a turning point in the situation (you have/haven't yet found your pencil, adjusted your camera, smoothed your hair, put on your spectacles). In B you are waiting for something to happen: in A you're just asking how things are.

---

17. Is that all?

S1: ဒါပဲလား။	Is that all? Is that the lot?	Da-bèh-là?
S2: ဒါပါပဲ။	That's it.	Da-ba-bèh.
or		
S2: ရှိပါသေးတယ်။	There's more.	Shí-ba-dhè-deh.

Notes

This question is one a shopkeeper might use to a customer to see if he wanted to buy anything more; or a teacher to a student to see if he had any other questions.

ဒါ (da) means "that," and the suffix –ပဲ (-bèh) means "only," so ဒါပဲလား (Da-bèh-là?) literally means "That only?" The *Yes* answer means "That only." The *No* answer includes the verb ရှိ– (shí-) meaning "there is," and the suffix –သေး (-dhè) meaning "still, further."

═══════════════════════════════

18. Do you understand?

S1: နား လည်သလား။	Do you understand?	Nà leh-dhǎ-là?
S2: နား လည်ပါတယ်။	Yes, I do.	Nà leh-ba-deh.
or		
S2: နား မလည်ပါဘူး။	No, I don't.	Nà mǎleh-ba-bù.

Notes

နား (nà) means "ear," and လည်– (leh-) means "to go round," so the verb နား လည်– (nà leh-) "to understand" originally meant "the ear goes round," "the ear encompasses."

The suffixes in this exchange illustrate three formulae common in verb sentences:

[verb]–သလား။	[verb]-dhǎ-là?	Does/did [someone] [verb]?
[verb]–ပါတယ်။	[verb]-ba-deh.	[Someone] does/did [verb].
မ–[verb]–ပါဘူး။	mǎ-[verb]-ba-bù.	[Someone] does/did not [verb].

═══════════════════════════════

19. May I leave now?

S1: ခွင့် ပြုပါအုံး။	May I leave now?	K'wín pyú-ba-oùn.
S2: ဟုတ်ကဲ့။ or ကောင်းပါပြီ။	Certainly.	Houq-kéh or Kaùn-ba-bi.

Notes

ခွင့်	permission, authorization	k'wín
ပြု–	to do, give	pyú-

It follows that ခွင့် ပြုပါအုံး (K'wín pyú-ba-oùn) means "Please give me permission" — in other words, "Please allow me to leave." The phrase is deferential way of announcing your impending departure, often preceded or followed by သွားပါအုံးမယ် (thwà-ba-oùn-meh) "Goodbye," or some similar phrase.

═══════════════════════════════

20. I enjoyed talking to you.

S1: စကား ပြောလို့ ကောင်းပါတယ်။	I enjoyed talking to you.	Săgà pyàw-ló kaùn-ba-deh.
S2: ဟုတ်ကဲ့။	I agree.	Houq-kéh.
or S2: ကောင်းပါတယ်။	Me too.	Kaùn-ba-deh.

Notes

စကား	word, speech, language	săgà
ပြော–	to speak, talk, tell, say	pyàw-
စကား ပြော–	to talk	săgà pyàw-
ကောင်း–	to be good	kaùn-
[verb]–လို့ ကောင်း–	to be good [verb]-ing	[verb]-ló kaùn

As you see from the component words, the phrase means something like "talking was good," hence "[I] enjoyed talking [with you]." A useful signal of impending goodbyes. The response ကောင်းပါတယ် (Kaùn-ba-deh) means "Yes, it was good," like saying "I enjoyed our conversation too."

SECTION 3.   REFERENCE

Teacher instructions

ဝင်ပါ။	Please come in.	Win-ba.
ဝင်ခဲ့ပါ။ /–ခဲ့ဘာ/	Please come in.	Win-géh-ba.
ထိုင်ပါ။	Please sit down.	T'ain-ba.
ဒီမှာ ထိုင်ပါ။	Please sit here.	Di-hma t'ain-ba.
ပြောပါ။	Please say, speak.	Pyàw-ba.
ပြန်ပြောပါ။	Please say that again.	Pyan-pyàw-ba.
ထပ်ပြောပါ။	Please say that again.	T'aq-pyàw-ba.
ကျယ်ကျယ် ပြောပါ။ /ကျယ်ကျယ်/	Say it loudly, more loudly.	Ceh-jeh pyàw-ba.
မြန်မြန် ပြောပါ။	Say it fast, faster	Myan-myan pyàw-ba.
ဗမာလို့ ပြောပါ။	Say it in Burmese./Talk Burmese.	Băma-lo pyàw-ba.
အင်္ဂလိပ်လို့ မပြောပါနဲ့။ /အင်း–/	Don't say it in English. Don't talk English.	Ìn-găleiq-lo măpyàw-ba-néh.
မေးပါ။	Please ask.	Mè-ba.
ပြန်မေးပါ။	Please ask that again.	Pyan-mè-ba.
ဖြေပါ။	Please answer./Reply.	P'ye-ba.
လိုက်ဆိုပါ။	Repeat after me.	Laiq-s'o-ba.
နားထောင်ပါ။	Listen.	Nà-t'aun-ba.
ကြည့်ပါ။ /ကျို–/	Look.	Cí-ba.
ဒီမှာ ကြည့်ပါ။	Look here.	Di-hma cí-ba.
လေ့ကျင့်ခန်း နံပါတ်–၃ ကြည့်ပါ။	Look at Exercise N° 3.	Lé-cín-gàn nan-baq-thoùn cí-ba.

စာမျက်နှာ နံပါတ်–ကို ကြည့်ပါ။	Look at page 9.	Sa-myeq-hna nan-baq-kò cí-ba.
စာအုပ် ဖွင့်ပါ။	Open the book.	Sa-ouq p'wín-ba.
စာအုပ် ပိတ်ပါ။	Close the book.	Sa-ouq peiq-ba.
စာအုပ် မဖွင့်ပါနဲ့။	Don't open the book.	Sa-ouq măp'wín-ba-néh.
စာအုပ် မကြည့်ပါနဲ့။	Don't look at the book.	Sa-ouq măcí-ba-néh.
ဖတ်ပါ။	Please read.	P'aq-pa.
ရေးပါ။	Please write.	Yè-pa.
အိမ်စာ ပေးပါ။ /–ဇာ/	Please give me your homework.	Ein-za pè-pa.

Grammar

| [verb]–ပါ။ | Please [verb]: see grammar | [verb]-ba. |
| မ–[verb]–ပါနဲ့။ | Please don't [verb]: see grammar | Mă[verb]-ba-néh. |

Variations

[verb]–ကြပါ။	Please [verb] everyone.	[verb]-já-ba.
	Please [verb], all of you.	
[verb]–လိုက်ပါ။	Please just [verb].	[verb]-laiq-pa.

(suggests that what you have to do is not laborious, and can be done quickly and easily)

Examples:

ထိုင်ကြပါ။	Please sit down everyone.	T'ain-já-ba.
နားထောင်ကြပါ။	Listen, all of you.	Nà-t'aun-já-ba.
စာအုပ် ပိတ်လိုက်ပါ။	Close the book.	Sa-ouq peiq-laiq-pa.

Teacher comments

ကောင်းပါတယ်။	That's good.	Kaùn-ba-deh.
မှန်ပါတယ်။	That's right.	Hman-ba-deh.
ဟုတ်ပါတယ်။	That's it./That is so.	Houq-pa-deh.
တော်ပါတယ်။	You are talented/capable.	Taw-ba-deh.
မှားပါတယ်။	That's wrong.	Hmà-ba-deh.
အသံ ပီပါတယ်။	Your pronunciation is good.	Ăthan pi-ba-deh.
အသံ ဝဲပါတယ်။	Your pronunciation is wrong.	Ăthan wèh-ba-deh.
လက်ရေး လှပါတယ်။	Your handwriting looks good.	Leq-yè hlá-ba-deh.

မမှန်ပါဘူး။	That's not right.	Măhman-ba-bù.
မဟုတ်ပါဘူး။	That's not it/not so.	Măhouq-ba-bù.
မဆိုးပါဘူး။	That's not bad.	Măs'ò-ba-bù.

မမှန်သေးပါဘူး။	That's not right yet.	Măhman-dhè-ba-bù.
မဟုတ်သေးပါဘူး။	That's not it yet.	Măhouq-thè-ba-bù.
မပီသေးပါဘူး။	That's not the right pronunciation yet.	Măpi-dhè-ba-bù.

| သိပ်တော်ပါတယ်။ | You are very talented/capable. | Theiq taw-ba-deh. |
| သိပ်ကောင်းပါတယ်။ | That's very good. | Theiq kaùn-ba-deh. |

သိပ်မှန်ပါတယ်။	That's absolutely right.	Theiq hman-ba-deh.
အသံ သိပ်ပီပါတယ်။	Your pronunciation is very good.	Ăthan theiq pi-ba-deh.
လက်ရေး သိပ်လှပါတယ်။	Your handwriting looks very good.	Leq-yè theiq hlá-ba-deh.

သိပ်တော်တာပဲ။	You are very talented/capable.	Theiq taw-da-bèh.
သိပ်ကောင်းတာပဲ။	That's very good.	Theiq kaùn-da-bèh.
သိပ်မှန်တာပဲ။	That's absolutely right.	Theiq hman-da-bèh.
အသံ သိပ်ပီတာပဲ။	Your pronunciation is very good.	Ăthan theiq pi-da-bèh.
လက်ရေး သိပ်လှတာပဲ။	Your handwriting looks very good.	Leq-yè theiq hlá-da-bèh.

တော်လိုက်တာ။	You are amazing!	Taw-laiq-ta.
ကောင်းလိုက်တာ။	That's wonderful!	Kaùn-laiq-ta.
လှလိုက်တာ။	How beautiful!	Hlá-laiq-ta.

Grammar

Note that "to be right" and "to be good" and so on are verbs in Burmese.

Also that Burmese does not always need to use words for "that" and "you" and so on.

[verb]–ပါတယ်။	[It] is [verb]: see grammar	[verb]-ba-deh.
သိပ် [verb]–ပါတယ်။	[It] is very [verb].	Theiq [verb]-ba-deh.
သိပ် [verb]–တာပဲ။	[It] is very [verb] [exclamatory].	Theiq [verb]-da-bèh.
မ–[verb]–ပါဘူး။	[It] isn't [verb].	Mă[verb]-ba-bù.
မ–[verb]–သေးပါဘူး။	[It] isn't [verb] yet.	Mă[verb]-dhè-ba-bù.
[verb]–လိုက်တာ။	How [verb]!	[verb]-laiq-ta.

Question and answer

A: နား လည်သလား။ /လယ်/	Do you understand?	Nà leh-dhălà?
B1: နား လည်ပါတယ်။	I do understand.	Nà leh-ba-deh.
B2: နား မလည်ပါဘူး။	I don't understand.	Nà măleh-ba-bù.
B3: နား မလည်သေးပါဘူး။	I don't understand yet.	Nà măleh-dhè-ba-bù.
A: သိသလား။	Do you know?	Thí-dhălà?
B1: သိပါတယ်။	I do know.	Thí-ba-deh.
B2: မသိပါဘူး။	I don't know.	Măthí-ba-bù.
A: မှတ်မိသလား။	Do you remember?	Hmaq-mí-dhălà?
B1: မှတ်မိပါတယ်။	I do remember.	Hmaq-mí-ba-deh.
B2: မမှတ်မိပါဘူး။	I don't remember.	Măhmaq-mí-ba-bù.
A: မှန်သလား ဆရာမ။	Is that right, Teacher?	Hman-dhălà, S'ăya-má?
B: သိပ် မှန်ပါတယ်။	It's entirely correct.	Theiq hman-ba-deh.
A: မေးစရာ ရှိပါတယ်။	I have a question.	Mè-zăya shí-ba-deh.
B: မေးပါ။	Ask it.	Mè-ba.

Grammar

| [verb]–သလား။ | Is [it] [verb]? Does [it] [verb]? | [verb]-dhălà? |

PART 2: DIALOGUES

INTRODUCTION

1 Scope

Part 2 "Dialogues" covers the following twelve Topics:

1.	Asking the way	7.	Travel: past trips
2.	Taking photographs	8.	Travel: trips in prospect
3.	Taking a taxi	9.	Travel: the current trip
4.	Cafés and Restaurants	10.	You and yours
5.	Shops	11.	To meet again
6.	Your command of Burmese	12.	Making a phone call

The first twelve Lessons give you a minimal competence in coping with the situation or conversation which forms the subject of each Topic. After all twelve Topics have been covered in this rudimentary way you move to Level 2, where you learn to say and understand a little more about each of the Topics in turn. Level 3 extends your competence still further, Topic by Topic, and so you go on. The highest Level you reach in Part 2 is Level 5.

Scenes with Customs and Immigration officials, with hotel staff, and with doctors, are standard elements in many language courses. In *BISL* they are deliberately omitted, as in Burma those who act in them speak English, mostly very well.

You should bear in mind that features of the Burmese scene that are subject to change — prices are the most obvious example — were correct at the time of writing, but will probably have changed by the time you come to use the course. The rate of inflation was estimated at 36% in 1992. Another example is house hunting. *Beginning Burmese,* by Cornyn and Roop, first published in 1968, has several sections on this topic. I deliberately omitted it from my list on the grounds that nowadays few foreigners stay in Burma long enough to want to rent a house; but in the few months before the press deadline I came across several foreign families who were renting houses and flats in Rangoon.

Be warned that you may find the content of many of the dialogues unexciting. There are no snake bites, kidnappings, forest fires, or other dramas, nor any slapstick. The words and phrases you learn to use, and the sentiments they express, have been chosen because they are used with high frequency in the situations and conversations you are most likely to encounter as a newcomer to Burma and the Burmese language.

As you listen to the tapes you may notice that when an extra male voice is needed for a dialogue, one of the parts is spoken by the author. It is true that he is not a native speaker, but as he mostly plays the part of a foreigner, and as it is perfectly natural to have a foreigner speaking the part of a foreigner, no excuses are offered for his participation.

2 Lesson structure

The procedure for a typical Lesson (a few Lessons differ) is as follows:

A. Learning new words and structures

1. You read through the list of New Words in the text.
2. You listen to the Sample Dialogue on the tape, at the same time following both text and translation in the book.
3. The tape introduces you to the New Words, giving you opportunities to say them yourself, and to do Exercises if appropriate.
4. You listen again to the Sample Dialogue, this time repeating the phrases after the speakers.

B. Using the new words and structures

5. You take part in a series of Practice Dialogues. When it is your turn to speak, you will hear a Prompt, which indicates what you should say next. The kind of information you bring with you to each situation in real life (such as what you want to buy and what price you are prepared to pay, or what your name is, where you come from and how long you have been in Burma) is set out for a list of hypothetical individuals in the text for each Lesson. In the Practice Dialogues, you play the part of each of the individuals named in the list. In some of the Dialogues you have to put questions to elicit information (such as the speaker's name, occupation and so on). You make a note of what you are told, usually in the blanks provided in the text, and at the end of the Lesson check that it agrees with the Key.

For convenience in reviewing, there is a separate tape containing the Sample Dialogues only from each Lesson. You can listen to these to refresh your memory without having to plough through all the explanations and Exercises and Practice Dialogues again.

3 Using Part 2 with a teacher

The text and the tapes are written with the needs of self-study students in mind, so they provide a lot of homework activity. This should enable you to develop a good speaking ability on your own. If you are learning with a teacher, there are two things you and your classmates can do with the course. One comes after you have worked through the exercises and practice on the tapes by yourself. When you come to the classroom you can acquire extra practice by acting out the survival situations detailed in the text (Mr. X takes a taxi to the Sule Pagoda, and so on), and you can make up others. In some of the lessons in the course you will find suggestions for other activities for classroom practice. For the conversation topics, you can either talk about your own lives and experiences (Have you ever been to France? and so on), or play the part of the characters listed in the text (Mrs. Y is a doctor who lives in Barnet and has three children aged 8, 10 and 13, and so on).

The other activity that some students find helpful comes before you have worked on the tapes for the next lesson. The teacher introduces and practises with you the material you will be working on after the class. After this first exposure to the new material, you should find that the homework is easier to work through.

4 Free-range speech

Exercises like those in Part 1 must have precisely predictable responses. The response of the recorded speaker must use language the learner knows, otherwise she/he won't understand it; and the response of the learner must be predictable so that the recorded speaker can confirm it. Real life is different. People don't always say "I don't know" when they can't answer your question. They may instead say "I couldn't say" or "I can't tell you I'm afraid" or "Haven't the foggiest" or "You've picked the wrong man" or "Ask him" or something else. I call these unpredictable responses "free-range speech" to distinguish them from the carefully controlled speech of the recorded exercises.

Many learners find free-range speech bewildering. It drains their confidence and induces panic. The long-term solution is to learn more words and phrases. In the short term there are several things the learner can do to reduce the disturbing impact of free-range speech. Here are some:

1. Deliberately keep cool and resist the temptation to abandon the exchange.
2. Listen intently to pick out words and phrases you do know from among those you don't.
3. Make full use of the speaker's gestures and facial expressions to interpret the message.
4. Ask checking questions (like "Is it 30 kyats?") to elicit answers couched in words you do know, and ask meaning questions (like "What does mǎwin-yá mean?")

BISL offers some measures designed to reduce the shock of the transition from carefully controlled exercises to free-range speech. In some responses the recorded speaker deliberately uses words and phrases the learner has not yet learned. The intention is to provide practice for the learner in picking out words he or she knows as the stream of speech flows by. The prompts for these exercises try to give some indication of expressions and gestures. Learners also acquire a set of questions like "What did you say?" and "It's this way. Is that right?" to help them grope their way out of the darkness of answers they can't yet understand. Finally, the inclusion of free-range speech is intended to demonstrate to learners, by giving them the experience of facing it, that it is not always an insuperable obstacle; and the confidence thus gained should help them to avoid panic and despair when they face free-range speech in conversation with live speakers.

LEVEL 1, TOPIC 1   ASKING THE WAY

First read through the New Words and the Sample Dialogue.
Then turn on the tape.

New words

ဒီမှာ ခင်ဗျာ။	Excuse me please [male speaker] 1	Di-hma k'in-bya. 4
ဒီမှာ ရှင်။	Excuse me please [female speaker] 1	Di-hma shin.
ဘယ်လို	how, in what way	beh-lo
— ဘယ်လို သွားရမလဲ။ 5	How should I go? 2	beh-lo thwà-yá-mǎlèh?
ဘက်	direction, way	beq
— ဒီဘက်	this way	di-beq
— ဘယ်ဘက်	which way?	beh-beq
သိ–	to know	thí-
ဆောရီး	Sorry [from English]	S'àw-rì
— ဆောရီးနော်	"Sorry" 3	S'àw-rì-naw

1. Literally "Here, Sir/Madam": used to attract someone's attention.
2. Used where English might say "How do I get there? Which way should I go?"
3. Much the same as plain ဆောရီးပဲ, but with the additional hint that you hope the inquirer will understand and excuse your predicament.
4. By the time you start Part 2 you should have learned how to read Burmese script. Romanized versions of the New Words and Sample Dialogues are provided as a concession to slow learners, but you will find that romanizations are not regularly provided in the Notes and Exercises.
5. Entries in the New Words section that are preceded by a long dash are sub-entries for the preceding entry. They may be compound words, or sentence examples, showing how the word is used, or smaller components of a longer word.

Some new places —

တူးရစ်ဘားမားရုံး	Tourist Burma office 4	Tù-riq Bà-mà Youn
— ရုံး	office	youn
သံရုံး	embassy ["voice, envoy-office"]	than-youn
အမေရိကန်သံရုံး	American Embassy	Byí-tí-shá than-youn
ဗြိတိသျှသံရုံး /ဗျိုတိရှ္ဃ–/	British Embassy	Ăme-rí-kan than-youn
သြစတြေးလျသံရုံး /အောစတရေးလယာ–/	Australian Embassy	Àw-sătrè-lǎyá than-youn

4. The name was officially changed in 1989 to "Myanmar Travel and Tours," but many Rangoon residents still use the earlier name.

Sample Dialogue

Scene: a street in Rangoon. S1 goes up to S2 to ask the way.

S1: ဒီမှာ ခင်ဗျာ॥	Excuse me please.	Di-hma k'in-bya.
S2: ဟုတ်ကဲ့॥ [1]	Yes?	Houq-kéh.
S1: သံတမန်ကုန်တိုက်	I want to go to the	Than-dăman Koun-daiq
သွားချင်ပါတယ် ခင်ဗျာ॥	Diplomatic Store.	thwà-jin-ba-deh k'in-bya.
ဘယ်လို သွားရမလဲ॥	How can I get there?	Beh-lo thwà-yá-mălèh?

FORK *

branch 1 (the person knows the way)

S2: ဒီဘက် သွားပါ॥	Go this way.	Di-beq thwà-ba.
S1: ကျေးဇူး တင်ပါတယ် ခင်ဗျာ॥	Thank you.	Cè-zù tin-ba-deh k'in-bya.
S2: ရပါတယ်॥	That's all right.	Yá-ba-deh.
ကိစ္စ မရှိပါဘူး॥	No trouble.	Keiq-sá măshí-ba-bù.

branch 2 (the person doesn't know the way)

S2: မသိပါဘူး॥ ဆောရီးနော်॥	I don't know. I'm sorry.	Măthí-ba-bù. S'àw-rì-naw?
S1: အော်၊ ကိစ္စမရှိပါဘူး॥	Oh. Never mind.	Aw. Keiq-sá măshí-ba-bù.
ရပါတယ်॥	That's all right.	Yá-ba-deh.

* In the Sample Dialogues we use the word FORK to mark points at which the dialogue may branch off onto divergent paths.

1. There are many ways of responding to ဒီမှာ ခင်ဗျာ (Di-hma k'in-bya). We use ဟုတ်ကဲ့ (Houq-kéh) because it is one of the most frequent, but the ဟုတ်ကဲ့ may be followed, or replaced, by phrases like —

ပြောပါ॥ or just ပြော॥	Please speak.	Pyàw-(ba).
	in other words: Go ahead: I'm listening.	
ဆိုပါ॥ or just ဆို॥	[ditto]	S'o-(ba).
မေးပါ॥ or just မေး॥	Please ask.	Mè-(ba).
ဘာလဲ॥	What is it?	Ba-lèh?
ဘာ ကူညီရမလဲ॥	How can I help you?	Ba ku-nyi-yá-mălèh?
အေး॥	Yes. [from senior speaker]	È.

In the Exercises and Dialogues you will hear a range of options used.

Exercises on the new places

Ex. 1. Prompt: Ask Mr. Grey where he wants to go. (Read across from left to right)

L/S2: Mr. Grey ဘယ်သွားချင်သလဲ॥	S1: တူးရစ်ဘားမားရုံး သွားချင်ပါတယ်॥
L/S2: တူးရစ်ဘားမားရုံးလား॥	S1: ဟုတ်ကဲ့ တူးရစ်ဘားမားရုံးပါ॥

Ex. 2. S1: Mrs. Brown ဘယ်သွားချင်သလဲ॥   L/S2: သြစတြေးလျသံရုံး သွားချင်ပါတယ်॥

For the Practice Dialogues

Follow the prompt on the tape.

name	wants to go to	name	wants to go to
Mr. Black	Theingyi Market	Ms. Green	American Embassy
Mrs. White	National Museum	Mr. Ross	British Embassy
Mr. Grey	Tourist Burma office	Mrs. Brown	Australian Embassy

A street intersection in Rangoon

Exercise for written answer

In the two brief dialogues below the lines have been put in the wrong order. Reorder them so that each dialogue makes sense. The speakers do not necessarily speak alternate lines. Needless to say, covering the Key before you start makes the Exercise more effective.

Dialogue 1 jumbled

၁။ S1: ကိစ္စမရှိပါဘူး ရှင်။

၂။ S2: တူးရစ်ဘားမားရုံး မသိပါဘူး ခင်ဗျာ။

၃။ S1: ဒီမှာ ရှင်။

၄။ S2: ဆောရီးနော်။

၅။ S1: ဘယ်လို သွားရမလဲ။

၆။ S2: ဟုတ်ကဲ့ ခင်ဗျာ။

၇။ S1: တူးရစ်ဘားမားရုံး သွားချင်ပါတယ်။

Dialogue 2 jumbled

၁။ S1: ကျေးဇူး တင်ပါတယ် ခင်ဗျာ။

၂။ S2: ဟုတ်ကဲ့ ရှင်။

KEY TO THE WRITTEN EXERCISE

Dialogue 1 key

၃။ S1: ဒီမှာ ရှင်။

၆။ S2: ဟုတ်ကဲ့ ခင်ဗျာ။

၇။ S1: တူးရစ်ဘားမားရုံး သွားချင်ပါတယ်။

၅။ S1: ဘယ်လို သွားရမလဲ။

၂။ S2: တူးရစ်ဘားမားရုံး မသိပါဘူး ခင်ဗျာ။

၄။ S2: ဆောရီးနော်။

၁။ S1: ကိစ္စမရှိပါဘူး ရှင်။

Dialogue 2 key

၅။ S1: ဒီမှာ ခင်ဗျာ။

၂။ S2: ဟုတ်ကဲ့ ရှင်။

၃။ S1: ဘယ်လို သွားရမလဲ။

၄။ S2: ရပါတယ်။

၅။ S1: ဒီမှာ ခင်ဗျာ။

၆။ S2: ဒီဘက် သွားပါ ရှင်။

၇။ S1: ဂျပန်သံရုံး သွားချင်ပါတယ်။

၇။ S1: ဂျပန်သံရုံး သွားချင်ပါတယ်။

၃။ S1: ဘယ်လို သွားရမလဲ။

၆။ S2: ဒီဘက် သွားပါ ရှင်။

၁။ S1: ကျေးဇူး တင်ပါတယ် ခင်ဗျာ။

၄။ S2: ရပါတယ်။

LEVEL 1, TOPIC 2   TAKING PHOTOGRAPHS

First read through the New Words and the Sample Dialogue.
Then turn on the tape.

New words

ဓါတ်ပုံ ရိုက်– /ဒတ်ပုံ ယိုက်–/	to take a photograph	daq-poun yaiq-
– ဓါတ်ပုံ	photograph	daq-poun
– ရိုက်–	to hit, beat, stamp, make imprint	yaiq-
ရ–	to get, manage, be successful, be possible	yá-
– ရတယ်နော်။	It's all right, isn't it?	Yá-deh-naw?
– ရပါတယ်။	It's fine. No problem. OK.	Yá-ba-deh.
– မရဘူး။	You can't do it. It's not all right.	Măyá-bù.
သွားမယ်နော်။	I'll be off then. Goodbye.	Thwà-meh-naw.
	["go-*future*-OK?"]	

A lacquerware shop, Nyaung-U

Sample Dialogue

Scene: somewhere in Burma. S2 is a lady in a photogenic spot, and S1 wants to take a photograph of the scene.

S1: ဒီမှာ ခင်ဗျာ။	Excuse me, please.	Di-hma k'in-bya.
S2: ဟုတ်ကဲ့။	Yes?	Houq-kéh.
S1: ဓါတ်ပုံ ရိုက်ချင်ပါတယ်။	I'd like to take a photograph.	Daq-poun yaiq-c'in-ba-deh.
ရတယ်နော်။	It's all right, isn't it?	Yá-deh-naw?

FORK

branch 1 (the person doesn't mind)

S2: ရပါတယ်။ ရိုက်ပါ။	It's OK. Go ahead.	Yá-ba-deh. Yaiq-pa.

S1 takes photograph.

S1: ကဲ။ ပြီးပြီ။	Right. I've taken it.	Kèh. Pì-bi.
ကျေးဇူး တင်ပါတယ် ခင်ဗျာ။	Thank you.	Cè-zù tin-ba-deh k'in-bya.
S2: ရပါတယ်။	That's all right.	Yá-ba-deh.
ကိစ္စ မရှိပါဘူး။	No trouble.	Keiq-sá măshí-ba-bù.
S1: သွားမယ်နော်။	Goodbye then.	Thwà-meh-naw?
S2: ဟုတ်ကဲ့။ ကောင်းပါပြီ။	Goodbye.	Houq-kéh. Kaùn-ba-bi.

branch 2 (the person doesn't want a photograph taken)

S2: မရဘူး။ မရိုက်ပါနဲ့။	No it isn't. Don't take one.	Măyá-bù. Măyaiq-pa-néh.
S1: အော်၊ ကောင်းပါပြီ။	Oh. Fine.	Aw. Kaùn-ba-bi.
မရိုက်ပါဘူး။	I won't then.	Măyaiq-pa-bù.

For the Practice Dialogues

Follow the prompt on the tape.

Dialogue 1. Banana stall.

Dialogue 2. Cane basket carrier.

Dialogue 3. Men playing chinlone.

Dialogue 4. Meditator.

Exercise for written answer

In the dialogue below the lines have been put in the wrong order. Reorder them so that the dialogue makes sense. The speakers do not necessarily speak alternate lines. It is prudent to cover the Key before you start.

၁။ S1: ကျေးဇူး တင်ပါတယ် ခင်ဗျာ။	KEY TO THE WRITTEN EXERCISE
၂။ S2: ရိုက်ပါ။	၃။ S1: ဒီမှာ ခင်ဗျာ။
၃။ S1: ဒီမှာ ခင်ဗျာ။	၆။ S2: ရှင်။ ဘာလဲ။
၄။ S2: ကိစ္စ မရှိပါဘူး။	၉။ S1: ဓါတ်ပုံ ရိုက်ချင်ပါတယ်။
၅။ S1: သွားမယ်နော်။	၇။ S1: ရတယ်နော်။
၆။ S2: ရှင်။ ဘာလဲ။	၁၂။ S2: ရပါတယ် ရှင်။
၇။ S1: ရတယ်နော်။	၂။ S2: ရိုက်ပါ။
၈။ S2: ကောင်းပါပြီ ရှင်။	၁၁။ S1: ကဲ။ ပြီးပြီ။
၉။ S1: ဓါတ်ပုံ ရိုက်ချင်ပါတယ်။	၁။ S1: ကျေးဇူး တင်ပါတယ် ခင်ဗျာ။
၁၀။ S2: ရပါတယ်။	၁၀။ S2: ရပါတယ်။
၁၁။ S1: ကဲ။ ပြီးပြီ။	၄။ S2: ကိစ္စ မရှိပါဘူး။
၁၂။ S2: ရပါတယ် ရှင်။	၅။ S1: သွားမယ်နော်။
	၈။ S2: ကောင်းပါပြီ ရှင်။

LEVEL 1, TOPIC 3   TAKING A TAXI

First read through the New Words and the Sample Dialogue.
Then turn on the tape.

A taxi in Rangoon

New words

တက်–	to go up, get on board,	teq-
	also to attend (school, meeting)	
– တက်ပါ။	Get in. Get inside the taxi.	Teq-pa.
ပေး–	to give	pè-
– ၂၀/– ပေးပါ။	Give me K20. I'll charge K20.	Hnǎs'eh pè-ba.

Some new places —

အင်းယားလိပ် ဟိုတယ်	Inya Lake Hotel	Ìn-yà Leiq Ho-teh
ကရဝိက် ဟိုတယ် /ကရဝိတ်–/	Karaweik Hotel	Kǎrǎweiq Ho-teh.

The ကရဝိက် is a mythical bird, often depicted in paintings. The Karaweik Hotel is built in the shape of a Karaweik bird, and stands in the Royal Lake (ကန်တော်ကြီး). The Burmese word ဟိုတယ် doesn't always mean the same sort of establishment as the English word "hotel." In some cases, including this one, a ဟိုတယ် offers a restaurant and bar but no accommodation.

ဘူတာကြီး /–ဒါ–/	the main station	Bu-da-jì
မင်္ဂလာဒုံ လေဆိပ် /–ဇိတ်/	Mingaladon Airport	Min-gǎla-doun Le-zeiq

– လေ	air [for "air transport, aeroplane"]	le
– ဆိပ်	transport stopping place, jetty, port, station	s'eiq

Sample Dialogue

Scene: a street in Rangoon. S1 is a taxi driver, and S2 has just hailed the taxi.

S1: ဘယ် သွားမလဲ။	Where are you going?	Beh thwà-mălèh?
S2: ဗိုလ်ချုပ်ဈေး သွားမယ်။	I'm going to Bogyoke Market.	Bo-jouq Zè thwà-meh.
S1: ရပါတယ်။ တက်ပါ။	OK. Climb in.	Yá-ba-deh. Teq-pa.

Before he gets in S2 asks:

S2: ဘယ်လောက် ပေးရမလဲ။[1]	How much shall I have to pay? like saying: What will you charge?	Beh-lauq pè-yá-mălèh?
S1: ၃၀/– ပေးပါ။	Give me K30.	Thoùn-zeh pè-ba.
S2: ကောင်းပါပြီ။ [2]	All right.	Kaùn-ba-bi.

S2 gets in, and they drive to their destination. When the taxi stops, S2 gets out and says:

S2: ၃၀/– နော်။	It was K30 wasn't it?	Thoùn-zeh-naw?
S1: ဟုတ်ပါတယ်။	Yes.	Houq-pa-deh.
S2: ပိုက်ဆံ ဒီမှာ။[3]	Here's the money.	Paiq-s'an di-hma.
သွားမယ်နော်။ [4]	Goodbye.	Thwà-meh-naw?
S1: ဟုတ်ကဲ့။ ကောင်းပါပြီ။	Goodbye.	Houq-kéh. Kaùn-ba-bi.

1. *Variant:* people also say: ဘယ်လောက် ကျမလဲ။ "How much will it come to? What will it cost?" (Beh-lauq cá-mălèh?)
2. S2 here accepts the taxi driver's fare. Many taxi drivers ask for more than they expect to get, and if you know the current rates you can usually negotiate a lower price. That will come on later levels.
3. More often than not people hand over their money without saying anything; but if you feel the need for some words to accompany the action ပိုက်ဆံ ဒီမှာ will do.
4. Tips. It is not customary to give tips to waiters or taxi drivers, but occasionally people will tell them to keep the change. Phrases to use:

မအမ်းပါနဲ့တော့။	Don't bother with the change. ["not-give change-*polite*-request-any more"]	Măàn-ba-néh-dáw.
ပိုတာ ယူလိုက်ပါ။	Keep the surplus. ["exceed-thing—take-quickly-*polite*"]	Po-da yu-laiq-pa.

   Variants: in place of ပိုတာ "the surplus" people say အနုတ် (ănouq) or အကြွေ (ăcwe) both meaning "change." In place of ယူလိုက်ပါ you may hear ယူထားလိုက်ပါ (yu-t'à-laiq-pa) "take and keep."

Exercises on the new places

Ex. 1. Prompt: Ask Mr. Farmer where he's going to go.

L/S2: Mr. Farmer ဘယ်သွားမလဲ။	S1: အင်းယားလိပ် ဟိုတယ် သွားမယ်။
L/S2: အင်းယားလိပ် ဟိုတယ်လား။	S1: ဟုတ်ကဲ့။ အင်းယားလိပ် ဟိုတယ်ပါ။

Ex. 2. S1: Mrs. Sawyer ဘယ်သွားမလဲ။ L/S2: ဘူတာကြီး သွားမယ်။

For the Practice Dialogues

Cover the Key column below before you start the Practice Dialogues. Speak after the prompt and make a note of the fare each person pays. When you've worked through all the dialogues uncover the Key and compare your answers with those you find there.

name	wants to go to	fare	KEY
Mrs. Shepherd	President Hotel	K...	K50
Mr. Farmer	Inya Lake Hotel	K...	K80
Ms. Carter	Karaweik Hotel	K...	K35
Mr. Miller	Mingaladon Airport	K...	K120
Mrs. Sawyer	the main station	K...	K25

Exercise for written answer

Reorder the lines below to make up two brief exchanges between a taxi driver and his passenger, and show which character speaks which lines (S1: ... S2: ...). The speakers do not necessarily speak alternate lines. Cover the Key before you start.

		KEY TO THE WRITTEN EXERCISE	
၁॥	ကဲ॥ ဒါက အင်းယားလိပ်ဟိုတယ်ပါ॥	၆॥	S1: ဘယ် သွားမလဲ ခင်ဗျာ॥
၂॥	အင်းယားလိပ်လား॥	၄॥	S2: အင်းယားလိပ်ဟိုတယ် သွားမယ်॥
၃॥	ဟုတ်ပါတယ် ခင်ဗျာ॥	၂॥	S1: အင်းယားလိပ်လား॥
၄॥	အင်းယားလိပ်ဟိုတယ် သွားမယ်॥	၇॥	S1: ရပါတယ်॥ တက်ပါ॥
၅॥	သွားမယ်နော်॥	၁၁॥	S2: ဘယ်လောက် ပေးရမလဲ॥
၆॥	ဘယ် သွားမလဲ ခင်ဗျာ॥	၁၀॥	S1: ၈၀/– ပေးပါ ခင်ဗျာ॥
၇॥	ရပါတယ်॥ တက်ပါ॥	၁၃॥	S2: ကောင်းပါပြီ॥
၈॥	ပိုက်ဆံ ဒီမှာ॥	၁॥	S1: ကဲ॥ ဒါက အင်းယားလိပ်ဟိုတယ်ပါ॥
၉॥	အော်॥ ဟုတ်ကဲ့॥ ၈၀/– နော်॥	၉॥	S2: အော်॥ ဟုတ်ကဲ့॥ ၈၀/– နော်॥
၁၀॥	၈၀/– ပေးပါ ခင်ဗျာ॥	၃॥	S1: ဟုတ်ပါတယ် ခင်ဗျာ॥
၁၁॥	ဘယ်လောက် ပေးရမလဲ॥	၈॥	S2: ပိုက်ဆံ ဒီမှာ॥
၁၂॥	ကောင်းပါပြီ॥	၅॥	S2: သွားမယ်နော်॥
၁၃॥	ကောင်းပါပြီ॥	၁၂॥	S1: ကောင်းပါပြီ॥

LEVEL 1, TOPIC 4 CAFÉS AND RESTAURANTS

First read through the New Words and the Sample Dialogue.
Then turn on the tape.

New words

မှာ-	to order, instruct	hma-
— ဘာ မှာမလဲ။	What are you going to order? What would you like to have?	Ba hma-mălèh?
ခွက်	cup, glass	k'weq
ပုလင်း /ပလင်း/	bottle	pălìn
လုံး or အလုံး [1]	round(-ish) object [2]	(ă)loùn
ဘယ်နှစ် /ဘယ်နှ-/	how many	beh-hnă-
— ကော်ဖီ ဘယ်နှစ်ခွက်လဲ။	How many cups of coffee?	Kaw-p'i beh-hnăk'weq-lèh?
သောက်-	to drink	thauq-
— ကော်ဖီ ဘယ်နှစ်ခွက် သောက်သလဲ။	How many cups of coffee did you drink?	Kaw-p'i beh-hnăk'weq thauq-thălèh?
ပိုက်ဆံ	money	paiq-s'an
ရှင်း-	to clear, clarify, settle up; be clear	shìn-
— ပိုက်ဆံ ရှင်းမယ်။	We'll settle the bill.	Paiq-s'an shìn-meh.
ကျ-	to fall, fall in place, amount to	cá-
— ဘယ်လောက် ကျသလဲ။	How much does that come to?	Beh-lauq cá-dhălèh?

Some drinks [3] —

ကော်ဖီ	coffee	kaw-p'i
လက်ဖက်ရည် /လဖက်ယေ/	tea	lăp'eq-ye
— အရည် /အယေ/ [1]	juice	ăye
လိမ်မော်ရည် /-ယေ/	orange juice	lein-maw-ye
— လိမ်မော်	orange [cf. Portuguese *limão*, English *lemon*]	lein-maw
ကိုကာကိုလာ	Coca-cola	Ko-ka-ko-la
ပက်စီ	Pepsi-cola	Peq-si
စပါကလင်	Sparkling [a bottled drink like Lilt, Seven-up and similar]	Săpa-kălin

1. For a note on the appearance and disappearance of the prefix အ- see Part 1 Lesson 35.
2. လုံး is used for counting spherical or cylindrical objects, even cubes, sometimes used in place of ပုလင်း။
3. For a longer list of drinks found in cafés see Appendix 6, section 7.

The menu from a cold drinks bar

ရသာစုံ၊အအေးဆိုင်

Golden Land Cold Drink Shop.

No-542, 80th Street Bet: 32×33 St, Mandalay. Phone - 21116/25553.

၁	ကြက်ဥပူတင်း	1	Pudding (Egg Cuatar I)
၂	စတော်ဘယ်ရီ ရေခဲမုန့်	2	Strawberry Ice Cream
၃	ကရင်ဆိုဒါ ရေခဲမုန့်	3	Cream Soda Ice Cream
၄	ချော့ကလက် ရေခဲမုန့်	4	Cocoa Ice Cream
၅	ရိုးရိုးဗယ်နီလာ ရေခဲမုန့်	5	Milk Ice Cream
၆	ရိမ်းဘိုး ရေခဲမုန့်	6	Rainbow Ice Cream
၇	မလိုင်ဖွာလူဒါ	7	Faluda Dessert
၈	သစ်သီးစုံ	8	Fruit Cocktail
၉	နွားမလိုင်	9	Full Cream Milk
၁၀	ရေခဲသုတ်	10	Cocktail Ice Ball
၁၁	နို့ချဉ်	11	Yought (Luxsee)
၁၂	နို့အေး	12	Cold Milk
၁၃	သံပုရာရည်	13	Fresh Lime
၁၄	သင်္ဘောသီး ဖျော်ရည်	14	Papaya Milk Shake
၁၅	ငှက်ပျော်သီး ဖျော်ရည်	15	Banana Milk Shake
၁၆	* ဒူးရင်းသီးဖျော်ရည်	16	* Durian Milk Shake
၁၇	* စတော်ဘယ်ရီ(စက်ဖျော်)	17	* Strawberry Milk Shake
၁၈	* စတော်ဘယ်ရီ(လက်ဖျော်)	18	* Strawberry Dessert
၁၉	* သရက်သီးဖျော်ရည်	19	* Mango Juice
၂၀	* စပျစ်သီး ဖျော်ရည်	20	* Grape Juice
၂၁	* နာနတ်သီး(စက်ဖျော်)	21	* Pineapple Juice
၂၂	* နာနတ်သီး(လက်ဖျော်)	22	* Sliod Pineapple
၂၃	ဘာလီဖျော်ရည်	23	Barley Juice
၂၄	ဇီးဖျော်ရည်	24	
၂၅	သံဗူးရည်	25	
၂၆	ဟောလစ်နို့အေး	26	Horlick Milk Shake
၂၇	အိုဗာတင်းနို့အေး	27	Ovaltine Milk Shake
၂၈	ကိုကိုးနို့အေး	28	Cocoa Milk Shake
၂၉	ကြက်ဥနို့အေး	29	Egg Milk Shake
၃၀	ဒိုင်းမွန်း ဘိလပ်ရည်	30	Rangoon Mineral Water
၃၁	ကျောက်ကျောရည်	31	Jelly
၃၂	ဆေးကုလားမရည်	23	Jeinglan
၃၃	လစ်ပို	33	Lipovitan-D
၃၄	7-up	34	7-up
၃၅	Cocacola	35	Cocacola
၃၆	ပေါင်မုန့်ရေခဲညှပ်	36	

Sample Dialogue

Scene: a café in Burma. S1 is a waiter, and S2 is a customer.

S1: ဘာ မှာမလဲ။ [3]	What would you like to order?	Ba hma-mălèh?
S2: ကော်ဖီ နှစ်ခွက် [4] ပေးပါ။ [5]	Two cups of coffee, please.	Kaw-p'i hnăk'weq pè-ba.
S1: ကောင်းပါပြီ။	Fine.	Kàun-ba-bi.
S2 drinks; then —		
S2: ပိုက်ဆံ ရှင်းမယ်။	We'll settle up now.	Paiq-s'an shìn-meh.
ဘယ်လောက် ကျသလဲ။	What does it come to?	Beh-lauq cá-dhălèh?
S1: ၈/-ပါ။ (or ၈/- ပေးပါ။)	K8. (or: Give me K8.)	Shiq-caq-pa or Shiq-caq-pè-ba.
S2: ပိုက်ဆံ ဒီမှာ။	Here's the money.	Paiq-s'an di-hma.
သွားမယ်နော်။ [6]	Goodbye.	Thwà-meh-naw?
S1: ဟုတ်ကဲ့။ ကောင်းပါပြီ။	OK. Fine.	Houq-kéh. Kaùn-ba-bi.

3. *Variants:*

S1: ဘာ ယူမလဲ။	What will you take?	Ba yu-mălèh?
S1: ဘာ စားမလဲ။	What will you eat?	Ba sà-mălèh?
S1: ဘာ သောက်မလဲ။	What will you drink?	Ba thauq-mălèh?
S1: ဘာ ယူပေးရမလဲ။	What should I bring you?	Ba yu-pè-yá-mălèh?

4. Note the order of elements:

ကော်ဖီ နှစ်ခွက်	"coffee two cup"	two cups of coffee	kaw-p'i hnăk'weq
လက်ဖက်ရည် သုံးခွက်	"tea three cup"	three cups of tea	lăp'eq-ye thoùn-gweq
ပက်စီ လေးပုလင်း	"Pepsi four bottle"	three bottles of Pepsi	peq-si lè-pălìn
စပါကလင် တစ်လုံး	"Sparkling one object"	one bottle of Sparkling	Săpa-kălin tăloùn

This order neatly parallels the order of round-number phrases, as in:

ပေါင် သုံးဆယ်	"pounds three ten"	thirty pounds	paun thoùn-zeh
ဒေါ်လာ ငါးရာ	"dollar five hundred"	five hundred dollars	daw-la ngà-ya

5. ပေးပါ "Please give us/me": used where in England one might say "Could we please have …"

6. The need to say something as you pay up and leave is felt less strongly in Burma than it is in the West. It is not unusual for a customer to pay and leave without using any words at all. A look or a smile is enough.

Exercises on the new words

Ex. 1. Prompt: Ask what U Thaw Kaung ordered.

L/S1: ဦးသော်ကောင်း ဘာမှာသလဲ။ — S1: ကော်ဖီ မှာပါတယ်။

Prompt: Ask how many cups he ordered.

L/S1: ကော်ဖီ ဘယ်နှစ်ခွက် မှာသလဲ။ — S1: နှစ်ခွက်ပါ။

Prompt: Check that.

L/S1: ကော်ဖီနှစ်ခွက်လား။ — S1: ဟုတ်ကဲ့ပါ။ ကော်ဖီနှစ်ခွက်။

For the Practice Dialogues

You are reminded of the point made in the note in Section 2 of the Introduction to
Part 1: that statements about the individuals named in this and other lists in *BISL*
have no relation to any real persons bearing the same names.

Cover the Key column below before you start the Practice Dialogues. Speak after the prompt
and make a note of the cost of each café visit when you hear it. When you've worked
through all the dialogues uncover the Key and compare your answers with those you find
there.

name	နာမည်	drink	how many	cost		KEY
U Thaw Kaung	ဦးသော်ကောင်း	coffee	2 cups	K...		K8
Daw Khin Than	ဒေါ်ခင်သန်း	tea	4 cups	K...		K16
San San Me	စမ်းစမ်းမေ	orange juice	1 glass	K...		K5
Ko Aung Khin	ကိုအောင်ခင်	Coca-cola	3 bottles	K...		K24
Awin	အဝင်း	Pepsi	5 bottles	K...		K40
Ko So Thein	ကိုစိုးသိန်း	Sparkling	2 "objects"	K...		K12

Exercise for written answer

The two brief exchanges below are spoken by a café waiter (S1) and a customer (S2). Cover the
Key and supply the missing words.

Dialogue 1

1. S1: ... သောက်မလဲ။
2. S2: လက်ဖက်ရည်လေး... ပေးပါ။
3. S1: ရပါ... ခင်ဗျာ။

KEY TO THE WRITTEN EXERCISE

S1: **ဘာ** သောက်မလဲ။
S2: လက်ဖက်ရည်လေး**ခွက်** ပေးပါ။
S1: ရပါ**တယ်** ခင်ဗျာ။

Dialogue 2

4. S2: ပိုက်ဆံ ...မယ်။
5. S2: ဘယ်လောက် ...သလဲ။
6. S1: ၁၆–ကျပ် ကျ...တယ်။
7. S2: ၁၆–ကျပ်။ ...မှာ။
8. S2: ...မယ်နော်။
9. S1: ကောင်းပါ... ခင်ဗျာ။

S2: ပိုက်ဆံ **ရှင်း**မယ်။
S2: ဘယ်လောက် **ကျ**သလဲ။
S1: ၁၆/–ကျ**ပါ**တယ်။
S2: ၁၆–ကျပ်။ **ဒီ**မှာ။
S2: **သွား**မယ်နော်။
S1: ကောင်းပါ**ပြီ** ခင်ဗျာ။

LEVEL 1, TOPIC 5   SHOPS

First read through the New Words and the Sample Dialogue.
Then turn on the tape.

New words

ယူ–	to take	yu-
— ယူမယ်	I'll take it. I'll have it.	Yu-meh.
ကြည့်– /ကျိ/	to look, look around, look at	cí-
— ကြည့်မယ်။	I'll look around.	Cí-meh.
— ကြည့်အုံးမယ်။	I'll carry on looking around.	Cí-oùn-meh.
— ကြည့်အုံးမယ်နော်။	I'll carry on looking, if you don't mind.	Cí-oùn-meh-naw?

Vegetable stall in a market

Sample Dialogue

Scene: a shop in Burma. S1 is a customer, and S2 is the shopkeeper.

S1: ဒါ ဘယ်လောက်လဲ။	How much is that/this?	Da beh-lauq-lèh?
S2: ၁၅/–ပါ။	K15.	S'éh-ngà-jaq-pa.

FORK

branch 1 (the price is acceptable)

S1: ကောင်းပါပြီ။ ယူမယ်။	Right. I'll take it.	Kaùn-ba-bi. Yu-meh.
ဒီမှာ။ [1]	Here you are.	Di-hma.
သွားမယ်နော်။	Goodbye.	Thwà-meh-naw.

217

S2: ကောင်းပါပြီ॥	Goodbye.	Kaùn-ba-bi.

branch 2 (the price is too high) [2]

S1: အော်॥	Oh.	Aw.
ကျေးဇူး တင်ပါတယ်॥	Thanks.	Cè-zù tin-ba-deh.
ကြည့်အုံးမယ်နော်॥	I'll keep looking around.	Cí-oùn-meh-naw?
S2: ကောင်းပါပြီ॥ ရပါတယ်॥	OK. Fine.	Kaùn-ba-bi. Yá-ba-deh.

1. As noted before, it is not unusual to say nothing at this point: some people simply hand over the money and leave without feeling obliged to say anything.
2. As with taxi fares, you can often negotiate a lower price if you think the shopkeeper's price is unreasonably high. You will find words for bargaining on Level 2.

For the Practice Dialogues

Follow the Prompt.

name	*item*	*ceiling price*		
ဆရာဝင်း	ပို့စကဒ်	၅/–	pó-săkaq	Saya Win
တင်တင်ဝင်း	ဘောပင်	၆/–	bàw-pin	Tin Tin Win
ကိုရဲမြင့်	ဖလင်	၄၀၀/–	p'ălin	Ko Ye Myint
မခင်ရီ	စာအိတ်	၁/၅၀	sa-eiq	Ma Khin Yee
ကိုဌေးလှိုင်	ဘီစကွတ်	၁၂/–	bi-săkuq	Ko Htay Hlaing
ကိုဆုမြိုင်	ကိုကာကိုလာ	၄၅/–	Ko-ka-ko-la	Ko Hsu Myaing

Exercise for written answer

Reorder the sentences in Column B below so that each forms a natural sequel to the sentence in Column A. In some cases both A and B are spoken by the same speaker, in others by different speakers. Example:

| ၁॥ ဘယ်လို သွားရမလဲ॥ | ၁၁॥ ဒီဘက် သွားပါ॥ |

Use the Key below to check your answers.

Column A	Column B
၁॥ ဘယ်လို သွားရမလဲ॥	၁॥ ရပါတယ်॥ ရိုက်ပါ॥
၂॥ သိမ်ကြီးဈေး သွားချင်ပါတယ်॥	၂॥ ဆောရီးနော်॥
၃॥ မသိပါဘူး॥	၃॥ ရပါတယ်॥ တက်ပါ॥
၄॥ ဓါတ်ပုံ ရိုက်ချင်ပါတယ်॥ ရတယ်နော်॥	၄॥ ကောင်းပါပြီ မရိုက်ပါဘူး॥
၅॥ ရပါတယ်॥ ရိုက်ပါ॥	၅॥ ဘယ်လောက် ကျသလဲ॥
၆॥ မရဘူး॥ မရိုက်ပါနဲ့॥	၆॥ အော်॥ ကြည့်အုံးမယ်နော်॥
၇॥ ဘူတာကြီး သွားမယ်॥	၇॥ စပါကလင် တစ်လုံး ပေးပါ॥
၈॥ ဘယ် သွားမလဲ॥	၈॥ ဘယ်လို သွားရမလဲ॥
၉॥ ဘာ မှာမလဲ॥	၉॥ မင်္ဂလာဒုံ လေဆိပ် သွားမယ်॥
၁၀॥ ပိုက်ဆံ ရှင်းမယ်॥	၁၀॥ ကောင်းပါပြီ ယူမယ်॥
၁၁॥ ၂၅–ကျပ်ပါ॥	၁၁॥ ဒီဘက် သွားပါ॥
၁၂॥ ၇၅–ကျပ်ပါ॥	၁၂॥ ကဲ॥ ပြီးပြီ॥

KEY TO THE WRITTEN EXERCISE

၁॥	ဘယ်လို သွားရမလဲ॥	၁၁॥	ဒီဘက် သွားပါ॥
၂॥	သိမ်ကြီးဈေး သွားချင်ပါတယ်॥	၈॥	ဘယ်လို သွားရမလဲ॥
၃॥	မသိပါဘူး॥	၂॥	ဆောရီးနော်॥
၄॥	ဓာတ်ပုံ ရိုက်ချင်ပါတယ်॥ ရတယ်နော်॥	၁॥	ရပါတယ်॥ ရိုက်ပါ॥
၅॥	ရပါတယ်॥ ရိုက်ပါ॥	၁၂॥	ကဲ॥ ပြီးပြီ॥
၆॥	မရဘူး॥ မရိုက်ပါနဲ့॥	၄॥	ကောင်းပါပြီ॥ မရိုက်ပါဘူး॥
၇॥	ဘူတာကြီး သွားမယ်॥	၃॥	ရပါတယ်॥ တက်ပါ॥
၈॥	ဘယ် သွားမလဲ॥	၉॥	မင်္ဂလာဒုံ လေဆိပ် သွားမယ်॥
၉॥	ဘာ မှာမလဲ॥	၇॥	စပါကလင် တစ်လုံး ပေးပါ॥
၁၀॥	ပိုက်ဆံ ရှင်းမယ်॥	၅॥	ဘယ်လောက် ကျသလဲ॥
၁၁॥	၂၅–ကျပ်ပါ॥	၁၀॥	ကောင်းပါပြီ॥ ယူမယ်॥
၁၂॥	၇၅–ကျပ်ပါ॥	၆॥	အော်॥ ကြည့်အုံးမယ်နော်॥

LEVEL 1, TOPIC 6 YOUR COMMAND OF BURMESE

First read through the New Words and the Sample Dialogue.
Then turn on the tape.

New words

ဗမာစကား	Burmese	Băma săgà
	["Burmese-words/speaking"]	
ပြော–	to speak, say, tell, talk	pyàw-
— ဗမာစကား ပြောတယ်	to speak Burmese	Băma sgà pyàw-deh.
— ဗမာစကား ပြောတာ	speaking Burmese,	Băma săgà pyàw-da.
	command of spoken Burmese	

The suffix -တာ (-da) turns a verb (like *speak*) into a noun (like *speaking, speech*). [1]

ကောင်း–	to be good	kaùn-
ပိ–	to be correctly, authentically pronounced	pi-
— ဗမာစကား ပြောတာ ကောင်းပါတယ်॥	Your spoken Burmese is good.	Băma sgà pyàw-da kaùn-ba-deh.
— ဗမာစကား ပြောတာ ပိပါတယ်॥	Your spoken Burmese is well pronounced. [= You have a good pronunciation in Burmese.]	Băma sgà pyàw-da pi-ba-deh.
သိပ်	very	theiq
အရမ်း	terrifically, fantastically	ăyàn
— သိပ် ကောင်းတယ်॥	It is very good.	Theiq kaùn-deh.
— အရမ်း ကောင်းတယ်॥	It is incredibly good.	Ăyàn kaùn-deh.
[verb]–တာပဲ [1]	[verb]-da-bèh	[similar to [verb]–ပါတယ် (-ba-deh) but a little more exclamatory —]
— သိပ် ကောင်းတာပဲ॥	It is really very good!	Theiq kaùn-da-bèh.
— အရမ်း ကောင်းတာပဲ॥	It is really incredibly good!	Ăyàn kaùn-da-bèh.

219

တကယ်	really, in truth, actually, in fact	tăgeh
— တကယ်ပဲ။	Really. I mean it.	Tăgeh-bèh.
— တကယ်ပဲလား။	Really? Do you mean it?	Tăgeh-bèh-là?

The suffix –ပဲ (-bèh) adds a little emphasis. Compare ရယ်ဒီပဲ (Reh-di-bèh) and ဆောရီးပဲ (S'àw-rì-bèh), and [verb]–တာပဲ (-da-bèh) above.

ဟုတ်–	1. to be so, to be the case	houq-
	(as in ဟုတ်ကဲ့ and related phrases)	
	2. to be as good as it possibly could be, right on, spot on, on target, on the ball, hot stuff, high class, real cool	
— မဟုတ်ပါဘူး။ [with meaning 2]	It's not perfect.	Măhouq-pa-bù.
— မဟုတ်သေးပါဘူး။	It's not perfect yet.	Măhouq-thè-pa-bù.
	မ–[verb]–သေးပါဘူး means "not [verb] yet"	
— သိပ် မဟုတ်သေးပါဘူး။	It's not really perfect yet.	Theiq măhouq-thè-pa-bù.
	[See also S2's variants in the Sample Dialogue.]	

1. Note that you meet here two different functions of [verb]–တာ။ One is a way of making a noun from a verb, and the other is part of an exclamatory sentence ending.

Sample Dialogue

S1 is Burmese and S2 is a foreigner who is learning the language.

S1: ဗမာစကား ပြောတာ	You speak Burmese	Băma săgà pyàw-da
သိပ် ကောင်းတာပဲ။	very well.	theiq kaùn-da-bèh.

or:

S1: ဗမာစကား ပြောတာ	You have fantastically	Băma săgà pyàw-da
အရမ်း ပီတာပဲ။	good pronunciation.	ăyàn pi-da-bèh.
S2: အော်။ တကယ်ပဲလား။	Oh. Really?	Aw. Tăgeh-bèh-là?
ကျေးဇူးတင်ပါတယ်။	Thank you.	Cè-zù tin-ba-deh.
သိပ် မဟုတ်သေးပါဘူး။	It's not really high class yet.	Theiq măhouq-thè-ba-bù.

Variants:

S2: သိပ် မကောင်းသေးပါဘူး။	It's not very good yet.	Theiq măkaùn-thè-ba-bù.
S2: သိပ် မပီသေးပါဘူး။	It's not very well pronounced yet.	Theiq măpi-thè-ba-bù.
S2: သိပ် မရသေးပါဘူး။	I haven't really mastered it yet.	Theiq măyá-thè-ba-bù.

Most Burmese are delighted to meet someone who takes enough interest in Burma to learn the language, and (unlike the people of some nations you may have met) they make great efforts to encourage you. So this dialogue is one you are likely to take part in many times as soon as you start using your Burmese with native Burmese speakers. Needless to say, it is not the sort of dialogue that follows a set sequence, so you will encounter many variations of the compliment —

ဗမာစကား ပြောတာ သိပ် ကောင်းတာပဲ။	Băma săgà pyàw-da theiq kaùn-da-bèh.
ဗမာစကား ပြောတာ အရမ်း ပီတယ်။	Băma săgà pyàw-da ăyàn pi-deh.
ဗမာစကား ပြောတာ သိပ် ပီတာပဲ။	Băma săgà pyàw-da theiq pi-da-bèh.
ဗမာစကား ပြောတာ အရမ်း ကောင်းတယ်။	Băma săgà pyàw-da ăyàn kaùn-deh.
ဗမာစကား ကောင်းကောင်း ပြောတတ်ပါကလား။	Băma săgà kaùn-gaùn pyàw-daq-pa-gălà!

and so on. As a learner of Burmese you don't need to be able to *say* all these variants: you only need to be able to recognize what the speaker is telling you. The surest clues will be in the situation (that you have just said something in your impeccable Burmese, that the speaker looks impressed, and so on), and other clues to look for are conjunctions of words like ဗမာစကား, ပြော-, ကောင်း-, ပီ- and the rest (Băma săgà, pyàw-, kaùn-, pi-). If you can pick up a few clues like these you can deduce that you are being paid a compliment, and you will then know how to respond.

Your response likewise is variable. The selection of words and sentiments you choose to deliver depends on your personality (timid, pushy, …), your mood (buoyant, irritable, …), and your relationship to the speaker (you like or dislike him/her). The three responses shown in the Sample Dialogue don't have to be used all together and all in that order. You can use just one, or two, or all three, and vary the order to suit the situation.

Exercise for written answer

One of the syllables in each of the following sentences is inappropriate. Cross it out and supply the right syllable, as in the following model:

> Wrong sentence: ဗမာစကား ပြောပြီ သိပ် ကောင်းတာပဲ။
> Corrected sentence: ဗမာစကား ပြောပြီ**တာ** သိပ် ကောင်းတာပဲ။

၁။ ဗမာစကား ပီတာ သိပ် ကောင်းတာပဲ။
၂။ ဗမာစကား ပြောတာ အမှတ် ပီတာပဲ။
၃။ ဗမာစကေး ပြောတာ အရမ်း ပီတယ်။
၄။ ဗမာစကား ပြောတယ် သိပ် ပီတာပဲ။
၅။ ဗလစကား ပြောတာ အရမ်း တင်တယ်။
၆။ အော်။ ကျေးဇူး ရပါတယ်။ သိပ် မဟုတ်သေးပါဘူး။
၇။ အော်။ ကျေးဇူးတင်ပါတယ်။ သိပ် မပီတ်သေးပါဘူး။
၈။ အော်။ တလုံးပဲလား။ ကျေးဇူးတင်ပါတယ်။
၉။ အော်။ တကယ်ပဲလား။ ကျေးဇူး ဟုတ်ပါတယ်။

KEY TO THE WRITTEN EXERCISE
၁။ ဗမာစကား ပြောတာ သိပ် ကောင်းတာပဲ။
၂။ ဗမာစကား ပြောတာ အရမ်း ပီတာပဲ။
၃။ ဗမာစကား ပြောတာ အရမ်း ပီတယ်။
၄။ ဗမာစကား ပြောတာ သိပ် ပီတာပဲ။
၅။ ဗမာစကား ပြောတာ အရမ်း ကောင်းတယ်။
၆။ အော်။ ကျေးဇူးတင်ပါတယ်။ သိပ် မဟုတ်သေးပါဘူး။
၇။ အော်။ ကျေးဇူးတင်ပါတယ်။ သိပ် မကောင်းသေးပါဘူး။
၈။ အော်။ တကယ်ပဲလား။ ကျေးဇူးတင်ပါတယ်။
၉။ အော်။ တကယ်ပဲလား။ ကျေးဇူးတင်ပါတယ်။

LEVEL 1, TOPIC 7   TRAVELS: PAST TRIPS

First read through the New Words and the Sample Dialogue.
Then turn on the tape.

New words

နိုင်ငံခြား /–ဂျား/	foreign country, abroad ["country-separate"]	nain-ngan-jà
ရောက်–	to get to, reach, arrive at	yauq-
ရောက်ဖူး–	to have reached before, to have been to	yauq-p'ù-
အခေါက်	trip, journey [mainly used in counting: "How many times have you been?"]	ăk'auq
— ဘယ်နှစ်ခေါက်	how many trips?	beh-hnăk'auq
— သုံးခေါက်	three trips	thoùn-gauq
— သုံးခေါက် ရောက်ဖူးပါတယ်။	I've been there three times.	Thoùn-gauq yauq-p'ù-ba-deh.
ခဏခဏ /ခဏ ခဏ/	frequently, often, many times	k'ăná-k'ăná

Sample Dialogue

Scene: somewhere outside Burma. S1 is Burmese and S2 is a foreigner.

S1: ဗမာပြည် ရောက်ဖူးသလား။	Have you ever been to Burma?	Băma-pye yauq-p'ù-dhălà?

FORK

branch 1 (the person hasn't been)

S2: မရောက်ဖူးပါဘူး။	I haven't.	Măyauq-p'ù-ba-bù.
or: မရောက်ဖူးသေးပါဘူး။ [1]	I haven't yet. [1]	Măyauq-p'ù-dhè-ba-bù.

branch 2 (the person has been)

S2: ရောက်ဖူးပါတယ်။	I have.	Yauq-p'ù-ba-deh.
S1: ဘယ်နှစ်ခေါက် ရောက်ဖူးသလဲ။	How many times have you been?	Beh-hnăk'auq yauq-p'ù-dhălèh?
S2: လေးခေါက် ရောက်ဖူးပါတယ်။	I've been four times.	Lè-gauq yauq-p'ù-ba-deh.
or: S2: ခဏခဏ ရောက်ဖူးပါတယ်။	I've been many times.	K'ăná-k'ăná yauq-p'ù-ba-deh.

If you start with နိုင်ငံခြား the dialogue could take this route:

Scene: somewhere in Burma. S1 is a foreigner and S2 is Burmese.

S1: နိုင်ငံခြား ရောက်ဖူးသလား။	Have you ever been abroad?	Nain-ngan-jà yauq-p'ù-dhălà?
S2: ရောက်ဖူးပါတယ်။	I have.	Yauq-p'ù-ba-deh.
S1: ဘယ်နိုင်ငံ ရောက်ဖူးသလဲ။	What country have you been to?	Beh-nain-ngan yauq-p'ù-dhălèh?
S2: ထိုင်းနိုင်ငံ ရောက်ဖူးပါတယ်။	I have been to Thailand.	T'aìn-nain-ngan yauq-p'ù-ba-deh.
S1: ဘယ်နှစ်ခေါက် ရောက်ဖူးသလဲ။	How many times have you been?	Beh-hnăk'auq yauq-p'ù-dhălèh?
S2: တစ်ခေါက် ရောက်ဖူးပါတယ်။	I've been once.	Tăk'auq yauq-p'ù-ba-deh.

1. The longer alternative (incorporating –သေး (-thè) "yet") implies, as in English, that the speaker plans to go sometime.

At Mingaladon airport

For the Practice Dialogues

Dialogues Set 1. You ask the questions and make a note of the answers.

နာမည်	*country*	*n° of times*	*name*
ဒေါက်တာဦးကျော်စိန်	...	...	Dr. U Kyaw Sein
ဒေါ်စိန်စိန်	...	...	Daw Sein Sein
ကိုဝင်းမောင်	...	...	Ko Win Maung
မခင်သန်းသန်း	...	...	Ma Khin Than Than
ဆရာဘစောမြင့်	...	...	Saya Ba Saw Myint
မစံလေး	...	...	Ma San Lay

Dialogues Set 2. You use the list below to answer the questions.

name	*country*	*n° of times*	*name*	*country*	*n° of times*
Ms. Tailor	Burma	1	Mr. Dyer	Thailand	0
Mr. Draper	Burma	2	Ms. Tanner	Indonesia	3
Mrs. Weaver	Burma	0	Mr. Fuller	Singapore	many

Exercise for written answer

Supply the missing words in the following exchange. By now you will not need a reminder about covering the Key before you start.

1. S1: နိုင်ငံခြား ရောက်...သလား။
2 S2: ဟုတ်ကဲ့။ ...ပါတယ်။
3. S1: ...နိုင်ငံ ရောက်ဖူးသလဲ။

KEY TO THE WRITTEN EXERCISE

1. S1: နိုင်ငံခြား ရောက်ဖူးသလား။
2. S2: ဟုတ်ကဲ့။ ရောက်ဖူးပါတယ်။
3. S1: ဘယ်နိုင်ငံ ရောက်ဖူးသလဲ။

4. S2: ထိုင်း... ရောက်ဖူးပါတယ်။	4. S2: ထိုင်းနိုင်ငံ ရောက်ဖူးပါတယ်။
5. S1: ...ခေါက် ရောက်ဖူးသလဲ။	5. S1: ဘယ်နှစ်ခေါက် ရောက်ဖူးသလဲ။
6. S2: တစ်... ရောက်ဖူးပါတယ်။	6. S2: တစ်ခေါက် ရောက်ဖူးပါတယ်။

KEY TO THE PRACTICE DIALOGUE

name	country	n° of times	name	country	n° of times
ဒေါက်တာဦးကျော်စိန်	-	-	မခင်သန်းသန်း	Japan	1
ဒေါ်စိန်စိန်	America	2	ဆရာဘစောမြင့်	-	-
ကိုဝင်းမောင်	Australia	many	မစံလေး	Hong Kong	3

LEVEL 1, TOPIC 8   TRAVELS IN PROSPECT

First read through the New Words and the Sample Dialogue.

Then turn on the tape.

New words

အစီအစဉ် /-စဉ်/	plan, programme	ăsi-ăsin
အစီအစဉ် ရှိ-	to have a plan, intend	ăsi-ăsin shí-
[verb]-ဖို့ အစီအစဉ် ရှိ-	to have a plan, intend, to [verb]	-bó ăsi-ăsin shí-
— ကား ဝယ်ဖို့	Are you thinking of	Kà weh-bó
အစီအစဉ် ရှိသလား။	buying a car?	ăsi-ăsin shí-dhălà?
— ဟုတ်ကဲ့။ ရှိပါတယ်။	Yes, I am.	houq-kéh. Shí-ba-deh.
— မရှိပါဘူး။	No, I'm not.	Măshí-ba-bù.
[verb]-မလို့	thinking of [verb]-ing, planning to [verb]	-măló
— ကား ဝယ်မလို့လား။	Are you thinking of buying a car?	Kà weh-măló-là?
— ဟုတ်ကဲ့။ ဝယ်မလို့ပါ။	Yes, I am.	Houq-kéh. Weh-măló-ba.
— ဘာကား ဝယ်မလို့လဲ။	What car are you thinking of buying?	Ba-kà weh-măló-lèh?
နောက်ထပ် [verb]	[verb] again, further, more	nauq-t'aq

Although [verb]-ဖို့ အစီအစဉ် ရှိ- (-bó ăsi-ăsin shí-) and [verb]-မလို့ (-măló) both express plans and intentions, there is an important difference in grammatical status between them. The ရှိ- (shí-) at the end of the first is a verb, and so can be used with all the suffixes that are attached to verbs: ရှိပါတယ် , ရှိသလား , မရှိပါဘူး (shí-ba-deh, shí-dhălà, măshí-ba-bù), and the like; but the second ([verb]-မလို့ -măló) does not end in a verb: grammatically it is an unfinished sentence that has come to be used without its verb. As the examples above show, [verb]-မလို့ (-măló) may be followed by -လား (-là) or -ပါ (-ba) or -လဲ (-lèh) (and some other suffixes), but *not* by the verb suffixes -ပါတယ် , -သလား , မ-ပါဘူး (-ba-deh, -dhălà, mă—ba-bù), and the others. In particular note that there is no *No* answer to [verb]-မလို့လား (-măló-là). People usually resort to the အစီအစဉ် (ăsi-ăsin) version of the expression and answer အစီအစဉ် မရှိပါဘူး (ăsi-ăsin măshí-ba-bù). See the Sample Dialogue below.

Sample Dialogue

Scene: somewhere outside Burma. S1 is Burmese and S2 is a foreigner.

S1: ဗမာပြည် သွားဖို့
  အစီအစဉ် ရှိသလား။

Are you planning
  to go to Burma?

Băma-pye thwà-bó
  ăsi-ăsin shí-dhălà?

S2: ဟုတ်ကဲ့။

Yes.

Houq-kéh.

  သွားဖို့ အစီအစဉ် ရှိပါတယ်။

  I am planning to go.

  Thwà-bó ăsi-ăsin shí-ba-deh.

or: အစီအစဉ် မရှိသေးပါဘူး။

I don't have any plans so far.

Ăsi-ăsin măshí-dhè-ba-bù.

Variant

S1: ဗမာပြည် သွားမလို့လား။

Are you thinking of
  going to Burma?

Băma-pye thwà-măló-là?

S2: ဟုတ်ကဲ့။ သွားမလို့ပါ။

Yes, I am.

Houq-kéh. Thwà-măló-ba.

or: အစီအစဉ် မရှိသေးပါဘူး။

I don't have any plans so far.

Ăsi-ăsin măshí-dhè-ba-bù.

Other variants

S1: နောက်ထပ် သွားဖို့
  အစီအစဉ် ရှိသလား။

Are you planning to go again?

Nauq-t'aq thwà-bó
  ăsi-ăsin shí-dhălà?

S2: သွားချင်ပါတယ်။

I would like to go.

Thwà-jin-ba-deh.

For the Practice Dialogues

It is possible to give a fuller or a shorter answer to a question (for some examples see the notes in Part 1, Lesson 29). You may find in some of the Practice Dialogues that the speaker on the tape who echoes what you say uses a longer or shorter version of the answer than you did. Don't worry about this unduly. Your version was probably just as acceptable as the tape version.

Dialogues Set 1. You use the list below to answer the questions.

name	been to Burma	plans to go
Sarah	many times	yes
Chris	2 times	yes
Elizabeth	0 times	no
Arnd	1 times	no
Dindy	0 times	yes
Raymond	3 times	no

Dialogues Set 2. You ask the questions and make a note of the answers.
  Cover up the Key columns below while you work through the Practice Dialogues and fill in the blanks. When you have filled in all the blanks, uncover the Keys and compare your answers.

နာမည်	been abroad	plans to go	name	KEY been	plans
ဦးစိန်လွင်	...	...	U Sein Lwin	4 times	no
ဒေါ်မြမြသိန်း	...	...	Daw Mya Mya Thein	0 times	yes
ဦးချစ်ဆွေ	...	...	U Chit Swe	3 times	yes
ဒေါ်စီစီဝင်း	...	...	Daw Si Si Win	1 times	no
ဦးထွန်းအောင်ချိန်	...	...	U Tun Aung Chain	many times	yes
ဒေါ်ခင်မာလေး	...	...	Daw Khin Mar Lay	0 times	no

Exercise for written answer

The words and syllables in the following sentences have been jumbled. Rearrange them to form
good sentences, and insert spacing and punctuation.

1. S1: –အစဉ်–ဖို့–ဗမာ–အစီ–ရှိ–ပြည်–သလား–သွား
2. S1: –လား–ပြည်–မလို့–သွား–ဗမာ
3. S1: –ထပ်–ရှိ–ဖို့–အစဉ်–နောက်–သွား–သလား–အစီ

4. S2: –ရှိပါ–ကဲ့–အစီ–ဟုတ်–ဖို့–တယ်–အစဉ်–သွား
5. S2: –အစီ–ပါဘူး–အစဉ်–သေး–မရှိ
6. S2: –ဟုတ်–မလို့–သွား–ကဲ့–ပါ
7. S2: –ပါတယ်–ချင်–သွား

KEY TO THE WRITTEN EXERCISE
1. S1: –ဗမာ–ပြည် –သွား–ဖို့ –အစီ–အစဉ် –ရှိ–သလား။
2. S1: –ဗမာ–ပြည် –သွား–မလို့–လား။
3. S1: –နောက်–ထပ် –သွား–ဖို့ –အစီ–အစဉ် –ရှိ–သလား။

4. S2: –ဟုတ်–ကဲ့။ –သွား–ဖို့ –အစီ–အစဉ် –ရှိပါ–တယ်။
5. S2: –အစီ–အစဉ် –မရှိ–သေး–ပါဘူး။
6. S2: –ဟုတ်–ကဲ့။ –သွား–မလို့–ပါ။
7. S2: –သွား–ချင်–ပါတယ်။

LEVEL 1, TOPIC 9   TRAVELS: CURRENT TRIP

First read through the New Words and the Sample Dialogue.
Then turn on the tape.

New words

လူမျိုး	race, nationality ["person-kind, type"]	lu-myò
နိုင်ငံသား	national, citizen ["country-son, member"]	nain-ngan-dhà
	See note below.	

Sample Dialogue

Scene: somewhere in Burma. S1 is Burmese and S2 is a foreigner.

S1: ဘယ်နိုင်ငံက လာသလဲ။   What country do you come from?   Beh nain-ngan-gá la-dhălèh?

S2: ကနေဒါကပါ။   From Canada.   Kăne-da-gá-ba.

S1: ဘယ်နိုင်ငံကလဲ။   What country are you from?   Beh nain-ngan-gá-lèh?

S2: ကနေဒါကပါ။   From Canada.   Kăne-da-gá-ba.

S1: ဘာလူမျိုးလဲ။   What's your nationality?   Ba lu-myò-lèh?

S2: ကနေဒါလူမျိုးပါ။   Canadian.   Kăne-da lu-myò-ba.

Scene: somewhere outside Burma. S1 is from the host country and S2 is Burmese.

S1: ဗမာပြည်ကလား။   Are you from Burma?   Băma-pye-gá-là?

S2: ဟုတ်ကဲ့။   Yes.   Houq-kéh.

S1: ဗမာလူမျိုးလား။   Are you Burmese?   Băma lu-myò-là?

S2: ဟုတ်ကဲ့။   Yes.   Houq-kéh.

or: S2: I beg your pardon?

Burmese children meet foreign tourists at Sagaing

"Country" and "nationality"

As a rule the Burmese words for country and nationality are the same; for example:

မြန်မာနိုင်ငံ၊ မြန်မာလူမျိုး   Burma, Burmese (Myanmar)   Myan-ma nain-ngan, Myan-ma lu-myò

အိန္ဒိယနိုင်ငံ၊ အိန္ဒိယလူမျိုး /အိန်ဒီယာ/   India, Indian   Ein-dí-yá nain-ngan, Ein-dí-yá lu-myò

ဂျပန်နိုင်ငံ၊ ဂျပန်လူမျိုး   Japan, Japanese   Jăpan nain-ngan, Jăpan lu-myò

တရုပ်နိုင်ငံ၊ တရုပ်လူမျိုး   China, Chinese   Tăyouq nain-ngan, Tăyouq lu-myò

227

Common exceptions are —

အင်္ဂလန်နိုင်ငံ၊ အင်္ဂလိပ်လူမျိုး [1]	England, English	In-gălan nain-ngan, Ìn-găleiq lu-myò
ဗြိတိန်နိုင်ငံ၊ ဗြိတိသျှလူမျိုး /–ရှား/	Britain, British	Byí-tein nain-ngan, Byí-tí-shá lu-myò
အမေရိကနိုင်ငံ၊ အမေရိကန်လူမျိုး [2]	America, American	Ăme-rí-ka nain-ngan, Ăme-rí-kan lu-myò
ဂျာမနီနိုင်ငံ၊ ဂျာမန်လူမျိုး	Germany, German	Ja-măni nain-ngan, Ja-man lu-myò

1. Note tones: /အင်ဂလန်/ but /အင်းဂလိပ်/ (In-gălan: Ìn-găleiq)
2. People also say အမေရိကန်နိုင်ငံ (Ăme-rí-kan nain-ngan)

Other exceptions depend on the speaker's command of English: speakers with less English will use the same word for both country and nationality, and speakers with more will use a different word if English has one; for example:

ဆွစ်ဇလန်နိုင်ငံ၊ ဆွစ်ဇလန်လူမျိုး or ဆွစ်လူမျိုး	Switzerland, Swiss	Swiq-zălan: Swiq
အီတလီနိုင်ငံ၊ အီတလီလူမျိုး or အီတာလျန်လူမျိုး	Italy, Italian	I-tăli, I-ta-lăyan
နယ်သာလင်နိုင်ငံ၊ နယ်သာလင်လူမျိုး or ဒတ်ချ်လူမျိုး	Netherlands, Dutch	Neh-dha-lin: Daq-(c')
အိုင်ယာလန်နိုင်ငံ၊ အိုင်ယာလန်လူမျိုး or အိုင်ရစ်လူမျိုး	Ireland, Irish	Ain-ya-lan: Ain-riq

"Nationality" and "race"

In contexts where it is necessary to make a distinction, you use နိုင်ငံသား ("country-son, member") for "nationality, citizenship" and လူမျိုး for "race"; for example:

မြန်မာနိုင်ငံသား၊	Burmese national,	Myan-ma nain-ngan-dhà,
ရှမ်းလူမျိုး	Shan by race	Shàn lu-myò
ဗြိတိသျှနိုင်ငံသား၊	British national,	Byí-tí-shá nain-ngan-dhà,
စကော့လူမျိုး	Scot by race	Săkáw lu-myò
အမေရိကန်နိုင်ငံသား၊	American national,	Ăme-rí-kan nain-ngan-dhà,
တရုတ်လူမျိုး	Chinese by race	Tăyouq lu-myò

But in ordinary conversation, like the Sample Dialogues above, ဘာလူမျိုးလဲ (Ba lu-myò-lèh?) asks the same question as ဘယ်နိုင်ငံကလဲ (Beh nain-ngan-gá-lèh?). The questioner is not asking you to specify race rather than citizenship.

For the Practice Dialogues

Use the list below to answer the questions.

name	*country*
Mr. Bull	England
Ms. Doe	America
Mr. Keating	Australia
Mrs. Mount	Canada
Mr. Wellington	New Zealand

Exercise for written answer

Fill in the gaps in the following sentences. In some cases a "…" will be filled by "[nil]": that is, it does not mark a gap at all.

၁။ ဘယ်နိုင်ငံ… လာသလဲ။
၂။ ဘယ်မြို့… နေသလဲ။
၃။ ဘယ်နိုင်ငံ… သွားမလို့လဲ။
၄။ နိုင်ငံခြား ရောက်…သလား။

KEY TO THE WRITTEN EXERCISE

၁။ ဘယ်နိုင်ငံ**က** လာသလဲ။
၂။ ဘယ်မြို့**မှာ** နေသလဲ။
၃။ ဘယ်နိုင်ငံ[**nil**] သွားမလို့လဲ။
၄။ နိုင်ငံခြား ရောက်**ဖူး**သလား။

၅။ ဘယ်နှစ်... ရောက်ဖူးလဲ။		၅။ ဘယ်နှစ်**ခေါက်** ရောက်ဖူးလဲ။	
၆။ သွား... အစီအစဉ် ရှိသလား။		၆။ သွား**ဖို့** အစီအစဉ် ရှိသလား။	
၇။ Mr. Jones–က ဘာ လူ...လဲ။		၇။ Mr. Jones–က ဘာ လူ**မျိုး**လဲ။	
၈။ ဘယ်အချိန်... လာမလို့လဲ။		၈။ ဘယ်အချိန်[**nil**] လာမလို့လဲ။	
၉။ ကျမ နာမည်က မပွင့်... ခေါ်ပါတယ်။		၉။ ကျမ နာမည်က မပွင့်**လို့** ခေါ်ပါတယ်။	
၁၀။ အဲဒါ ဘယ်... ပေးရသလဲ။		၁၀။ အဲဒါ ဘယ်**လောက်** ပေးရသလဲ။	
၁၁။ တံခါး... ဖွင့်ရမလား။		၁၁။ တံခါး[**nil**] ဖွင့်ရမလား။	

LEVEL 1, TOPIC 10A — YOU AND YOURS

First read through the New Words and the Sample Dialogue.
Then turn on the tape.

New words

ကျမ [noun]	my [noun] (woman speaking)	cămá
– ဒါ ကျမ ဘောပင်ပါ။	That's my pen (woman speaking)	Da cămá bàw-pin-ba.
ကျနော့် [noun][1]	my [noun] (man speaking)	cănáw
– ဒါ ကျနော့် ဘောပင်ပါ။	That's my pen (man speaking)	Da cănáw bàw-pin-ba.

Some relatives [2]—

အမျိုးသား	husband, fiancé, boyfriend (also "gentleman")	ămyò-thà (or -dhà)
အမျိုးသမီး	wife, fiancée, girlfriend (also "lady")	ămyò-dhămì
သား	son	thà
သမီး	daughter	thămì
အဖေ	father	ăp'e
အမေ	mother	ăme
မိတ်ဆွေ	friend	meiq-s'we

1. One of the words for "I" used by male speakers is ကျွန်တော် (cun-daw "honoured servant"), pronounced /ကျွန်ဒေါ်/ in careful speech, but often contracted to /ကျနော်/ and written to match (cun-daw, cănaw). Its possessive form is the original ကျွန်တော် (ကျနော်) with the last syllable converted from low tone to creaky tone: pronounced /ကျွန်ဒေါ့၊ (ကျနော့)/ (cun-dáw/cănáw). When writing the possessive form in the script you don't replace the low tone (ေ–ာ်) by a creaky tone (ေ–ာ့) as you might expect: instead you acknowledge the word's derived status by retaining the original low tone (ေ–ာ်) and adding to it the sign of the creaky tone (–့). You write ကျွန်တော့် (ကျနော့်) , not ကျွန်တော့ (ကျနော့).

The corresponding word for "I" used by female speakers is ကျွန်မ (cun-má), often contracted to ကျမ (cămá). Since the last syllable is a creaky tone anyway, it can't be converted to creaky to indicate possessive, so the possessive form is the same as the original form: ကျွန်မ or ကျမ။

Although you do need to use words for "my" fairly often, you rarely need, as you know, to use a word for "I." Where it can be inferred from the context, you leave it out.

2. For a full list of terms for relatives, see Appendix 6, section 17.

For reference: some other words for husband and wife (not practised on the tape)

ယောက်ျား (/ယောက်ကျား/)၊ မိန်းမ	less refined and classy	yauq-cà, meìn-má
	(also = "man" and "woman")	
ခင်ပွန်း (/-ပွန်း/)၊ ဇနီး	more refined and classy	k'in-bùn, zănì
ခင်ပွန်းသည်၊ ဇနီးသည် (/-သုယ်/)	=ခင်ပွန်း၊ ဇနီး	k'in-bùn-dheh, zănì-dheh

Another word useful in this context is:

ရည်းစား (/ယီးဇာ/)	fiancé/e, boy/girlfriend	yì-zà

အမျိုးသား၊ အမျိုးသမီး are chosen as the safest for beginners: ယောက်ျား၊ မိန်းမ may grate on the listener's ear as lacking in respect, and ခင်ပွန်:(သည်)၊ ဇနီး:(သည်) can sound too obsequious.

အမျိုးသား၊ အမျိုးသမီး and ယောက်ျား၊ မိန်းမ (sometimes abbreviated to ကျား၊ မ) are often seen written over the entrances to toilets and other sexually segregated facilities. They correspond neatly to the English *Gentlemen* and *Ladies,* and *Men* and *Women,* respectively.

Etymologically အမျိုးသား ["son of the race"] corresponds well with the English word *gentleman* ["man of the race"]; but it is more likely that the word was made up on the analogy of the corresponding Pali word kulaputta (also "son of the race").

Sample Dialogue

Scene: S2 is showing some family photographs to S1.
Woman speaking

S1: ဒါ ဘယ်သူလဲ။ — Who is that? — Da beh-dhu-lèh?

S2: ဒါက ကျမ အမျိုးသားပါ ရှင်။ — That's my husband. — Da-gá cămá ămyò-dhà-ba, shin.

S1: နာမည် ဘယ်လို ခေါ်သလဲ။ — What is his name? — Nan-meh beh-lo k'aw-dhălèh?

S2: ကိုမြင့်မောင်လို့ ခေါ်ပါတယ်။ — It's Ko Myint Maung. — Ko Myín Maun-ló k'aw-ba-deh.

Man speaking

S1: ဒါ ဘယ်သူလဲ။ — Who is that? — Da beh-dhu-lèh?

S2: ဒါက ကျနော့်
အမျိုးသမီးပါ ခင်ဗျာ။ — That's my wife. — Da-gá cănáw
ămyò-dhămì-ba, k'in-bya.

S1: နာမည် ဘယ်လို ခေါ်သလဲ။ — What is her name? — Nan-meh beh-lo k'aw-dhălèh?

S2: မခင်မေလို့ ခေါ်ပါတယ်။ — She's called Ma Khin May. — Má K'in Me-ló k'aw-ba-deh.

The same with checking questions

S1: ဒါ ဘယ်သူလဲ။ — Who is that? — mm

S2: ဒါက ကျနော့်
အမျိုးသမီးပါ ခင်ဗျာ။ — That's my wife. — Da-gá cănáw
ămyò-dhămì-ba k'in-bya.

S1: အော်။ အမျိုးသမီးလား။ * — Oh. It's your wife, is it? * — Aw. Ămyò-dhămì-là?

S2: ဟုတ်ကဲ့ ခင်ဗျာ။ — Yes. — Houq-kéh, k'in-bya.

S1: နာမည် ဘယ်လို ခေါ်သလဲ။ — What is her name? — Nan-meh beh-lo k'aw-dhălèh?

S2: မခင်မေလို့ ခေါ်ပါတယ်။ — She's called Ma Khin May. — Má K'in Me-ló k'aw-ba-deh.

S1: မခင်မီလား။ — Ma Khin Mi? — Má K'in Mi-là?

S2: မဟုတ်ပါဘူး ခင်ဗျာ။
မခင်မေပါ။ — No.
Ma Khin May. — Măhouq-pa-bù, k'in-bya.
Má K'in Me-ba.

S1: အော်။ မခင်မေ။ — Oh. Ma Khin May. — Aw. Má K'in Me.

Variants

1. S2: ကိုမြင့်မောင်ပါ။ — Ko Myint Maung. — Ko Myín Maun-ba.

Variant for:

S2: ကိုမြင့်မောင်လို့ ခေါ်ပါတယ်။ — His name is Ko Myint Maung. — Ko Myín Maun-ló k'aw-ba-deh.

2. S1: ကိုမြင့်မောင် ဟုတ်လား။ — Ko Myint Maung — is that right? — Ko Myín Maun, houq-là?

Variant for:

S1: ကိုမြင့်မောင်လား။ — Ko Myint Maung? — Ko Myín Maun-là?

Did you say "Ko Myint Maung"?

* This is a good example of a question that takes the same form as a checking question, but doesn't really need an answer. It is used like "Oh, I see" statements in English: "Oh, so this is your wife, is it? Well, well" and so on. When we need to refer to questions of this type again, we shall call it an "Oh I see" question.

For the Practice Dialogues

Format for Dialogue 1

Prompt: Point to n° 1 and ask who it is:

L/S1: ဒါ ဘယ်သူလဲ။

L/S1: အော်။ အဖေလား။ ("Oh I see" question)

L/S1: နာမည် ဘယ်လို ခေါ်သလဲ။

L/S1: ဦးခင်မောင်ဒင် ဟုတ်လား။

Now fill in the name in the blank below.

S2: ဒါက ကျနော့် အဖေပါ ခင်ဗျာ။

S2: ဟုတ်ကဲ့ ခင်ဗျာ။

S2: ဦးခင်မောင်ဒင်လို့ ခေါ်ပါတယ်။

S2: ဟုတ်ကဲ့။

Dialogue 1. You ask the questions and make a note of the answers.

		Speaker A (male)	Speaker B (female)
		name	*name*
1.	father	...	...
2.	mother	...	...
3.	spouse	...	...
4.	son	...	...
5.	daughter	...	...
6.	friend	...	...

Dialogue 2. You use the family tree below to answer the questions.

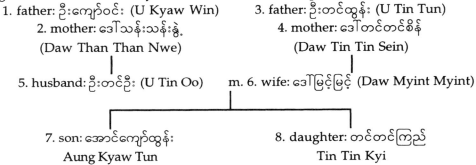

1. father: ဦးကျော်ဝင်း (U Kyaw Win)   3. father: ဦးတင်ထွန်း (U Tin Tun)
2. mother: ဒေါ်သန်းသန်းနွဲ့   4. mother: ဒေါ်တင်တင်စိန်
(Daw Than Than Nwe)   (Daw Tin Tin Sein)

5. husband: ဦးတင်ဦး (U Tin Oo)   m. 6. wife: ဒေါ်မြင့်မြင့် (Daw Myint Myint)

7. son: အောင်ကျော်ထွန်း   8. daughter: တင်တင်ကြည်
Aung Kyaw Tun   Tin Tin Kyi

Dialogue 3. Imagine you are introduced to someone. Cover up the Key columns while you fill in the blanks from the tape.

	relationship	*name*	**KEY**		
			reln	နာမည်	*name*
Person 1:	...	...	mother	ဒေါ်ခင်မူ	Daw Khin Mu
Person 2:	...	...	husband	ဦးစိန်ဦး	U Sein Oo
Person 3:	...	...	daughter	ညွန့်တင်	Nyunt Tin
Person 4:	...	...	friend	ဒေါ်စံစံမြ	Daw San San Mya
Person 5:	...	...	father	ဦးမြင့်ကျော်	U Myint Kyaw
Person 6:	...	...	son	ရန်နိုင်	Yan Naing

Exercise for written answer

Using the family tree provided for Dialogue 2, complete the following sentences to match this model:

(Nº 4 Daw Tin Tin Sein speaking)

၀။ ဒေါ်မြင့်မြင့်က ...

ဒေါ်မြင့်မြင့်က ကျမ သမီးပါ။

(Nº 6 Daw Myint Myint speaking)

၁။ ဦးတင်ဦးက ...

၂။ ဒေါ်တင်တင်စိန်က ...

၃။ အောင်ကျော်ထွန်းက ...

(Nº 5 U Tin U speaking)

၄။ ဦးကျော်ဝင်းက ...

၅။ ဒေါ်မြင့်မြင့်က ...

၆။ တင်တင်ကြည်က ...

KEY TO THE WRITTEN EXERCISE

ဦးတင်ဦးက ကျမ အမျိုးသားပါ။

ဒေါ်တင်တင်စိန်က ကျမ အမေပါ။

အောင်ကျော်ထွန်းက ကျမ သားပါ။

ဦးကျော်ဝင်းက ကျနော့် အဖေပါ။

ဒေါ်မြင့်မြင့်က ကျနော့် အမျိုးသမီးပါ။

တင်တင်ကြည်က ကျနော့် သမီးပါ။

KEY TO DIALOGUE 1

		Speaker A (male) *name*	Speaker B (female) *name*
1.	father	ဦးခင်မောင်ခင်	ဦးညွန့်သောင်း
2.	mother	ဒေါ်တင်တင်မြင့်	ဒေါ်နဲ့နဲ့
3.	spouse	မသိန်း	ကိုဝင်း
4.	son	မင်းဦး	မျိုးမင်း
5.	daughter	မာလေး	စံတင့်
6.	friend	ကိုစိန်လင်း	မသောင်းခင်

LEVEL 1, TOPIC 10B   YOU AND YOURS continued

First read through the New Words and the Sample Dialogue.
Then turn on the tape.

New words

မိတ်ဆက်– or မိတ်ဆက်ပေး:–	to introduce ["friend-connect-give"]	meiq-s'eq-(pè)-
N–နဲ့ မိတ်ဆက်ပေးချင်ပါတယ်။	I want to introduce you to N.	N-néh meiq-s'eq-pè-jin-ba-deh.
N–နဲ့ မိတ်ဆက်ပေးမယ်နော်။	I'll introduce you to N — all right?	N-néh meiq-s'eq-pè-meh-naw?
N–နဲ့ မိတ်ဆက်ပေးပါအုံး။	Please introduce me to N.	N-néh meiq-s'eq-pè-ba-oùn.
[verb]–ပါအုံး is a slightly more friendly, more coaxing, alternative to [verb]–ပါ။		-ba-oùn
ဝမ်းသာ– [1]	to be happy ["stomach—be pleasant"]	wùn-tha- [1]
တွေ့–	to meet [also = see, notice, find]	twé-
— တွေ့ရတယ်	has the opportunity to meet [note new meaning of verb+ရ–]	twé-yá-deh
— တွေ့ရတာ	the having the opportunity to meet	twé-yá-da
— တွေ့ရတာ ဝမ်းသာပါတယ်။	I am happy at having the opportunity to meet you.	Twé-yá-da wùn-tha-ba-deh.
[noun]–လဲ [5]	[noun] also, [noun] too	-lèh

[noun]–ကော or [noun]–ရော	how about [noun]?	-gàw, -yàw
	[Refers back to preceding question or statement: see Common Phrases in Part 1 and Format for Dialogue 1 below]	
မိတ်ဆွေ	friend; also used = "you" and "your" when you don't yet know a person's name	meiq-s'we

Some new relatives — 2

အကို 3	older brother	ăko
အမ 3	older sister	ămá
ဦးလေး 3, 4	uncle	ù-lè
အဒေါ် 3, 4	aunt	ădaw

1. Sometimes, specially on formal occasions, pronounced wàn-tha- rather than wùn-tha-.

2. Kin terms are used in Burmese much more frequently than in English. Firstly, they are used where English uses "you" and "your." So, for example, if you found a ballpoint pen and wanted to ask your older sister if were hers, you'd say

ဒါ အမ ဘောပင်လား။   Is that sister's pen?   Da ămá bàw-pin-là?

= Is that your pen?

Secondly, kin terms are used for calling people, and attracting their attention, where English would use the person's name. So if you were calling your sister to come and answer the phone, or if you wanted to gain her attention in a conversation, you would say အမ "Sister," where English would use her name.

Another factor that multiplies the frequency of use of kin terms in Burmese is that people use them a lot not only for their actual relatives, but also for friends who are not related to them, and even for complete strangers. You will be introduced to these extended uses in the appropriate place.

For a full list of terms for relatives, see Appendix 6, section 17.

3. Notice the connection between the new words for relatives and the prefixes you find before names: ကို၊ မ၊ ဦး၊ ဒေါ် (Ko, Má, Ù, Daw).

4. Uncles and aunts. In earlier times there was a more extensive set of words for uncles and aunts: there were different terms for father's siblings and mother's, and for aunts and uncles older or younger than the parent. Many of these terms still survive today, more in some parts of the country than in others, though their definitions are not uniform among all regions and all speakers. As you learn more Burmese you will come across terms from this extended set, but for all practical purposes you can use ဦးလေး and အဒေါ် just as you use "uncle" and "aunt" in English.

5. The officially approved spelling of –လဲ is –လည်း, but we use –လဲ here as this is the spelling most people use when writing in colloquial style.

Sample Dialogue

Scene: a social occasion. S1 is introduced by S2 to S3.

Dialogue 1

S1 casts a glance at S2's companion and says:

S1: မိတ်ဆက်ပေးပါအုံး။ | Please introduce me. | Meiq-s'eq-pè-ba-oùn.
| = Why don't you introduce me? |

S2: အော်။ ဟုတ်ကဲ့။ | Oh. Yes. | Aw. Houq-kéh.
ဒါက ကျွမ အဖေပါ။ | This is my father. | Da-gá cămá ăp'e-ba.

S1: တွေ့ရတာ | I'm happy to meet you. | Twé-yá-da
ဝမ်းသာပါတယ် ခင်ဗျာ။ | | wùn-tha-ba-deh, k'in-bya.

S3: ကျွနော်လဲ | And I'm happy | Cănaw-lèh
ဝမ်းသာပါတယ် ခင်ဗျာ။ | (to meet you) too. | wùn-tha-ba-deh, k'in-bya.

S1: နံမည် ဘယ်လို ခေါ်သလဲ။ | What is your name? | Nan-meh beh-lo k'aw-dhălèh?

S3: ရဲမြင့်ပါ။ [1] | Ye Myint. | Yèh Myín-ba.

S1: အော်။ ဦးရဲမြင့်လား။ | Oh. U Ye Myint, is it? | Aw. Ù Yèh Myín-là?

S3: ဟုတ်ကဲ့။ မိတ်ဆွေ နာမည် | Yes. | Houq-kéh. Meiq-s'we nan-meh
ဘယ်လို ခေါ်သလဲ။ | What's your name? | beh-lo k'aw-dhălèh?

S1: ကျွနော့ နာမည်က ပီတာပါ။ | My name is Peter. | Cănáw nan-meh-gá Pi-ta-ba.

S3: တွေ့ရတာ | I'm pleased | Twé-yá-da
ဝမ်းသာပါတယ် ခင်ဗျာ။ | to have met you. | wùn-tha-ba-deh, k'in-bya.

Dialogue 2

S2: ကျွမ အမေနဲ့ | I'll introduce you to | Cămá ăme-néh
မိတ်ဆက်ပေးမယ်နော်။ [2] | my mother — OK? | meiq-s'eq-pè-meh-naw?

S1: ဟုတ်ကဲ့။ မိတ်ဆက်ပေးပါ။ | Yes, do. | Houq-kéh. Meiq-s'eq-pè-ba.

S2 calls her mother over

S2: အမေ။ ဒါက | Mother. This is | Ăme. Da-gá
ကျွမ မိတ်ဆွေ ကိုပီတာ။ | my friend Ko Peter. | cămá meiq-s'we Ko Pi-ta.

[to Peter] ဒါက ကျွမ အမေပါ။ | This is my mother. | Da-gá cămá ăme-ba.

S1: အော်။ တွေ့ရတာ | Oh. I am happy | Aw. Twé-yá-da
ဝမ်းသာပါတယ် ခင်ဗျာ။ | to have met you. | wùn-tha-ba-deh, k'in-bya.

S3: ကျွမလဲ ဝမ်းသာပါတယ် ရှင်။ | And I'm happy | Cămá-lèh wùn-tha-ba-deh, shin.
| (to have met you) too. |

S3: ကျွမ နာမည်က ခင်မေရီပါ။ | My name is Khin Me Yi. | Cămá nan-meh-gá
| | K'in Me Yi-ba.

1. Notice that when you are telling someone your own name you often omit the prefix. You say ရဲမြင့် (Yèh Myín) rather than ဦးရဲမြင့် (Ù Yèh Myín), and so on — just as English speakers identify themselves as (say) "Tom Hanks" rather than "Mr. Hanks."

2. *Variant:*

ကျွမ အဖေနဲ့ | I'd like to introduce you | Cămá ăp'e-néh
မိတ်ဆက်ပေးချင်ပါတယ်။ | to my father. | meiq-s'eq-pè-jin-ba-deh.

For the Practice Dialogues

Dialogue 1. Format. Imagine you are speaking to S1, who has a companion with her.

Prompt: You are Tom. Ask to be introduced.

L/S2: မိတ်ဆက်ပေးပါအုံး။။

S1: အော်။။ ဟုတ်ကဲ့ ရှင်။။ ဒါက ကျမ ဦးလေးပါ။။

L/S2: အော်။။ ဦးလေးလား။။ တွေ့ရတာ ဝမ်းသာပါတယ် ခင်ဗျာ။။

S3: ကျနော်လဲ ဝမ်းသာပါတယ် ခင်ဗျာ။။

L/S2: နာမည် ဘယ်လို ခေါ်သလဲ။။

S3: ဦးဘသန်းပါ။။ မိတ်ဆွေ နာမည်ကော ဘယ်လို ခေါ်သလဲ။။

L/S2: ကျနော့် နာမည်က Tom ပါ။။

Now make a note of his name in the appropriate blank below. When Column A is filled, move on to Column B.

		Column A	Column B
your name	*relative*	*relative's name*	*relative's name*
Tom	uncle	...	...
Lucy	aunt	...	...
Sue	brother	...	...
John	sister	...	...

Dialogue 2. Use the family tree below to identify your relative. Note that you speak both for the introducer and the introduced. Format:

Prompt: S1 indicates person 2 on the tree.

S1: မိတ်ဆက်ပေးပါအုံး။။

L/S2: ဟုတ်ကဲ့။။ ဒါက ကျနော့် အဒေါ်ပါ။။

S1: တွေ့ရတာ ဝမ်းသာပါတယ် ရှင်။။

L/S3: ကျမလဲ ဝမ်းသာပါတယ် ရှင်။။

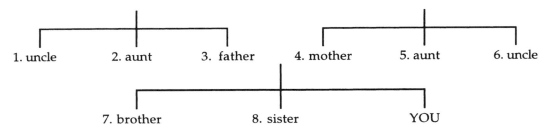

1. uncle   2. aunt   3. father   4. mother   5. aunt   6. uncle

7. brother   8. sister   YOU

Exercise for written answer

Translate the following dialogue into Burmese.

S1 is a Burmese man; S2 is a foreign woman, a friend of S1; S3 is a Burmese man, brother of S1.

	KEY TO THE WRITTEN EXERCISE
1. S1: I'll introduce you to my brother, OK?	ကျနော့် အကိုနဲ့ မိတ်ဆက်ပေးမယ်နော်။။
2. S2: Yes, please do.	ဟုတ်ကဲ့။။ မိတ်ဆက်ပေးပါ။။
3. S1: Brother: this is my friend Ma Laura.	အကို။။ ဒါက ကျနော့် မိတ်ဆွေ မလောရာ။။
4. S1: Ma Laura: this is my brother.	မလောရာ။။ ဒါက ကျနော့် အကိုပါ။။
5. S2: Oh. I am happy to meet you (+tag).	အော်။။ တွေ့ရတာ ဝမ်းသာပါတယ် ရှင်။။
6. S3: I'm happy to meet you too (+tag).	ကျနော်လဲ ဝမ်းသာပါတယ် ခင်ဗျာ။။

7. S2: What is your name?　　　　　　　　　နာမည် ဘယ်လို ခေါ်သလဲ။

8. S3: My name is Zaw Win.　　　　　　　　ကျနော့် နာမည်က ဇော်ဝင်းပါ။

9. S3: What country do you come from?　　　မလော်ရာ ဘယ်နိုင်ငံက လာသလဲ။

10. S2: From America.　　　　　　　　　　　အမေရိကကပါ။

Another meaning of အမျိုးသမီး

KEY TO THE DIALOGUE

		Speaker A (male)		Speaker B (female)	
yr name	*relative*	*rel's name*	*rel's name*	*rel's name*	*rel's name*
Tom	uncle	ဦးဘသန်း	U Ba Than	ဦးမြဖေ	U Mya Pe
Lucy	aunt	ဒေါ်စံစံနု	Daw San San Nu	ဒေါ်ခင်မျိုးသက်	Daw Khin Myo Thet
Sue	brother	ကိုစိုးတင့်	Ko So Tint	ကိုမောင်မောင်အေး	Ko Maung Maung Aye
John	sister	မအေးရီ	Ma Aye Yee	မသိန်းရှင်	Ma Thein Shin

LEVEL 1, TOPIC 11　　　　　　　　TO MEET AGAIN

First read through the New Words and the Sample Dialogue.
Then turn on the tape.

New words

တွေ့-	to meet [also = notice, find, see]	twé-
— တွေ့ရအောင်။	Let's meet. Shall we meet?	Twé-yá-aun.
— တွေ့ကြရအောင်။ [4]	Let's meet.	Twé-já-yá-aun.
နောက်ထပ်	again, more, further	nauq-t'aq
— နောက်ထပ် တွေ့ကြရအောင်။	Let's meet again.	Nauq-t'aq twé-já-yá-aun.
[noun]-လဲ	[noun] too, [noun] also	-lèh

— ကျွန်တော်လဲ တွေ့ချင်ပါတယ်။	I too would like to meet.	Cănaw-lèh twé-jin-ba-deh.
မနက်ဖြန် or မနက်ဖြင် or မနက်ဖန် [1]	tomorrow	măneq-p'yan, măneq-p'yin, măneq-p'an
နက်ဖြန် or နက်ဖြင် or နက်ဖန် [1]	tomorrow	neq-p'yan, neq-p'yin, neq-p'an
လုပ်စရာ	things that have to be done	louq-săya
များ-	to be many, much	myà-
— လုပ်စရာ များပါတယ်။	I have a lot to do.	Louq-săya myà-ba-deh.
နဲနဲ [5]	a little, a bit	nèh-nèh
— လုပ်စရာ နဲနဲ များပါတယ်။	I have rather a lot to do.	Louq-săya nèh-nèh myà-ba-deh.
— လုပ်စရာ နဲနဲ များနေပါတယ်။	I have rather a lot to do at the moment.	Louq-săya nèh-nèh myà-ne-ba-deh.
လောလောဆယ် /-ဇယ်/	recently, currently, for the time being	làw-làw-zeh
— လောလောဆယ် လုပ်စရာ နဲနဲ များ(နေ)ပါတယ်။	I have rather a lot to do at the moment.	Làw-làw-zeh louq-săya nèh-nèh myà-ne-ba-deh.
— လောလောဆယ် သွားစရာ နဲနဲ များ(နေ)ပါတယ်။	I have rather a lot of "going" to do at the moment.	Làw-làw-zeh thwà-zăya nèh-nèh myà-ne-ba-deh.
စီစဉ်- /စီဇင်/	to arrange, fix up	si-zin-
— စီစဉ်ရအောင်။	Let's arrange.	Si-zin-yá-aun.
— စီစဉ်ကြရအောင်။ [4]	Let's arrange.	Si-zin-já-yá-aun.
နောက်မှ	later, not till later	nauq-hmá
— နောက်မှ စီစဉ်ကြရအောင်။	Let's fix up something later. [2]	Nauq-hmá si-zin-já-yá-aun.
— နောက်မှပဲ [3] စီစဉ်ကြရအောင်။	Let's fix up something later.	Nauq-hmá-bèh si-zin-já-yá-aun.

1. All six versions are used. Each speaker tends to prefer one form over the rest.

2. = "Let's leave it till later to fix something up," "Let's not do it now."

3. The suffix –ပဲ is attached to a noun and adds emphasis, focusses attention on it. Compare:

ဒီမှာ ထိုင်ကြရအောင်။	Let's sit here	Di-hma t'ain-já-yá-aun.
ဒီမှာပဲ ထိုင်ကြရအောင်။	Let's sit right here, in this very spot	Di-hma-bèh t'ain-já-yá-aun.

4. [verb]-ကြ- (-já-) is often (but not obligatorily) used when the verb has a plural subject.

5. The officially approved spelling of this word is နည်းနည်း, but we use နဲနဲ here as this is the spelling that most people use when writing in colloquial style.

Sample Dialogue

Scene: S1 and S2 have just met each other. They have had a short conversation, and are now about to part.

A. S2 is willing to meet again.

Version 1

S1: နောက်ထပ် တွေ့ကြရအောင်။	Let's meet again.	Nauq-t'aq twé-já-yá-aun.
S2: ဟုတ်ကဲ့။ တွေ့ချင်ပါတယ်။	Yes. I'd like to.	Houq-kéh. Twé-jin-ba-deh.

Version 2

S1: နောက်ထပ် တွေ့ချင်ပါတယ်။	I'd like to meet you again.	Nauq-t'aq twé-jin-ba-deh.
S2: ကျမလဲ တွေ့ချင်ပါတယ်။	I'd like to too [female speaker].	Cămá-lèh twé-jin-ba-deh.
or S2: ကျနော်လဲ တွေ့ချင်ပါတယ်။	I'd like to too [male speaker].	Cănaw-lèh twé-jin-ba-deh.

Variants:

S1: မနက်ဖန် တွေ့ကြရအောင်။	Let's meet tomorrow.	Măneq-p'an twé-já-yá-aun.
S1: မနက်ဖန် ထပ်တွေ့ကြရအောင်။	Let's meet again tomorrow.	Măneq-p'an t'aq-twé-já-yá-aun.
S1: နောက်ထပ် တွေ့ကြအုံးစို့လား။ [1]	How about us meeting again?	Nauq-t'aq twé-já-oùn-zó-là.
S2: တွေ့တာပေါ့။ [2]	By all means let's meet.	Twé-da-báw.

1. The verb suffixes –စို့ and –စို့လား have much the same effect as –ရအောင်။ The difference is that [verb]–ရအောင် is a little more like "Would you like to ... ?", "Shall we ... ?" (with an element of consultation), whereas [verb]–စို့ and [verb]–စို့လား are more like "Let's ... " (assuming willingness on the part of the listener).
2. One of the functions of [verb]–တာပေါ့ /–ဒါဘော့/ is to convey an enthusiastic response to an invitation or suggestion.

B. S2 declines the suggestion.

S1: နောက်ထပ် တွေ့ကြရအောင်။	Let's meet again.	Nauq-t'aq twé-já-yá-aun.
S2: လောလောဆယ် လုပ်စရာ နဲ့နဲ့ များပါတယ်။	I have rather a lot to do at the moment.	Làw-làw-zeh louq-săya nèh-nèh myà-ba-deh.
or: လောလောဆယ် သွားစရာ နဲ့နဲ့ များပါတယ်။	I have rather a lot of "going" to do at the moment.	Làw-làw-zeh thwà-săya nèh-nèh myà-ba-deh.
S2: နောက်မှပဲ စီစဉ်ကြရအောင်။	Let's fix up something later.	Nauq-hmá-bèh si-zin-já-yá-aun.
S1: ကောင်းပါပြီ။	All right.	Kaùn-ba-bi.

Variant:

S2: နောက် ကြုံအုံးမှာပါ။	We'll come across each other later (so we don't need to fix a date now).	Nauq coun-oùn-hma-ba.
– ကြုံ–	to meet, to fall in with each other, to turn up in the same place	coun-
– ကြုံအုံးမယ်	our paths will cross again	Coun-oùn-meh.
– ကြုံအုံးမှာပါ	[same as preceding, but with a hint of reassurance: as if you were saying "don't worry"]	Coun-oùn-hma-ba.

Needless to say, there are many different ways of saying "Let's meet again." The list above gives a small selection. For practical purposes, if you can pick out a combination of words like နောက်ထပ် "again" or မနက်ဖန်/နက်ဖြန်/မနက်ဖြန် "tomorrow" and တွေ့– "to meet," and add that to any non-verbal clues you may see, you can guess with some confidence that a further meeting is being suggested. For your own use, you will find the first wording adequate. Similar considerations apply to declining the invitation.

For the Practice Dialogues

Cover up the Key columns while you fill in the blanks.

နာမည်	*wants to meet again?*	*name*	**KEY**

Dialogues Set 1. You make the suggestion.

ဒေါ်ကြည်ကြည်ရင်	...	Daw Kyi Kyi Yin	Yes
ဦးအောင်ခင်မြင့်	...	U Aung Khin Myint	No
ဒေါ်မေစု	...	Daw Me Suu	No
ဦးမြသိန်း	...	U Mya Thein	Yes

Dialogues Set 2. You respond to the suggestion.

ဒေါ်ခင်မေကြည်	Yes	Daw Khin Me Kyi
ဦးသိန်းလွင်	No	U Thein Lwin
ဒေါ်သိန်းနီ	Yes	Daw Thein Ni
ဦးအောင်သန်း	Yes	U Aung Than
ဒေါ်ခင်မေ	No	Daw Khin Me
ဦးစိုးသိန်း	No	U So Thein

From the magazine မျက်ခင်းသစ်, Sept. 1992
(with the words adapted for our purpose).

Exercise for written answer

Translate the following sentences into Burmese. They illustrate the sequence [verb]–ကြရအောင်
"Let's [verb]."

	KEY TO THE WRITTEN EXERCISE
1. Let's sit here.	၁။ ဒီမှာ ထိုင်ကြရအောင်။
2. Let's go to the market.	၂။ ဈေး သွားကြရအောင်။
3. Let's settle the bill.	၃။ ပိုက်ဆံ ရှင်းကြရအောင်။
4. Let's take a photograph.	၄။ ဓါတ်ပုံ ရိုက်ကြရအောင်။
5. Let's close the window.	၅။ ပြတင်းပေါက် ပိတ်ကြရအောင်။
6. Let's buy a map.	၆။ မြေပုံ ဝယ်ကြရအောင်။
7. Let's meet again.	၇။ နောက်ထပ် တွေ့ကြရအောင်။
8. Let's go to the market again.	၈။ နောက်ထပ် ဈေး သွားကြရအောင်။
9. Let's fix up something (not till) later.	၉။ နောက်မှပဲ စီစဉ်ကြရအောင်။
10. Let's meet again (not till) later.	၁၀။ နောက်မှပဲ တွေ့ကြရအောင်။
11. Let's go to the market (not till) later.	၁၁။ နောက်မှပဲ ဈေး သွားကြရအောင်။
12. Let's take a photograph (not till) later.	၁၂။ နောက်မှပဲ ဓါတ်ပုံ ရိုက်ကြရအောင်။

LEVEL 1, TOPIC 12   MAKING A PHONE CALL

First read through the New Words and the Sample Dialogue.
Then turn on the tape.

New words

ဟလို or ဟယ်လို။	Hallo.	Hălo, Heh-lo
အမိန့် ရှိပါ။	Please speak.	Ămeín shí-ba.
	["order, instruction—have"; used as an alternative or addition to ဟလို]	
ရှိ-	to be [in some place]	shí-
	also = have, there is	
— ဦးတင်လှိုင် ရှိလား။	Is U Tin Hlaing there?	Ù Tin Hlain shí-là?
စကား ပြော-	to talk, speak with	săgà pyàw- ["word—say"]
[noun]–နဲ့	with [noun], [speak] to [person]	-néh
— ဦးတင်လှိုင်နဲ့	I'd like to speak	Ù Tin Hlain-néh
စကားပြောချင်ပါတယ်။	to U Tin Hlaing.	săgà pyàw-jin-ba-deh.

[verb]–နေ–	to be [verb]-ing,	-ne-
	[verb] for the time being; examples:	
— အပြင်မှာ ထိုင်ပါတယ်။	They sat outside.	Ăpyin-hma t'ain-ba-deh.
— အပြင်မှာ ထိုင်နေပါတယ်။	They were sitting outside.	Ăpyin-hma t'ain-ne-ba-deh.
— မြေပုံ ကြည့်ပါတယ်။	They look at the map.	Mye-boun cí-ba-deh.
— မြေပုံ ကြည့်နေပါတယ်။	They are looking at the map.	Mye-boun cí-ne-ba-deh.
— ဦးတင်လှိုင် စကားပြောပါတယ်။	U Tin Hlaing speaks.	Ù Tin Hlain săgà pyàw-ba-deh.
— ဦးတင်လှိုင် စကားပြောနေပါတယ်။	U Tin Hlaing is speaking.	Ù Tin Hlain săgà pyàw-ne-ba-deh.

ခေါ်–	to fetch [also = call, be called]	k'aw-
သွားခေါ်–	to go and fetch	thwà-k'aw-
— သွားခေါ်မယ်။	I'll go and fetch him.	Thwà-k'aw-meh.
— သွားခေါ်ပေးမယ်။	I'll go and fetch him [for you].[1]	Thwà-k'aw-pè-meh.
— သွားခေါ်ခဲ့မယ်။	I'll go and fetch him [and bring him here].[1]	Thwà-k'aw-géh-meh.
— သွားခေါ်လိုက်မယ်။	I'll go and fetch him [and it won't take long].[1]	Thwà-k'aw-laiq-meh.
ကိုင်–	to grasp, hold	kain-
ကိုင်ထား–	to hold [and keep hold] [1]	kain-t'à-
— ခဏ ကိုင်ထားပါ။	Please hold on a minute.	K'ăná kain-t'à-ba.

1. The difference between the English verbs *write* and *write out*, *sit* and *sit down*, *read* and *read through*, is subtle and elusive to describe, but appreciable nonetheless. The difference made to a Burmese verb by adding the suffix –ပေး– or –ခဲ့– or –ထား– or –လိုက်– (-pè, -k'éh, -t'à, -laiq) is of the same order. The meaning suggested by the suffixes is indicated by the words bracketed in the list above, but to use the bracketed words in a translation would be to give too much weight to the additional meaning conveyed by the suffix.

241

Format for the Exercise

Prompt: He sat here.   L/S2: ဒီမှာ ထိုင်တယ်။

Prompt: He was sitting here.   L/S2: ဒီမှာ ထိုင်နေတယ်။

Sample Dialogue

Scene: S2 dials. S1 answers.

The sign ± is used to indicate that any one (or two) of the utterances given to a Speaker may be omitted. And (apart from ဟုတ်ကဲ့ or ဟယ်လို, which come first) the utterances may be used in any order.

±S1: ဟုတ်ကဲ့။   Yes?   Houq-kéh.

±S1: ဟယ်လို။   Hallo.   Heh-lo.

±S1: အမိန့် ရှိပါ။   Hallo?   Ămeín shí-ba.

±S2: ဟုတ်ကဲ့။   Yes.   Houq-kéh.

±S2: ဦးတင်လှိုင် ရှိလား ခင်ဗျာ/ရှင်။   Is U Tin Hlaing there?   Ù Tin Hlain shí-là, k'in-bya/shin.

±S2: ဦးတင်လှိုင်နဲ့ စကား   I'd like to speak   Ù Tin Hlain-néh săgà
      ပြောချင်ပါတယ် ခင်ဗျာ/ရှင်။   to U Tin Hlaing.   pyàw-jin-ba-deh, k'in-bya/shin.

FORK

branch 1

±S1: ဟုတ်ကဲ့။   Yes.   Houq-kéh?

±S1: ကျနော် ဦးတင်လှိုင် စကား   U Tin Hlaing speaking.   Cănaw Ù Tin Hlain săgà
      ပြောနေပါတယ် ခင်ဗျာ။   pyàw-ne-ba-deh, k'in-bya.

S2: အော်။ ဦးတင်လှိုင်လား။   Oh: is that U Tin Hlaing? Aw. Ù Tin Hlain-là?

    စိုးမြင့်ပါ။ [1]   This is So Myint. [1]   Sò Myín-ba.

branch 2

±S1: သွားခေါ်ပေးမယ်။   I'll go and fetch him.   Thwà-k'aw-pè-meh.

    (or သွားခေါ်လိုက်မယ် and the like) (Thwàk'aw-laiq-meh and the like)

±S1: ခဏ ကိုင်ထားပါ။   Please hold on a minute.   K'ăná kain-t'à-ba.

±S2: ဟုတ်ကဲ့။   OK.   Houq-kéh.

±S2: ကောင်းပါပြီ။   Fine.   Kaùn-ba-bi.

±S2: ကိုင်ထားပါမယ်။   I'll hold.   Kain-t'à-ba-meh.

Then back to branch 1, where S1 is now U Tin Hlaing.

1. When you are identifying yourself on the phone, you often omit the prefix before your name: you say စိုးမြင့် rather than ဦးစိုးမြင့် (Ù Sò Myín)

For the Practice Dialogues

Dialogues Set 1. You answer the phone (use ဟုတ်ကဲ့).

Dialogues Set 2. You make the phone call.

Caller	ဒေါ်မေအုံး	ဦးဝင်းနိုင်	မဝင်းဝင်းမေ	ကိုမြင့်ဆွေ	ဒေါ်သီတာအောင်
Asks for	ဒေါ်သန်းဟန်	ဦးလူမော်	ကိုတင်ကျော်လှိုင်	မစောရီ	ဦးတင်ထွန်း

Caller	Daw Me Ohn	U Win Naing	Ma Win Win Me	Ko Myint Swe	Daw Thida Aung
Asks for	Daw Than Han	U Lu Maw	Ko Tin Kyaw Hlaing	Ma Saw Yi	U Tin Tun

■ ကျွန်တော် ပေးပို့ထားသော ကြော်ငြာ များ ပါ၊ မပါ သတင်းစာ ကြည့်နေစဉ် တယ်လီဖုန်း ခေါ်င်းလောင်းသံ မြည်သည်။ သတင်းစာကို စားပွဲပေါ်တင်၍ ဘယ်လက်က တယ်လီဖုန်း စကားပြောခွက်ကို မ,သည်။

"ဟဲလို..အမိန့်ရှိပါခင်ဗျ....၊ မနောသုခ ကြော်ငြာလုပ်ငန်းက ဆွေမျိုး စကားပြော နေပါတယ်"

" ... "

"ဩော်..ဟုတ်ကဲ့..၊ ဘယ်လိုကြော်ငြာ ဖြစ်ဖြစ် ဆောင်ရွက်ပေးပါတယ်ခင်ဗျ။ လူကြီး မင်း အနေနဲ့ ရုပ်မြင်သံကြားမှာ ကြော်ငြာ ချင်သလား၊ ရေဒီယိုမှာ ကြော်ငြာချင်သလား၊ သတင်းစာ–မဂ္ဂဇင်းနဲ့ စာစောင်တွေမှာ ကြော် ငြာချင်သလား၊ ဒါမှမဟုတ် လမ်းဘေးမှာ ဆိုင်းဘုတ်ကြီးတွေ စိုက်ထူ ချင်သလား၊ အဆောက်အဦတွေပေါ်မှာ ဆိုင်းဘုတ်ချိတ် ချင်သလား။ ပိုစတာရိုက်ချင်သလား၊ စတစ် ကာ(ကပ်ခွာ) လုပ်ချင်သလား၊ သော့ချိတ်တို့ လိပ်စာကတ်တို့ လုပ်ချင်သလား၊ ကြော်ငြာ

နည်းပေါင်းစုံ ရှိပါတယ်ခင်ဗျ။ ကျွန်တော် ဆောင်ရွက်ပေးနိုင်ပါတယ်"

" ... "

"ဟုတ်ကဲ့...လာခဲ့ပါခင်ဗျ။ ကျွန်တော်နဲ့ တွေ့ဆုံဆွေးနွေး ရတော့ ပိုကောင်းပါတယ်။ ၃၅လမ်း၊ အလယ်ဘလောက်မှာ ရုံးခန်းရှိပါ တယ်။ မနောသုခလို့ ဆိုင်းဘုတ် ချိတ်ထား ပါတယ်။ ဒါပေမယ့် မွန်းလွဲ ၁နာရီနဲ့ ၂နာရီ ကြားလောက်မှာ မလာပါနဲ့၊ နိုင်ငံခြားကုမ္ပဏီ တစ်ခုက ညည်သည်နဲ့၊ ကြော်ငြာစ္ စကား ပြောဖို့ ချိန်းထားပါတယ်။ ညနေ ၄နာရီခွဲနဲ့ ၆နာရီကြားလည်း မလာပါနဲ့ခင်ဗျာ။ စန္တယာ သိန်းမြင့်သန်း စတူဒီယိုမှာ ရေဒီယိုကြော်ငြာ တစ်ခု အသံသွင်းတာ သွားရောက် ကြည့်ရှု ဖို့ ရှိပါတယ်။ ကျန်တဲ့အချိန်တွေမှာ လာပါ။

ကျွန်တော့် ရုံးခန်းမှာ ည ၁ဝနာရီအထိ ရှိပါတယ်"

" ... "

"ဟုတ်ကဲ့ခင်ဗျာ...ကျေးဇူးပါဲ" စကားပြောခွက်ကို ပြန်ချသည်။

A telephone conversation between an advertizing agency manager and a prospective client. From the magazine မြန်မာ့ဓန nº 31, Jan. 1993, p.32

Exercise for written answer

Translate the following dialogue into Burmese. When writing polite tags: S1 and S2 are male, and S3 is female.

1. S1: Yes? Please go ahead.
2. S2: I'd like to speak to Daw Than Han.
3. S2: Is she at home?
4. S1: Yes, she is.
5. S1: I'll go and fetch her for you.
6. S1: Please hold on a minute (+tag).
7. S2: Yes, fine.
8. S3: Yes?
9. S3: This is Than Han speaking (+tag).
10. S2: Oh. Is that you?
11. S2: This is (= "I am") Myint Swe.

KEY TO THE WRITTEN EXERCISE
ဟုတ်ကဲ့။ အမိန့် ရှိပါ။
ဒေါ်သန်းဟန်နဲ့ စကား ပြောချင်ပါတယ်။
အိမ်မှာ ရှိလား။
ရှိပါတယ်။
သွားခေါ်ပေးမယ်။
ခဏ ကိုင်ထားပါ ခင်ဗျာ။
ဟုတ်ကဲ့။ ကောင်းပါပြီ။
ဟုတ်ကဲ့။
သန်းဟန် စကား ပြောနေပါတယ် ရှင်။
အော်။ ဒေါ်သန်းဟန်လား။
ကျနော်က မြင့်ဆွေပါ။

APPENDIX 1   THE SOUND SYSTEM OF BURMESE

THE SOUNDS OF THE SPOKEN LANGUAGE
AND THE ROMAN LETTERS USED TO REPRESENT THEM

Burmese syllables can be divided into five parts:
for example, the syllable myín မြင့် contains —

1.	a consonant:	m
2.	a medial consonant	y
3.	a vowel:	i
4.	a tone:	´
5.	a final consonant:	n

The sounds of Burmese, and the symbols used in *BISL* to represent them, are listed below in five groups corresponding to these divisions. Remember that there is no standard method of representing Burmese sounds in the roman alphabet: other books and courses use a variety of different conventions.

1. Consonants

roman	script	description
b	ဗ	as in English *bore*
c	ကျ	as in Italian *ciao*, or *'cello*;
		something like *ch* in English *chore*, but made with the flat of the tongue (not the tip) against the palate; and made without aspiration: see under Aspirates below
c'	ချ	see under Aspirates below
d	ဒ	as in English *door*
dh	[ဓ]	like *th* in English *this, there*
g	ဂ	as in English *gore*
h	ဟ	as in English *hoar*
hl	လှ	see under Aspirates below
hm	မှ	" " " "
hn	နှ	" " " "
hng	ငှ	" " " "
hny	ညှ	" " " "
hw	၀ှ	" " " "
j	ဂျ	like *gi* in Italian *Giorgio*;
		something like *j* in English *jaw*, but made with the flat of the tongue (not the tip) against the palate
k	က	like *c* in French *corps*: see under Aspirates below
k'	ခ	like *c* in English *core*: see under Aspirates below
l	လ	as in English *law*
m	မ	as in English *more*

n	၌	as in English *nor;* see also under Final consonants below
ng	င	like *ng* in English *long oar*
ny	ည	like *gn* in Italian *gnocchi;*
		something like *ni* in English *senior,* but made with the flat of the tongue (not the tip) against the palate
p	ပ	as in French *port:* see under Aspirates below
p'	ဖ	as in English *pore:* see under Aspirates below
q	[ဝ်]	see under Final consonants below
r	ရ	as in English *raw* (mostly in foreign words)
s	စ	as in English *soar:* see under Aspirates below
s'	ဆ	see under Aspirates below
sh	ရှ	as in English *shore*
t	တ	as in French *tort:* see under Aspirates below
t'	ထ	as in English *tore:* see under Aspirates below
th	သ	as in English *thaw*
w	ဝ	as in English *war;* and see under Medial consonants below
y	ယ	as in English *your;* and see under Medial consonants below
z	ဇ	as in English *zone*

Aspirate consonants

Burmese has two sets of corresponding pairs of consonants:

k'	t'	p'	c'	s'		ခ	ထ	ဖ	ဆျ	ဆ
k	t	p	c	s		က	တ	ပ	ကျ	စ

Those on the first line are known as "aspirate" consonants, and those on the second are known as the corresponding "plain" or "unaspirated" consonants. The difference between the two sets is that the aspirate consonants have a short puff of breath expelled after the consonant is pronounced and before the vowel begins; while after a plain consonant there is no audible breath: the vowel begins immediately the consonant has been pronounced.

Put this way, this distinction may sound unfamiliar, but you have probably heard examples of both aspirate and plain consonants, perhaps without being aware of the difference. Most speakers of English use aspirate consonants in words like *kill, till, pill.* To a Burmese ear these words sound like k'ill, t'ill, p'ill. Plain consonants on the other hand are used in French and Italian: think of French words like *casse, tasse, passe.* French and Italian speakers (and Indians and Pakistanis even more noticeably) often use these plain consonants when they speak English — a habit that helps to make their English sound "foreign." They say kill, till, pill instead of k'ill, t'ill, p'ill. Burmese uses both sets and gives equal status to each. Careful listening to the tapes will help you recognize and pronounce the two sets differently.

The paired aspirate and plain consonants in the other group are these:

hng	hn	hm	hny	hl	hw		ှင	ှန	ှမ	ှည	ှလ	ှဝ
ng	n	m	ny	l	w		င	န	မ	ည	လ	ဝ

Those on the first line are sometimes called breathed or voiceless consonants. They are pronounced like the plain set, but with breath expelled quietly through the nose (through the mouth for hl hw) before voicing begins.

h m is like	English *hmm*	in *"Hmm — let me see"*
h l is like	Welsh *ll*	in *Llandudno*
h w is like	English *wh*	in "breathy" pronunciations of *what, where,* and the like.

The remaining consonants in this set — hng, hn, hny — are produced by the same mechanism as h m.

2. Medial consonants

Some consonants may be followed by a "medial" consonant: y or w; for example:

	y	in Daw Myá Myá	(name)	ဒေါ်မြမြ
and	w	in mwè-né	birthday	မွေးနေ့

3. Vowels

(for descriptions of -q and -n see under Final consonants below)

roman	script	description
ă	[အ]	like *a* in English *about*
a	အာ	like *a* in English *car,*
		but closer to *a* in French *car*
a in aq and an	အတ်၊ အန်	like *a* in English *cat* and *can*
ai in aiq and ain	အိုက်၊ အိုင်	like *i* in English *site* and *sine*
au in auq and aun	အောက်၊ အောင်	like *ou* in English *lout* and *lounge*
e	အေ	like *é* in French *élève*
e in eh	အယ်	like *e* in English *sell*
e in eq	အက်	like *e* in English *set*
ei in eiq and ein	အိတ်၊ အိန်	like *a* in English *late* and *lane*
i	အီ	like *i* in English *ravine*
i in iq and in	အစ်၊ အည်/အင်	like *i* in English *sit* and *sin*
aw	အော်	like *aw* in English *saw*
o	အို	like *eau* in French *peau*
ou in ouq and oun	အုတ်၊ အုန်	like *o* in English *tote* and *tone*
u	အူ	like *u* in English *Susan*
u in uq and un	အွတ်၊ အွန်	like *oo* in English *foot* and *full*

4. Tones

Tones are marked in the *BISL* transcription by accents (or absence of accent) placed over the vowel. They are illustrated here with the vowel a.

a	အာ	low pitch, called "low" tone
		(marked here by having no printed accent):
à	အား	high pitch spoken with normal or relaxed throat: "plain high tone"
á	အာ့	high pitch spoken with a tightened throat: "creaky high tone"

There are two other kinds of syllable in Burmese. Though they don't have a place in the three-way contrast just described, they are listed here for completeness.

aq   အတ်   high pitch, followed by a glottal stop, called a "stopped" syllable (may be pronounced with low pitch when followed by a high tone)

ă   [အ]   low pitch, only on the vowel ă,
called a "weak" syllable (may be pronounced with high pitch if sandwiched between two high tones). Also called "reduced" or "unstressed" syllable.

Schematically, the tones can be arranged like this:

	plain	creaky	stopped	weak
high pitch	à အား	á အာ့/အ	aq အတ်	—
low pitch	a အာ	—	—	ă [အ]

It should be understood that "low pitch" and "high pitch" are relative terms:
       "low"   means lower than neighbouring highs, and
       "high"   means higher than neighbouring lows.
A syllable spoken in isolation can't readily be identified as having either high or low pitch (though it may be distinguished by features other than pitch, namely creakiness, glottal stop, or weak vowel).

The pronunciation exercises on the tapes will help you distinguish the tones.
Here are some examples:

tone	roman	meaning	script
low	sa-ba-deh	compares	စာပါတယ်
high plain	sà-ba-deh	eats	စားပါတယ်
high creaky	sá-ba-deh	begins	စပါတယ်
high stop	saq-pa-deh	is hot to taste	စပ်ပါတယ်
weak (low)	săne-nan	Saturday name	စနေနံ
low	da paun-ba	that's a pound	ဒါ ပေါင်ပါ
high plain	da zeì-ba	that's a market	ဒါ ဈေးပါ
high creaky	da s'ín-ba	that's a cent	ဒါ ဆင့်ပါ
high stop	da eiq-pa	that's a bag	ဒါ အိတ်ပါ
weak (low)	da Băma-ba	that's a Burman	ဒါ ဗမာပါ

5. Final consonants

-n   –င် –ည် –န် –မ်   represents nasalization, as in French *un, bon, vin, Jean*
-q   –က် –စ် –တ် –ပ်   represents a glottal stop,
                                 as in "Cockney" English *"The ca' sa' on the ma' ,"*
                                 or (in our transcription) "The caq saq on the maq."

APPENDIX 2 LANGUAGE-LEARNING AIDS

BURMESE LANGUAGE-LEARNING MATERIALS

The following is a list of some other learning aids you may find useful. It covers material published up to 1992. Most teachers of Burmese supplement published work with unpublished materials they have written themselves, and you may be able to obtain lists and copies of further material from them.

Course books and grammars

The script

An Introduction to the Burmese Writing System, by H. D. Roop. New Haven, Yale University Press, 1972. A programmed, teach-yourself course, that assumes you are already familiar with the pronunciation.

Burmese: An Introduction to the Script, by John Okell. Parallel with this volume. With tapes. Includes appendices on handwriting forms, display types, alphabetical order, abbreviations, and other topics.

Some spoken language courses also contain sections on the script: see below.

The spoken language (entries are in date order, most recent first)

(a) for speakers of English

Burmese: An Introduction to the Spoken Language, Book 2, by John Okell. Continuation from *Book 1.* All in script, with tapes. Sample dialogues and practice dialogues for a set of 12 situations, including survival (shops, taxis and so on) and social (Where are you from? Are you married? Shall we meet again? and so on)

First Steps in Burmese, by John Okell. London, SOAS, 1989. Text and vocabulary with 5 x 90 min. tapes. A brief foundation course, designed to develop fluency and comprehension. Mainly exercises for practising question and answer, using vocabulary appropriate to the classroom (timetables, calendars, maps, price lists and so on). Script is used alongside romanized versions, but not taught in the book. Superseded by this course.

Burmese Phrase Book, by David Bradley. South Yarra, Australia, Lonely Planet, 1988. 125 pp. Very compact: 3.5 x 5 inches. Has roman and Burmese script. Sections on: pronunciation, grammar, greetings, smalltalk, accommodation, getting around, around town, in the country, food, shopping, health, times and dates, numbers. No tapes.

Beginning Burmese, by W. S. Cornyn and H. D. Roop. 1987 reprint. See full entry below.

Burma: a Seven Day Burmese Language Survival Guide on cassette, by Robin Carter *alias* Hla Aung: £5.95 from the author at 27 Oval Road, East Croydon, Surrey CR0 6BJ. ?1987. One tape of words and phrases with notes. No script.

Spoken Burmese, by W. S. Cornyn. 1979 reprint. See full entry below.

Spoken Burmese, by U Khin. Washington DC, Dept of State, Foreign Service Institute, 2 volumes, 1976. 643 and 479 pp.

A Reference Grammar of Colloquial Burmese, by John Okell. London, Oxford University Press, 2 volumes, 1969. A description, no exercises, no training in script. Volume 2 is a list of grammatical forms with translations and examples.

Beginning Burmese, by W. S. Cornyn and H. D. Roop. New Haven, Yale University Press, 1968. 501pp, reprinted 1987. Book and 25 tapes including exercises. Dialogues, explanations and exercises, including sections introducing the script; copious drills. Helpful explanations of grammar. Tapes available separately.

Lessons in Spoken Burmese, by Emily Ballard. Rangoon, Burma Baptist Convention, 1961. A well set out introduction, with exercises, and a good section introducing the script. Some Christian missionary content.

Burmese: Basic Course, by U.S. Defense Language Institute. Monterey CA, Dept of Defense, 1957. Well presented, thorough drills. Some military content.

Spoken Burmese, by W. S. Cornyn. New York, Henry Holt, 2 volumes, 1945; reprinted Ithaca NY, Spoken Language Services, 1979. With tapes. U.S. War Dept Education Manual 541-542, designed for U.S. Army personnel in wartime; forerunner of Beginning Burmese; uses pre-decimal coinage, discourteous style, but has good exercises. No script.

(b) for speakers of other languages

Manuel de birman, by Denise Bernot, Marie-Hélène Cardinaud, Daw Yin Yin Myint. Paris, L'Asiathèque, volume 1, 1990. 246 pp and 2 tapes.

Burmesisches Übungsbuch, by Annemarie Esche and Eberhardt Richter, unter Mitarbeit von U Khin Maung Saw. Leipzig, VEB Verlag. 1988. 12 Units and tape: to accompany Richter's *Lehrbuch*. Enables learner to conduct simple conversations.

Biruma-go yonshukan (Burmese in four weeks), by Ono Toru. Tokyo, Daigaku Shorin, 1986. 274pp. Explanations in Japanese.

Lehrbuch des modernen Burmesisch, by E. Richter. Leipzig, VEB Verlag, 1983. 405pp. Script and colloquial. Hard work as a course book, but sound and useful as a reference grammar.

Eigo taisho Biruma-go kaiwa ("Burmese conversation with English equivalents"), by Ono Toru. Tokyo, Daigaku Shorin, 1982. A phrase book, arranged by situations ("At the post office" and so on), in 3 columnss: Japanese, Burmese (in Burmese script), English. No explanations.

Deutsch-Burmesisches Gesprächsbuch, by E. Richter and Maung Than Zaw. Leipzig, VEB, 1969. 306pp. A phrase book, German-Burmese, "Occupations" and so on.

The literary language

Burmese: An Introduction to the Literary Style, by John Okell. Parallel with this course. Texts and exercises. Assumes a modest command of colloquial style, and ability to read the script.

A Reference Grammar of Literary and Colloquial Burmese, by Anna J. Allot and John Okell. In preparation at SOAS.

Other study aids

Readers

Burmese Chrestomathy, by W. S. Cornyn. Washington, ACLS, 1957. A selection of texts, colloquial and literary: narrative, dialogue, short stories, radio broadcasts, newspaper extracts, and so on. Typewritten text.

Burmese Glossary, by W. S. Cornyn and J. K. Musgrave. Washington, ACLS, 1958. About 11,000 entries. A glossary of words and phrases found in the Chrestomathy, sometimes also handy as a supplement to other dictionaries.

Unpublished: SOAS has a set of texts provided with notes and vocabularies, including comics, novels, short stories, memoirs, personal correspondence. For distribution to students.

Listening

Unpublished: SOAS has a set of tapes provided with notes and vocabularies, including radio interviews, radio plays and feature programs. For distribution to students.

Viewing

Video tapes made in Burma can be used in teaching, but so far there do not seem to be any provided with study aids.

Dictionaries

Burmese-Burmese

မြန်မာ အဘိဓာန် အကျဉ်းချုပ် *(Concise Burmese Dictionary)*, by မြန်မာစာအဖွဲ့။ Rangoon, Myanmar Language Commission, 5 volumes, 1978-80. About 28,000 entries. A reduced and completed version of the unfinished တက္ကသိုလ် မြန်မာအဘိဓာန်. Accurate and comprehensive, with pronunciation and diagrams. Very useful.

တက္ကသိုလ် မြန်မာအဘိဓာန် *(University Burmese Dictionary)*, by U Wun and others. Rangoon, Government Printing, parts 1-5, 1952-1964. Incomplete: covers letters က to ဆ. Accurate and more detailed than the အကျဉ်းချုပ် , with quotations and references, but no guide to pronunciation.

မြန်မာ အဘိဓာန် *(Burmese Dictionary)*, by မြန်မာစာအဖွဲ့။ Rangoon, Myanmar Language Commission, 1991. Estimated 28,000 entries. An improved version of the မြန်မာ အဘိဓာန် အကျဉ်းချုပ် . Printed in one volume, with improved alphabetical order, full etymologies, and pronunciation as before. Very useful.

Burmese-other languages

Burmese-English

မြန်မာ–အင်္ဂလိပ်အဘိဓာန် *(Myanmar-English Dictionary)*, by မြန်မာစာအဖွဲ့။ Rangoon, Myanmar Language Commission, 1993. The best available: up to date, concise, and accurate.

A Dictionary, Burmese and English, by A. Judson. 1st ed. Maulmain, ABM Press, 1852, followed by many revisions and reprints. 10th ed. Rangoon, Burma Baptist Board, 1966. 1200 pp. Most recent reprint: Hotaka Book Co Ltd (2-43 Kanda Jimbo-cho, chiyoda-ku, Tokyo), 1989. 643 pp: reprint of 1883. About 18,000 entries. The standard B-E dictionary for over a century. Last revised in 1914, so now very dated but still useful.

A *Burmese-English Dictionary*, by J. A. Stewart et al. London, Luzac (vols 1-2), SOAS (vols 3-6), 1941-80. Unfinished: covers all words beginning with the syllable အ. Accurate, detailed, academic, with pronunciation, quotations, and references.

The Universal Burmese-English-Pali Dictionary, by Hoke Sein. Rangoon, Myitzu-thaka, 1981. 1066pp. About 68,000 entries. Large and up to date, but only gives one or two translation equivalents for each Burmese word, so does not give a rounded picture of the range of meanings of the word. The compounds listed help to make up for this shortcoming. Strong on terms from law and administration. Also gives the Pali equivalent.

The Thalun Burmese-English Pocket Dictionary, by U Tint Win Naing. Rangoon, Dipa-mye, 1989. 485 pp. The coverage is gappy, as it is intended for Burmese needing an English word, and does not have entries for all the obvious words.

Burmese-French

Dictionnaire birman-français (Burmese-French dictionary), by Denise Bernot. Paris, SELAF, 15 volumes, 1978-1993. About 40,000 entries. Concise and up to date, very comprehensive, with pronunciation and diagrams.

Burmese-Chinese

Mu-fen Mien-hua ta-tz'u-tien (A model Burmese-Chinese dictionary) by Chen Yi Sein. Tokyo, Toyo Bunko, 1970. 1st ed. Rangoon, Chen Yi Sein, 1962.

Miàn Hàn Cí-diǎn (Burmese-Chinese dictionary), by Burmese Language Teaching and Research Office, Dept of Eastern Languages and Literatures, Beijing University. Beijing, Commercial Press, 1990. About 1200 pp. Gives word-class in Burmese, pronunciation in roman, meaning in Chinese.

Burmese-German

Wörterbuch Burmesisch-Deutsch (Burmese-German dictionary) by Annemarie Esche. Leipzig, VEB, 1976. About 17,000 entries. Up to date and useful, but not comprehensive.

Burmese-Russian

Birmansko-Russkiy slovar' (Burmese-Russian dictionary) by G. F. Minina and U Kyaw Zaw. Moscow, Russkii Iazyk, 1976. About 29,000 entries. Good coverage, with appendices on grammar, names, abbreviations and other topics.

Burmese-Japanese

Biruma-go joyo 6,000-go (Burmese-Japanese vocabulary) by Ono Toru. Tokyo, Daigaku Shorin, 1984. 525pp. Actually contains about 9,000 entries.

Biruma-go Jiten (Burmese dictionary) by Harada Masaharu and Ono Toru. Tokyo, Nihon Biruma Bunka Kyo-kai, 1979.

Other languages-Burmese

English-Burmese

The University English Burmese Dictionary, by Ba Han. Rangoon, Hanthawaddy Press, 2 vols, 1951-1952; reprinted in one vol. 1966. The largest EB dictionary

A Dictionary, English and Burmese, by A. Judson. 1st ed. Maulmain, ABM Press, 1849; 10th ed. Rangoon, The Baptist Board of Publication, 1966.

The Student's English-Burmese Dictionary, by U Tun Nyein. Rangoon, Myo Nyunt, 1971; 1st ed. 1906. 1192pp.

and many other E-B dictionaries published in Burma.

Russian-Burmese

Karmannyj Russko-birmanskij slovar', by U Kyin We and A J Borovikov.   Moscow, Gosudarstvennoe Izdatel'stvo Inostrannuikh i Natsional'nuikh Slovarei, 1962. 756 pp.

Japanese-Burmese

ဂျပန်မြန်မာ အဘိဓာန် by U E Cho and Ono Toru. Rangoon, Universities' Press, 1982. 728pp

Biruma-go kiso 1500-go by Toru Ono. Tokyo, Daigaku Shorin, 1980. 130 pp, 1500 entries.

French-Burmese

Dictionnaire de base français-birman, by Emmanuel Guillon and Claude Delachet. Rangoon, 1972. Compiled for use in French language teaching in Rangoon.

Pali-Burmese

ပါဠိအဘိဓာန်ချုပ် [ရေးသူ] လယ်တီပဏ္ဍိတ။ 2nd imp., Rangoon, Ledi Taya Thadinza Press, no date (around1908). 627 pp.

Other reference sources

The Pali Text Society's Pali-English Dictionary, by T. W. Rhys Davids and W. Stede. Chipstead, The Pali Text Society, 1925. 203 pp. Comprehensive and authoritative.

Pali-English Dictionary, by A. P. Buddhadatta. 2nd ed. Colombo, Colombo Apothecaries' Company, 1958. Compact and useful.

Dictionary of Pali Proper Names, by G. P. Malalasekara. London, Luzac for the Pali Text Society, 1960. 1162 + 1370 pp. Indispensable for references to Pali names of people, places and texts.

Burma (World bibliographical series 132), by P. Herbert. Oxford, Clio Press, 1991. 327 pp. A very informed and informative bibliography.

Bibliography and Index of Mainland Southeast Asian Languages and Linguistics, by F. E. Huffman.   New Haven and London, Yale University Press, 1986.   640 pp. Comprehensive.

မြန်မာ့စွယ်စုံကျမ်း။ (Burmese encyclopedia). Rangoon, Burma Translation Society, 15 volumes, 1954-1976. Mainly committed to informing the Burmese reader about the world, but the entries on Burmese topics (music, literature, places, people and others) are very useful.

စာဆိုတော်များအတ္ထုပ္ပတ္တိ (Lives of literary figures) [ရေးသူ] မောင်သုတ။ Rangoon, Shumawa Press, 1962 and later reprints. 634 pp. Brief accounts of the lives and works of 168 Burmese authors from early to recent times.

Alphabetical Order in Burmese, by John Okell. Journal of the Burma Research Society 51, 145-171, 1968.   Describes the main systems in use and makes suggestions for improvements.

A Guide to the Romanization of Burmese, by John Okell. London, Luzac for the Royal Asiatic Society, 1971.   69 pp.   Surveys the main approaches and makes recommendations among them.

APPENDIX 3   ROMANIZING BURMESE

3.1   Burmese written in Burmese script

Burmese is written in its own script, and although you can learn to speak a little without learning to read the script, it makes learning much easier if you can read it. You are strongly advised to learn the script as quickly as you can. There is an introduction to the script parallel with this course.

3.2   Burmese written in roman letters

Most people, understandably, want to start learning to speak some Burmese while they are still learning the script and before they can yet read it comfortably. For this transition phase we need some way of presenting Burmese words on the page in the familiar roman letters. This is easier said than done. Burmese pronunciation includes sounds that the roman alphabet is not normally asked to represent.

Traditional romanization

Traditionally people who have needed to write Burmese words and names in roman letters (journalists, travellers, mapmakers, ...) have done the best they can to match the unmatchable. Over time certain conventions have become established as to which Burmese sounds are represented by which roman letters, and for non-linguistic purposes this rough and ready "traditional romanization" serves its purpose.

For a language learner, however, the traditional romanization is far from adequate. Words romanized in the ad hoc traditional way don't show tone, they don't reliably show whether a consonant is aspirated or not, and they don't always distinguish one vowel from another. As a result, the syllable written "pe" (for example) in the traditional romanization, may represent any one of 12 different syllables in pronunciation:

ေပ   ေပ့   ေပး   ဖယ်   ဖဲ့   ဖဲ

ေဖ   ေဖ့   ေဖး   ပယ်   ပဲ့   ပဲ

For the learner of the language, ambiguity of this order is intolerable. It is like providing, for a foreign learner of English, one written syllable to cover the sounds of the eight English words *pat, bat, pet, bet, pad, bad, ped,* and *bed*.

A further deficiency is that traditional romanization often offers two, or sometimes three, different ways of romanizing the same sound. So the Burmese word ေမ, for example, may be romanized *me,* or *may,* or *mae,* or *mai*. This inconsistency is particularly rife in Burmese personal names, where some people deliberately adopt a variant spelling for their own name in order to make it more distinctive.

Systematic romanization

To remedy this weakness, foreign students and scholars have applied themselves to the task of devising a romanization in which each sound of the language is unambiguously distinguished. Such a romanization is called a "systematic romanization." Devising a systematic romanization means allotting to some of the roman letters values they don't normally carry, and that makes the matching of letters and sounds more or less arbitrary. As a result, almost every scholar who has written about Burmese has come up with a romanization that is different from those of his predecessors. Each writer finds some elements of the other systems illogical, or hard to remember, or implausible, and makes his own attempts to improve on them, so there is still no widely accepted standard system for the systematic romanization of Burmese. (For more on this topic, see my booklet *A Guide to the Romanization of Burmese.*)

The system used in this course differs in some respects from those in other courses. I introduced the changes because I hoped they would make the romanization easier for learners to use. However, all romanizations have their shortcomings, and I strongly recommend that you learn to use the script as soon as you can.

3.3   Showing pronunciation

Like English, Burmese is a language in which the pronunciation has changed in various ways since the writing system was established. The result is that many words written in Burmese script look as if they should be read with one pronunciation, but in practice are spoken and read with a different one (there are many parallels in English; for example, the word you write "plumber" and read "plummer"). So books for language learners need a way of indicating the pronunciation of such words. One way of doing this is to write the systematic romanization for the word alongside the script version. Another is to respell the word in Burmese script, using the normal values for the Burmese letters.

Most English dictionaries give a guide to the pronunciation of each entry by respelling it in letters that have defined values; for example:

| head | hed | [not the heed you would expect on the basis of "bead"] |
| who | hoo | [not the wō you would expect on the basis of "which" and "go"] |

A similar respelling system exists in Burmese, and in some ways it is easier to use than a systematic romanization. It entails assigning fewer unconventional values to the letters. When words are respelled to show their pronunciation, the respelled word is placed between slashes; for example:

script	*pronunciation in script*
ရွှေတိဂုံ	/ရွှေဒဂုန်/
ဘုရား	/ဖယား/

The Burmese respelling system was first presented in the *Concise Burmese Dictionary* compiled and published by the Burma Language Commission (မြန်မာအဘိဓာန် အကျဉ်းချုပ်။ မြန်မာစာအဖွဲ့.). It is set out again in the Script course parallel with this Spoken Language course.

In this course we rewrite Burmese words in two ways: (a) in a systematic romanization (for those who can't yet read the script, and to show pronunciation); and (b) respelled in Burmese script (to show pronunciation for those who find this easier to read than the systematic roman transcription).

3.4   Romanized names of Burmese people and places

Traditional romanization

Most books and press reports about Burma in foreign languages write the the names of people and places in *traditional* romanization. In some cases, this version of a name may differ markedly from the *systematic* romanization. So when Burmese names come up in this course, you will find them presented in four different versions:

	Example:
1. in Burmese script	စိုလ်ချုပ်
2. in Burmese script rewritten (to show the pronunciation)	/ဗိုဂျုတ်/
3. in systematic romanization (ditto), and	Bo-jouq
4. in traditional romanization (to help you recognize the name)	Bogyoke

Established foreign equivalents

A further complication for place names is that in some cases a version of the name has gained currency in English (and other languages) which suggests a pronunciation that diverges considerably from the sound of the Burmese name. It is not obviously close to either the systematic romanization or the traditional romanization. An example is the name of the capital city, which is —

> written: ရန်ကုန်
>
> pronounced: /ယန်ဂုန်/ Yan-goun
>
> and has the established foreign equivalent: Rangoon

The established English equivalent *Munich* for the German name *München* is a parallel case.

Revised foreign equivalents

In 1989 the Burmese government ruled that the established foreign equivalents for such names should be replaced by a traditional romanization of the Burmese form of the name. So in place of "Rangoon," people are urged to write "Yangon." For examples of more place names with established foreign equivalents, see Lesson 19.

> Dr. Mason had consulted with the Secretariat on the question of an uniform scheme of Burmese transliteration to be employed in the forthcoming work. He pointed out that no recognized system was at present in force: every Government servant was at liberty to follow his own method; the result being that the English equivalents for even the commonest vernacular names were very rarely alike in two publications. ... I have seen the name of a large district in the Tenasserim Division transliterated in the following ways: — Shwegheen, Shwaygheen, Shwaygyen, Shwayghen, Shwaygyen, Showegyen, Showegyeen.
>
> From: *Burmese Transliteration*, by H. L. St. Barbe. Journal of the Royal Asiatic Society, vol. 10, 1878, p. 229.

APPENDIX 4

INDEX TO NOTES AND MAPS IN BOOK 1
Figures refer to Lessons

APPENDIX 5   VOCABULARIES

This section lists words introduced in all parts of Book 1: Part 1 (Groundwork), the Common Phrases Supplement, and Level 1 of Part 2 (Dialogues). The vocabulary list appears three times, each time with a different element at the head of each entry, which determines the order in which the entries are listed:

   5.1. Burmese-English, headed by the entry word in Burmese script. This list is in Burmese alphabetical order.

   5.2. Burmese-English, headed by the entry word in roman transcription, for users who cannot yet read Burmese script. This list is in roman alphabetical order.

   5.3. English-Burmese, in roman alphabetical order.

5.1 Burmese-English vocabulary (entry words in Burmese script)

Conventions

The elements of each entry below are illustrated in the following sample entry:

ခါတ်ပုံ	the entry word. A hyphen after an entry word shows it is a verb. Suffixes to sentences and phrases are shown preceded by S- and P- respectively.
/ဒတ်ပုံ/	indication of pronunciation in script, where not easily predictable from the spelling
daq-poun	pronunciation shown in romanization
>	sign showing end of entry word and start of translation or explanation
photograph	translation or explanation
["technical-picture"]	note on the meanings of the parts of the entry word
D2	reference to the point in Book 1 where the word is introduced or commented on. G5 = Groundwork, Lesson 5; CP5 = Common Phrases, Section 5; D3 = Dialogues, Level 1, Topic 3.
◊	sign showing that an example (or compound) follows
ခါတ်ပုံ ရိုက်–	example or compound
to take a photograph	translation of preceding

------------- က – ခ – ဂ – ဃ – င ---------------

က in: [place]–က လာ– [place]-gá la- > to come from [place] G31

ကရဝိက် ဟိုတယ် /ကရဝိတ်–/ Kărăweiq Ho-teh > Karaweik Hotel D3

ကဲ kèh > There. Right. Well. ◊ ကဲ။ ရပြီ။ Kèh. Yá-bi. There. Got it. CP14; ကဲ။ ပြီးပြီ။ Kèh. Pì-bi. > There. That's done. CP14

ကော in: [noun]–ကော or [noun]–ရော -gàw, -yàw > How about [noun]? CP4, D10B

ကော်ဖီ kaw-p'i > coffee D4

ကော်ဖီမှုန့် kaw-p'i-hmoún > instant coffee ["coffee-powder"] G40

ကို Ko > (prefix for names of younger men) G24

ကိုကာကိုလာ Ko-ka-ko-la > Coca-cola D4

ကိုရီးယား Ko-rì-yà > Korea G34

257

ကိုး kò > nine G4

ကောင်း– kaùn- > to be good D6; ◊ ကောင်းပါပြီ Kaùn-ba-bi > Goodbye CP5, CP11; Very well. Fine. OK. CP12, CP19

ကိုင်– kain- > to grasp, hold D12; ခဏ ကိုင်ထားပါ။ K'ăná kain-t'à-ba. > Please hold on a minute. D12

ကိစ္စ keiq-sá > business, matter, affair, activity; ◊ ကိစ္စ မရှိပါဘူး။ Keiq-sá măshí-ba-bù. > No problem. CP8, CP9; It doesn't matter. CP13

ကုန် koun > goods, merchandise G3

ကုန်တိုက် /–ဒိုက်/ koun-daiq > department store G35

ကုန်သည်လမ်း /–သုယ်–/ Koun-dheh Làn > Merchant Street G7

ကမ်းနားလမ်း Kàn-nà Làn > Strand Road G7

ကျ– cá- > to fall, fall in place, amount to D4; ◊ ဘယ်လောက် ကျသလဲ။ Beh-lauq cá-dhălèh? > How much does that come to? D4

ကျနော့် cănáw > my (man speaking) D10A; ◊ ဒါ ကျနော့်ဘောပင်ပါ။ Da cănáw bàw-pin-ba. That's my pen (man speaking). D10A

ကျမ cămá > I, my (woman speaking) D10A; ◊ ဒါ ကျမဘောပင်ပါ။ Da cămá bàw-pin-ba. That's my pen (woman speaking). D10A

ကျေးဇူး တင်ပါတယ်။ Cè-zù tin-ba-deh. > Thank you. CP9

ကျပ် caq > kyat G32

ကြည့်– /ကျိ/ cí- > to look, look around, look at D5; ◊ ကြည့်အုံးမယ်နော်။ Cí-oùn-meh-naw? > I'll carry on looking, if you don't mind. D5

ကွာလာလမ်ပူ Kwa-la Lan-pu > Kuala Lumpur G15

ကျွန်တော့် cun-dáw > full form of ကျနော့် cănáw G32

ကျွန်မ cun-má > full form of ကျမ cămá G32

ခဏ k'ăná > moment; ◊ ခဏလေးနော်။ K'ăná-lè-naw? > Just a moment, OK? CP8, CP14

ခဏခဏ /ခနှ ခနှ/ k'ăná-k'ăná > frequently, often, many times D7

ခုနစ် k'ú-niq, k'ú-hniq, k'un > seven G4, G6

ခဲ့ in: [verb]–ခဲ့– -géh-/-k'éh > used with verbs involving movement "from somewhere else to here"; ◊ သွားခေါ်ခဲ့မယ်။ Thwà-k'aw-géh-meh. > I'll go and fetch him [and bring him here]. D12. In other contexts –ခဲ့– -géh-/-k'éh implies that the action takes place (a) somewhere other than here ("How long did you spend there?"); or (b) in the past ("Burma was ruled by Burmese kings.")

ခေါ်– k'aw- > to call, to be called G36; to fetch D12; ◊ သွားခေါ်– thwà-k'aw- > to go and fetch D12

ခင်ဗျာ K'in-bya > (polite tag, like Monsieur/Madame, used by male speakers) CP10

ချင်– in: [verb]–ချင်– [verb]-jin- > to want to [verb] G42

ခြောက် c'auq > six G4

ခွဲ -gwèh/-k'wèh > - and a half G37, G38; ◊ တစ်နာရီခွဲ tăna-yi-gwèh 1.30 ["one hour and a half"]; ◊ သုံးနာရီခွဲ thoùn-na-yi-gwèh 3.30 ["three hours and a half"]; ◊ သုံးကျပ်ခွဲ thoùn-jaq-k'wèh K3.50 ["three kyats and a half"]

ခွက် k'weq > cup, glass D4

ခွင့် k'wín > permission, authorization; ◊ ခွင့်ပြုပါအုံး။ K'wín pyú-ba-oùn. > May I leave now? CP19

ဂျပန်နိုင်ငံ Jăpan Naing-ngan > Japan G13

ဂျာမနီ Ja-măni > Germany G34

ငါး ngà > five G2

ငါးမူး ngà-mù > half a kyat G38

-------------- စ – ဆ – ဇ – ဈ – ည --------------

စကား ပြော– săgà pyàw- > to talk, speak, have conversation; ◊ စကား ပြောလို့ ကောင်းပါတယ်။ Săgà pyàw-ló kaùn-ba-deh. > I enjoyed talking to you. CP20; ◊ ဗမာစကား ပြောတာ ကောင်းပါတယ်။ Băma săgà pyàw-da kaùn-ba-deh. > Your spoken Burmese is good. D6; ◊ ဦးတင်လှိုင်နဲ့ စကားပြောချင်ပါတယ်။ Ù Tin Hlain-néh săgà pyàw-jin-ba-deh. > I'd like to speak to U Tin Hlaing. D12

စထရင်းဟိုတယ် Săt'ărìn Ho-teh > Strand Hotel G5

စပါကလင် Săpa-kălin > Sparkling [a bottled drink like Lilt, Seven-up and similar] D4

စရာ in: [verb]–စရာ [verb]-săya > things that have to be [verb]-ed; ◊ လုပ်စရာ များပါတယ်။ Louq-săya myà-ba-deh. I have a lot to do. D11

စာကြည့်တိုက် /–ကျိဒိုက်/ sa-cí-daiq > library G35

စာရွက် sa-yweq > writing paper ["paper-sheet"] G40

စာအိတ် sa-eiq > envelope ["letter-bag"] G40

စားပွဲ /စပွဲ/ săbwèh > table, desk G43

စားသောက်ခန်း sà-thauq-k'àn > eating room, canteen G35

စီစဉ်– /စီဇင်/ si-zin- > to arrange, fix up D11

စင်္ကာပူ /စင်ဂါ/ Sin-ga-pu > Singapore G34

စစ်ကိုင်း /ဇဂိုင်း/ Săgaìn > Sagaing G19

ဆရာ S'ăya > Teacher (male and generic) CP2

ဆရာမ S'ăya-má > Teacher (female) CP2

ဆူးလေဘုရား /–ဖယား/ S'ù-le P'ăya > Sule Pagoda G5; ◊ ဆူးလေဘုရားလမ်း S'ù-le P'ăyà Làn > Sule Pagoda Road G9

ဆောရီး s'àw-rì > sorry; ◊ ဆောရီးပဲ။ S'àw-rì-bèh. > Sorry! CP13; ◊ ဆောရီးနော် S'àw-rì-naw > Sorry! D1

ဆင့် s'ín > cent G26

ဆယ် s'eh > ten G4

ဆယ်လိုတိပ် s'eh-lo-teiq > sellotape/Scotchtape [from English] G40

ဈေး /ဇေး/ zè > market G1

-------------- တ – ထ – ဒ – ဓ – န --------------

တကယ် tăgeh > really, in truth, actually, in fact D6; ◊ တကယ်ပဲလား။ Tăgeh-bèh-là? > Really? Do you mean it? D6

တရုပ်နိုင်ငံ or တရုတ်နိုင်ငံ Tăyouq Naing-ngan > China G13

တာ da in: [verb] –တာ > turns a verb (like *speak*) into a noun (like *speaking, speech*); ◊ ဗမာစကား ပြောတာ ကောင်းပါတယ်။ Băma săgà pyàw-da kaùn-ba-deh. > Your spoken Burmese is good. D6

တာ in: [verb]–တာပဲ [verb]-da-bèh > similar to [verb]–ပါတယ် -ba-deh, but a little more exclamatory D6; ◊ သိပ် ကောင်းတာပဲ။ Theiq kaùn-da-bèh. > It is really very good! D6

တူးရစ်ဘားမားရုံး Tù-riq Bà-mà Yoùn > Tourist Burma office D1

တဲ့ in: [name]–တဲ့ [name]-déh > it is called [name] G36

တိုကျို To-co > Tokyo G15

တက်– teq- > to go up, get on board (taxi and so on); to attend (school, meeting) D3

တိုက် taiq > building G35

တောင်ကြီး /–ကျီး/ Taun-jì > Taunggyi G19

တစ် tiq > one G2

တစ်ဆယ် tăs'eh > ten G4

တိပ်ခွေ teiq-k'we > tape ["tape-reel"] G40

တံခါး /ဒဂါး/ dăgà > door G43

တယ်လီဖုန်း teh-li-p'oùn > telephone G6

တွေ့– twé- > to see, meet, find, notice; ◊ တွေ့သေးတာပေါ့။ Twé-dhè-da-báw. See you later/next time. CP6; ◊ တွေ့ရတာ ဝမ်းသာပါတယ်။ Twé-yá-da wùn-tha-ba-deh. I am happy at having the opportunity to meet you. D10B; ◊ နောက်ထပ် တွေ့ကြရအောင်။ Nauq-t'aq twé-já-yá-aun. > Let's meet again. D11

ထောင် -t'aun > thousand G10

ထိုင်– t'ain- > to sit G43

ထိုင်းနိုင်ငံ T'aìn Naing-ngan > Thailand G13

ထပ်ပြောပါအုံး။ /–တာ–/ T'aq-pyàw-ba-oùn. > Please say that again. G13

ဒါ da > this, that G1; ◊ ဒါပဲလား။ Da-bèh-là? > Is that all? Is that the lot? CP17; ဒါပါပဲ။ Da-ba-bèh. > That's it, that's all. CP17; ရှိပါသေးတယ်။ Shí-ba-dhè-deh. > There's more. CP17

ဒီ–[noun] di-[noun] > this [noun] G7

ဒီမှာ di-hma > in this [place], here G20; Excuse me please D1

ဒေါ် Daw > (prefix for names of older women) G22

ဒေါ်လာ daw-la > dollar G23

ဒက္ကား Deq-kà > Dacca G15

ဓာတ်ပုံ /ဒတ်ပုံ/ daq-poun > photograph D2; ◊ ဓာတ်ပုံ ရိုက်– daq-poun yaiq- > to take a photograph D2

နယူးဒေလီ Năyù De-li > New Delhi G15

နာမည် /နန်မယ်/ nan-meh in colloquial style, but /နာမျိ/ na-myi in reading style > name G27

နာရီ na-yi > hour G33

နား လည်– nà leh- > to understand CP18

နေ– ne- > to live, remain G27

နေ– in: [verb]–နေ– -ne- > to be [verb]-ing, [verb] for the time being D12; ◊ မြေပုံ ကြည့်နေပါတယ်။ Mye-boun cí-ne-ba-deh. > They are looking at the map. D12

နေကောင်း– ne-kaùn- > to be well CP3; ◊ နေကောင်းရဲ့လား။ Ne-kaùn-yéh-là? How are you? ◊ နေကောင်းပါတယ်။ Ne-kaùn-ba-deh. I'm fine.

နေရာ ne-ya > place G35

နဲနဲ nèh-nèh > a little, a bit D11

နဲ့ in: [noun]–နဲ့ -néh > with [noun] G14; [speak] to [person] D12; ◊ ဦးတင်လှိုင်နဲ့ စကားပြောနေပါတယ်။ Ù Tin Hlain-néh săgà pyàw-ne-ba-deh. He is talking to U Tin Hlaing. D12

နို့မှုန့် nó-hmoún > milk powder ["milk-powder"] G40

နက်ဖြန် or နက်ဖြင် or နက်ဖန် neq-p'yan, neq-p'yin, neq-p'an > tomorrow D11

နောက်ထပ် [verb] nauq-t'aq > [verb] again, further, more D8

နောက်မှ nauq-hmá > later, not till later D11; ◊ နောက်မှပဲ စီစဉ်ကြရအောင်။ Nauq-hmá-bèh si-zin-já-yá-aun. Let's fix up something later. D11

နိုင်ငံ naing-ngan > country, state G13

နိုင်ငံခြား /–ဂျား/ nain-ngan-jà > foreign country, abroad ["country-separate"] D7

နိုင်ငံသား nain-ngan-dhà > national, citizen ["country-son, member"] D8

နံပါတ် /–ဗတ်/ nan-baq > number G2

နှစ် hniq > two G2

-------------- ပ–ဖ–ဗ–ဘ–မ --------------

ပါ– in: [verb]–ပါ– [verb]-ba- > to [verb] (polite) G42

ပါအုံး in: [verb]–ပါအုံး။ [verb]-ba-oùn > a slightly more friendly, more coaxing, alternative to [verb]–ပါ; ◊ အဖေနဲ့ မိတ်ဆက်ပေးပါအုံး။ Ăp'e-néh meiq-s'eq-pè-ba-oùn. Please introduce me to your father. D10B

ပီ– pi- > to be correctly, authentically pronounced D6; ◊ ဗမာစကား ပြောတာ ပီပါတယ်။ Băma sgà pyàw-da pi-ba-deh. > Your spoken Burmese is well pronounced. [= You have a good pronunciation in: Burmese.] D6

ပီကင်း Pi-kìn > Peking/Beijing G15

ပုဂံ /ဗဂန်/ Păgan > Pagan (Bagan) G19

ပုလင်း /ပလင်း/ pălìn > bottle D4

ပေး– pè- > to give D3

ပေး in: [verb]–ပေး– -pè- > implies that the action of the verb is undertaken for someone else's benefit; ◊ သွားခေါ်ပေးမယ်။ Thwà-k'aw-pè-meh. > I'll go and fetch him [for you]. D12

ပေးရ– [price] pè-yá- > to pay [price], have to give G39

ပဲခူး /ဗဂိုး/ Păgò > Pegu (Bago) G19

ပဲနီ pèh-ní > penny G26

ပို့စကဒ် /–ကတ်/ pó-săkaq > postcard [from English] G40

ပက်စီ Peq-si > Pepsi-cola D4

ပိုက်ဆံ paiq-s'an > money D4

ပေါင် paun > pound G23

ပိတ်– peiq- > to close, turn off G43

ပန်ကာ pan-ka > fan G43

ပန်းခြံ /–ဂျန်/ pàn-jan > park, garden G1

ပန်းဆိုးတန်း /ဆိုး or ဇိုး/ Pàn-s'ò-dàn (s'ò or zò) > Pansodan Street G9

ပြတိုက် /ပြဒိုက်/ pyá-daiq > museum G1

ပြတင်းပေါက် /ပဒင်းဇောက်/ pădìn-bauq > window G43

ပြား pyà > pya (or English penny) G25

ပြီး– pì- > to finish; ◊ ပြီးပြီလား။ Pì-bi-là? Have you finished? CP15; ◊ ပြီးပြီ။ Pì-bi. I have finished. CP15; ◊ မပြီးသေးပါဘူး။ Măpì-dhè-ba-bù. I haven't finished yet. CP15

ပြော– pyàw- > to speak, say, tell, talk D6

ပြင်သစ်နိုင်ငံ Pyin-thiq Nain-ngan > France G34

ပြည် /ပျေ/ or /ပို့/ Pye > Prome (Pyi/Pyay) G19

ပြန်ပြောပါအုံး။ /–တာ–/ Pyan-pyàw-ba-oùn. > Please say that again. G13

ဖလင် p'ălin > film [from English] G40

ဖိလစ်ပိုင်နိုင်ငံ P'í-liq-pain Naing-ngan > Philippines G13

ဖို့ in: [verb]–ဖို့ အစီအစဉ် ရှိ– -bó ăsi-ăsin shí- > to have a plan, intend, to [verb] D8

ဖွင့်– p'wín- > to open, turn on G43

ဗမာစကား Băma săgà > Burmese ["Burmese-words/speaking"] D6

ဗမာပြည် Băma-pye > Burma G13

ဗမာလို Băma-lo > in Burmese ["Burmese-way"] G40

ဗီယက်နမ်နိုင်ငံ Bi-yeq-nan Naing-ngan > Vietnam G13

ဗိုလ်အောင်ကျော်လမ်း /ဗို အောင်ကျော်–/ **Bo Aun Jaw Làn** > Bo Aung Kyaw Street G9

ဗိုလ်ချုပ်ဈေး /ဗိုဂျုပ်ဇေး/ **Bo-jouq Zè** > Bogyoke Market G5

ဗိုလ်ချုပ်ပန်းခြံ /ဗိုဂျုပ်ပန်းဂျန်/ **Bo-jouq Pàn-jan** > Bogyoke Park G5

ဗိုလ်ချုပ်ပြတိုက် /ဗိုဂျုပ်ပျာ့ဒိုက်/ **Bo-jouq Pyá-daiq** > Bogyoke Museum G5

ဗိုလ်ချုပ်လမ်း /ဗိုဂျုပ်–/ **Bo-jouq Làn** > Bogyoke Street G7

ဘာ **ba** > what G1; ဘာ–[noun] **ba-[noun]** > what [noun] G5

ဘီစကွတ် **bi-săkuq** > biscuit [= cookie; from English] G40

ဘုရား /ဖယား:/ **p'ăyà** > lord, pagoda, Buddha image G1

ဘုရားလမ်း /ဖယား–/ **P'ăyà Làn** > Shwedagon Pagoda Road G9

ဘူတာကြီး /–ဒါ–/ **Bu-da-jì** > the main station D3

ဘောပင် **bàw-pin** > ballpoint pen [from English] G40

ဘက် **beq** > direction, way D1; ◊ ဒီဘက် **di-beq** > this way D1; ◊ ဘယ်ဘက် **beh-beq** > which way? D1

ဘင်္ဂလားဒေ့ရှ်နိုင်ငံ /ဗင်ဂ–/ **Bin-gălà-désh Naing-ngan** > Bangladesh G13

ဘန်ကောက် **Ban-kauq** > Bangkok G15

ဘယ်–[noun] **beh-[noun]** > which [noun] G11; ဘယ် သွားသလဲ။ **Beh thwà-dhălèh?** > Where did they go? G34

ဘယ်နှစ် /ဘယ်န–/ **beh-hnă-** > how many D4; ◊ ကော်ဖီ ဘယ်နှစ်ခွက်လဲ **kaw-p'i beh-hnăk'weq-lèh?** > How many cups of coffee? D4

ဘယ်မှာ **beh-hma** > in which [place], where G20

ဘယ်လို **beh-lo** > how, in what way G36, D1

ဘယ်လောက် **beh-lauq** > how much, what (number, price) G6, 23

ဘယ်သူ **beh-dhu** > who G21

မ **Má** > (prefix for names of younger women) G24

မနီလာ **Măni-la** > Manila G15

မနက်ဖြန် or မနက်ဖြင် or မနက်ဖန် **măneq-p'yan, măneq-p'yin, măneq-p'an** > tomorrow D11

မလေးရှားနိုင်ငံ **Mălè-shà Naing-ngan** > Malaysia G13

မလို့ in: [verb]–မလို့ **-măló** > thinking of [verb]-ing, planning to [verb] D8; ◊ ဘာကား ဝယ်မလို့လဲ။ **Ba-kà weh-măló-lèh?** What car are you thinking of buying? D8

မဟာဗန္ဓုလပန်းခြံ /ဗန်ဒုလ္လာပန်းဂျန်/ **Măha Ban-dú-lá Pàn-jan** > Maha Bandoola Park G5

မဟာဗန္ဓုလလမ်း /ဗန်ဒုလ္လာ–/ **Măha Ban-dú-lá Làn** > Maha Bandoola Street G7

မဟုတ်ပါဘူး /–ဘူး/ **Măhouq-pa-bù.** > It is not so. G3

မိနစ် /မိနစ်–မင်းနစ်–မနစ်/ **mí-niq, mìn-niq, măniq** (the pronunciation of the first syllable varies with the speed of the speaker) > minute G37

မီး **mì** > fire, light G43

မေမြို့ **Me-myó** > Maymyo G19

မော်လမြိုင် **Maw-lămyain** > Moulmein (Mawlamyine) G19

မင်္ဂလာ **min-găla** > blessing, auspiciousness CP1; ◊ မင်္ဂလာပါ **Min-găla-ba** Good morning/afternoon

မင်္ဂလာဒုံ လေဆိပ် /–ဇိတ်/ **Min-găla-doun Le-zeiq** > Mingaladon Airport D3

မတ် **maq** > quarter G38

မိတ်ဆက်– or မိတ်ဆက်ပေး– **meiq-s'eq-(pè)-** > to introduce ["friend-connect-give"] D10B; ◊ N-နဲ့ မိတ်ဆက်ပေးချင်ပါတယ်။ **N-néh meiq-s'eq-pè-jin-ba-deh.** I want to introduce you to N. D10B

မိတ်ဆွေ **meiq-s'we** > friend D10A; also used = "you" and "your" when you don't yet know a person's name D10B

မန္တလေး /မန်းဒလေး/ **Màn-dălè** > Mandalay G19

များ– **myà-** > to be many, much D11; ◊ လုပ်စရာ များပါတယ်။ **Louq-săya myà-ba-deh.** I have a lot to do. D11

မြေပုံ /–ဗုံ/ **mye-boun** > map ["earth picture"] G40

မြို့ **myó** > town G15

မြို့နယ် **myó-neh** > township G29

မြစ်ကြီးနား **Myiq-cì-nà** > Myitkyina G19

မြန်မာနိုင်ငံ **Myan-ma Naing-ngan** > Burma/Myanmar G13

မှာ– **hma-** > to order, instruct D4

မှာ in: [place]–မှာ နေ– [place]-hma ne- > to live
in [place] G27, 29, 30; in: [time]–မှာ [verb]
[time]-hma [verb] > to [verb] at [time] G33

---------------- ယ – ရ – လ – ၀ ----------------

ယူ– yu- > to take D5; ◊ ယူမယ် Yu-meh. > I'll
take it. I'll have it. D5

ရ– yá- > to get, manage, be successful, be
possible, to be all right, to be acceptable, to
manage CP7; ◊ ရတယ်နော်။ Yá-deh-naw? >
This is all right, isn't it? CP7, CP12, D2;
ရပါတယ်။ Yá-ba-deh. > Yes, it is all right; ;
That's all right. CP7, D2, CP8, CP9, CP13;
◊ မရဘူး။ Mǎyá-bù. > No, it's not all right.
CP12, D2; ◊ ရပြီလား။ Yá-bi-là? > All set?
Ready? ရပြီ။ Yá-bi. > Yes, I am. CP16;
မရသေးပါဘူး။ Mǎyá-dhè-ba-bù. > No, I'm not
ready yet. CP16

ရ– in: [verb]–ရ– [verb]-yá- > to have to [verb]
G45

ရာ -ya > hundred G8

ရေနံချောင်း /ယေနန်ကျောင်း/ Ye-nan-jaùn >
Yenangyaung G19

ရော in: [noun]–ကော or [noun]–ရော -gàw, -yàw >
How about [noun]? CP4, D10B

ရောက်– yauq- > to get to, reach, arrive at D7;
◊ ရောက်ဖူး– yauq-p'ù- > to have reached
before, to have been to D7

ရိုက်–yaiq- > to hit, beat, stamp, make imprint
D2; ◊ ဓါတ်ပုံ ရိုက်– /ဒတ်ပုံ ယိုက်–/ daq-
poun yaiq- > to take a photograph D2

ရတ်ရှား Raq-shà > Russia G34

ရန်ကုန် /ယန်ဂုန်/ Yan-goun > Rangoon/Yangon
G15, G19

ရပ် or ရပ်ကွက် yaq or yaq-kweq > Quarter (in a
town) G29

ရုံး youn > office D1

ရှိ– shí- > to be [in some place]; also = have, there
is D12; ◊ ဦးတင်လှိုင် ရှိလား။ Ù Tin Hlain shí-
là? > Is U Tin Hlaing there? D12

ရှင် Shin > (polite tag, like Monsieur/Madame,
used by female speakers) CP10

ရှင်း– shìn- > to clear, clarify, settle up; be clear
D4; ◊ ပိုက်ဆံ ရှင်းမယ်။ Paiq-s'an shìn-meh.
> We'll settle the bill. D4

ရှစ် shiq > eight G4

ရွှေဘုံသာလမ်း Shwe-boun-dha Làn >
Shwebontha Street G9

ရွှေတိဂုံဘုရား /ရွှေဒဂုန်ဖယား:/ Shwe-dǎgoun
P'ǎyà > Shwedagon Pagoda G5

လာ– la- > to come G31, 34

လား in: [noun]–လား။ [noun]-là > Did you say
[noun]? Was that [noun]? G6

လူမျိုး lu-myò > race, nationality ["person-kind,
type"] D9

လေး lè > four G2

လဲ in: [noun]–လဲ -lèh > [noun] also, [noun] too
D10B; ◊ ကျွန်တော်လဲ တွေ့ချင်ပါတယ်။
Cǎnaw-lèh twé-jin-ba-deh. I too would like
to meet. D11

လောလောဆယ် /–ဆယ်/ làw-làw-zeh > recently,
currently, for the time being D11

လို့ in: [name]–လို့ ခေါ်– [name]-ló k'aw- > to call,
be called [name] G36

လက်ဖက်ရည် /လဖက်ယေ/ lǎp'eq-ye > tea D4

လိုက် in: [verb]–လိုက်– -laiq- > implies that
action of the verb will not be onerous or
prolonged; ◊ သွားခေါ်လိုက်မယ်။ Thwà-k'aw-
laiq-meh. > I'll go and fetch him [and it
won't take long or be any trouble]. D12

လိပ်စာ leiq-sa > address G29

လုပ်– louq- > to do D11; ◊ လုပ်စရာ များပါတယ်။
Louq-sǎya myà-ba-deh. I have a lot to do.
D11

လမ်း Làn > road, street G7

လိမ်မော်ရည် /–ယေ/ lein-maw-ye > orange juice
D4

လုံး or အလုံး (ǎ)loùn > round(-ish) object D4

ဝမ်းသာ– wùn-tha- > to be happy ["stomach—be
pleasant"] D10B

ဝယ်– weh- > to buy G41

----------------သ – ဟ – င – အ ----------------

သမီး thǎmì > daughter D10A

သား thà > son D10A

သိ– thí- > to know D1

သုည thoun-nyá > zero G6

သေး in: မ–[verb]–သေးပါဘူး mǎ-[verb]-thè-pa-bù
> not [verb] yet; ◊ မရောက်သေးပါဘူး။ mǎ-
yauq-thè-pa-bu. They haven't arrived yet.
D6

သောက်– thauq- > to drink D4

သောင်း -thaùn > ten thousand G10

သန်း -thàn > million G10

သိန်း -theìn > hundred thousand G10

သိပ် theiq > very D6; ◊ သိပ် ကောင်းတယ်။ Theiq kaùn-deh. It is very good. D6

သံတမန် /–ဒမန်/ than-dăman > diplomatic G35; ◊ သံတမန်ကုန်တိုက် /–ဒမန် –ဒိုက်/ than-dăman koun-daiq > Diplomatic Store G35

သံတွဲ /–ဒွဲ/ Than-dwèh > Sandoway (Thandwe) G19

သမ္မတဟိုတယ် /သမဒ]/ Thămădá Ho-teh > President Hotel G5

သံရုံး than-youn > embassy ["voice, envoy-office"] D1

သိမ်ကြီးဈေး /သိန်ဂျီးဇေး/ Thein-jì-zè > Thein-gyi Market G5

သုံး thoùn > three G2

သွား– thwà- > to go G34, 35; ◊ သွားခေါ်မယ်။ Thwà-k'aw-meh. > I'll go and fetch him. D12; ◊ သွားပါအုံးမယ် Thwà-ba-oùn-meh > Goodbye CP5; ◊ သွားမယ်နော်။ Thwà-meh-naw? > Goodbye (less formal) CP11, D2

ဟနွိုင်း Hănwaìn > Hanoi G15

ဟလို or ဟယ်လို။ Hălo, Heh-lo > Hallo D12

ဟိုတယ် ho-teh > hotel [from English] G1

ဟုတ်– houq- > (a) to be so, to be the case; ◊ ဟုတ်ကဲ့။ Houq-kéh. Yes, that is so; Yes, I agree. G3, CP19; ◊ မဟုတ်ပါဘူး။ Măhouq-pa-bù. No, that is not so. G3; (b) to be as good as it possibly could be, right on, spot on, on target, on the ball, hot stuff, high class, real cool D6; ◊ ဗမာစကား ပြောတာ သိပ် ဟုတ်သေးပါဘူး။ Băma săgà pyàw-da theiq măhouq-thè-pa-bù. > His spoken Burmese isn't perfect yet. D6

ဟယ်လို or ဟလို။ Heh-lo, Hălo > Hallo D12

အကို ăko > older brother D10B

အခေါက် ăk'auq > trip, journey [mainly used in counting] D7; ◊ သုံးခေါက် ရောက်ဖူးပါတယ်။ Thoùn-gauq yauq-p'ù-ba-deh. > I've been there three times. D7

အချိန် ăc'ein > time G33

အစီအစဉ် /–စင်/ ăsi-ăsin > plan, programme D8; ◊ အစီအစဉ် ရှိ– ăsi-ăsin shí- > to have a

plan, intend; ◊ ကား ဝယ်ဖို့ အစီအစဉ် ရှိသလား။ Kà weh-bó ăsi-ăsin shí-dhălà? Are you thinking of buying a car? D8

အဒေါ် ădaw > aunt D10B

အနော်ရထာလမ်း /ယထာ or ရထာ/ Ănaw-yăt'a Làn (yă or ră) > Anawrahta Street G7

အပြင် ăpyin > outside, out G35

အဖေ ăp'e > father D10A

အမ ămá > older sister D10B

အမေ ăme > mother D10A

အမေရိကနိုင်ငံ Ăme-rí-ká Nain-ngan > America G34

အမိန့် ရှိပါ။ Ămeín shí-ba. > Please speak (used as an alternative or addition to ဟလို on the phone). D12

အမျိုးသမီး ămyò-dhămì > wife, fiancée, girlfriend (also "lady") D10A

အမျိုးသား ămyò-thà (or -dhà) > husband, fiancé, boyfriend (also "gentleman") D10A

အမျိုးသားပြတိုက် /–ပျူဒိုက်/ Amyò-thà Pyá-daiq > National Museum G5

အမှတ် ăhmaq > number G29

အရမ်း ăyàn > terrifically, fantastically D6; ◊ အရမ်း ကောင်းတယ်။ Ăyàn kaùn-deh. It is incredibly good. D6

အလုံး or လုံး (ă)loùn > round(-ish) object D4

အင်္ဂလန်နိုင်ငံ /အင်္ဂလန်/ In-gălan Nain-ngan > England G34

အင်းယားလိပ် ဟိုတယ် Ìn-yà Leiq Ho-teh > Inya Lake Hotel D3

အိုင်ယာလန် Ain-ya-lan > Ireland G34

အိန္ဒိယနိုင်ငံ /အိန်ဒိယာ–/ Ein-dí-yá Naing-ngan > India G13

အိမ် ein > house G29

အိမ်သာ/–သွာ/ ein-dha > toilet G35

ဦး /အူး/ Ù > (prefix for names of older men) G22

ဦးလေး ù-lè > uncle D10B

အဲဒါ èh-da > that (nearer you) G39

ဩစတြေးလျှနိုင်ငံ /အောစတရေးလျှာ/ Àw-sătrè-lyá > Australia G34, D1

ဩ် Aw > Oh G5

5.2 Burmese-English vocabulary (entry words in roman transcription)

This list is in roman alphabetical order. The letter ă listed after the letter a, and a consonant followed by -' is listed before its counterpart without -'; thus c'- precedes c-, and so on.

Àw-sătrè-lyá Nain-ngan ဩစတြေးလျနိုင်ငံ /အောစတရေးလျှ့/ > Australia G34, D1

Ain-ya-lan အိုင်ယာလန် > Ireland G34

Amyò-thà Pyá-daiq အမျိုးသားပြတိုက် /-ပျှ့ဒိုက်/ > National Museum G5

Aw အော် > Oh G5

ăc'ein အချိန် > time G33

ădaw အဒေါ် > aunt D10B

ăhmaq အမှတ် > number G29

ăk'auq အခေါက် > trip, journey [mainly used in counting] D7; ◊ သုံးခေါက် ရောက်ဖူးပါတယ်။ Thoùn-gauq yauq-p'ù-ba-deh. > I've been there three times. D7

ăko အကို > older brother D10B

ăloùn or loùn လုံး or အလုံး > round(-ish) object D4

ămá အမ > older sister D10B

ăme အမေ > mother D10A

Ăme-rí-ká Nain-ngan အမေရိကနိုင်ငံ > America G34

Ămeín shí-ba. အမိန့် ရှိပါ။ > Please speak (used as an alternative or addition to ဟလို on the phone). D12

ămyò-dhămì အမျိုးသမီး > wife, fiancée, girlfriend (also "lady") D10A

ămyò-thà အမျိုးသား > husband, fiancé, boyfriend (also "gentleman") D10A

Ănaw-yăt'a Làn အနော်ရထာလမ်း /ယထာ or ရထာ/ > Anawrahta Street G7

ăp'e အဖေ > father D10A

ăpyin အပြင် > outside, out G35

ăsi-ăsin အစီအစဉ် /-စင်/ > plan, programme D8; ◊ အစီအစဉ် ရှိ- ăsi-ăsin shí- > to have a plan, intend; ◊ ကား ဝယ်ဖို့ အစီအစဉ် ရှိသလား။ Kà weh-bó ăsi-ăsin shí-dhălà? Are you thinking of buying a car? D8

ăyàn အရမ်း > terrifically, fantastically D6; ◊ အရမ်း ကောင်းတယ်။ Ăyàn kaùn-deh. It is incredibly good. D6

ba ဘာ > what G1

ba-[noun] ဘာ-[noun] > what [noun] G5

ba-ပါ- in: [verb]-ပါ- [verb]-ba- > to [verb] *(polite)* G42

ba-oùn ပါအုံး in: [verb]-ပါအုံး။ [verb]-ba-oùn > a slightly more friendly, more coaxing, alternative to [verb]-ပါ; ◊ အဖေနဲ့ မိတ်ဆက်ပေး-ပါအုံး။ Ăp'e-néh meiq-s'eq-pè-ba-oùn. Please introduce me to your father. D10B

bàw-pin ဘောပင် > ballpoint pen [from English] G40

Ban-kauq ဘန်ကောက် > Bangkok G15

Băma săgà ဗမာစကား > Burmese ["Burmese-words/speaking"] D6

Băma-lo ဗမာလို > in Burmese ["Burmese-way"] G40

beh-[noun] ဘယ်-[noun] > which [noun] G11; ဘယ် သွားသလဲ။ Beh thwà-dhălèh? > Where did they go? G34

beh-dhu ဘယ်သူ > who G21

beh-hma ဘယ်မှာ > in which [place], where G20

beh-hnă- ဘယ်နှစ် /ဘယ်နှ-/ > how many D4; ◊ ကော်ဖီ ဘယ်နှစ်ခွက်လဲ kaw-p'i beh-hnă-k'weq-lèh? > How many cups of coffee? D4

beh-lauq ဘယ်လောက် > how much, what (number, price) G6, 23

beh-lo ဘယ်လို > how, in what way G36, D1

beq ဘက် > direction, way D1; ◊ ဒီဘက် di-beq > this way D1; ◊ ဘယ်ဘက် beh-beq > which way? D1

bi-săkuq ဘီစကွတ် > biscuit [= cookie; from English] G40

Bi-yeq-nan Naing-ngan ဗီယက်နမ်နိုင်ငံ > Vietnam G13

Bin-gălà-désh Naing-ngan ဘင်္ဂလားဒေ့ရှ်နိုင်ငံ /ဗင်ဂ-/ > Bangladesh G13

Bo Aun Jaw Làn ဗိုလ်အောင်ကျော်လမ်း /ဗို အောင်ကျော်-/ > Bo Aung Kyaw Street G9

Bo-jouq Làn ဗိုလ်ချုပ်လမ်း /ဗိုဂျုပ်-/ > Bogyoke Street G7

Bo-jouq Pàn-jan ဗိုလ်ချုပ်ပန်းခြံ /ဗိုဂျုပ်ပန်းဂျန်/ > Bogyoke Park G5

Bo-jouq Pyá-daiq ဗိုလ်ချုပ်ပြတိုက် /ဗိုဂျုပ်ပျှ့ဒိုက်/ > Bogyoke Museum G5

Bo-jouq Zè ဗိုလ်ချုပ်ဈေး /ဗိုဂျုပ်ဇေး/ > Bogyoke Market G5

bó see p'ó

Bu-da-jì ဘူတာကြီး /‐ခါ‐/ > the main station D3

c'auq ခြောက် > six G4

c'in/‐jin‐ ချင်‐ in: [verb]‐ချင်‐ [verb]> to want to [verb] G42

cá‐ ကျ‐ > to fall, fall in place, amount to D4; ◊ ဘယ်လောက် ကျသလဲ။ Beh‐lauq cá‐dhălèh? > How much does that come to? D4

caq ကျပ် > kyat G32

cămá ကျမ > I, my (woman speaking) D10A; ◊ ဒါ ကျမ ဘောပင်ပါ။ Da cămá bàw‐pin‐ba. That's my pen (woman speaking). D10A

cănáw ကျနော့် > my (man speaking) D10A; ◊ ဒါ ကျနော့် ဘောပင်ပါ။ Da cănáw bàw‐pin‐ba. That's my pen (man speaking). D10A

Cè‐zù tin‐ba‐deh. ကျေးဇူး တင်ပါတယ်။ > Thank you. CP9

cun‐dáw ကျွန်တော့် > full form of ကျနော့် cănáw G32

cun‐má ကျွန်မ > full form of ကျမ cămá G32

cí‐ ကြည့်‐ /ကျို/ > to look, look around, look at D5; ◊ ကြည့်အုံးမယ်နော်။ Cí‐oùn‐meh‐naw? > I'll carry on looking, if you don't mind. D5

da ဒါ > this, that G1; ◊ ဒါပဲလား။ Da‐bèh‐là? > Is that all? Is that the lot? CP17; ဒါပါပဲ။ Da‐ba‐bèh. > That's it, that's all. CP17; ရှိပါသေးတယ်။ Shí‐ba‐dhè‐deh. > There's more. CP17

da တာ in: [verb] ‐တာ [verb]‐da > turns a verb (like *speak*) into a noun (like *speaking, speech*); ◊ ဗမာစကား ပြောတာ ကောင်းပါတယ်။ Băma săgà pyàw‐da kaùn‐ba‐deh. > Your spoken Burmese is good. D6

da‐bèh in: [verb]‐တာပဲ [verb]‐da‐bèh > similar to [verb]‐ပါတယ် ‐ba‐deh, but a little more exclamatory D6; ◊ သိပ် ကောင်းတာပဲ။ Theiq kaùn‐da‐bèh. > It is really very good! D6

daq‐poun ဓာတ်ပုံ /ဒတ်ပုံ/ > photograph D2; ◊ ဓာတ်ပုံ ရိုက်‐ /ဒတ်ပုံ ယိုက်‐/ daq‐poun yaiq‐ > to take a photograph D2

Daw ဒေါ် > (prefix for names of older women) G22

daw‐la ဒေါ်လာ > dollar G23

déh တဲ့ in: [name]‐တဲ့ [name]‐déh > it is called [name] G36

Deq‐kà ဒက္ကား > Dacca G15

di‐[noun] ဒီ‐[noun] > this [noun] G7

di‐hma ဒီမှာ > in this [place], here G20; Excuse me please D1

dăgà တံခါး /ဒဂါး/ > door G43

èh‐da အဲဒါ > that (nearer you) G39

ein အိမ် > house G29

ein‐dha အိမ်သာ /‐သာ/ > toilet G35

Ein‐dí‐ya Naing‐ngan အိန္ဒိယနိုင်ငံ /အိန်ဒိယာ‐/ > India G13

gá in: [place]‐က လာ‐ [place]‐gá la‐ > to come from [place] G31

gàw, ‐yàw in: [noun]‐ကော or [noun]‐ရော [noun]‐gàw, [noun]‐yàw > How about [noun]? CP4, D10B

géh‐ see ‐k'éh

gwèh see ‐k'wèh

Hălo or Heh‐lo ဟလို or ဟယ်လို။ > Hallo D12

Hănwain ဟန္ဟိုင်း > Hanoi G15

Heh‐lo or Hălo ဟလို or ဟယ်လို။ > Hallo D12

hma မှာ in: [place]‐မှာ နေ‐ [place]‐hma ne‐ > to live in [place] G27, 29, 30; in: [time]‐မှာ [verb] [time]‐hma [verb] > to [verb] at [time] G33

hma‐ မှာ‐ > to order, instruct D4

hniq နှစ် > two G2

ho‐teh ဟိုတယ် > hotel [from English] G1

houq‐ ဟုတ်‐ > (a) to be so, to be the case; ◊ ဟုတ်ကဲ့။ Houq‐kéh. Yes, that is so; Yes, I agree. G3, CP19; ◊ မဟုတ်ပါဘူး။ Măhouq‐pa‐bù. No, that is not so. G3; (b) to be as good as it possibly could be, right on, spot on, on target, on the ball, hot stuff, high class, real cool D6; ◊ ဗမာစကား ပြောတာ သိပ် ဟုတ်သေးပါဘူး။ Băma săgà pyàw‐da theiq măhouq‐thè‐pa‐bù. > His spoken Burmese isn't perfect yet. D6

In‐gălan Nain‐ngan အင်္ဂလန်နိုင်ငံ /အင်ဂလန်/ > England G34

Ìn‐yà Leiq Ho‐teh အင်းယားလိပ် ဟိုတယ် > Inya Lake Hotel D3

Ja‐măni ဂျာမနီ > Germany G34

Jăpan Naing‐ngan ဂျပန်နိုင်ငံ > Japan G13

jin see ‐c'in‐

k'aw‐ ခေါ်‐ > to call, to be called G36; to fetch D12; ◊ သွားခေါ်‐ thwà‐k'aw‐ > to go and fetch D12

k'ăná ခဏ > moment; ◊ ခဏလေးနော်။ **K'ăná-lè-naw?** > Just a moment, OK? CP8, CP14

k'ăná-k'ăná ခဏခဏ /ခန့ ခနဲ့/ > frequently, often, many times D7

k'éh-/-géh ခဲ့ in: [verb]—ခဲ့— > used with verbs involving movement "from somewhere else to here"; ◊ သွားခေါ်ခဲ့မယ်။ **Thwà-k'aw-géh-meh.** > I'll go and fetch him [and bring him here]. D12. In other contexts —ခဲ့— -géh-/-k'éh implies that the action takes place (a) somewhere other than here ("How long did you spend there?"); or (b) in the past ("Burma was ruled by Burmese kings.")

K'in-bya ခင်ဗျာ > (polite tag, like Monsieur/Madame, used by male speakers) CP10

k'ú-niq, k'ú-hniq, k'un ခုနစ် > seven G4, G6

k'wèh/-gwèh ခွဲ > - and a half G37, G38; ◊ တစ်နာရီခွဲ **tăna-yi-gwèh** 1.30 ["one hour and a half"]; ◊ သုံးနာရီခွဲ **thoùn-na-yi-gwèh** 3.30 ["three hours and a half"]; ◊ သုံးကျပ်ခွဲ **thoùn-jaq-k'wèh** K3.50 ["three kyats and a half"]

k'weq ခွက် > cup, glass D4

k'wín ခွင့် > permission, authorization; ◊ ခွင့် ပြုပါအုံး။ **K'wín pyú-ba-oùn.** > May I leave now? CP19

Kàn-nà Làn ကမ်းနားလမ်း > Strand Road G7

kain- ကိုင်– > to grasp, hold D12; ခဏ ကိုင်ထားပါ။ **K'ăná kain-t'à-ba.** > Please hold on a minute. D12

kaùn- ကောင်း– > to be good D6; ◊ ကောင်းပါပြီ **Kaùn-ba-bi** > Goodbye CP5, CP11; Very well. Fine. OK. CP12, CP19

kaw-p'i ကော်ဖီ > coffee D4

kaw-p'i-hmoún ကော်ဖီမှုန့် > instant coffee ["coffee-powder"] G40

Kărăweiq Ho-teh ကရဝိက် ဟိုတယ် /ကရဝိတ်–/ > Karaweik Hotel D3

kèh ကဲ > There. Right. Well. ◊ ကဲ။ ရပြီ။ **Kèh. Yá-bi.** There. Got it. CP14; ကဲ။ ပြီးပြီ။ **Kèh. Pì-bi.** > There. That's done. CP14

keiq-sá ကိစ္စ > business, matter, affair, activity; ◊ ကိစ္စ မရှိပါဘူး။ **Keiq-sá măshí-ba-bù.** > No problem. CP8, CP9; It doesn't matter. CP13

Ko ကို > (prefix for names of younger men) G24

Ko-ka-ko-la ကိုကာကိုလာ > Coca-cola D4

Ko-rì-yà ကိုရီးယား > Korea G34

kò ကို: > nine G4

koun ကုန် > goods, merchandise G3

koun-daiq ကုန်တိုက် /–ဒိုက်/ > department store G35

Koun-dheh Làn ကုန်သည်လမ်း /–သွယ်–/ > Merchant Street G7

Kwa-la Lan-pu ကွာလာလမ်ပူ > Kuala Lumpur G15

la- လာ– > to come G31, 34

là လား in: [noun]—လား။ [noun]-là > Did you say [noun]? Was that [noun]? G6

làn လမ်း > road, street G7

làw-làw-zeh လောလောဆယ် /–ဇယ်/ > recently, currently, for the time being D11

laiq- လိုက် in: [verb]—လိုက်— [verb]-laiq- > implies that action of the verb will not be onerous or prolonged; ◊ သွားခေါ်လိုက်မယ်။ **Thwà-k'aw-laiq-meh.** > I'll go and fetch him [and it won't take long or be any trouble]. D12

lăp'eq-ye လက်ဖက်ရည် /လဖက်ယေ/ > tea D4

lè လေး > four G2

lèh လဲ in: [noun]—လဲ -lèh > [noun] also, [noun] too D10B; ◊ ကျွန်တော်လဲ တွေ့ချင်ပါတယ်။ **Cănaw-lèh twé-jin-ba-deh.** I too would like to meet. D11

lein-maw-ye လိမ်မော်ရည် /–ယေ/ > orange juice D4

leiq-sa လိပ်စာ > address G29

ló လို့ in: [name]—လို့ ခေါ်– [name]-ló k'aw- > to call, be called [name] G36

loùn or ăloùn လုံး or အလုံး > round(-ish) object D4

louq- လုပ်– > to do D11; ◊ လုပ်စရာ များပါတယ်။ **Louq-săya myà-ba-deh.** I have a lot to do. D11

lu-myò လူမျိုး > race, nationality ["person-kind, type"] D9

Má မ > (prefix for names of younger women) G24

Màn-dălè မန္တလေး /မန်းဒလေး/ > Mandalay G19

maq မတ် > quarter (of a kyat) G38

Maw-lămyain မော်လမြိုင် > Moulmein (Mawlamyine) G19

Măha Ban-dú-lá Làn မဟာဗန္ဓုလလမ်း /ဗန်ဒုလာ–/ > Maha Bandoola Street G7

Mǎha Ban-dú-lá Pàn-jan မဟာဗန္ဓုလပန်းခြံ /ဗန်ဒုလ္လာ့ပန်းကျန်/ > Maha Bandoola Park G5

Mǎhouq-pa-bù. မဟုတ်ပါဘူး /–ဇူး/ > It is not so. G3

Mǎlè-shà Naing-ngan မလေးရှားနိုင်ငံ > Malaysia G13

mǎló မလို့ in: [verb]–မလို့ [verb]-mǎló > thinking of [verb]-ing, planning to [verb] D8; ◊ ဘာကား ဝယ်မလို့လဲ။ Ba-kà weh-mǎló-lèh? What car are you thinking of buying? D8

mǎneq-p'yan, mǎneq-p'yin, mǎneq-p'an မနက်ဖြန် or မနက်ဖြင် or မနက်ဖန် > tomorrow D11

Mǎni-la မနီလာ > Manila G15

Me-myó မေမြို့ > Maymyo G19

meiq-s'eq-(pè)- မိတ်ဆက်– or မိတ်ဆက်ပေး:– > to introduce ["friend-connect-give"] D10B; ◊ N–နဲ့ မိတ်ဆက်ပေးချင်ပါတယ်။ N-néh meiq-s'eq-pè-jin-ba-deh. I want to introduce you to N. D10B

meiq-s'we မိတ်ဆွေ > friend D10A; also used = "you" and "your" when you don't yet know a person's name D10B

min-gǎla မင်္ဂလာ > blessing, auspiciousness CP1; ◊ မင်္ဂလာပါ Min-gǎla-ba Good morning/afternoon

Min-gǎla-doun Le-zeiq မင်္ဂလာဒုံ လေဆိပ် /– ဇိတ်/ > Mingaladon Airport D3

myà- များ:– > to be many, much D11; ◊ လုပ်စရာ များပါတယ်။ Louq-sǎya myà-ba-deh. I have a lot to do. D11

Myan-ma Naing-ngan မြန်မာနိုင်ငံ > Burma/Myanmar G13

mye-boun မြေပုံ /–ပုံ/ > map ["earth picture"] G40

Myiq-cì-nà မြစ်ကြီးနား > Myitkyina G19

myó မြို့ > town G15

myó-neh မြို့နယ် > township G29

mí-niq, mìn-niq, mǎniq မိနစ် /မိနစ်–မင်းနစ်– မနစ်/ (the pronunciation of the first syllable varies with the speed of the speaker) > minute G37

mì မီး > fire, light G43

na-yi နာရီ > hour G33

nà leh- နား လည်– > to understand CP18

nain-ngan-dhà နိုင်ငံသား > national, citizen ["country-son, member"] D8

nain-ngan-jà နိုင်ငံခြား /–ဂျား/ > foreign country, abroad ["country-separate"] D7

naing-ngan နိုင်ငံ > country, state G13

nan-baq နံပါတ် /–ဗတ်/ > number G2

nan-meh နာမည် /နန်မယ်/ nan-meh in colloquial style, but /နာမျို/ na-myi in reading style > name G27

nauq-hmá နောက်မှ > later, not till later D11; ◊ နောက်မှပဲ စီစဉ်ကြရအောင်။ Nauq-hmá-bèh si-zin-já-yá-aun. Let's fix up something later. D11

nauq-t'aq နောက်ထပ် [verb] > [verb] again, further, more D8

Nǎyù De-li နယူးဒေလီ > New Delhi G15

ne- နေ– > to live, remain G27

ne- နေ– in: [verb]–နေ– [verb]-ne- > to be [verb]-ing, [verb] for the time being D12; ◊ မြေပုံ ကြည့်နေပါတယ်။ Mye-boun cí-ne-ba-deh. > They are looking at the map. D12

ne-kaùn- နေကောင်း:– > to be well CP3; ◊ နေကောင်းရဲ့လား။ Ne-kaùn-yéh-là? How are you? ◊ နေကောင်းပါတယ်။ Ne-kaùn-ba-deh. I'm fine.

ne-ya နေရာ > place G35

néh နဲ့ in: [noun]–နဲ့ [noun]-néh > with [noun], [speak] to [person] D12; ◊ ဦးတင်လှိုင်နဲ့ စကားပြောနေပါတယ်။ Ù Tin Hlain-néh sǎgà pyàw-ne-ba-deh. He is talking to U Tin Hlaing. D12

nèh-nèh နဲနဲ > a little, a bit D11

neq-p'yan, neq-p'yin, neq-p'an နက်ဖြန် or နက်ဖြင် or နက်ဖန် > tomorrow D11

ngà ငါး > five G2

ngà-mù ငါးမူး > half a kyat G38

nó-hmoún နို့မှုန့် > milk powder ["milk-powder"] G40

p'ǎlin ဖလင် > film [from English] G40

P'ǎyà Làn ဘုရားလမ်း /ဖယား:–/ > Shwedagon Pagoda Road G9

p'ǎyà ဘုရား /ဖယား:/ > lord, pagoda, Buddha image G1

p'ó/bó ဖို့ in: [verb]–ဖို့ အစီအစဉ် ရှိ– -bó ǎsi-ǎsin shí- > to have a plan, intend, to [verb] D8

p'wín- ဖွင့်– > to open, turn on G43

P'í-liq-pain Naing-ngan ဖိလစ်ပိုင်နိုင်ငံ > Philippines G13
pàn-jan ပန်းခြံ /–ဂျန်/ > park, garden G1
Pàn-s'ò-dàn (s'ò or zò) ပန်းဆိုးတန်း /ဆိုး or ဇိုး/ > Pansodan Street G9
paiq-s'an ပိုက်ဆံ > money D4
pan-ka ပန်ကာ > fan G43
paun ပေါင် > pound G23
pădìn-bauq ပြတင်းပေါက် /ပဒင်းဗောက်/ > window G43
Păgan ပုဂံ /ဗဂန်/ > Pagan (Bagan) G19
Păgò ပဲခူး /ဗဂိုး/ > Pegu (Bago) G19
pălìn ပုလင်း /ပလင်း/ > bottle D4
pè- ပေး in: [verb]—ပေး— -pè- > implies that the action of the verb is undertaken for someone else's benefit; ◊ သွားခေါ်ပေးမယ်။ Thwà-k'aw-pè-meh. > I'll go and fetch him [for you]. D12
pè- ပေး– > to give D3
pè-yá- ပေးရ– [price] > to pay [price], have to give G39
pèh-ní ပဲနီ > penny G26
peiq- ပိတ်– > to close, turn off G43
Peq-si ပက်စီ > Pepsi-cola D4
pi- ပီ– > to be correctly, authentically pronounced D6; ◊ ဗမာစကား ပြောတာ ပီပါတယ်။ Băma sgà pyàw-da pi-ba-deh. > Your spoken Burmese is well pronounced. [= You have a good pronunciation in Burmese.] D6
Pi-kìn ပီကင်း > Peking/Beijing G15
pó-săkaq ပို့စကဒ် /–ကတ်/ > postcard [from English] G40
pyá-daiq ပြတိုက် /ပြဒိုက်/ > museum G1
pyà ပြား > pya (or English penny) G25
pyàw- ပြော– > to speak, say, tell, talk D6
Pyan-pyàw-ba-oùn. ပြန်ပြောပါအုံး။ /–ဗာ–/ > Please say that again. G13
Pye ပြည် /ပျေ/ or /ပြီ/ > Prome (Pyi/Pyay) G19
Pyin-thiq Nain-ngan ပြင်သစ်နိုင်ငံ > France G34
pì- ပြီး– > to finish; ◊ ပြီးပြီလား။ Pì-bi-là? Have you finished? CP15; ◊ ပြီးပြီ။ Pì-bi. I have finished. CP15; ◊ မပြီးသေးပါဘူး။ Măpì-dhè-ba-bù. I haven't finishsed yet. CP15
Raq-shà ရုရှား > Russia G34
s'àw-rì ဆောရီး > sorry; ◊ ဆောရီးပဲ။ S'àw-rì-bèh. > Sorry! CP13; ◊ ဆောရီးနော် S'àw-rì-naw > Sorry! D1
S'ăya ဆရာ > Teacher (male and generic) CP2
S'ăya-má ဆရာမ > Teacher (female) CP2
s'eh-lo-teiq ဆယ်လိုတိပ် > sellotape/Scotchtape [from English] G40
S'ù-le P'ăya ဆူးလေဘုရား /–ဖယား/ > Sule Pagoda G5; ◊ ဆူးလေဘုရားလမ်း S'ù-le P'ăyà Làn > Sule Pagoda Road G9
s'eh ဆယ် > ten G4
s'ín ဆင့် > cent G26
sa-cí-daiq စာကြည့်တိုက် /–ကျိဒိုက်/ > library G35
sa-eiq စာအိတ် > envelope ["letter-bag"] G40
sa-yweq စာရွက် > writing paper ["paper-sheet"] G40
sà-thauq-k'àn စားသောက်ခန်း > eating room, canteen G35
săbwèh စားပွဲ /စဗွဲ/ > table, desk G43
săgà pyàw- စကား ပြော– > to talk, speak, have conversation; ◊ စကား ပြောလို့ ကောင်းပါတယ်။ Săgà pyàw-ló kaùn-ba-deh. > I enjoyed talking to you. CP20; ◊ ဗမာစကား ပြောတာ ကောင်းပါတယ်။ Băma săgà pyàw-da kaùn-ba-deh. > Your spoken Burmese is good. D6; ◊ ဦးတင်လှိုင်နဲ့ စကားပြောချင်ပါတယ်။ Ù Tin Hlain-néh săgà pyàw-jin-ba-deh. > I'd like to speak to U Tin Hlaing. D12
Săgaìn စစ်ကိုင်း /ဇဂိုင်း/ > Sagaing G19
Săpa-kălin စပါကလင် > Sparkling [a bottled drink like Lilt, Seven-up and similar] D4
Săt'ărìn Ho-teh စထရင်းဟိုတယ် > Strand Hotel G5
săya in: [verb]–စရာ [verb]-săya > things that have to be [verb]-ed; ◊ လုပ်စရာ များပါတယ်။ Louq-săya myà-ba-deh. I have a lot to do. D11
Shin ရှင် > (polite tag, like Monsieur/Madame, used by female speakers) CP10
shiq ရှစ် > eight G4
Shwe-boun-dha Làn ရွှေဘုံသာလမ်း > Shwebontha Street G9
Shwe-dăgoun P'ăyà ရွှေတိဂုံဘုရား /ယွှေဒဂုန်ဖယား/ > Shwedagon Pagoda G5

shí- ရှိ– > to be [in some place]; also = have, there is D12; ◊ ဦးတင်လှိုင် ရှိလား။ Ù Tin Hlain shí-là? > Is U Tin Hlaing there? D12

shìn- ရှင်း– > to clear, clarify, settle up; be clear D4; ◊ ပိုက်ဆံ ရှင်းမယ်။ Paiq-s'an shìn-meh. > We'll settle the bill. D4

si-zin- စီစဉ်– /စီဇင်/ > to arrange, fix up D11

Sin-ga-pu စင်္ကာပူ /စင်ဂါ/ > Singapore G34

t'ain- ထိုင်– > to sit G43

T'aq-pyàw-ba-oùn. ထပ်ပြောပါအုံး။ /–တာ–/ > Please say that again. G13

t'aun ထောင် > thousand G10

T'aìn Naing-ngan ထိုင်းနိုင်ငံ > Thailand G13

taiq တိုက် > building G35

Taun-jì တောင်ကြီး /–ကြီး/ > Taunggyi G19

tăgeh တကယ် > really, in truth, actually, in fact D6; ◊ တကယ်ပဲလား။ Tăgeh-bèh-là? > Really? Do you mean it? D6

tăs'eh တစ်ဆယ် > ten G4

Tăyouq Naing-ngan တရုပ်နိုင်ငံ or တရုတ်နိုင်ငံ > China G13

teh-li-p'oùn တယ်လီဖုန်း > telephone G6

teiq-k'we တိပ်ခွေ > tape ["tape-reel"] G40

teq- တက်– > to go up, get on board (taxi and so on); to attend (school, meeting) D3

thà သား > son D10A

thàn သန်း > million G10

Than-dwèh သံတွဲ /–တွဲ/ > Sandoway (Thandwe) G19

than-dăman သံတမန် /–ဒမန်/ > diplomatic G35; ◊ သံတမန်ကုန်တိုက် /–ဒမန် –ဒိုက်/ than-dăman koun-daiq > Diplomatic Store G35

than-yoùn သံရုံး > embassy ["voice, envoy-office"] D1

thaùn သောင်း > ten thousand G10

thauq- သောက်– > to drink D4

thè- သေး in: မ–[verb]–သေးပါဘူး mă-[verb]-thè-pa-bù > not [verb] yet; ◊ မရောက်သေးပါဘူး။ mă-yauq-thè-pa-bu. They haven't arrived yet. D6

Thein-jì-zè သိမ်ကြီးဈေး /သိန်ကျီးဇေး/ > Thein-gyi Market G5

theiq သိပ် > very D6; ◊ သိပ် ကောင်းတယ်။ Theiq kaùn-deh. It is very good. D6

theìn သိန်း > hundred thousand G10

thoùn သုံး > three G2

thoun-nyá သုည > zero G6

thwà- သွား– > to go G34, 35; ◊ သွားခေါ်မယ်။ Thwà-k'aw-meɲ. > I'll go and fetch him. D12; ◊ သွားပါအုံးမယ် Thwà-ba-oùn-meh > Goodbye CP5; ◊ သွားမယ်နော်။ Thwà-meh-naw? > Goodbye (less formal) CP11, D2

Thămădá Ho-teh သမ္မတဟိုတယ် /သမဒ/ > President Hotel G5

thămì သမီး > daughter D10A

thí- သိ– > to know D1

tiq တစ် > one G2

To-co တိုကျို > Tokyo G15

Tù-riq Bà-mà Yoùn တူးရစ်ဘားမားရုံး > Tourist Burma office D1

twé- တွေ့– > to see, meet, find, notice; ◊ တွေ့သေးတာပေါ့။ Twé-dhè-da-báw. See you later/next time. CP6; ◊ တွေ့ရတာ ဝမ်းသာပါတယ်။ Twé-yá-da wùn-tha-ba-deh. I am happy at having the opportunity to meet you. D10B; ◊ နောက်ထပ် တွေ့ကြရအောင်။ Nauq-t'aq twé-já-yá-aun. > Let's meet again. D11

Ù ဦး /အူး/ > (prefix for names of older men) G22

ù-lè ဦးလေး > uncle D10B

weh- ဝယ်– > to buy G41

wùn-tha- ဝမ်းသာ– > to be happy ["stomach—be pleasant"] D10B

ya ရာ > hundred G8

yá- ရ– > to get, manage, be successful, be possible, to be all right, to be acceptable, to manage CP7; ◊ ရတယ်နော်။ Yá-deh-naw? > This is all right, isn't it? CP7, CP12, D2; ရပါတယ်။ Yá-ba-deh. > Yes, it is all right; ; That's all right. CP7, D2, CP8, CP9, CP13; ◊ မရဘူး။ Măyá-bù. > No, it 's not all right. CP12, D2; ◊ ရပြီလား။ Yá-bi-là? > All set? Ready? ရပြီ။ Yá-bi. > Yes, I am. CP16; မရသေးပါဘူး။ Măyá-dhè-ba-bù. > No, I'm not ready yet. CP16

yá- ရ– in: [verb]–ရ– [verb]-yá- > to have to [verb] G45

yaiq- ရိုက်–> to hit, beat, stamp, make imprint D2; ◊ ဓါတ်ပုံ ရိုက်– /ဒတ်ပုံ ယိုက်–/ daq-poun yaiq- > to take a photograph D2

Yan-goun ရန်ကုန် /ယန်ဂုန်/ > Rangoon/Yangon G15, G19

269

yaq ရပ် or ရပ်ကွက် or yaq-kweq > Quarter (in a town) G29

yauq- ရောက်– > to get to, reach, arrive at D7; ◊ ရောက်ဖူး– yauq-p'ù- > to have reached before, to have been to D7

Ye-nan-jaùn ရေနံချောင်း /ယေနန်ချောင်း/ > Yenangyaung G19

yoùn ရုံး > office D1

yu- ယူ– > to take D5; ◊ ယူမယ် Yu-meh. > I'll take it. I'll have it. D5

zè ဈေး /ေဈး/ > market G1

5.3 English-Burmese vocabulary

abroad, foreign country > နိုင်ငံခြား /–ဂျား/ nain-ngan-jà D7

address > လိပ်စာ leiq-sa G29

again: [verb] again, further, more > နောက်ထပ် [verb] nauq-t'aq D8; Please say that again. > ထပ်ပြောပါအုံး။ /–တာ–/ T'aq-pyàw-ba-oùn or ပြန်ပြောပါအုံး။ /–တာ–/ Pyan-pyàw-ba-oùn. G13

all right: It is all right > ရပါတယ်။ Yá-ba-deh. CP7, D2, CP8, CP9, CP13

all, in: Is that all? > ဒါပဲလား။ Da-bèh-là? > Is that all? Is that the lot? CP17; ဒါပါပဲ။ Da-ba-bèh. That's it, that's all. CP17; ရှိပါသေးတယ်။ Shí-ba-dhè-deh. > There's more. CP17

also, in: [noun] also > [noun]–လဲ -lèh D10B, D11

America > အမေရိကနိုင်ငံ Ă me-rí-ká Nain-ngan G34

amount to > ကျ– cá- D4

Anawrahta Street > အနော်ရထာလမ်း /ယထာ or ရထာ/ Ănaw-yăt'a Làn (yă or ră) G7

arrange > စီစဉ်– /စီဇင်/ si-zin- D11

arrive at, get to, reach > ရောက်– yauq- D7

at, in, on [place or time] > [place]–မှာ [place]-hma G27, 29, 30; [time]–မှာ [time]-hma G33

aunt > အဒေါ် ădaw D10B

Australia > ဩစတြေးလျနိုင်ငံ /ဩစတရေးလျာ/ Àw-sătrè-lyá G34, D1

back there > ခဲ့ in [verb]–ခဲ့– -géh-/-k'éh > used with verbs involving movement "from somewhere else to here" D12

Bago (Pegu) > ပဲခူး /ဗဂို:/ Păgò G19

ballpoint pen > ဘောပင် bàw-pin G40

Bangkok > ဘန်ကောက် Ban-kauq G15

Bangladesh > ဘင်္ဂလားဒေ့ရှ်နိုင်ငံ /ဗင်္ဂ–/ Bin-gălà-désh Naing-ngan G13

be [in some place] > ရှိ– shí- D12

been to: to have been to > ရောက်ဖူး– yauq-p'ù- D7

biscuit, cookie > ဘီစကွတ် bi-săkuq G40

bit: a bit > နဲနဲ nèh-nèh D11

Bo Aung Kyaw Street > ဗိုလ်အောင်ကျော်လမ်း /ဗို အောင်ကျော်–/ Bo Aun Jaw Làn G9

Bogyoke Market > ဗိုလ်ချုပ်ဈေး /ဗိုဂျုပ်ေဈး/ Bo-jouq Zè G5

Bogyoke Museum > ဗိုလ်ချုပ်ပြတိုက် /ဗိုဂျုပ်ပျာ့ဒိုက်/ Bo-jouq Pyá-daiq G5

Bogyoke Park > ဗိုလ်ချုပ်ပန်းခြံ /ဗိုဂျုပ်ပန်းဂျန်/ Bo-jouq Pàn-jan G5

Bogyoke Street > ဗိုလ်ချုပ်လမ်း /ဗိုဂျုပ်–/ Bo-jouq Làn G7

bottle > ပုလင်း /ပလင်း/ pălìn D4

boyfriend, husband, fiancé > အမျိုးသား ămyò-thà (or -dhà) D10A

brother (older) > အကို ăko D10B

building > တိုက် taiq G35

Burma/Myanmar > ဗမာပြည် Băma-pye, မြန်မာနိုင်ငံ Myan-ma Nain-ngan G13

Burmese (language) > ဗမာစကား Băma săgà D6; in Burmese > ဗမာလို Băma-lo G40

business > ကိစ္စ keiq-sá CP8, CP9, CP13

busy, to have a lot to do > လုပ်စရာ များပါတယ်။ Louq-săya myà-ba-deh. D11

buy > ဝယ်– weh- G41

call: to be called [name] > [name]–လို့ ခေါ်– [name]-ló k'aw- G36; [name]–တဲ့ [name]-déh G36

canteen, eating room > စားသောက်ခန်း sà-thauq-
k'àn G35

cent > ဆင့် s'ín G26

China > တရုပ်နိုင်ငံ or တရုတ်နိုင်ငံ Tăyouq Naing-
ngan G13

close, turn off > ပိတ်– peiq- G43

Coca-cola > ကိုကာကိုလာ Ko-ka-ko-la D4

coffee > ကော်ဖီ kaw-p'i D4

come > လာ– la- G31, 34

converse > စကား ပြော– săgà pyàw- CP20, D12

cookie, biscuit > ဘီစကွတ် bi-săkuq G40

correctly pronounced > ပီ– pi- D6

country, state > နိုင်ငံ naing-ngan G13

cup, glass > ခွက် k'weq D4

currently, recently, for the time being >
လောလောဆယ် /–ဇယ်/ làw-làw-zeh D11

Dacca > ဒက္ကား Deq-kà G15

daughter > သမီး thămì D10A

Daw (prefix for names of older women) > ဒေါ်
Daw G22

department store > ကုန်တိုက် /–ဒိုက်/ koun-daiq
G35

desk, table > စားပွဲ /စဗွဲ/ săbwèh G43

diplomatic > သံတမန် /–ဒမန်/ than-dăman G35;
◊ Diplomatic Store > သံတမန်ကုန်တိုက် /–
ဒမန် –ဒိုက်/ than-dăman koun-daiq G35

direction, way > ဘက် beq D1

do > လုပ်– louq- D11; have a lot to do > လုပ်စရာ
များပါတယ်။ Louq-săya myà-ba-deh. D11

dollar > ဒေါ်လာ daw-la G23

door > တံခါး /ဒဂါး/ dăgà G43

drink > သောက်– thauq- D4

eating room, canteen > စားသောက်ခန်း sà-thauq-
k'àn G35

eight > ရှစ် shiq G4

embassy > သံရုံး than-yoùn D1

England > အင်္ဂလန်နိုင်ငံ /အင်ဂလန်/ In-gălan
Nain-ngan G34

envelope > စာအိတ် sa-eiq G40

Excuse me please > ဒီမှာ di-hma D1

fall > ကျ– cá- D4

fan > ပန်ကာ pan-ka G43

father > အဖေ ăp'e D10A

fetch > ခေါ်– k'aw- D12

film > ဖလင် p'ălin G40

Fine! > ကောင်းပါပြီ Kaùn-ba-bi

finish > ပြီး– pì- ◊ ပြီးပြီလား။ Pì-bi-là? Have you
finished? CP15; ◊ ပြီးပြီ။ Pì-bi. I have
finished. CP15; ◊ မပြီးသေးပါဘူး။ Mӑpì-dhè-
ba-bù. I haven't finishsed yet. CP15

fire, light > မီး mì G43

five > ငါး ngà G2

four > လေး lè G2

France > ပြင်သစ်နိုင်ငံ Pyin-thiq Nain-ngan G34

frequently > ခဏခဏ /ခန့ ခန့/ k'ăná-k'ăná D7

friend > မိတ်ဆွေ meiq-s'we D10A

from [place] > [place]–က G31

garden, park > ပန်းခြံ /–ဂျန်/ pàn-jan G1

Germany > ဂျာမနီ Ja-măni G34

get to, reach, arrive at > ရောက်– yauq- D7

girlfriend, wife, fiancée > အမျိုးသမီး ămyò-
dhămì D10A

give > ပေး– pè- D3

glass, cup > ခွက် k'weq D4

go > သွား– thwà- G34, 35

go up, get on board (taxi and so on) > တက်– teq-
D3

Good morning/afternoon (in schools) > မင်္ဂလာပါ
Min-găla-ba CP1

good: to be good > ကောင်း– kaùn- D6; to be
excellent, top class > ဟုတ်– houq- D6

Goodbye > သွားပါအုံးမယ် Thwà-ba-oùn-meh
CP5; (less formal) သွားမယ်နော်။ Thwà-meh-
naw? CP11, D2

goods > ကုန် koun G3

half a kyat > ငါးမူး ngà-mù G38

half, and a half > ခွဲ -gwèh/-k'wèh G37, G38

Hallo > ဟလို or ဟယ်လို Hălo, Heh-lo D12;
Please speak > အမိန့် ရှိပါ။ Ӑmeín shí-ba.
(used as an alternative or addition to ဟလို on
the phone). D12

Hanoi > ဟနွိုင်း Hănwaìn G15

happy: to be happy > ဝမ်းသာ– wùn-tha- D10B

have to [verb] > [verb]–ရ– [verb]-yá- G45

here, in this place > ဒီမှာ di-hma G20

hold > ကိုင်– kain- D12

hotel > ဟိုတယ် ho-teh G1

hour > နာရီ na-yi G33

house > အိမ် ein G29

How about [noun]? > [noun]–ကော or [noun]–ရော -
gàw, -yàw CP4, D10B

how many > ဘယ်နှစ် /ဘယ်နှ–/ beh-hnă- D4

how much, what (number, price) > ဘယ်လောက် beh-lauq G6, 23

how, in what way > ဘယ်လို beh-lo G36, D1

hundred > –ရာ -ya G8

hundred thousand > –သိန်း -theìn G10

husband, fiancé, boyfriend > အမျိုးသား ămyò-thà (or -dhà) D10A

I, my (woman speaking) > ကျမ cămá D10A

in, on, at [place or time] > [place]–မှာ [place]-hma G27, 29, 30; [time]–မှာ [time]-hma G33

India > အိန္ဒိယနိုင်ငံ /အိန်ဒိယာ–/ Ein-dí-yá Naing-ngan G13

instant coffee > ကော်ဖီမှုန့် kaw-p'i-hmoún G40

intend: to have a plan, intend, to [verb] > [verb]–ဖို့ အစီအစဉ် ရှိ– -bó ăsi-ăsin shí- D8

introduce > မိတ်ဆက်– or မိတ်ဆက်ပေး– meiq-s'eq-(pè)- D10B

Inya Lake Hotel > အင်းယားလိပ် ဟိုတယ် Ìn-yà Leiq Ho-teh D3

Ireland > အိုင်ယာလန် Ain-ya-lan G34

Japan > ဂျပန်နိုင်ငံ Jăpan Naing-ngan G13

Karaweik Hotel > ကရဝိက် ဟိုတယ် /ကရဝိတ်–/ Kărăweiq Ho-teh D3

know > သိ– thí- D1

Ko (prefix for names of younger men) > ကို Ko G24

Korea > ကိုရီးယား Ko-rì-yà G34

Kuala Lumpur > ကွာလာလမ်ပူ Kwa-la Lan-pu G15

kyat > ကျပ် caq G32

later, not till later > နောက်မှ nauq-hmá D11; See you later > တွေ့သေးတာပေါ့။ Twé-dhè-da-báw CP6

library > စာကြည့်တိုက် /–ကျိဒိုက်/ sa-cí-daiq G35

light, fire > မီး mì G43

little: a little > နဲနဲ nèh-nèh D11

live > နေ– ne- G27

look, look around, look at > ကြည့်– /ကျိ/ cí- D5

Ma (prefix for names of younger women) > မ Má G24

Maha Bandoola Park > မဟာဗန္ဓုလပန်းခြံ /ဗန်ဒု– လ္လပန်းဂျန်/ Măha Ban-dú-lá Pàn-jan G5

Maha Bandoola Street > မဟာဗန္ဓုလလမ်း /ဗန်ဒုလာ–/ Măha Ban-dú-lá Làn G7

Malaysia > မလေးရှားနိုင်ငံ Mălè-shà Naing-ngan G13

Mandalay > မန္တလေး /မန်းဒလေး/ Màn-dălè G19

Manila > မနီလာ Măni-la G15

many: to be many, much > များ– myà- D11

map > မြေပုံ /–ဗုံ/ mye-boun G40

market > ဈေး /ဇေး/ zè G1

Maymyo > မေမြို့ Me-myó G19

meet (also: see, find, notice) > တွေ့– twé- CP6, D10B, D11; Happy to meet you တွေ့ရတာ ဝမ်းသာပါတယ်။ Twé-yá-da wùn-tha-ba-deh. D10B; နောက်ထပ် တွေ့ကြရအောင်။ Nauq-t'aq twé-já-yá-aun. D11

merchandise > ကုန် koun G3

Merchant Street > ကုန်သည်လမ်း /–သွယ်–/ Koun-dheh Làn G7

milk powder > နို့မှုန့် nó-hmoún G40

million > –သန်း -thàn G10

Mingaladon Airport > မင်္ဂလာဒုံ လေဆိပ် /–ဇိတ်/ Min-găla-doun Le-zeiq D3

minute > မိနစ် /မိနစ်–မင်းနစ်–မနစ်/ mí-niq, mìn-niq, măniq (the pronunciation of the first syllable varies with the speed of the speaker) G37

moment > ခဏ k'ăná CP8, CP14

money > ပိုက်ဆံ paiq-s'an D4

mother > အမေ ăme D10A

Moulmein (Mawlamyine) > မော်လမြိုင် Maw-lămyain G19

much: to be a lot > များ– myà- D11

museum > ပြတိုက် /ပြဒိုက်/ pyá-daiq G1

my (man speaking) > ကျနော့် cănáw D10A

my, I (woman speaking) > ကျမ cămá D10A

Myanmar/Burma > မြန်မာနိုင်ငံ Myan-ma Naing-ngan or ဗမာပြည် Băma Pye G13

Myitkyina > မြစ်ကြီးနား Myiq-cì-nà G19

name > နာမည် /နန်မယ်/ nan-meh in colloquial style, but /နာမျိ/ na-myi in reading style G27

National Museum > အမျိုးသားပြတိုက် /–ပျာဒိုက်/ Amyò-thà Pyá-daiq G5

national, citizen > နိုင်ငံသား nain-ngan-dhà D8

nationality, race > လူမျိုး lu-myò D9

New Delhi > နယူးဒေလီ Năyù De-li G15

nine > ကိုး kò G4

No (that is not so) > မဟုတ်ပါဘူး။ Măhouq-pa-bù. G3

No problem > ကိစ္စ မရှိပါဘူး။ Keiq-sá mǎshí-ba-
bù. CP8, CP9, CP13

not: It is not so. > မဟုတ်ပါဘူး /–ဗူး/ Mǎhouq-pa-
bù. G3

number > နံပါတ် /–ဗတ်/ nan-baq G2; အမှတ်
ǎhmaq G29

office > ရုံး youn D1

often > ခဏခဏ /ခန့ ခနာ/ k'ǎná-k'ǎná D7

Oh > အော် Aw G5

OK: That's fine > ကောင်းပါပြီ Kaùn-ba-bi CP 5,
CP11, CP12

OK: It is all right > ရပါတယ်။ Yá-ba-deh. CP7,
D2, CP8, CP9, CP13

on, in, at [place or time] > [place]–မှာ [place]-
hma G27, 29, 30; [time]–မှာ [time]-hma G33

one > တစ် tiq G2

open, turn on > ဖွင့်– p'wín- G43

orange juice > လိမ်မော်ရည် /–ရေ/ lein-maw-ye
D4

order, instruct > မှာ– hma- D4

outside, out > အပြင် ǎpyin G35

Pagan (Bagan) > ပုဂံ /ဗဂန်/ Pǎgan G19

pagoda, lord, Buddha image > ဘုရား /ဗယား/
p'ǎyà G1

Pansodan Street > ပန်းဆိုးတန်း /ဆိုး or ဇိုး/ Pàn-
s'ò-dàn (s'ò or zò) G9

park, garden > ပန်းခြံ /–ဂျန်/ pàn-jan G1

pay [price], have to give > ပေးရ– [price] pè-yá-
G39

Pegu (Bago) > ပဲခူး /ဗဂိုး/ Pǎgò G19

Peking/Beijing > ပီကင်း Pi-kìn G15

penny > ပဲနီ pèh-ní G26

Pepsi-cola > ပက်စီ Peq-si D4

permission, authorization > ခွင့် k'wín CP19

Philippines > ဖိလစ်ပိုင်နိုင်ငံ P'í-liq-pain Naing-
ngan G13

photograph > ဓါတ်ပုံ /ဒတ်ပုံ/ daq-poun D2;
◊ take a photograph > ဓါတ်ပုံ ရိုက် /ဒတ်ပုံ
ယိုက်/ daq-poun yaiq- D2

place > နေရာ ne-ya G35

plan, programme > အစီအစဉ် /–စင်/ ǎsi-ǎsin D8;
to have a plan, intend, to [verb] > [verb]–ဖို့
အစီအစဉ် ရှိ– -bó ǎsi-ǎsin shí- D8

postcard > ပို့စကဒ် /–ကတ်/ pó-sǎkaq G40

pound > ပေါင် paun G23

President Hotel > သမ္မတဟိုတယ် /သမဒ၁/
Thǎmǎdá Ho-teh G5

problem, in: No problem > ကိစ္စ မရှိပါဘူး။ Keiq-sá
mǎshí-ba-bù.CP8, CP9, CP13

Prome (Pyi/Pyay) > ပြည် /ပျေ/ or /ပှီ/ Pye G19

pya (or English penny) > ပြား pyà G25

Quarter (in a town) > ရပ် or ရပ်ကွက် yaq or yaq-
kweq G29

quarter (of kyat or other unit) > မတ် maq G38

race, nationality > လူမျိုး lu-myò D9

Rangoon/Yangon > ရန်ကုန် /ယန်ရုန်/ Yan-goun
G15, G19

ready: I am ready > ရပြီ။ Yá-bi. CP16

really > တကယ် tǎgeh D6

recently, currently, for the time being >
လောလောဆယ် /–ဇယ်/ làw-làw-zeh D11

Right! > ကဲ kèh CP14

road, street > လမ်း làn G7

Russia > ရုတ်ရှား Raq-shà G34

Sagaing > စစ်ကိုင်း /ဇဂိုင်း/ Sǎgaìn G19

Sandoway (Thandwe) > သံတွဲ /–ဒွဲ/ Than-dwèh
G19

Scotchtape, sellotape > ဆယ်လိုတိပ် s'eh-lo-teiq
G40

sellotape, Scotchtape > ဆယ်လိုတိပ် s'eh-lo-teiq
G40

settle up, pay up > ရှင်း– shìn- D4

seven > ခုနှစ် k'ú-niq, k'ú-hniq, k'un G4, G6

Shwebontha Street > ရွှေဘုံသာလမ်း Shwe-boun-
dha Làn G9

Shwedagon Pagoda > ရွှေတိဂုံ ဘုရား
/ယွှေဒဂုန်ဗယား/ Shwe-dǎgoun P'ǎyà G5;
Shwedagon Pagoda Road > ဘုရားလမ်း
/ဗယား–/ P'ǎyà Làn G9

Singapore > စင်္ကာပူ /စင်ဂါ/ Sin-ga-pu G34

sister (older) > အမ ǎmá D10B

sit > ထိုင်– t'ain- G43

six > ခြောက် c'auq G4

son > သား thà D10A

sorry > ဆောရီး s'àw-rì, ဆောရီးပဲ။ S'àw-rì-bèh
CP13; ဆောရီးနော် S'àw-rì-naw D1

Sparkling > စပါကလင် Sǎpa-kǎlin D4

speak, say, tell, talk > ပြော– pyàw- D6; have a
conversation > စကား ပြော– sǎgà pyàw-
CP20, D12

273

station: the main railway station > ဘူတာကြီး /–ဒါ–/ Bu-da-jì D3

Strand Hotel > စထရင်းဟိုတယ် Săt'ărìn Ho-teh G5

Strand Road > ကမ်းနားလမ်း Kàn-nà Làn G7

street, road > လမ်း làn G7

Sule Pagoda > ဆူးလေဘုရား /–ဖယား/ S'ù-le P'ăya G5; Sule Pagoda Road > ဆူးလေဘုရားလမ်း S'ù-le P'ăyà Làn G9

table, desk > စားပွဲ /စပွဲ/ săbwèh G43

take > ယူ– yu- D5

take a photograph > ဓါတ်ပုံ ရိုက်– /ဒတ်ပုံ ယိုက်–/ daq-poun yaiq- D2

talk, speak, say, tell > ပြော– pyàw- D6; have a conversation > စကား ပြော– săgà pyàw- CP20, D12

tape > တိပ်ခွေ teiq-k'we G40

Taunggyi > တောင်ကြီး /–ဂျီး/ Taun-jì G19

tea > လက်ဖက်ရည် /လဖက်ယေ/ lăp'eq-ye D4

Teacher > (male and generic) ဆရာ S'ăya; (female) ဆရာမ S'ăya-má CP2

telephone > တယ်လီဖုန်း teh-li-p'oùn G6

ten > တစ်ဆယ်၊ ဆယ် tăs'eh, s'eh G4

ten thousand > –သောင်း -thaùn G10

terrifically, fantastically > အရမ်း ăyàn D6

Thailand > ထိုင်းနိုင်ငံ T'aìn Naing-ngan G13

Thank you. > ကျေးဇူး တင်ပါတယ်။ Cè-zù tin-ba-deh. CP9

that, this > ဒါ da G1; that (nearer you) > အဲဒါ èh-da G39

Thein-gyi Market > သိမ်ကြီးဈေး /သိန်ဂျီးဇေး/ Thein-jì-zè G5

There! > ကဲ kèh CP14

this, that > ဒါ da G1; this [noun] > ဒီ– [noun] di-[noun] G7

thousand > –ထောင် -t'aun G10

three > သုံး thoùn G2

time > အချိန် ăc'ein G33

to, in: speak to [person] > [person]–နဲ့ စကား ပြော– တယ်။ [person]-néh săgà pyàw-deh. D12

toilet > အိမ်သာ/–သာ/ ein-dha G35

Tokyo > တိုကျို To-co G15

tomorrow > မနက်ဖြန် or မနက်ဖြင် or မနက်ဖန် măneq-p'yan, măneq-p'yin, măneq-p'an,

or နက်ဖြန် or နက်ဖြင် or နက်ဖန် neq-p'yan, neq-p'yin, neq-p'an D11

too, in: [noun] too > [noun]–လဲ -lèh D10B, D11

Tourist Burma office > တူးရစ်ဘားမားရုံး Tù-riq Bà-mà Yoùn D1

town > မြို့ myó G15

township > မြို့နယ် myó-neh G29

trip, journey > အခေါက် ăk'auq D7

turn off, close > ပိတ်– peiq- G43

turn on, open > ဖွင့်– p'wín- G43

two > နှစ် hniq G2

U (prefix for names of older men) > ဦး /အူး/ Ù G22

uncle > ဦးလေး ù-lè D10B

understand > နား လည်– nà leh- CP18

Very well > ကောင်းပါပြီ Kaùn-ba-bi

very > သိပ် theiq D6

Vietnam > ဗီယက်နမ်နိုင်ငံ Bi-yeq-nan Naing-ngan G13

want to [verb] > [verb]–ချင်– [verb]-jin- G42

Well! > ကဲ kèh CP14

well: to be well > နေကောင်း– ne-kaùn- CP3

what > ဘာ ba G1; what [noun] ဘာ–[noun] ba-[noun] G5

where, in which place > ဘယ်မှာ beh-hma G20

which [noun] > ဘယ်–[noun] beh-[noun] G11

who > ဘယ်သူ beh-dhu G21

wife, fiancée, girlfriend > အမျိုးသမီး ămyò-dhămì D10A

window > ပြတင်းပေါက် /ပဒင်းဘောက်/ pădìn-bauq G43

with [noun] > [noun]–နဲ့ -néh G14

writing paper > စာရွက် sa-yweq G40

Yangon/Rangoon > ရန်ကုန် /ယန်ဂုန်/ Yan-goun G15, G19

Yenangyaung > ရေနံချောင်း /ယေနန်ချောင်း/ Ye-nan-jaùn G19

Yes > ဟုတ်ကဲ့။ Houq-kéh G3, CP19

yet > သေး in: မ–[verb]–သေးပါဘူး mă-[verb]-thè-pa-bù; ◊ မရောက်သေးပါဘူး။ mă-yauq-thè-pa-bu. They haven't arrived yet. D6

you, your (when you don't know the person's name) > မိတ်ဆွေ meiq-s'we "friend" D10B

zero > သုည thoun-nyá G6

Burmese (Myanmar):
An Introduction to the Spoken Language Book 1

ERRATA ET CORRIGENDA

Reference	Text	Amend to
p 20 nᵒ 7	p'ăya	p'ăyà
p 50 line 11 & 36	အိန္ဒိယ	အိန္ဒိယ
p 51 nᵒ 10	Ein-dì-yá	Ein-dí-yá
p 104 line 5	Shiq-s'éh ngà-Làn	K'un-năs'éh ngà-Làn
p 106 line 10 from end	*road*	*country*
p 106 line 3 from end	Mr. Cruz	Mrs. Cruz
p 108 and p 109	Ex. 4	Ex. 3
p 118 2 from end	ရွှေတိဂုံဘုရား	ဆူးလေဘုရား
p 125 ex 1	L/S2male	L/S2
p 127 line 4 from end	55 minutes	25 minutes
p 200 line 3	peiq-ba	peiq-pa
p 200 line 7	yè-pa	yè-ba
p 200 line 8	pè-pa	pè-ba
p 205 line 5 from end	Byí-tí-shá	Ăme-rí-kan
p 205 line 4 from end	Ăme-rí-kan	Byí-tí-shá
p 219 lines 19, 12, 10 from end	sgà	săgà
p 231 line 15	mm	Da beh-dhu-lèh?
p 235 line 13	နံမည်	နာမည်